Towards a Socioanalysis Finance and Capitalism

The current global financial crisis has raised awareness of the impact the world of finance has on the economy and the future of democracy. Following the crisis, this book aims at a deep understanding of the human psychosocial dynamics beneath the surface of the financial industry, its markets and institutions. It seeks to understand why the seemingly rational world of economic behaviour, with its calculated models and predictions, at times goes horribly wrong.

This book uses the discipline of socioanalysis to explore the meaning of money, markets and the broad financial world that so strongly affects our daily lives. Socioanalysis contributes to an awareness and understanding of underlying unconscious desires, fantasies and illusions that bring about the irrational inflation of faith and trust in the world of money, finance and capital(ism). The insight that the financial crisis 'was essentially psychological in origin' (Robert Shiller) and that the world of finance is broadly shaped if not determined by irrational, often unconscious factors is not yet broadly shared. This book appears to be one of the first, if not *the* first, to explicitly focus on what is beneath the surface of money, finance and capital. It invites the reader to explore the financial world in depth.

The aim of this book is to provide businesses, organizational consultants, students, researchers and interested persons more broadly with a detailed exploration of the psychosocial dynamics of the financial industry as it exists currently within the capitalist system. The contributors to this book come from Australia, Denmark, France, Germany, Hungary, Sweden, the Netherlands, the United Kingdom and the United States.

Susan Long is an adjunct Professor at RMIT University in Melbourne, Australia, where she supervises research students and conducts organizational research. She is currently President of the Psychoanalytic Studies Association of Australasia and is a past President of the International Society for the Psychoanalytic Study of Organizations and the founding president of Group Relations Australia.

Burkard Sievers is Professor Emeritus of Organization Development in the Schumpeter School of Business and Economics at Bergische Universität Wuppertal, Germany. He is a past President of the International Society for the Psychoanalytic Study of Organizations.

Routledge international studies in money and banking

Towards a Socioanalysis of Money, Finance and Capitalism

Beneath the surface of the financial industry

Edited by Susan Long and Burkard Sievers

Routledge
Taylor & Francis Group

LONDON AND NEW YORK

First published 2012
by Routledge
2 Park Square, Milton Park, Abingdon, Oxon OX14 4RN

Simultaneously published in the USA and Canada
by Routledge
711 Third Avenue, New York, NY 10017

First issued in paperback 2013

Routledge is an imprint of the Taylor & Francis Group, an informa business

British Library Cataloguing in Publication Data
A catalogue record for this book is available from the British Library

Library of Congress Cataloging in Publication Data
Towards a socioanalysis of money, finance and capitalism : beneath the
surface of the financial industry / edited by Susan Long and
Burkard Sievers.
  p. cm.
  Includes bibliographical references and index.
  1. Money–Psychological aspects. 2. Finance–Psychological aspects.
  3. Financial crises–Psychological aspects. 4. Capitalism–Psychological
  aspects. I. Long, Susan, 1948- II. Sievers, Burkard, 1942–
  HG222.3.T69 2011
  306.3–dc22
                                                        2011002339

ISBN: 978-0-415-60031-6 (hbk)
ISBN: 978-0-415-71060-2 (pbk)
ISBN: 978-0-203-80815-3 (ebk)

Typeset in Times
by Wearset Ltd, Boldon, Tyne and Wear

Contents

Figures and table

Figures

Table

Contributors

Seth Allcorn, PhD, is a university and health care executive, organizational consultant and an Associate of the University of Missouri Truman School of Public Affairs Center for the Study of Organizational Change. He is a founding member of the International Society for the Psychoanalytic Study of Organizations (ISPSO). He is the co-author of a new book with Michael Diamond, *Private Selves in Public Organizations: The psychodynamics of organizational diagnosis and change* (Palgrave Macmillan, 2009).

Jesper Blomberg is Associate Professor at the Stockholm School of Economics, where he also earned his PhD. His current research includes project management, with both an instrumental and a critical stance, as well as organizational analysis of the financial sector. He has published several books and articles covering organizational theory, project management and organizational finance.

Amy L. Fraher is Associate Professor, Chief Pilot and Director, International Team Training Center, at San Diego Miramar College. She is a retired US Navy Commander, Naval Aviator and former United Airlines pilot and crisis management expert with almost thirty years of leadership experience in high-risk fields. Dr Fraher is a member of the *Washington Post* 'Leadership Panel' who consults internationally with a broad range of organizations; her focus is on improving team performance in high-risk organizations. She has published in books and professional journals such as *History of Psychology*, *Human Relations*, *Socio-Analysis* and *Organisational and Social Dynamics*.

Alison Gill is the co-founder and joint CEO of Crelos Ltd. She leads strategic organizational change projects consulting with boards and executive teams on organizational development, team dynamics and behavioural change. She brings creativity and insight to help strengthen relationships, enhance decision making about people and organizational issues, and improve workplace productivity. Alison is a fellow of the Association of Business Psychologists, a fellow of the Royal Society of Arts and a board member of Bvalco Ltd. She is currently studying for a DBA at Henley Business School and is a much-sought-after commentator and author on behavioural change.

Larry Hirschhorn, PhD, is a principal with CFAR, a management consulting firm in Philadelphia, Pennsylvania. He is also an instructor in the Organization Dynamics Program at the University of Pennsylvania, and a Professor of Human and Organization development at Fielding Graduate University. He is a founding member and past President of the International Society for the Psychoanalytic Study of Organizations. He has published several books on organizational psychodynamics.

Angelien Kemna is Professor of Corporate Governance and Financial Econometrics, Erasmus School of Economics/Finance Group, Rotterdam, the Netherlands. As of November 2009, Angelien Kemna is also Chief Investment Officer of the investment company APG, which looks after about €200 billion worth of assets, primarily on behalf of Dutch civil pension fund ABP.

Douglas Kirsner, PhD, has a personal chair in philosophy and psychoanalytic studies at Deakin University, Melbourne. His publications include *Unfree Associations: Inside psychoanalytic institutes, The Schizoid World of Jean-Paul Sartre and R.D. Laing*, edited collections and many articles in psychoanalytic journals. He lectures widely at psychoanalytic institutes and associations. He is Associate Editor of the *International Journal of Applied Psychoanalytic Studies* and *Organisational and Social Dynamics*, editorial adviser to *Psychoanalysis and History*, and an editorial board member of *Psychotherapy in Australia*. He founded the Freud Conference in 1977 and directed it for the next twenty years.

Hans Kjellberg is Associate Professor at the Department of Marketing and Strategy, Stockholm School of Economics. His research interests concern economic organizing in general and the shaping of markets and economic exchange in particular. Current research projects concern mundane market practices, the performativity of marketing theories, and how investment banks shape the financial markets. Recent publications include articles in *Industrial Marketing Management, Marketing Theory, Journal of Cultural Economy* and the edited volume *Reconnecting Marketing to Markets* (Oxford University Press, 2010).

Matthias Klaes is Professor of Commerce and Head of the School of Management at Keele University in the United Kingdom. He has served as an adviser both to industry and to the public sector, and is a board member of the International Network for Economic Method, as well as a Senior Research Fellow of SCEME at Stirling University in the United Kingdom, which he founded in 2003. He is on the editorial board of the *Journal of Economic Methodology*, which he served five years as Managing Editor, and part of the Evolutionary Economics Research Group of the German Economic Association (Verein für Socialpolitik).

W. Gordon Lawrence is founder and director of Social Dreaming Solutions Ltd, London. A former member of the Tavistock Institute scientific staff and a Visiting Professor at Cranfield University in the United Kingdom, he is now Visiting Professor at the New Bulgarian University, Sofia. Dr Lawrence is a Distinguished Member of the International Society for the Psychoanalytic Study of Organizations and is on the editorial boards of *Free Associations* (UK), *Freie Assoziation* (Germany), *Organizational and Social Dynamic* (UK) and *Socio-Analysis* (Australia). He has published over a hundred articles and several books.

Marc Lenglet is Assistant Professor of Management at the European Business School (EBS) and Chaired Professor of Socially Responsible Corporate Behaviour. He holds a PhD in Management Sciences from Paris-Dauphine University, a Master's degree in Philosophy from Paris-Sorbonne University and an MBA from ESSEC Business School. His research focuses on social studies of finance, the anthropology of financial regulation and compliance, and financial innovation. Before joining EBS, he worked as an Equities Compliance Officer in a European brokerage house.

David P. Levine is a Professor in the Josef Korbel School of International Studies at the University of Denver. He is the author of numerous books and articles in the fields of political economy, political psychology and group dynamics, most recently *Object Relations, Work and the Self* (Routledge, 2010) and *The Capacity for Civic Engagement: Public and private worlds of the self* (Palgrave Macmillan, 2011). Professor Levine was educated at Yale University (PhD in economics) and the Colorado Center for Psychoanalytic Studies (Certificate in Psychoanalytic Scholarship).

Geoff Lightfoot is Senior Lecturer in Entrepreneurship and Accounting at the University of Leicester, School of Management. Dr Lightfoot joined the School of Management in September 2004 after previously teaching at the University of Humanistics, Utrecht and Keele University. Prior to his studies at Kingston University, London School of Economics and the Open University, Geoff worked for the United Kingdom's civil service. His research is wide-ranging but may perhaps be broadly grouped around the exploration of aspects of representation and markets.

Simon Lilley, PhD, is Professor of Organization and Information and Head of the University of Leicester, School of Management. He has taught previously at the Universities of Keele, Edinburgh, Glasgow and Lancaster, at the International Business School, Budapest, and at the Manchester School of Management, UMIST. Simon is editor of the journal *Culture and Organization*. His research interests turn around the relationships between (human) agency, technology and performance, and are reflected in a focus on the use of information technologies and strategic models in organizations and investigation of the regulation and conduct of financial and commodity derivatives trading.

Susan Long, PhD, is a Melbourne-based organizational consultant and researcher using a socioanalytic perspective. Previously Professor of Creative and Sustainable Organization at RMIT University, Melbourne, she now teaches and leads research as an Adjunct Professor. She is currently President of the Psychoanalytic Studies Association of Australasia and vice-president of the National Institute of Organisation Dynamics Australia (NIODA). She is a past President of the International Society for the Psychoanalytic Study of Organizations and of Group Relations Australia. She has published five books and many articles in scholarly journals.

Ian S. Miller, PhD, MBA, is a psychoanalytically trained business consultant based in New York, where he is Principal of the Accord Advisory Group (www.accordadvisorygroup.com). He teaches globally as Professor of Industrial-Organizational Psychology and Human Relations in the International Masters' Programs of Baruch College, City University of New York.

Richard Morgan-Jones is an organizational consultant and a psychoanalytic psychotherapist with a practice in Eastbourne, UK. His original education was at Cambridge, Oxford and Exeter Universities in Anthropology, Theology and Education. He trained as a psychotherapist at the London Centre for Psychotherapy, of which he is a full member. He is a member of the Organisation for Promoting the Understanding of Society (OPUS), the International Society for the Psychoanalytic Study of Organizations (ISPSO), the European Business Ethical Network (EBEN), and the Restorative Justice Consortium (RJC). He directs Work Force Health: Consulting and Research.

Claudia Nagel, who holds a PhD in Organizational Psychology and an MBA, trained as a Jungian analyst at ISAP, Zurich. She began her professional career as a Director of the Institute of Business Ethics. After extensive experience in international management consulting and in different leadership positions in banking (Goldman Sachs, Credit Suisse), she founded her own management consulting company (Nagel & Co.) focusing on the psychodynamic development of corporate strategy and change management processes. She is a board member of the International Society for the Psychoanalytic Study of Organizations and has worked and studied in New York, London, Paris and in Germany.

Peter Pelzer has studied economics, with an emphasis on planning and organization, and philosophy, in Wuppertal, Germany. He has spent most of his professional life working in and for banks, currently as an independent consultant. Dr Pelzer is also Visiting Professor at the University for Humanistics, Utrecht, the Netherlands. He wrote a book that explored the question of what postmodern philosophers and aesthetic thinking can contribute to organization theory. He is very much interested in understanding the processes he experiences during his projects beyond the textbook knowledge of organization and management theory.

Howard S. Schwartz's bachelor's degree is in philosophy from Antioch College. He studied philosophy as a graduate student at the University of

Pittsburgh and organizations at the University of California, San Diego. His PhD is in Organizational Behavior from Cornell University, Ithaca, New York. He is Professor of Organizational Behavior at Oakland University, Rochester, Michigan. His published works include *Narcissistic Process and Corporate Decay: The theory of the organization ideal* (1991), *The Revolt of the Primitive: An inquiry into the roots of political correctness* (2003) and *Society against Itself: Political correctness and organizational self-destruction* (2010). He was one of the founders of the International Society for the Psychoanalytic Study of Organizations (ISPSO).

Allan Shafer, MA (Clin. Psych.), D. Litt. et Phil., a clinical psychologist and socioanalyst, has over thirty years' experience as a psychoanalytic psycho-therapist and twenty years' as an organization consultant, primarily in Perth, Western Australia, but relocating to Melbourne in 2011. He is President of the Association for Psychoanalytic Psychotherapy of Western Australia, a member of the Psychoanalytic Psychotherapy Association of Australasia and a founding member of Group Relations Australia. He has consulted to mental health, educational and religious organizations in Australia, South Africa and the United States and directed and consulted on the staff of group relations conferences in Australia, Israel and the United Kingdom.

Mannie Sher is a Principal Social Scientist and Director of the Group Relations Programme at the Tavistock Institute of Human Relations, London. He manages organizational development projects and consults to boards and top teams on the role of leadership in effecting strategic change. His work focuses on the impact of thought on the dialectic relationship between social construc-tivism, the unconscious and liberal democracy. A practising psychoanalytical psychotherapist, e has published on consultancy, leadership, organizational development, ethics and corruption. He is a member of the board of the Inter-national Society for the Psychoanalytic Study of Organizations (ISPSO) and the Israel Association for the Study of Group and Organizational Processes (OFEK).

Burkard Sievers is Professor Emeritus of Organization Development in the Schumpeter School of Business and Economics at Bergische Universität Wuppertal in Germany. Dr Sievers' research focuses on unconscious dynamics in management and organization from a socioanalytic and systemic perspective. In 1995, he was awarded the international prize for participation by the HBK Bank in Antwerp, Belgium, for his book *Work, Death and Life Itself: Essays on management and organization* (de Gruyter, 1994). He is a past President of the International Society for the Psychoanalytic Study of Organizations (ISPSO).

Howard F. Stein, PhD, a psychoanalytic and organizational anthropologist, and psychohistorian, is Professor and Special Assistant to the Chair in the Depart-ment of Family and Preventive Medicine, University of Oklahoma Health Sciences Center, Oklahoma City, where he has taught since 1978. He is a long-time member of the International Psychohistorical Association. He has co-authored a book and several articles with Seth Allcorn. His most recent book is *Insight and Imagination* (University Press of America, 2008).

Sándor Takács, PhD, is Associate Professor at the Department of Organizational Behaviour at Corvinus University of Budapest, Hungary. He is director of the Human Resource Management programme and leader of various MBA and MSc courses. He has fifteen years' of training, coaching and consulting experience in organizational development and change management projects (as Ideas and Solutions Consulting) at various Hungarian and multinational companies (Deutsche Telekom, Hewlett-Packard, Siemens, Tetra Pak and Unilever) in Hungary and Central-Eastern Europe. He is a member of the Hungarian Psychodrama Association and the International Society for the Psychoanalytic Study of Organizations (ISPSO).

Emre Tarim is a PhD student in Sociology at the University of Edinburgh. His research interests are on sociology of financial markets and role of narratives in cognition, decision making and legitimation.

Erik van de Loo is Professor of Leadership and Behaviour at the Free University of Amsterdam and visiting Clinical Professor of Leadership and Programme Director at the INSEAD Global Leadership Centre, Fontainebleau, France. He holds a PhD in Social Sciences from Leiden University. He is a partner in and co-founder of Phyleon, the centre for leadership and change, The Hague, the Netherlands, and specializes in the interrelated change processes at individual, group and organizational levels. Erik van de Loo, a licensed clinical psychologist and psychoanalyst, is a member of the International Psychoanalytical Association, the Dutch Society of Psychoanalysis and the International Society for the Psychoanalytic Study of Organizations.

Hans van den Hooff is an organizational consultant, executive coach and a practising psychoanalyst in London and Amsterdam. He has twenty years of experience in working with organizations and executives. Dr Van den Hooff was Partner with the management consulting firm Arthur D. Little and has worked for Shell in Europe and the United States. He has a PhD in Physics and qualified as a Jungian psychoanalyst in London. He has been writing and lecturing internationally in the fields of executive coaching and interpersonal organizational dynamics. His publications include articles on analytical psychology, unconscious processes in organizations and leadership.

Karin Winroth holds a PhD in Business Administration and is currently assistant professor at Sodertorn University. Among her research interests are issues of professional culture and leadership in professional service firms, especially in relation to construction of identity and the organizing of work. She has published on management in law firms and is currently working on a project about the organizing of investment banks, especially the organizing of expert work and their contributions to the financial markets. She also takes an interest in the expression and construction of corporate brands.

Byron Woollen, PhD, is the founder and President of Podia Consulting, an organizational consulting firm based in New York City. His degrees are in English and the combined fields of psychology and religion, and he has a doctorate in clinical psychology. He is a member of the International Society for the Psychoanalytic Study of Organizations (ISPSO).

Laura Yu is a Systems, Processes and Training Professional at an education technology company in New York City. She received a BA focused in Political Economy from Evergreen State College in Olympia, Washington, and a Master's degree in Leadership Studies at the University of San Diego. Since her introduction to group relations at the University of San Diego, she has participated in the conference experience and training group at the International Team Training Center (ITTC) at San Diego Miramar College and in a video about the group relations conference experience created by the University of San Diego, Calfornia, and the A.K. Rice Institute, Rainier, Washingtom.

Acknowledgements

The authors acknowledge all who gave support to this project, including: in Chapter 5, the many respondents who generously gave of their time and their thoughts, whether they have been supportive or critical; Chapter 7: Rose Mersky for help in editing; Chapter 16: Bipin Patel, who organized the meeting at the Working Men's College and the thirty people who participated; Franca La Nave, John Wilkes and Stephen Fitzpatrick and Bipin Patel, who worked as hosts; Dr Victoria Hamilton for her insight and editing.

Chapter 3 was published in an earlier form as 'Greed' in *Psychodynamic Practice*, 15(3): 245–59. The section on 'greed seen developmentally' was first presented in an earlier form in *The Perverse Organisation and its Deadly Sins* Karnac, London 2008.

Chapter 7 was first partly published as 'Beneath the surface of the financial crisis: the psychoanalytic perspective', in H. Brunning and M. Perini (eds) (2010) *Psychoanalytic Perspectives on a Turbulent World*, London: Karnac: 117–37.

Chapter 13 was written as part of the research project 'Handlingar som skapar finansmarknaen' funded by the Bank of Sweden Tercentenary Fund, project no. P2006-0797.

1   Introduction

Burkard Sievers and Susan Long

As the disastrous consequences of the collapse of Lehman Brothers emerged, so did the illusionary belief that the United States was suffering a crisis comparable to a hurricane, tsunami or a hundred-year flood or earthquake; catastrophes that periodically recall to mankind 'its precariousness, of its land frailty' (Miller 2008: 4). The reality that this crisis was, however, 'human-made' appeared for some time unthinkable. Perceiving the crisis as an unavoidable stroke of fate avoided dealing with it from a state of mind (the depressive state) accepting of the human failures and frailties involved. Resigning to the crisis as 'fate' meant that further thought about collective responsibilities and/or guilt was avoided. Blame was projected outward onto market forces or failures in economic models of risk.

What triggered our decision to edit a book on this subject was the experience of the current financial crisis and its aftermath up to 2010. A call for papers was sent out on 2 August 2009. While the consequences of the crisis were unpredictable at that point in time, when the world appeared almost irrevocably changed, it now (December 2010) appears as if the crisis is regarded as a past episode. Take our home countries, for instance. In Germany, a new economic upturn is hailed in the media and claimed as a success by the current government. In Australia, where the economic crisis was perhaps weathered more favourably than elsewhere, government has also claimed credit for saving the country from vast unemployment through its stimulus packages. The US economy is weak but showing uncertain signs of recovery.

It appears that the euro crisis of 2010 and its unforeseeable worldwide implications have pushed the experience of the previous crisis into the background. While several European (the English, French and German) governments are contemplating severe reductions of their national budgets, the United States is primarily concerned with increasing consumption in order to reduce the enormous amount of state debts and fiscal deficit. European governments are reproached by the United States for their lack of solidarity in fiscal policy, and Germany in particular is accused of living on the costs of other countries, owing to its main emphasis of (and dependency on) exports. Greece and Ireland appear to be suffering their own 'crises' requiring support from the European Union.

It is unpredictable how the world economy will look when this book is published. Times and economic destinies change rapidly. Whereas optimism about future economic development appears to prevail, there are voices that express concern that an even bigger catastrophe may soon happen; the present economic recovery may well be but a 'ridge of high pressure' to be followed by gloomy times.

While (academic) publications on the financial crisis were small in number during the middle of 2009 at the time of our call for papers, they have now increased, along with seminars, conferences and special journal issues.

Our intentions with the book

Our call for papers emphasized the need for a socioanalytic perspective on the financial industry because 'since the earliest part of the twentieth century, anything psychoanalytic with regard to economic or financial studies remains banished' (Shaw 2005: 293).

Although it is too early to produce a general socioanalytic theory of money, finance and capital(ism), our aim for this book is to deepen the psycho- and socioanalytic study of the world of finance, the financial industry and the meaning and unconscious function of money and capital as fundamental concerns of contemporary societies.

Rationale

The present global financial crisis and its aftermath have made us alarmingly aware of the impact and dominance that the world of finance has on the economy, the future of democracy and the world at large. Not only does the financial crisis put into question recently taken-for-granted paradigms such as economic rationality and the notion of a free market, but also it has proven that the strategies and actions of many role-holders in the financial system have to a large extent been based on ignorance and flawed understanding. Moreover, both economists and politicians are struggling to adequately perceive and understand the current crisis. Given that academic debate on the causes of the Great Depression continues, it is also likely that an adequate understanding of the unconscious dynamics that led to the current financial crisis – not to mention its aftermath – will also continue to be sought.

The discourse about the financial crisis and its outcome has been broadly restricted to financial-economic facts and explanations, apportioning of blame towards apparently responsible parties and the consideration of appropriate measures to prevent the very worst. The insight that the financial crisis – like all bubbles and busts of financial markets – 'was essentially psychological in origin' (Shiller 2008: 24) is not broadly shared, either in the media or in much of the literature. The attempt at a deeper understanding of immediate crises and the world of finance from a socioanalytic perspective thus appears to be 'handicapped ... by economists' understanding of human beings' (Bain 2009: 1).

While attention to and about the financial industry is primarily restricted to the trading of financial instruments for distribution and accumulation of money and capital, the thinking behind it and the state of mind on which it is based favour a supposed rationality and objectivity of fact and figures, instruments, strategies, risk calculation and management derived from superficially sophisticated mathematical models. Further-reaching attempts at understanding the world of finance and the 'rules of its games' from a social science perspective are in a state of early adolescence. Although the present boom in behavioural economics as a supposed promising new discipline with the intent to 'increase the explanatory power of economics by providing it with more realistic psychological foundations' (Camerer and Loewenstein 2002) has meanwhile led to behavioural finance as a subdiscipline, it appears to be restricted to theoretical and rational explanations of *behaviour* in situations of decision, uncertainty and time pressure. Financial markets, in particular, have to date 'not been paid much attention by sociologists' (Knorr Cetina and Preda 2005: 3; cf. Hessling and Pahl 2006).

In addition, there are some few further attempts to reconceptualize finance and public finance. Critical finance studies, for example, is based on the mission of 'putting philosophy and art to work on financial ideas, theories and practices, in order to create concepts that will make it possible to think and use finance altogether differently' (Critical Finance Studies), and social studies of finance is 'the application to financial markets of social-science disciplines such as sociology, anthropology, and social studies of science' (Social Studies of Science). From a psychoanalytic perspective, Tuckett and Taffler (2005, 2008) and Taffler and Tuckett (2007) propose 'an interdisciplinary set of theories presently labelled *emotional finance*' (Tavistock Policy Seminars 2008).

Moreover, publications that explicitly deal with money or the world of finance from a psychodynamic or socioanalytic perspective seem to be scarce so far (e.g. Arnaud 2003; Kirsner 1990; Levine 2008; Shafer 2001; Sievers 2003, 2009a, b; Stein 2000, 2003, 2004, 2007; Wolfenstein 1993; Young 1998). However, there is, as Sievers (Chapter 7) elaborates, quite a body of theory, for example, on corruption and perversion (Chapman 1999; Chapman and Long 2009; Levine 2005; Long 2008), on narcissistic process and corporate decay (Schwartz 1990a, b), and on toxicity and miasma (Gabriel 2008; Stein 2008) that may be of further help in developing an understanding of some of the unconscious dynamics of the financial world and the present financial crisis in particular.

The attempt at a deeper understanding of the unconscious dynamics of the financial industry and fiscal world will make us face gaps in our field of study. In addition to viewing money, finance, and capital in depth, such an attempt may raise further reaching questions such as the broadly unconscious implications of risk and risk management (e.g. Hirschhorn 1999; Pelzer 2007, 2009; Pelzer and Case 2007; Stein 2003); whether and, if so, to what extent the financial system as a societal or global subsystem is at present serving as a kind of container (and a 'scapegoat' or cover story) for various other virulent issues and broadly neglected problems, both on the level of societies and on that of the world at large; and the range and deeper meaning of discontents with capitalism in its present form, which often seems to be equated with civilization itself.

What is socioanalysis?

Socioanalysis is a social science discipline in the making. The notion of applied psychoanalysis seems to suggest the application of insights gained in clinical research. Socioanalysis, however, with its emphasis on the study of the social, i.e. of social, cultural and political phenomena and dynamics, yet with recourse to clinical concepts and theories from psychoanalysis, aims at the development of specific means of observation, research and hypotheses, concepts and theories that contribute to a deeper understanding of the 'social fabric' of organizations and society.

Compared to the more common term of organizational psychodynamics (e.g. Cilliers and Koortzen 2000; Czander 1993; Diamond 2009; Diamond and Allcorn 2009; Hirschhorn 1990; Hirschhorn and Barnett 1993; Kets de Vries and Balazs 1998) or psychoanalytic study of organizations – as offered by the International Society for the Psychoanalytic Study of Organizations (ISPSO) (e.g. Gould 1988/2009; Sievers 2009c) – socioanalysis provides a more extensive frame that goes beyond the perception of social systems as organizations and/or groups in so far as it perceives these as embedded in a social, cultural and global environment and investigates issues at the global level, for instance the economy, the financial industry, 'the market' or politics or society at large.

Socioanalysis, as an approach to study, emerged in the late 1990s. In 1999 the first edition of the journal *Socio-Analysis* was published in Melbourne, co-edited by Susan Long and Allan Shafer. It is at the confluence of certain disciplines, theories and approaches of experiential learning: psychoanalysis, group relations, social systems thinking, social dreaming and organizational behaviour (Bain 1999). While authors like Melanie Klein, Donald W. Winnicott, Wilfred R. Bion or those formerly affiliated with the Tavistock Institute of Human Relations in London, such as W. Gordon Lawrence, Eric Miller, Isabel E. P. Menzies, A.K. Rice or Pierre Turquet, have either directly or indirectly laid much of the ground for this new discipline, various others, not least several members of ISPSO, of which each of us in the past has been president, have meanwhile contributed further leading research, writings and insights. While rooted in psychoanalysis, socioanalysis aims to go beyond its traditional focus of the individual and its narrower frame of object relations. In a sense, socioanalysis adds a further dimension to Freud's (1917) statement that the ego is no longer the master of its own house, in so far as it inverts the relation between master and house. Using Freud's metaphoric frame, it might be stated that socioanalysis regards the master as being like a tenant who has rented his house, while the house itself is owned either by a landlord or a bank.

Bain (1999) sees the origin of socioanalysis in the work of Bion, Rickman and Foulkes at the Hollymoor Hospital, Northfield, Birmingham, in 1943 (Harrison 2000; Harrison and Clarke 1992; Main 1946). The broadening of the psychoanalytic perspective to groups and institutions is mainly attributed to Wilfred R. Bion and the learnings he derived from his experience of the Northfield Experiments (Bion 1946, 1948a, b, 1961). Even though the respective theory was not yet available at the time, Bion first contributed a 'systemic' perspective to psychoanalytic thinking. His work with groups was based on the hypothesis that groups are led in general by 'primitive' phantasies of an unconscious nature, which are an expression of psychotic anxieties. This led him to the assumption that the traditional emphasis on the individual or triadic part of the Greek myth of Oedipus, termed by Freud and most of his successors the 'Oedipus complex', could be extended to the social and political dimension. Emphasizing the other part of the myth, i.e. the Sphinx and its riddle – 'What is the creature that walks on four legs in the morning, two legs at noon and three in the evening?' – Bion (1961: 8; cf. Kernberg and Ahumada 2000; Lawrence 1999) suggested a 'binocular' vision as an indispensable prerequisite for the psychoanalytic study of groups – and thus the social. While 'the project of Oedipus' stands for the classical domain of psychoanalysis in the dyadic setting of analyst and analysand, 'the project of the Sphinx' refers to the social context, which constitutes consciousness and meaning in organizations (Lawrence 1999: 104; cf. Sievers 1999). The Sphinx represents the capacity to illuminate and question the predominant (unconscious) fantasies and the psychotic thinking in groups in order to allow reality-testing required for the 'work group'. Socioanalysis 'coheres around the centering of Sphinx, with Oedipus as a secondary but linked consideration. In short, Sphinx is "figure" in the study of organizations and Oedipus is "ground"' (Lawrence 1999: 106).

The primary focus of socioanalysis is the impact of 'the social' on individuals and their inner world. This becomes evident, for example, in the hypothesis that the thinking (and behaviour) of role-holders in organizations and other social systems is understood as *socially* induced by the system and/or its environment and influences them to (re)act in, for example, a neurotic, psychotic or perverse manner more than they would in other (systemic) contexts (Lawrence 1995, 1998). By adding, for example, the drama at work (put on stage in the organization or broader social context) as an additional dimension of experience, thinking and fantasy (Sievers 1995), the drama rooted in infancy (Klein 1959/1988) may be broadened to a *social* drama that not only reactivates significant protagonists of the past but activates and is activated by others in the present as well.

A secondary, but equally important, focus of socioanalysis is the 'function' that organizations and other social systems have for the individual – that is, how individual role-holders make use of 'the social' (or abuse it), for example by identification, or projection/introjection for their own often unconscious anxieties, defences, fantasies, desires, etc. There often is a mutual relation between systemic structures and dynamics on the one hand and individual 'predispositions' on the other (Menzies 1967; cf. Jaques 1955). Individual dramas of childhood have, for example, a decisive impact on the choice of profession and organization.

Though the main emphasis of socioanalysis may – like that of psychoanalysis – be to reveal the 'dysfunctional' impact of unconscious dynamics that obstruct or jeopardize both the effectiveness of social systems and the quality of working life for its members, the concern for organizational structures, processes, instruments, etc. that may increase a system's capacity for containment and are supportive of its effectively pursuing its primary task are of equal importance and certainly require further attention and research (e.g. Jaques 1997; cf. Kirsner 2006).

We have endeavoured to have our focus on organisational rather than personal or individual centred issues because that is what socio-analysis is about. However, system or organisational issues are expressed through individuals and groups; that is how they are examined. The philosophy of science supporting this study is different from traditional empiricist or positivist philosophies, although some of the researchers in the field may at times work within these traditions. A primary philosophy of science supporting socioanalysis is that propounded by Charles Sanders Pierce, a late 19th century philosopher who introduced the idea of 'abductive logic' (Burch 2010). He examined scientific discovery as moving through stages of abductive, deductive and inductive logic. Abductive logic is involved in the early stages of hypothesis creation. At this stage, argument by metaphor leads to the creative development of what we call 'working hypotheses' that can then be examined against new cases. This underlies the method of 'negative case analysis' as practised in many sociological investigations. We recognise that socioanalysis relies heavily on abductive logic as well as deductive and inductive logic. This may be due to its 'youth' as a discipline; but we believe it is also due to the nature of its subject – the unconscious dynamics of groups and organisations, where individualised exploration of systems is paramount.

The major research methodology in our discipline is the case study, hence the many cases related in this book. The reasons for this include the complexity of concepts with non-linear causality; the use of narrative, qualitative, descriptive methods rather than experimental, quantitative methods; the use of action research which – because of the changing, systemic nature of organizations – utilises a social and political intervention alongside an exploratory method; and the use of abductive logic in the development of working hypotheses that aid in thinking through case material and organizational change.

As with psychoanalysis, the great strength of socioanalysis is not so much its answers as its questions. Socioanalysis

> is, most of all, a point of view that probes beneath the surface of the obvious and raises questions about what we have comfortably assumed.... The questioning dialogue, rather than the definitive diagnosis, is the hallmark of the psychoanalytic method and of its benefits and virtues.
>
> (Wachtel 2003: 103)

Outline of the book

The perspective of this book is largely socioanalytic as described in the previous section. However, some of our authors come from more specifically sociological backgrounds. In accepting responses to our call for chapters, we considered those who focused on looking 'beneath the surface' from a variety of perspectives.

Hence, we broaden our perspective in this book to all those efforts that examine the surface phenomena of the financial industry to find those dynamics that occur at an unconscious level.

Money

The traditional psychoanalytic view of money developed by Freud and his immediate followers links anal eroticism to the accumulation of money. Personality types based on the anal character were seen not only as demonstrating excessive cleanliness, but also as having a hoarding and acquisitive nature as a defence against anal eroticism.

This is extensively developed in the social context through the work of Norman O. Brown (1959, 1966). Money, seen as a representation of human faeces, is a product of the body, and the control, even repression, of bodily functions is regarded as central to the civilizing function of society. Hence, money can be seen as both a representation of and a defence against anal eroticism – the exact recipe for sublimation. Moreover, in its capacity to unconsciously both represent the desired immortal body and its restraint, money is not simply a tool of economic exchange but a deeply emotional link between the personal and the cultural. On the one hand, in fantasy it represents the capacity to fulfil all desires – the nature of everlasting consumerism – and on the other hand, control of money in fantasy represents control of the body, control of the bodies of others, and, ultimately, control of culture and society.

A socioanalysis of money is focused on the meaning of money to individuals, groups, institutions and society most broadly. Freudian psychoanalysis as described understands this meaning to originate in early relations involving early eroticism, and, at a social level, to involve the struggle between eros and civilization. Socioanalysis extends this analysis through incorporating an additional sociological perspective.

Later writers such as Giddens (1990) stress the current nature of interpersonal and social relations and the role played by trust in institutions. Money to Giddens is a form of trust. He regards our modern society as characterized by disembedded social relations evidenced in a reliance on abstract, distanced systems of technology and impersonal expertise. True, we use internet banking, for example, rather than having direct relationship with a banker. But this is just the latest step in the evolution of money from a barter system to the use of commodities such as gold, through to a representational paper money system and eventually to numbers in an electronic system. This all indicates an increasing reliance on trust that the system involved will eventually translate into paying the bills and, more deeply, fulfilling desires.

Trust can be and at times is violated. Socioanalysis looks at the systemic and institutionalized ways that this occurs at a level that is unconscious to the players in those systems.

In Part I of the book, titled 'Money', the authors look at the socioanalytic meaning of money. Allan Shafer in Chapter 2 proposes the idea that money can be a fantasy and the institutionalized power of money is currently a defence against rapidly increasing powerlessness and diminished faith in personal and institutional authoritative leadership.

The unconscious perverse dynamics surrounding money are explored by Susan Long (Chapter 3), who explores the socioanalysis of greed through an Australian case study, and Claudia Nagel (Chapter 4), who examines money as fetish. Here a detailed analysis of the consecutive stages of the financial market crisis demonstrates how different psychological mechanisms have been working together in a complex way. Alison Gill and Mannie Sher (Chapter 5), through their research interviews, explore how some of the central players in the financial sector think about money and finance. Also in Part I, Richard Morgan-Jones (Chapter 6) explores the links between money and time, utilizing ideas that inform the saying 'time is money'. He argues that money and time are increasingly scarce resources and that the link between them is at risk of being 'killed off'.

Finance

Finance, the subject of Part II of the book, involves the management of money and other assets, especially through institutions such as banks, investment companies, the stock market, other financial markets and funds management groups.

> Financial economics is the branch of economics concerned with the workings of financial markets, such as the stock market, and the financing of companies. It can be distinguished from other branches of economics by its concentration on monetary activities, in which money of one type or another is likely to appear on both sides of a trade. The questions addressed are typically framed in terms of time, uncertainty, options and information.
>
> (Zantrio)

Part II concerns socioanalytic explorations of finance and the finance industry. In this perspective, we examine the social dynamics affecting and affected by financial institutions and the players who work in and around this industry. Financial institutions play an increasingly dominant role in society. No one can escape their effects. Nowadays, not only are the great bulk of workers affected by financial markets but most people are significant players through their roles in superannuation schemes, government bonds, housing mortgages and other loans. It is this transformation of society by finance that brings about the 'financialization of everyday life' (Martin 2002; cf. Langley 2009), which is producing increased volatility in daily life and a decreased sense of democratic participation. In addition, although there may never have been a wide social comprehension of finance, recent complex financial 'products' have led to an even further decline in the comprehension of financial institutions.

In this part of the book our authors offer a variety of case studies and theoretical explanations about the nature of the finance industry, helping to explore the dynamic socioanalytic roots of the recent financial crisis and its effects. Burkard

Sievers in Chapter 7 sets the scene by introducing a theoretical overview of socioanalytic approaches to finance, setting the scene for the chapters that follow. In Chapter 8, Emre Tarim looks at the narrative performances of five Istanbul-based fund managers in April and May 2008. Examples of sense-making narratives from this observation period are given, which reveal the paradigmatic and vernacular knowledge these fund managers use in order to reach meaningful interpretations of past and present, and accurate predictions of the future.

From the United States, Seth Allcorn and Howard F. Stein explore in Chapter 9 the cultural psychodynamics of what former chairman of the Federal Reserve Alan Greenspan called 'irrational exuberance', showing how beneath the illusion of 'rational economic man' lurks a vast sea of irrationality rooted both in human nature and in the specific historical moment of American crisis.

Several chapters deal with the issues surrounding risk. Byron Woollen in Chapter 10 explores the dynamics affecting top financial leaders, who were dissociated from and, in some cases, hostile to evidence that their companies were taking unreasonable risks. Two cases studies from Woollen's consulting practice are offered as evidence of the way in which an unconscious belief about the protective powers of money (money as fetish) may distort the 'organization in the mind of the leader'. Peter Pelzer in Chapter 11 argues that 'risk' as a concept has replaced 'fate' and that the future has become commodified in financial products. In Chapter 12, Jesper Blomberg, Hans Kjellberg and Karin Winroth argue that while stock traders construct share identities based on external (market) influences and trading opportunities, risk managers translate shares into the currency of risk on the basis of both legal frameworks and internal procedures for risk assessment. These two different approaches render coordination between the two groups difficult.

Roles are again explored in Chapter 13, where Erik van de Loo and Angelien Kemna describe interactions between participants of the Dutch financial system, where the introduction of new rules and codes of governance intended to protect the system has constrained, if not eliminated, existing ways of communication between participants. Finally in the area of risk, Amy L. Fraher in Chapter 14 writes about the complicated interrelatedness of money and safety within the commercial airline industry in post-9/11 America. She demonstrates how a perverse culture emerged in which airlines' fixation on maximizing short-term profits at the expense of long-term safety, and government regulators' inability to curtail this culture, caused a shift in pilot demographics.

In Chapter 15, W. Gordon Lawrence describes a Social Dreaming Matrix that was convened at the Working Men's College, Camden Town, London, in July 2009. The working hypothesis employed was that whatever the conscious, historical and rational reasons for financial institutions, the resulting contemporary financial crisis has happened because banks, and related institutions, have been blinded to the demands of their original purpose because of their unconscious thinking and ideology, which border on delusion. The chapter describes the dreams reported and the associations made by those attending.

Sándor Takács in Chapter 16 explores how psychoanalytically informed research in organizations contributes to our understanding of financial institutions. He does this through examining the consumer credit boom (2004–8) and the changing roles of banks and their employees in Hungary, where 'consultants' became 'customer service' employees. Research using case studies is employed by Hans van den Hooff in Chapter 17. Here the phenomenon of steep career development and sudden burn-out in the financial industry is explored through an analysis using the Greek myth of Phaethon, who crashes his father's sun chariot. He proposes that one-to-one executive coaching is an efficient way of transforming organizations that are in danger of following their leader in his or her fall.

The final chapter in Part II, Chapter 18 by Marc Lenglet, argues that if we are to understand what lies beneath the surface of the financial industry, it may well be necessary to acknowledge that our cognitive map resembles an iceberg, where a large part of the financial reality remains unseen, and therefore unquestioned. Drawing on a series of examples, he focuses on market contexts where the compliance function, responsible for the framing of practices, interacts with market operators. In so doing, he seeks to provide a better understanding of how markets are framed and constituted.

Capitalism

The notion of 'capitalism' may at first be described relatively easily as 'the possession of capital or wealth' (*New Shorter Oxford* 1993: 333), with capital either simply regarded as 'assets available for use in the production of further assets' (*Free Dictionary*) or, in a more sophisticated conception, as a 'measure of the accumulated financial strength of an individual, firm, or nation, created by sacrificing present consumption in favor of investment to generate future returns above investment costs' (*Business Dictionary*). However, the answer to the nature of capitalism may, on second thought, echo the answer Saint Augustine (*Confessions* XI: 14) once gave when asking himself: 'What then is time?' His reply was 'If no one asks me, I know what it is. If I wish to explain it to someone who asks, I don't know.'

It appears as if the pretence of knowing what capitalism *is* broadly serves to conceal our not-knowing – both in everyday language and, to quite some extent, in economics. For example, Heinsohn (2009) states that 'the politics of economics … resemble emergency surgery without any knowledge of anatomy. We still deceive ourselves about the basics of interest, money and market'. Whereas we both profit and suffer from capitalism, more often than not we tend to displace our discontent; we broadly appear 'to accept capitalist society, equating it with civilization itself' (Hansen 1956, drawing on Marcuse's [1955] *Eros and Civilization*).

The following seven chapters, making up Part III, attempt to throw further light on what may be beneath the surface of contemporary capitalism and the current financial crisis in particular. Capitalism is often linked theoretically with Adam Smith's *Wealth of Nations* – the capitalist spirit seen as imbued with assertive, creative individualism on the positive side and with greed and profit at the expense of others by its critics. In this part of our book the authors examine some psychological and social dynamics within capitalism.

In Chapter 19 a distinction is drawn by David P. Levine between pathological forms of the capitalist spirit linked to wealth seeking and those forms that are consistent with respect for self-boundaries and regard for others. The distinction between these forms of the capitalist spirit is considered in relation to the creative and destructive aspects of fantasy life. A further understanding of psychological factors important in capitalism is pursued by Douglas Kirsner (Chapter 20), who considers the nature of trust. He argues that consumers and investors behave differently depending on their confidence or concern and need to have confidence in their financial institutions systems not to betray them. The situation facing the world at the global financial crisis, he claims, raises some fundamental issues about how to erect and maintain a secure foundation of trustworthy institutions.

Larry Hirschhorn in Chapter 21 suggests that 'the market' has become the projective screen for our imaginative capacities, but at the same time itself creates systemic risks that require the exercise of authority and the subordination of imagination to rules and regulations. The result is a tension between imagination and authority which, when poorly managed, leads to crises. Reflecting upon the financial crisis both from psychoanalytic and business experience, Ian S. Miller's chapter (Chapter 22) examines both the values of profit and competitive advantage as flexible, utilitarian business drivers and the systemic limitations of 'bounded rationality' in business enterprises. The chapter concludes with an understanding of business activity based in Robert Waelder's understanding of the ego's executive function – as the continuous permutation of multiple subsystem actions, both passive/active and internal/external.

Two cases studies follow, in Chapters 23 and 24. Contrasting 'oedipal' and 'anti-oedipal' worldviews, Howard S. Schwartz examines a study by the Boston Federal Reserve Bank which he argues is dominated by an 'anti-oedipal' worldview of political correctness. Through such a worldview, he argues, many facts about the mortgage risks of loans behind the sub-prime mortgage crisis in the United States were distorted, and hence our analyses of the situation are also distorted. Laura Yu in Chapter 24 considers the interface of market pressures and the democratic participatory environment of the world's largest worker cooperative: the Mondragon Corporation of Spain. Mondragon's expanding growth and market interactions challenge its important organizational balance between achieving competitiveness in the global market and maintaining the centrality of workplace democracy as supported by its Basic Cooperative Principles. The dynamics of this contentious balance are explored. In particular, a focus on how the anxiety caused by this organizational tension may also be at play in perpetuating these shifts highlights both the difficulty of and potential strategies for maintaining the integrity of the democratic workplace.

Focusing on narrative repertoires of alternative trading regimes, Matthias Klaes, Geoff Lightfoot and Simon Lilley in Chapter 25 examine how traders make sense of their activities at the same time as practically orienting them, and argue that compared to the widely acknowledged masculinity of open outcry trading, screen-based trading provides no less of an arena for expression of compulsory masculinity.

In a final chapter, we (Susan Long and Burkard Sievers, Chapter 26) present some of our ideas on capitalism as the current cultural container for money and finance in the context of learning from this book.

References

Arnaud, G. (2003) 'Money as signifier: a Lacanian insight into the monetary order', *Free Associations*, 10, part 1(53): 25–43.

Bain, A. (1999) 'On socio-analysis', *Socio-Analysis*, 1(1): 1–17. Online, available at: www.acsa.net.au/articles/onsocio-analysis.pdf (retrieved 2 June 2010).

Bain, A. (2009) 'The economic crisis as manic depression: a few thoughts', Online, available at: www.acsa.net.au/articles/The%20Economic%20Crisis%20as%20Manic%20Depression.pdf (retrieved 9 May 2009).

Bion, W.R. (1946) 'Leaderless group project', *Bulletin of the Menninger Clinic*, 10: 77–81.

Bion, W.R. (1948a) 'Psychiatry in a time of crisis', *British Journal of Medical Psychology*, 21: 81–9.

Bion, W.R. (1948b) 'Experiences in groups', *Human Relations*, 1–4, 1948–51. Reprinted in Bion, W.R (1961) *Experiences in Groups*, London: Tavistock Publications.

Bion, W.R. (1961) *Experiences in Groups*, London: Tavistock Publications.

Brown, N.O. (1959) *Life against Death: The psychoanalytic meaning of history*, Middletown, CT: Wesleyan University Press.

Brown, N.O. (1966) *Love's Body*, NewYork: Random House.

Burch, R. (2010) *Stanford Dictionary of Philosophy*. Online, available at http://plato.stanford.edu/entries/peirce/#dia (retrieved 31st August 2011).

Business Dictionary, 'Capital', Business Dictionary.com. Online, available at: www.businessdictionary.com/definition/capital.html (retrieved 26 November 2010).

Camerer, C.F. and Loewenstein, G. (2002) 'Behavioral economics: past, present, future' Online, available at: www.hss.caltech.edu/~camerer/ribe239.pdf (retrieved 25 November 2010).

Chapman, J. (1999) 'Hatred and corruption of task', *Socio-Analysis*, 1(2). Reprinted in *Organisational and Social Dynamics*, 2003, 3(1): 40–60.

Chapman, J. and Long, S. (2009) 'Role contamination: is the poison in the person or the bottle?' *Socio-Analysis*, 11(1): 53–66.

Cilliers, F. and Koortzen, P. (2000) 'The psychodynamic view on organizational behavior', *Society for Industrial and Organizational Psychology*. Online, available at: www.siop.org/TIP/backissues/TipOct00/08Cilliers.aspx (retrieved 27 February 2010).

Critical Finance Studies. Online, available at: www.criticalfinancestudies.org/?page_id=4 (retrieved 26 November 2010).

Czander, W.M. (1993) *The Psychodynamics of Work and Organization: Theory and application*, New York: Guilford Press.

Diamond, M.A. (2009) 'Organizational change and the analytic third: locating and attending to unconscious organizational psychodynamics', *Psychoanalysis, Culture and Society*, 12: 142–64.

Diamond, M.A. and Allcorn, S. (2009) *Private Selves in Public Organizations: The psychodynamics of organizational diagnosis and change*, New York: Palgrave Macmillan.

Free Dictionary, 'Capital', *The Free Dictionary by Farlex*. Online, available at: www. thefreedictionary.com/capital (retrieved 26 November 2010).

Freud, S. (1917) 'A difficulty in the path of psycho-analysis', *The Standard Edition of the Complete Psychological Works of Sigmund Freud*, vol. 17, London: Hogarth Press.

Gabriel, Y. (2008) 'Organizational miasma, purification and cleansing', in A. Ahlers-Niemann, U. Beumer, R. Redding Mersky and B. Sievers (eds) *Organisationsland-schaften. Sozioanalytische Gedanken und Interventionen zur normalen Verrücktheit in Organisationen/The Normal Madness in Organizations: Socioanalytic thoughts and interventions*, Bergisch-Gladbach, Germany: Verlag Andreas Kohlhage.

Giddens, A. (1990) *The Consequences of Modernity*, Cambridge: Polity Press.

Gould, L.J. (1988/2009) 'Psychoanalytic frameworks for organizational analysis and consultation: an overview and appraisal of theory and practice', in B. Sievers (ed.) *Psycho-analytic Studies of Organizations: Contributions from the International Society for the Psychoanalytic Study of Organizations (ISPSO)*, London: Karnac.

Hansen, J. (1956) 'A psychoanalyst looks for a sane society', *Fourth International*, 17(2): 65–9. Online, available at: www.marxists.org/archive/hansen/1956/xx/psych.htm (retrieved 18 May 2009).

Harrison, T. (2000) *Bion, Rickman, Foulkes and the Northfield Experiments: Advancing on a different front*, London: Jessica Kingsley.

Harrison, T. and Clarke, D. (1992) 'The Northfield Experiments', *British Journal of Psychiatry*, 160: 698–708.

Heinsohn, G. (2009) 'Die nächste Blase schwillt schon an', *Frankfurter Allgemeine Zeitung*, 20 May, no. 116: 31.

Hessling, A. and Pahl, H. (2006) 'The global system of finance: scanning Talcott Parsons and Niklas Luhmann for theoretical keystones', *American Journal of Economics and Sociology*, 65(1): 189–218.

Hirschhorn, L. (1990) *The Workplace Within: Psychodynamics of organizational life*, Cambridge, MA: MIT Press.

Hirschhorn, L. (1999) 'The primary risk', *Human Relations*, 52(1): 5–23.

Hirschhorn, L. and Barnett, C.K. (eds) (1993) *The Psychodynamics of Organizations*, Philadelphia: Temple University Press.

Jaques, E. (1955) 'Social systems as a defense against persecutory and depressive anxiety', in M. Klein, P. Heimann and R. Money-Kyrle (eds) *New Directions in Psychoanalysis*, New York: Basic Books.

Jaques, E. (1997) *Requisite Organization: A total system for effective managerial organization and managerial leadership for the 21st century*, Arlington, VA: Cason Hall.

Kernberg, O.F. and Ahumada, J.L. (2000) 'Bion, a binocular view: groups and individuals', *International Journal of Psycho-Analysis*, 81: 991–4.

Kets de Vries, M.F.R. and Balazs, K. (1998) 'Beyond the quick fix: the psychodynamics of organizational transformation and change', *European Management Journal*, 16(5), October: 611–22.

Kirsner, D. (1990) 'Illusion and the stock market crash: some psychoanalytic aspects', *Free Associations*, 19: 31–58. Online, available at: http://internationalpsychoanalysis. net/wp-content/uploads/2009/04/kirsnerillusion_21.pdf (retrieved 3 June 2009).

Kirsner, D. (2006): Guest editorial: 'The contributions of Elliott Jaques', *International Journal of Applied Psychoanalytic Studies*, 2(4): 315–17.

Klein, M. (1959/1988) 'Our adult world and its roots in infancy', in M. Klein (1988), *Envy and Gratitude and Other Works: 1921–1963*, London: Virago.

Knorr Cetina, K. and Preda, A. (2005) Introduction, in K. Knorr Cetina and A. Preda (eds) *The Sociology of Financial Markets*, Oxford: Oxford University Press.

Langley, P. (2009) *The Everyday Life of Global Finance: Saving and borrowing in Anglo-America*, Oxford: Oxford University Press.

Lawrence, W.G. (1995) 'The seductiveness of totalitarian states-of-mind', *Journal of Health Care Chaplaincy*, 7, October: 11–22.

Lawrence, W.G. (1998) 'Unconscious social pressures on leaders', in E.B. Klein, F. Gabelnick and P. Herr (eds) *The Psychodynamics of Leadership*, Madison, CT: Psychosocial Press.

Lawrence, W.G. (1999) 'Centring of the Sphinx for the psychoanalytic study of organisations', *Socio-Analysis*, 1(1): 99–126.

Levine, D.P. (2005) 'The corrupt organization', *Human Relations*, 58(6): 723–40.

Levine, D.P. (2008) *Politics without Reason*, New York: Palgrave Macmillan.

Long, S. (2008) *The Perverse Organisation and Its Deadly Sins*, London: Karnac.

Main, T.F. (1946) 'The hospital as a therapeutic institution', *Bulletin of the Menninger Clinic*, 10: 66–70.

Marcuse, H. (1955) *Eros and Civilization: A philosophical inquiry into Freud*, Boston: Bacon Press.

Martin, R. (2002) *Financialization of Daily Life*, Philadelphia: Temple University Press.

Menzies, I.E.P. (1967) 'The functioning of social systems as a defence against anxiety', Tavistock Pamphlet no. 3, London: Tavistock Publications. Reprinted in A.D. Coleman and W.H. Bexton (eds) *Group Relations Reader*, Washington, DC: A.K. Rice Institute, 1975.

Miller, J.-A. (2008) 'The financial crisis'. Online, available at: www.lacan.com/symptom/?page_id=299 (retrieved 30 November 2008).

New Shorter Oxford (1993) *The New Shorter Oxford English Dictionary on Historical Principles*, ed. L. Brown, Oxford: Clarendon Press.

Pelzer, P. (2007) 'The futility of excess, or the displaced world of rules and regulations', *Culture and Organization*, 13(2): 157–69.

Pelzer, P. (2009) 'The displaced world of risk: risk management as alienated risk (perception?)', *Society and Business Review*, 4(1): 26–36.

Pelzer, P. and Case, P. (2007) 'The displaced world of risk management: covert enchantment in a calculative world', in M. Kostera (ed.) *Mythical Inspirations and Storytelling for Organizational Realities*, Basingstoke, UK: Palgrave.

Schwartz, H.S. (1990a) 'Narcissism project and corporate decay: the case of General Motors'. Online, available at: www.sba.oakland.edu/faculty/schwartz/GMDecay.htm (retrieved 17 December 2008).

Schwartz, H.S. (1990b) *Narcissistic Process and Corporate Decay: The theory of the organization ideal*, New York: New York University Press.

Shafer, A. (2001) 'What is the value of money?', paper presented at Seminar for the Australian Institute of Socio-Analysis' series "Money Talks!", 30 November. Online, available at: www.allanshafer.com/docs/What%20is%20the%20Value%20of%20Money.doc (retrieved 18 May 2009).

Shaw, L. (2005) 'The uncanny and long term capital management', *International Journal of Applied Psychoanalytic Studies*, 2(3): 271–94.

Shiller, R.S. (2008) *The Subprime Solution: How today's global financial crisis happened, and what to do about it*, Princeton, NJ: Princeton University Press.

Sievers, B. (1995) 'Characters in search of a theatre: organization as theatre for the drama of childhood and the drama at work', *Free Associations*, 5, part 2(34): 196–220.

Sievers, B. (1999) 'Psychotic organization as a metaphoric frame for the socio-analysis of organizational and interorganizational dynamics', *Administration and Society*, 31(5): 588–615.

Sievers, B. (2003) '"Your money or your life?" Psychotic implications of the pension fund system: towards a socio-analysis of the financial services revolution', *Human Relations*, 56(2): 187–210.

Sievers, B. (2009a) 'Der "ganz normale" Wahnsinn. Zu einer Sozioanalyse der gegenwärtigen Finanzkrise', *texte*, 29(1): 81–106.

Sievers, B. (2009b) 'Beneath the surface of the financial industry: prolegomena to a socioanalysis of the present global financial crisis', paper presented at the 26th ISPSO Annual Meeting, Toledo, Spain, 22–28 June.

Sievers, B. (ed.) (2009c) *Psychoanalytic Studies of Organizations: Contributions from the International Society for the Psychoanalytic Study of Organizations (ISPSO) 1983–2008*, London: Karnac.

Social Studies of Finance. Online, available at: www.sociology.ed.ac.uk/finance/index. html (retrieved 26 November 2010).

Stein, M. (2000) 'The risk taker as shadow: a psychoanalytic view of the collapse of Barings Bank', *Journal of Management Studies*, 37(8): 1215–29.

Stein, M. (2003) 'Unbounded irrationality: risk and organizational narcissism at Long Term Capital Management', *Human Relations*, 56(5): 523–40.

Stein, M. (2004) 'The critical period of disasters: insights from sensemaking and psychoanalytic theory', *Human Relations*, 57(10): 1243–61.

Stein, M. (2007) 'Oedipus Rex at Enron: leadership, Oedipal struggles, and organizational collapse', *Human Relations*, 60(9): 1387–410.

Stein, M. (2008) 'Toxicity and the unconscious experience of the body at the employee–customer interface', *Organization Studies*, 28: 1223–41.

Taffler, R. and Tuckett, D. (2007) 'Emotional finance: understanding what drives investors', *Professional Investor*, Autumn: 18–20.

Tavistock Policy Seminars (2008) 'Markets, meaning and madness', 20 November, London: Tavistock and Portman NHS Foundation Trust.

Tuckett, D. and Taffler, R. (2005) 'A psychoanalytic interpretation of dot.com stock valuations', *SSRN Social Science Research Network*, 1 March. Online, available at: http:// papers.ssrn.com/sol3/papers.cfm?abstract_id=676635 (retrieved 11 May 2009).

Tuckett, D. and Taffler, R. (2008) 'Phantastic objects and the financial market's sense of reality: a psychoanalytic contribution to the understanding of stock market instability', *International Journal of Psychoanalysis*, 89: 389–412.

Wachtel, P.L. (2003) 'Full pockets, empty lives: a psychoanalytic exploration of the contemporary culture of greed', *American Journal of Psychoanalysis*, 63(2): 101–20.

Wolfenstein, E.V. (1993) *Psychoanalytic-Marxism: Groundwork*, London: Free Association Books; New York: Guilford Press.

Young, R.M. (1998) 'Some reflections on the psychodynamics of wealth'. Online, available at: www.human-nature.com/rmyoung/papers/pap106.html (retrieved 25 November 2010).

Zantrio 'Financial economics'. Online, available at: http://zantrio.com/dictionary/financial_economics.php (retrieved 25 November 2010).

Part I
Money

2   What is the value of money?

Allan Shafer

An article in a local newspaper curiously announced a 'charity walk'. These are usually held to raise funds. This one was called a 'Walk for Capitalism', which was rather surprising, as it is unusual for 'capitalism' to be raising funds in this way. Apparently only four people turned up. This ironic little tale poignantly introduces the complex and paradoxical topic of what the value of money might be or might have become. It is paradoxical in that money has complex real value but it also has great symbolic meaning.

The value of money is explored in this chapter from a primarily socioanalytic vertex. This focus reflects an interest not only in the social value of money (as an ethical concern) as well as the financial value (as a resource), but also in the relationship between the social and financial dimensions.

Philip Ball (1999), a freelance science writer and consultant editor to *Nature* magazine, proffers a useful definition of the value of money: 'One could say that the value of money is an emergent property of the system.'

Questions about value in the current emergent context are raised by Richard Sennett:

> How do we decide what is of lasting value in ourselves in a society which is impatient, which focuses on the immediate moment? How can long-term goals be pursued in an economy devoted to the short-term? How can mutual loyalties and commitments be sustained in institutions which are constantly breaking apart or continually being re-designed? These are the questions about character posed by the new, flexible capitalism.
>
> (1998: 11)

Flexible capitalism in essence means that a society has no long-term engagement with work and organizational life, and means a significant alteration to traditional hierarchical organizational structures. This perspective will be expanded later.

By 'character', Sennett is referring to enduring emotional experience and the value invested in socio-emotional engagement in balance with personal desire. He identifies allegiance and mutual obligation and delayed gratification. These qualities can be at odds with the short-term tendencies of the current value of money. Sennett is questioning the larger implications for the psychosocial capital of our society.

In writing as a socioanalyst I do not want to represent myself as a claimant to any economic expertise. Indeed, as John Kenneth Galbraith said on the Australian ABC National Radio Series *Money, Markets and the Economy* (2001), economists' 'prime interest is how money works .. economists assume money is neutral and erases distinction and simply acts as an intermediary between the buyer and the seller'. In contrast, the focus of interest here is in the non-neutral significance of money and its reach beyond merely being an intermediary. Indeed, money has very notable symbolic and emotional meaning outside of a purely economic model.

The ideas presented here have been influenced by Paul Hoggett (1992), a socioanalytic thinker, and Richard Sennett (1998), who comes close to being one.

To help us examine these issues, two interlinked hypotheses are offered (the second of which contains a number of implicit hypotheses), for which supporting arguments will be provided. There is undoubtedly a myriad of ways money functions symbolically and in reality in our lives. In this chapter, just a few will be investigated.

The hypotheses are:

1   Money can be a fantasy.
2   The institutionalized power of money is *currently* a defence against rapidly increasing powerlessness and diminished faith in personal and institutional authoritative leadership. (A corollary of this is that money is currently overvalued, to protect us against unpredictability.)

In considering these hypotheses, the contemporary global background – and in particular, world events since 11 September and the so-called global financial crisis – must be kept in mind, even though the origins of the ideas to be presented often predate this.

Hypothesis 1

To recap, hypothesis 1 is that *money can be a fantasy*. Hoggett (1992) suggests that fantasy is a means whereby thought takes us away from the real and from action. He says, 'Fantasy can subvert terror by being an act of defiance.... Subversive fantasy is an expression of autonomy.' But it does not alter the social nexus. 'Fantasy belongs to the realm of *impossibility*. By contrast, imagination is the vehicle of hope [i.e. the possible]; fantasy the vehicle of despair' (ibid.: 13).

Hoggett asks, 'How does an individual develop and maintain a sense of "the possible"; a durable conviction that reality *can* be changed, that the "given" *can* be subverted? And how do we block ourselves from developing this sense?' (1992: 11).

It is proposed here – in line with Hoggett – that when money operates as a fantasy, it blocks imagination, and that imagination is crucial to hope and change.

In examining the distinction between fantasy and imagination, Marx's ideas about production are relevant. His notion captures the process in a way that is similar to the psychoanalytic formulation (cited in Hoggett 1992: 17): 'At the end of every labour-process we get a result that already existed in the imagination of the laborer at its commencement.'

Marx (in Hoggett 1992: 17–18) described four components to the production process:

1   imaginative activity or an idea;
2   the 'material' of production;
3   a technology or tool;
4   a labourer.

The first, *imaginative activity*, occurs within a boundary set by two objects: the idea and the product (the objective and the outcome). Labour is a movement from conception to realization – from psychic to real. Second, the 'material' has its own laws and recalcitrance. 'Because it imposes constraints upon the realisation of need and desire, [to which I will return] it limits our independence and autonomy' (in Hoggett 1992: 18). Third, the *technology* or *tool* is a thing or complex of things interposed by the labourer 'between himself and the subject of his labour, which serves as the "conductor" of his activity' (ibid.). Fourth is the *labourer*, whose capacity to imagine is not to be assumed, but who is the source of the 'idea', which, according to Marx, 'gives the law' to activity.

Another way of putting this is that there is a task to be done (a 'what') and an idea in the mind of the worker of how to do it, which must take account of the resources – human and technical – as well as the barriers to transformation from an idea to an outcome.

Hoggett (1992) adds that our activity must be something that develops our own possibilities, lest the organization in which one participates feeds off the powerlessness of its members. And from psychoanalysis we know that the object is always a combination of our individual (and collective) projections and part of a shared reality.

Gosling in his examination of group behaviour explains the phenomenon:

> a world of shared creations of the mind, fantasies, attitudes, values, assumptions, and misgivings, that have little that is conclusive to show for themselves objectively, but by virtue of 'being held in common' have a great influence on the life of the group members and are in that sense real.
>
> (1979: 81)

This includes the object of labour, be it individual or collective. What if the 'object of production' is money? It is interesting how we commonly use the term 'to make money', yet the 'making of money' is primarily through the making of other 'objects'. Indeed, is the 'making of money' now the primary object of production?

In a world that has become increasingly narcissistic, we can recognize the constraints that narcissism imposes on production. I argue that this increasing trend may be a consequence – among other influences – of the new 'flexible capitalism'. The recalcitrance of the material and the technology confront our narcissism in particular ways; we are reminded of our neediness: we need materials and technologies to realize our idea. This reveals our lack and our dependence upon our environment. It also predicates envy.

Michael Rustin makes the point that in Thatcherite times, self-interest became prioritized over the common social good – 'a pervasive process of privatization and atomization of social interests' (1991: 146). Hoggett asks, 'What if we are unable to relate to the natural world with humility or respect?' (1992: 23). He quotes psychoanalyst Wilfred Bion (1975a): 'the flip-side of envy is arrogance' (Hoggett 1992: 24) – the feeling that there is nothing beyond oneself. This is the opposite of freedom. In such envy, one *cannot* need, because the desire is unbearable. Nor can one use objects effectively.

> Such an arrogant and omniscient attitude towards one's objects is clearly given support by a culture within which *money* is considered a universal good. Money's most essential property lies in its promise to overcome all obstacles, therefore it is a denial of the necessary recalcitrance of real objects.
>
> (Hoggett 1992: 25)

Indeed, it is a denial too of the need for imaginative transformation. Marx spoke of money as the 'pimp' between need and object. Need no longer requires realization through imaginative action. Hoggett uses the literal example of prostitution to dramatically illustrate this. The work of courting is obviated; there are no doubts about the recalcitrance of the object. 'No work is required on behalf of the client other than that involved in the monetary transaction. No concern is necessary as to the other's sense of value' (Marx, cited in Hoggett 1992: 25).

There may be

> relief in the knowledge that the other values only one's money. No doubt is involved, no element of chance. Money is indeed a magical thing. Its power of command is so immense that, without it, one is helpless and dependent.... Need no longer requires realization through imaginative action.
>
> ...One may be weak but money provides one with the appearance of strength. When one needs solace money promises to provide comfort. When one is lonely money can provide one with the appearance of companionship. When one feels empty money can provide one with the appearance of mystery. Money promises to transform every weakness, every lack into its opposite. Money is negation.... Money grants omnipotence.... Money abolishes the 'gap' between need and realization and thereby abolishes the imagination.
>
> (Hoggett 1992: 25)

Imagination, proposes Hoggett, is the vehicle of hope, while fantasy is the vehicle of despair.

Young (1998) makes similar observations in his description of money as a fetish when he describes fetishism as the substitution of something near the real thing or representing the real thing. Marx spoke of the fetishism of commodities as the treatment of the relations between people as though they were relations between things. 'The act of fetishization is the substitution for our commitment and emotional regard for relations between people of the relations between things.... The fetishism of money is an equally fantastical substitution' (Young 1998).

Imagination carries two realms: activity based on need and activity based on desire. The distinction between need and desire lies in the distinction between 'freedom from' and 'freedom to'. In both, imagination is impelled by absence. To satisfy need, that which is missing is known. To satisfy desire, creativity is required; the creation of something new. This is 'to do'. But, beyond this, 'to be' is another form of creative engagement. Improvisation is the creative expression of Being. Bion (1957b) takes psychoanalysis into this arena.

Before we consider the second hypothesis, two things should be noted. First, the term 'fantasy' is being used in a specific way – with an emphasis in this regard on the over-determination or hyper-cathexis of money. Undoubtedly, money in a more concrete sense can also lubricate other kinds of opportunities for creativity.

Second, money is also real. Just as fetishism may be seen as a substitute of relations with objects for relations with people, so we might regard the reality of money as predicated on how we relate to it – as a fetish/substitute object or as a thing in itself. The boundary between money as fantasy and money as reality rests on the nature of our relatedness to it. Hence, the reality of money is determined from an examination of that relatedness.

Consider now the second hypothesis.

Hypothesis 2

The second hypothesis is that *the institutionalized power of money is currently a defence against rapidly increasing powerlessness and diminished faith in personal and institutional authoritative leadership.* To explore ideas associated with this hypothesis, the work of Richard Sennett (1998) has been referenced, and in particular the notion of 'flexible capitalism'.

In contrast with the qualities of character referenced earlier, he describes the new flexible capitalism as having three elements:

1   Discontinuous reinvention of institutions – discontinuous change referring to ruptures that irreversibly alter our lives.
2   Flexible specialization of production: getting more varied products ever more quickly onto the market, responding rapidly to consumer demand – a strategy of permanent innovation: accommodation to ceaseless change,

rather than an effort to control it; letting the shifting demands of the outside world determine the inside structure of institutions; subordination of the state's bureaucracy to the economy, reducing the government's provision of a safety net. 'The operation of flexible production depends on how a society defines the common good' (Sennett 1998: 55).

3   Concentration without centralization of power – reorganizing an institution from the topdown into fragments and nodes in a network: 'to the economies of inequality the new order thus adds new forms of an unequal, arbitrary power within the organization' (ibid.: 55). 'The (bureaucratic) structure remains in the forces driving units or individuals to achieve; what is left open is how to do so, and the flexible organization's top seldom provides the answers' (ibid.: 56).

This is most palpably expressed in the popular management notion of teams. However, what is notable in Sennett's conception is a potentially significant effect on the social structure and dynamic of work. Uncertainty, lack of clarity and unpredictability prevail in all dimensions. While rigidity may stultify creativity, a degree of rigour and certainty may be crucial for the secure continuity of organizational life.

Also, the value of delayed gratification becomes null in a system whose institutions change rapidly, says Sennett; it becomes absurd to work long and hard for an employer who thinks only about selling up and moving, i.e. only about money.

Teamwork stressed as mutual responsiveness rather than personal validation, or an ethic of the group rather than of the individual, is the work ethic that suits the flexible economy. It is argued here that in modern management practice, when the team-leader 'facilitates' a solution or 'mediates' between client and team, his or her role is not so much that of leader as that of process manager, with the limited authority that is thus implied. In other words, the location of formal authority changes when decision making is regarded as within a team-managerial rather than a leadership domain. While this may have short-term functional usefulness (e.g. in some areas of project management), a significant consequence is the uncertainty of *the location of leadership accountability*. Workers, in other words, are uncertain about where to situate accountability – and in what role or form. The significance of this cannot be overemphasized. This point is proffered because of my observation of a recurrence of the inappropriate shift of location of accountability on two axes. The first extends from major corporations through to government. The second extends from the justice system through to abnegation of parental responsibility. The recent global financial crisis is a widespread case in point.

Sennett concludes that this negation of authority and responsibility affects all aspects of work life and he asserts that it 'frees those in control to shift, adapt, re-organize, without having to justify their acts' (1998: 115). 'Power without authority permits leaders of a team to dominate employees by denying legitimacy to [their] needs and desires' (ibid.: 115).

It is asserted here that the negation of authority not only permits but facilitates a breakdown in social and corporate accountability. There is a familiar social defence as described by Pierre Turquet in a seminal paper on the dynamics of large groups: 'The I.M. [individual member] is under constant threat of being converted into either becoming a membership individual (M.I.) where group membership predominates over individual self-definition with its associated loss of identity, or withdrawal into the singleton state of isolation' (1975: 91).

Survival then becomes a primary aim.

Sennett vividly articulates some consequences:

> The culture of the new order profoundly disturbs self-organization. It can divorce flexible experience from static personal ethics…. It can divorce easy, superficial labour from understanding and engagement…. It can make the constant taking of risks an exercise in depression…. Irreversible change and multiple fragmented activity may be comfortable for the new regime's masters … but it may disorient its servants.
>
> (1998: 117)

Sennett goes on to refer to 'masters … who dodge truthful engagement with their servants' (ibid.: 117). In essence, he is asserting that this new order can significantly split leadership and management from the organization as a whole. The organization becomes primarily focused on the making of money, leaving workers disengaged and constantly uncertain. A risk-management engineer to whom I consulted described how his experience of lodging a complaint against an incompetent manager met with a black hole of silence. Two months after refusing to work for that manager, he had not been responded to, even verbally. Similarly, at a university school to which I consulted – in an environment characterized by a cultural change from educational institution to business enterprise – urgent requests for essential resources remained unanswered for months.

In an unpublished seminar I gave for the (then) Australian Institute of Socio-Analysis on some of the consequences of electronic management in the electronic age, similar observations were made. The title of that seminar series, 'E-Management? Who Is in Charge Today?', drew attention to the question of the location or embodiment of the locus of authority, management and leadership. (In that paper, specific reference was made especially to the emergent use of electronic communication.) My observation of current organizations demonstrated an increasing feeling among staff in large corporations, both private and government,

> that they do not know who they work for; who is in charge; who is managing; who is making what decisions, and whether today's manager will be there tomorrow. This occurs especially when decisions affect their lives in a personal way. They feel, often, (in all meanings of the phrase) that they have lost their heads.
>
> (Shafer 2000: 1)

and

> I believe that there are significant processes of distanciation that operate cur-
> rently – outside of the awareness or intentionality of the individual. They
> are, I think, both a consequence of current market forces and processes and
> act cybernetically or systemically to exacerbate the experience of disembod-
> iment that I think increasingly characterises many dimensions of corporate
> life today.
>
> (ibid.: 3)

It is proposed here that flexible capitalism (as Sennett calls it), globalization,
market forces and other contemporary economic and political influences have contributed to a terrible loss of engagement. The massive development of electronic
technology has had a major influence on the nature, form and quality of engagement in organizations and in communities. Electronic communication has changed
the way members of organizations 'engage' with each other. This form of communication can split meaning and emotion. It enables de-personalized messages to be
sent, and can be a very powerful vehicle for unconscious projections.

Alongside, the global financial crisis has produced a greater sense of uncertainty and unpredictability both in the stability of major corporations and in the
integrity of their leadership. It is suggested that they have contributed:

*   To a literal experience of losing contact with people's corporeal and com-
    munal connections.
*   To a loss of engagement between leaders and the community, between
    senior management and workers (not that that is especially new; it is just far
    worse and on a bigger scale).
*   To a loss of self among managers and workers. By loss of self, I am speak-
    ing in the broadest sense about a number of things that contribute to the
    sense of self. I mean loss of relationship to the institution; loss of the rela-
    tionship between perpetrators and sufferers; loss of the connection to the
    institution itself. There is little doubt that the present one has so far brought
    with it a very great extent of disengagement and alienation.

It has been quite striking recently in Australia to observe a shift in the marketing of some banking services. One major bank states that its local managers are
very easily accessible, even to the extent of its advertised depiction of a family
in an overseas holiday crisis calling the bank manager directly on a Saturday to
arrange emergency funds. By contrast, the culture of banking for over a decade
has been to become more and more inaccessible, through the use of call centres
and automated responses, and a refusal to reveal even the telephone numbers of
local branches. What is illustrated here is the history of disengagement from
both staff and customers.

Gordon Lawrence (1995) extends this view through strong argument that contemporary managers are often caught between the paranoid-schizoid and depres-

sive positions because advancing capitalism has altered the primary tasks of institutions. The primary task or reason for existence has become more focused on making or saving money than on production of goods or services. The former induces paranoid-schizoid thinking, whereas a work-oriented task is a depressive one 'because the totality of activities are [*sic*] regarded as a complex whole, having meaning which transcends the simplicity of economics'. Earlier, it was proposed similarly, in accord with Hoggett, that there is an increasing pre-eminence of the impossibility of fantasy instead of the possible creativity of imagination.

Similar to the proposition here that money has been hyper-cathected, Lawrence suggests that economic survival has come to represent the narrow and pervasive interpretation of capitalism, while alternative economic models have been found wanting. Lawrence (1995) concludes that

> this gross simplification of human life can be seen as a world wide social system of defence against acknowledging the tragic and taking authority and responsibility for exercising the human ability to discriminate between what is patently good and what is incontrovertibly evil.

A position in support of the central hypotheses has been offered here. It has been argued:

- that money has acquired a value as a social defence against fundamental unpredictability and uncertainty which impedes creative thinking in the service of production;
- that in part it does so by supporting fantasy rather than imagination;
- that the immoderate ascription of power to money via the new flexible economy has severely impacted on the exercise of authority for leadership (at a personal and social level) and substituted power for authority.

It is greatly concerning that such investment in power – magical and real – reflects the political and economic, but also spiritual and moral, crises of these times. These crises are characterized by significant experiences of loss of emotional and social engagement. Indeed, the realms of politics, economics and religion have been dominated by the politics of divisiveness, not of engagement, and the value of money has in part been absorbed into this phenomenon.

References

Ball, P. (1999) 'The nature of money', Nature Publishing Group. 24 September. Online, available at: www.nature.com/news/1999/990924/full/news990930-2.html (retrieved 4 November 2010).

Bion, W.R. (1957a) 'On arrogance', *International Journal of Psycho-Analysis*, 39: 144–6. Reprinted in *Second Thoughts: Selected papers on psychoanalysis*, London: Heinemann, 1967.

Bion, W.R. (1957b) 'Differentiation of the psychotic from the non-psychotic personalities', in *Second Thoughts: selected papers on psychoanalysis*, London: Heinemann,
1967, 43–64.

Gosling, R.H. (1979) 'Another source of conservatism in groups', in W.G. Lawrence
(ed.) *Exploring Individual and Organisational Boundaries*, Chichester, UK: John
Wiley.

Hoggett, P. (1992) *Partisans in an Uncertain World: The psychoanalysis of engagement*,
London: Free Association Books.

Lawrence, W.G. (1995) 'The presence of totalitarian states-of-mind in institutions', paper
read at the inaugural conference on Group Relations, of the Institute of Human Relations, Sofia, Bulgaria. Online, available at: http://human-nature.com/free-associations/
lawren.html (retrieved 30 August 2010).

Money, Markets and the Economy (2001) ABC Radio series. Online, available at: www.
abc.net.au/money/vault/programs.htm (retrieved 30 August 2010).

Rustin, M. (1991) *The Good Society and the Inner World: Psychoanalysis, politics and
culture*, London: Verso.

Sennett, R. (1998) *The Corrosion of Character: The personal consequences of work in
the new capitalism*, New York: W.W. Norton.

Shafer, A.T. (2000) 'Disembodied managers and their disembodied staff: or, losing your
head in the corporate world', Australian Institute of Socio-Analysis Seminar series
(unpublished) 'E-Management? Who Is in Charge Today?

Turquet, P. (1975) 'Threats to identity in the large group', in L. Kreeger (ed.) *The Large
Group: Dynamics and therapy*, London: Karnac Books.

Young, R.M. (1998) 'Some reflections on the dynamics of wealth', paper delivered to
Merseyside Psychotherapy Institute Series on 'The Mystery of Money', Liverpool,
Study Day on 'The Construction of Money', 27 February. Online, available at: http://
human-nature.com/rmyoung/papers/pap106h.html (retrieved 2 November 2010).

3   Greed

Susan Long

Introduction

The headlines are full of stories of individual greed, especially on the part of chief executives who get huge bonuses whether or not they increase company capability. In the current time of economic crisis, major political leaders are calling for an end to this practice and instigating legislation to cap what the public sometimes regards as an obscenity. There is an increasing awareness, though, that what looks like the personal greed of the few at the top, supported by those in power, is a result of the whole current capitalist system – that an economic system that looked like the true path for democracy, through economic liberalism and (so-called) free markets, may in fact be too easily subject to enacted greed, unregulated cronyism and exploitation. This is a picture that describes a perverse culture which will be elaborated.

Following the description of perverse organizational dynamics illustrated by Company A, an argument will be postulated: that corporations have collective, mostly unconscious anxieties about running out of resources and /or a loss of power or knowledge. That is, a basic fear of loss. This fear is inherent in the profit motive. It is the 'shadow' of the desire to make gain. Such anxieties lead to a need to gather and hoard in order to guard against further loss; hence the inherent impetus for capital to accumulate. Money thus comes unconsciously to have a magical power to guard against loss. This, it is stressed is an unconscious group or organizational dynamic.

As with all group dynamics, this dynamic can only be expressed through individuals and may appear phenomenally as individual greed – a need to have more than is necessary. The intent of this chapter is not to judge the individual or to pursue a study of individual motives. No doubt such motives exist, but they are not the focus of this chapter. The intent here is to explore the collective dynamics. But first, a short story.

Early in 2008, Company A, a large stockbroking business in Australia, ceased trading and was put into receivership. The company provided margin lending for investment in shares to many companies and individuals. Company A customers seemed to disproportionately hold shares that were often illiquid and in small capitalized companies. What many of these customers didn't know was that the stocks that they thought were in their names were in fact in the names of the company's financiers; or, depending on who tells the story, stocks that were initially transferred into the name of Company A when the client joined, were then transferred to the names of Company A's financiers during its last few days as its managers desperately sought additional funding and the banks sought collateral. Regardless, many Company A investors were genuinely surprised when, as share prices fell, the banks called in their loans and, when customers could not pay, they sold shares to cover losses. Even more surprised were those customers who found their shares being sold by the banks even though they did not have a margin loan – and the value of their shares being used to offset overall Company A liabilities. In fact, not only did clients of Company A lose their shares, but in December 2008 many were identified as debtors of Company A and required to pay additional amounts to Company A as well as interest on those debts.

The fallout was significant for companies ranging through mobile phone companies, advertising, mining, online media, wholesale and retail businesses, and individuals. Some takeovers and mergers were derailed, and forced selling triggered price falls that triggered margin calls for other shareholders and led to further price falls, leading in turn to companies violating their lending covenants and facing bankruptcy.

The Australian newspaper, March 2008 reported:

> On the day the Australian stock market is expected to record its worst quarterly performance in more than 20 years, [Company A's] 1000-plus customers will be forced to watch helplessly as shares many thought they owned are sold to repay the firm's banks…. [Company A] was put into receivership on Thursday after directors identified 'irregularities' in a number of the firm's accounts. — and investment bank —, which together provided [Company A] with $1 billion to fund its margin lending business, are selling shares held on behalf of [Company A's] clients to recoup their money.

Following the story of the collapse, the details began to emerge. While overall clients were owed over $500 million, it was alleged that over the past months the company had favoured some clients over others. In this part of the story it emerged that one customer had borrowed huge amounts that alone had caused a large part of the collapse. He had a 95 per cent loan on his $200 million account. It was also alleged that Company A had moved millions of dollars offshore just prior to the collapse. In a strange off-side story, this led one of Melbourne's infamous underground figures to travel in a chase for the money, stating at the airport as he left that he was helping to get money back for some of the little people who had lost out. He himself was a Company A customer.

During the investigation, the stockbroking chief executive came under fire as a major player. The *Business Spectator* of 31 March 2008 reported:

> According to transcripts from a Federal Court hearing late on Friday, Mr — instructed staff to doctor the accounts of six affluent clients, providing

security for up to 200 million dollars against personal losses while their share portfolios lost value.

The transcripts contain allegations that Mr — was responsible for moving shares or by changing loan-to-valuation ratios so accounts could be made to look healthier, thereby avoiding margin calls that could have forced [Company A] clients to dump shares or inject extra cash.

[Company A] was also accused of deliberately selling off the shares of less-favoured clients. ASIC senior investigator Richard Vandeloo said that Mr — 'appeared to be a person that instituted a lot of the manipulation'.

This story can perhaps too readily be seen as one where individual blame is assigned and personal greed imputed. True, it may appear to be such a story, along with other stories like that of the Madoff company in the United States, which disguised a Ponzi scheme that ended in disaster. But the interest here lies not with the individuals concerned but with the systems surrounding them. The argument here is that the larger system surrounding Company A and other similar companies provides the stage upon which greed and corruption are possibilities: surface symptoms of an underlying perverse process.

The organization as perverse

We are working with an analogy – a 'what if'. What if an organization were like a person? Or, better put: what if the system that is 'organization' or 'corporation' has processes and structures in common with the system that is 'person'? That is, human systems, both person and organization, may have dynamics in common arising from their systemic nature; especially the nature of their *emotional content*. Or put in yet another way, the person may be a system where social dynamics are at play on an internal stage and the organization a system where emotions are at play on a large collective scale.

If we are to understand the perverse state-of-mind as a social system property (rather than an individual property), its essential system dynamics are more pertinent than its place in current popular or psychiatric classifications of individuals. What then are the indicators of a perverse system state-of-mind in psychodynamic terms?[1]

1   The perverse state of mind is not simply a deviation from normative morality. It has to do with individual pleasure at the expense of a more general good, often to the extent of not recognizing the existence of others or their rights. It reflects a state of primary narcissism.
2   The perverse state of mind acknowledges reality but, at the same time, denies it. This leads to a state of fixed ideation and phantasy to protect against the pain of seeing and not seeing at the same time.
3   The perverse state of mind engages others as accomplices in the perversion.
4   The perverse state of mind may flourish where instrumental relations have dominance in the society. This is because instrumentality ignores the rights

of others to have an independent existence. This in itself is abusive. The perverse state of mind turns a blind eye.

5 Perversion begets perversion. Abusive cycles are hard to break. Corruption breeds corruption because of the complicity of the accomplices and their subsequent denial and self-deception (Long 2008).

Translating these indicators into social and organizational terms means that perversion is exemplified by:

- The pleasure (viz. growth or profit) of the organization as gained at the expense of employees or customers (or, in broad social terms, at the expense of a more general good);
- the paradoxical dynamic of denial of reality, where what is known in the organization is at the same time not known (or, as an example in corporate terms, disparate and contradictory public and private images exist in parallel);
- the use of accomplices in an instrumental social relation – in corporate terms the accomplices are often the institutional auditors, investors or creditors;
- the self-perpetuation or closed-ness of the perverse dynamic – in terms of the corporate culture.

Greed is a complex notion linked to the medieval deadly sins of avarice and gluttony. In twenty-first-century corporate life, the idea of avarice is also associated with a greed for power: to be in that place that leads to gaining mass recognition, and the lifestyle of the rich and famous; the sometimes perverse culture of celebrity. The dividing line between a good eye for business and an over-reaching grasp for bigger and bigger profits in the financial world is often crossed on emotional impulse driven by the thrill of the gamble or the identity that riches bestow.

How can greed be understood? Some of the basic ideas within psychoanalysis and social science may help here in order to understand the nature of greed, how it is expressed in the individual and what might lie behind greed at a corporate level.

Greed seen developmentally

The analysis of greed here follows an analysis of the unconscious phantasies that become associated with 'wanting more'. Healthy babies have a lusty zest for life expressed through enthusiastic feeding. When hungry, the baby sometimes sucks greedily at breast or bottle as if wanting to empty it all at once. A hallmark of greed is the intent to find a supply and take as much as possible; to drain the supply, perhaps driven by the fear that there will be no more. The desire to have it 'all at once' sits with the phantasy that the supply may dry up or be withheld by an even greedier or persecuting presence.

Babies differ in their greediness. This is observable. And we should distinguish between (1) the desire for an object and (2) pursuit of that desire. Is greed a desirous state in itself or a pattern of reactions and behaviours in response to such desire? In this distinction the question of ethics arises. Greed is popularly seen as something that individuals should have some control over. Greed taken into action is popularly seen as an exemplification of the breakdown of self-control.

Development beyond infancy sees the further vicissitudes of greed. Gluttony is a form derived from infant greediness and exaggerates the sensuality of eating and drinking. It may unconsciously represent a need for physical comfort and closeness to the mother, but becomes consciously attached to the sensual activity associated with eating, including the taste and texture of food and the social context of eating, including its part in power dynamics and friendship.

Gluttony is an old-fashioned term. In this age of psychology, many modern formulations of ideas about gluttony centre round the eating disorders: obesity, anorexia and bulimia. Obesity is sometimes a psychological response to personal depression, but it may also be a sociological response to changing family economies and behavioural patterns, and economic depression in the midst of plenty.

Some corporate greed can be understood in this way, as a response to perceived psychological and economic depression. At times, corporate greed seems present in the ever-demanding cry for increased profits from shareholders, beyond reasonable steady growth. It is as if there is a fear that the source of plenty may dry up and must be exploited before it is withdrawn. This is supported in reality by knowledge that environmental resources are expendable and that irrevocable pollution of the environment is a real risk. Despite this knowledge, many corporations – or worse, governments – persist in denying their effects on the environment, or, perhaps more to the point, in denying that their behaviour in turn will rebound on them in the future. This blindness follows a greedy, selfish view that they are independent of, and can control, the wider system – a linking of pride with greed.

Perverse greed often continues to drive corporate behaviour in acquisitions beyond those necessary for reasonable growth. The dangers are both known and denied. Danger is courted and the phantastic belief in power over death and loss is maintained. This is the psychology of gambling at a corporate level.

The individually psychologically more serious disorders of anorexia nervosa and bulima, while superficially linked to issues of poor self-image, are more integrally connected to issues of power. The most primitive form of power is the control of bodily functions. In these eating disorders there is often a struggle between the individual and the social system (family or medical system) with regard to eating and body weight or shape. Many power issues become represented in this struggle of life and death. 'Gluttony' here is represented in binge eating, or negatively represented in the mixed fascination and abhorrence the anorexic has for food. Similarly, the power struggles for control of functions within corporations may unconsciously represent such struggles over the body corporate. Capital and money become the symbols of such control.

Money and power

Greed also has an anal form: the 'filthy lucre' analysed by Norman O. Brown (1959) in terms of the Freudian hypothesis that faeces unconsciously equals money. Brown's argument finds that wealth, created from surplus production and leading to commodification and the social division of labour with its inequities is based on the desexualization and negation of anality. This brings the projection of negated anality into culture. As a social historian, Brown rejects the idea that economic history is a direct result of the exchange value of money. Prior to its exchange value, money (or the pre-money barter symbols of crops, teeth or beads) first came to have sacred value – originally given to the gods as surplus and later hoarded as accumulated wealth by the priestly elite and privileged. Money/faeces thus are the symbols of power in society; rampant consumerism, the expression of infantile polymorphous perverse sexuality. Both are the expression of a wish for immortality and a denial of death.

> What the psychoanalytic paradox is asserting is that 'things' which are possessed and accumulated, the property and the universal condensed precipitate of property, money, are in their essential nature excremental … the infantile wish which sustains the money complex is for a narcissistically self-contained and self replenishing immortal body.
>
> (ibid.: 292–3)

Money and material goods come to represent a capacity to control the body (at first the anal sphincter) and its death in the face of a seemingly demanding civilization represented through the parents – the 'others' who first require such control. In such a phantasy, money comes to represent the power to buy all that is desired, as if the fires of desire might be quenched through a constant stream of consumer goods – although, in fact, this stream serves simply to feed the fire. To consume means to be consumed by fire, according to the *Oxford Dictionary*. The buying and consuming is inexorably linked to the exercise of power.

Giddens reminds us that, 'today, "money proper" is independent of the means whereby it is represented, taking the form of pure information lodged as figures in a computer printout' (1990: 25). In modernity, the accumulation of wealth is not simply sensual, seen and felt in coffers of gold or bolts of silk. It shows itself as pure symbol, removed far from the body. Modernity for Giddens is partly identified through the presence of systems that are disembedded from their local context. Globalization requires this, and modern monetary systems are examples of such disembeddedness. 'Money in its developed form is thus defined above all in terms of credit and debt and … is a means of bracketing time and so of lifting transactions out of a particular milieux of exchange' (ibid.: 24). Such a disembeddedness, while enabling a reaching out beyond the local, may in so doing also require a denial of the power of the local; perhaps a rejection of the body and its limitations.

The foundation of an abstract disembedded social system is trust, Giddens argues, an emotion on which modern societies rely and on which the modern psyche is predicated. It is a different form of trust from that found in pre-modern cultures, where kinship, community, religion and tradition formed the foundations for local face-to-face trust. Modern trust is evidenced in a reliance on abstract distanced systems of technology and impersonal expertise. This is almost a blind trust, instilled in us by those institutions on which we rely for everything in our everyday lives. And still, when trust is broken in these systems we feel shocked and betrayed because a fundamental connection to our sense of everyday life has been destroyed. When debts are not honoured, the rage evoked can lead to violence. A very primitive sense of injustice is aroused. That the system of 'money proper' is an expression of social trust may seem a travesty to those poor who seem mostly to enter that system through debt rather than credit. But, in a wry twist, they *can* count on or trust that others will demand their debts be paid. When corporations betray trust, do not pay their debts despite wringing as much profit as possible from the consumers, and when many suffer due to this, the sense of anger and betrayal is immense.

The contemporaneous presence and absence found in abstract systems of disembeddedness is most evident in modern monetary systems. The notes and coins in our pockets are but a few grains in the vast sea of computerized credits and debits. Money is present, yet absent. If we take Giddens and Brown together, money becomes both a symbol of trust and a symbol of the negation of the body and death. Together these seem to produce a deified symbol, aiding in denial of the existential angst that Giddens sees as lying within modernity. Contemporary money systems, then, are based on the dynamics of perversion as presented in this chapter: the dynamics of denial alongside the ambivalence about trust embedded in the relations between accomplices and their instrumental use of others.

Greed may also take expression in a phallic form: the greed for power over others, especially their sexuality and desire. The phallic culture of the Wall Street money traders has been described by Lewis (1990). In his account of the corporate culture of Salomon Brothers, adolescent phallic characteristics are described. The more aggressive aspects shown by the Long Term Capital Management traders in their international deals are examples (Long 2008). The picture of phallic greed links with that of phallic pride. Phallic pride desires to display before the other, perhaps to triumph over the shame of the other, so the other is forced to concede its superiority. The greed for power is a desire to dominate and control the other. At a whole-system level, while previously a Marxist analysis examined this in terms of capitalism as the domination of the system of production by a limited few, this has changed. Nowadays it is revealed in a system where many, through privatization linked to superannuation and government investment, no longer are simply and unambiguously the owners of labour (and in simple false consciousness), but also are the owners of production and so are insidiously tied in with their own wealth creation and simultaneously, their own domination.

Each of these forms of greed – gluttony, the relentless desire for riches and material goods, and the overwhelming desire for power – are developmental expressions of greed. Whereas appetite, pecuniary interest and assertion of self are the life-giving expressions of each of these impulses, the normal healthy forms that undergird social life are turned towards destructivity by perverse greed. The implication of unconscious volition is present. In the vicissitudes of greed, the passive process of division is not primary. The human psyche is constituted within a cultural context where responsibility, volition and accountability are key foundations. We must be held to account, if not for the development of our psyche and its desirous states, then for our *actions*. If greed is part of our instinctive inheritance, then its shape and enactment are learned in a cultural context where self-constraint may also be learned and adopted – or perhaps, more aptly, where the social forms of appetite, pecuniary interest and assertion of self are limited and contained.

Generosity

The impulse to share and be generous can be regarded as the opposite of, yet closely connected to, greed. Its development is linked to the growing infant's capacity to see its mother as a whole person rather than split into good and bad breast. Generosity is associated with a recognition and love of the other, feelings of guilt about destructive impulses towards the other, and a desire to repair past aggressive projections and splitting. A classic sign of peace and reconciliation is found in the communal meal or 'breaking/taking of bread together' – the giving and accepting of food. The words 'companion' and 'company' are derived from the Latin roots *com* (meaning 'with') and *panis* (meaning 'bread'). It means to draw sustenance with another. Generosity is a building block for relationship with others.

Generosity may be regarded as part of the wellspring of creativity – an impulse to create and give, inwardly to the self and outwardly to others. Generosity towards self helps in the building of confidence and ameliorates harsh self-judgements. This forms a basis for generosity towards others and a desire to share pleasures. Although some psychoanalysts focus on generosity in the form of reparation, infant development also shows signs of generosity in non-reparative, directly connective forms. It can be seen as part of the infant's openness to experience and willingness to develop trusting relationships (Hamilton 1982).

Some of history's most famous characters are marked out by their capacity to give of themselves to others, despite, seemingly, great costs to themselves. Yet the reward is in enrichment to self and is immeasurable in terms of spirit. Of course, all behaviour, including charitable behaviour, is the result of mixed motives, conscious and unconscious impulses, and learned character. Nonetheless, generosity is part of the impulse to generativity, charity and social enterprise (Gillin and Long 2004).

The analysis of the (sin) of avarice and the (virtue) of generosity seems to see them as two sides of a coin, two expressions of an impulse in the relation of self to other. Freudian analyses of the sexualization of greed in oral, anal and phallic stages trace its development in the individual body. Kleinian analysis considers the internal objects formed throughout this development, with a focus on the development of psychological defences against painful impulses and experiences (Klein, 196; 1957).

The thoughts, feelings and actions surrounding guilt and reparation, generosity, and recognition and love of others, unlike greed, are readily seen as linked to conscious volition. Such impulses are regarded within religious thinking as virtues to be achieved through a dedicated pursuit. They are taught in schools as part of community values and lauded in the community as an underpinning of voluntary and charitable work. They are not normally regarded as attitudes that we slip into unknowingly and unconsciously. Unconscious volition seems to sit more comfortably with the devil than the saints; more with the deadly sins than the virtues. This is another aspect of volition and intent; greed as desire is shameful and hidden.

Greed and the organization

At the beginning of this chapter I noted that, as a community, we often regard corporate corruption as primarily due to the conscious desires of greedy executives and board members. This is despite the beliefs of many executives caught in perverse organizational dynamics that they were just doing their best for the company. As a contrast, we may see how unconscious perverse dynamics pervade many aspects of our society and its institutions, including corporations and organizations. Systems can 'turn a blind eye' as a whole, not recognizing the blind spots and not experiencing the perversity in individual character but experiencing it in systemic roles with their associated thoughts and feelings. These are feelings that are *in* the person but not *of* the person: they are *of* the role and the system in the sense used by Armstrong (1995). It may be useful to think of the greediness or generosity of various organizational players as 'released' or enabled and expressed by individuals through particular social and political forces and dynamics at play. That is, they really emerge from the system. The emotions are released *from* the system and back *into* the system, much as adrenaline may be released in the body to pervade and influence muscular reactions which in turn stimulate the production of more adrenaline.

Psychological splitting, both of objects and of the ego, is a device to create structures for dealing with unbearable feelings so that thinking might occur, even if that thinking is limited, as in the paranoid-schizoid state described by Klein (1946). Different thoughts and feelings can be 'held' in different structures, perhaps to be reintegrated in new ways at a later time – Klein's depressive position. Division of labour in an organization can be understood in much the same way. Different parts of the organization not only execute different tasks but also 'hold' different thoughts and feelings on behalf of the organization (Long 2000). We can think also of power structures as divisions where different thoughts and feelings are held.

Of course, to argue in this way brings us head-on with the sticky issue of personal volition. Who causes what? Is it the individual or the social conditions?

Where is accountability: in the group or in the person? In the systemic approach given here, causes and effects are interwoven such that causality is never linear but circular, complex, perhaps chaotic. How is this dilemma dealt with in organizations? And why and where do the structures developed to deal with it fall down?

From an examination of recent corporate disasters and the responses of the media, such as the Company A story we can determine how corporate greed is understood socially. Quite often the social 'drama' as presented in the media and in popular discussion emerges as follows. A popular picture is first painted of the greedy executive or group of executives who dupe others with full personal intent. This view might be translated as *'personal greed gets the better of them'* and may satisfy a social desire to find individuals to blame. Alongside this is a picture of the seemingly duped auditors and bankers who on closer examination have failed in their duty to examine with due diligence the transactions in which they have engaged. This view might be translated as the *'"they just didn't know" scenario'*. Later, the law (quite correctly) has the proper task of teasing out the accountabilities and responsibilities of individuals, and judges their personal culpability; their intents and complicities. The media then give us a feast and blow-by-blow account of how all this proceeds.

In this way, most of our common language for understanding greed in organizations is directed towards the conscious intent of the players. But on further examination, and with the 'as if' (an organization could be seen as a person) stance, other impressions come into view. Greed may blind the whole organizational system and move beyond the specific organization to other, broader system players, enrolling them as accomplices. Hence, perverse greed distorts reason and undermines reasonable risk assessment. Such a wide system effect can be perceived in stock market behaviour as well as corporations.

Tuckett and Taffler (2008) argue that greed within the stock market creates a belief in a phantastic object. An infantile phantasy comes to dominate. It centres round the (unconscious) phantastic object that can bring about great wealth with little effort – the fairy-tale goose that lays the golden egg. They analyse the dotcom bubble of the late twentieth century in terms of this phantastic object. At that time, market players believed that the internet had begun a powerful social change that would transform the nature of consumerism beyond imagination. Companies associated with this phantastic object became idealized. Speculation in the dotcom companies accelerated and share prices rose to absurd heights. The perverse nature of this process was demonstrated in market players' refusal to heed warnings put out by some analysts, indeed by many market and financial authorities themselves, going outside the normal company assessments and accepting high valuations on companies with few or even no business plans. As Tuckett and Taffler say, the data were thin, yet belief in the possibilities high. A blind eye was turned to what was usually regarded as prudent and hopes were lodged in the belief in a 'new economy' where new rules prevailed.

Eventually, the bubble burst. The unrealistic, greedy dreams of the players came to nought. Stock prices crashed and players were left with their pockets empty and their psyches shamed.

So how can the Company A story be seen in terms of organizational or system perversion? On the whole, the story superficially appears primarily as one of greed and cronyism – a few people supporting each other to gain large returns from small inputs and securing this by drawing on unknowing others. But in taking a systemic perspective, consider the data.

1   Individual pleasure at the expense of a more general good. Company A and its favoured customers, it seems, were gaining at the expense of other customers, even though these customers themselves were allegedly unaware of what was happening. It seems that a vision of making much out of little led to poor decisions and practice within the company. The CEO (a former bank executive) allegedly directed staff to top up the accounts of six customers to save them from margin calls. But he also gave a personal guarantee to the creditor bank over all of his personal assets. He argued that his actions were simply poor judgement and that he made 'terrible mistakes'. The company survival and profits were at the expense of the greater good.

2   Denial and turning a blind eye. Allegedly, for some time, senior managers had been warning that the CEO's way of operating was wrong and would lead to trouble. It seems he didn't want to know. He was unable to maintain this denial, however. The warning signs became unavoidable when some investors wished to sell their stock and this could not be done immediately. Next came the cover-up. In the company, staff members were directed to cover up the losses of major clients and it was alleged also that the creditor covered up their exposure to Company A (*Canberra Times*, January 2009). Organizationally, there had been a desire to turn a blind eye to the failures of the business model that Company A was operating – a model that might be perceived to run against usual business practice and ethics. But the denial was basically in the possible arrogance of many players, led by Mr —, their view that they could take the financial risks that they did without problems arising. The denial, it might be argued was as much in the arrogance and pride lodged in the organizational culture as in the company's economic and business practices. Moreover, this was also the case with some of their customers. The customer who lost $2 million, for example, said he did not know what was going on. But one wonders about his judgement in leveraging 95 per cent of his borrowings.

3   Accomplices. Armstrong and Frances say that 'greed in one organization corrupted the morals of those with whom it had dealings' (2007: 16). Company A is a good example. The financial institutions were drawn in to lend huge margins. Of course, they did this by demanding collateral and taking on the shares of Company A customers. But their part in the story was one of poor judgement, perhaps also driven by the general culture of 'profits, profits, profits'. Too often in these stories, the financial institutions support large corporations with too little questioning.

A major bank involved has now agreed to improve compliance in various areas, including to review and, where necessary, remedy:

- poor reconciliation processes;
- a breakdown in proper compliance processes;
- inadequate resourcing and risk management;
- inaccurate and delayed responses to beneficial tracing notices; and
- a poor compliance culture, meaning that deficiencies in processes were not identified, escalated or remedied in an appropriate or timely manner.

4   Instrumentality. Company A, it appears, treated customers as instruments in the development of profit.
5   The issue of organizational perversity leading to further organizational perversity can be seen in terms of culture. The Company A story is set in a general culture of corporate greed which tends to be perpetuated. 'If [Company A] represents the worst side of greed, lack of transparency and poor regulation of the Australian financial system, then they are the first of many yet to be exposed' (*The Australian*, 29 March 2008).

Greed in the corporate world

Perhaps we take the question of greed for granted. It is easily assumed that the profit motive is the prime driver of greed – that the desire to increase profits at times oversteps decent and legal practice. Accordingly, the motive of personal gain at the individual level is most often (although perhaps mistakenly) popularly invoked. However, as Hirschhorn (Chapter 21 in this volume) points out, the behaviour of the individual may be as much due to an aggrieved sense of entitlement as to personal greed. At the social level, capitalist-system growth may be regarded as the central problem.

This chapter argues that we need to look beyond ideas of individual greed if we are to understand perverse dynamics at the organisational level. At the beginning of the chapter, it was stated that the organizational dynamics involved with anxieties of running out of resources and/or a loss of power or knowledge might lie behind corporate greed. What then can be made of such unconscious forces at social levels? At a more systemic level, it is hypothesized that the following may be occurring.

- There are the possible fears of running out of resources and associated lack of trust in others, hence the need to gather and hoard.
- There are the unconscious fears of having no power or knowledge, hence the phantasy that money can remedy this.
- Yet again, there is the symbolic power of money to mollify enemies, the gods and devils; a sacred gift. Corporate greed may well be the modern or post-modern expression of magical exculpation from the wrath of the gods and the fear that we may be left with nothing.
- Finally, there is the traditional psychoanalytic view that money and material goods represent faeces and, following Brown, come to represent a capacity

to control the body (at first the anal sphincter) and its death. Beyond this, developmentally, money may come to represent symbolically and unconsciously different bodily fluids and their control at different times for different people.[2] Giddens argues that money is a representation of trust. For the infant, milk is nourishment, security and linked to trust. It is given or withheld by the breast: a primitive form of exchange involving the dynamics of trust. So too is semen seen as a valuable exchange, given by one to another in sexual intercourse, certainly another form of trust.

Each of the above factors has associated unconscious psychological dynamics and motives beyond and less understood than simple personal monetary gain. Is there a need amongst some company directors to be seen as powerful and beneficent, hence opening the door to the perverse dynamics involving greed? Is what appears in some senior executives to be a motive for personal monetary gain, perhaps really a wish for power, sexual potency or even a denial of death? Not having access to the psychology of individuals in companies that appear to have perverse dynamics, we can only speculate. Moreover, such motivations, it has been argued here, are endemic to capitalist culture – the individuals being symptoms of that culture. More importantly, we do know that many companies who appear to have the perverse dynamics named earlier in this chapter gain the implicit trust of the banks and financial institutions that support them, beyond reasonable risk. Money seems to cast a spell of blindness.

If, as Joel Bakan (2004) says, the corporation is treated in law as a person, then as a consequence we are increasingly likely to use it projectively as a person. The corporation, through the motive of profit maximization, comes itself to be 'greedy' and this in turn is introjected by its owner shareholders and its employees. But there is a tension between the collective fear of lack – of resources, power, knowledge – and the unconscious powerful symbolic meaning of milk, faeces and semen, all bodily fluids that themselves seem to possess what is lacked. It is this tension that is the driver of greed and is expressed in the individual as the drive for personal gain, a sense of entitlement and in the social as growth in profit. It is as if we collectively attempt to ward off loss before it ever occurs because of our inherent experience of lack.

Notes

1 A full argument establishing the evidence for these indicators is available in Long (2008)
2 Bodily fluids can unconsciously represent life forces whose flow needs to be controlled. This unconscious belief is of course not scientific or justified, but is primitive and unconscious – expressed in a primitive form but the mediaeval theory of bodily 'humors'.

References

Armstrong, A. and Frances, R. (2007) 'An ethical climate is a duty of care', *Journal of Business Systems Governance and Ethics*, 3(3): 15–20.

Armstrong, D. (1995) 'The analytic object in organisational work', paper presented at Symposium of the International Society for the Psychoanalytic Study of Organisations, London, July.

Bakan, J. (2004) *The Corporation: The pathological pursuit of profit and power*, London: Constable.

Brown, N.O. (1959) *Life against Death: The psychoanalytic meaning of history*, Middletown, CT, Wesleyan University Press.

Giddens, A. (1990) *The Consequences of Modernity*, Cambridge: Polity Press.

Gillin, L. and Long, S.D. (2004) 'Integration of psychosocial theory', paper presented at the Conference of the Small Enterprise Association of Australia and New Zealand, Brisbane.

Hamilton, V. (1982) *Narcissus and Oedipus: The children of psychoanalysis*, London: Routledge & Kegan Paul.

Klein, M. (1946) 'Notes on Some Schizoid Mechanisms' in *The selected Melanie Klein* edited by Juliet Mitchell 1986 Harmondsworth: Penguin Books.

Klein, M. (1957) 'Envy and Gratitude' in *Envy and Gratitude and other works 1946–1963* New York: Dell Publishing Co.

Lewis, M. (1990) *Liar's Poker: Two cities, true greed*, London: Coronet.

Long, S.D. (2000) 'Cooperation and conflict: two sides of the same coin', in R. Wiesner and B. Millett (eds) *Management and Organisational Behaviour: Contemporary challenges and future directions*, Milton, Queensland: Jacaranda Wiley.

Long, S.D. (2008) *The Perverse Organisation and Its Deadly Sins*, London: Karnac.

Marx, K. (1992) *Capital: A critique of political economy*, London: Penguin Classics.

Tuckett, D. and Taffler, R. (2008) 'Phantastic objects and the financial market's sense of reality: a psychoanalytic contribution to the understanding of stock market instability', *International Journal of Psychoanalysis*, 89: 389–412.

4 Money as a fetish

The financial market crisis from a psychodynamic perspective

Claudia Nagel

Toward gold throng all,
To gold cling all,
Yes, all!

(Johann Wolfgang von Goethe)

Introduction

Through concentrating on establishing rules and regulations, the search for the causes of the financial market crisis in 2008/9 was quickly finalized. The culprits and their motivations were identified as the investment bankers and their greed. But what if the investment bankers were only a symptom of fundamental social psychodynamics?

I would like to advance the thesis that the cause of the financial market crisis is better explained by the psychodynamics of perversion which pervade the economic system in the sense of a state of mind or mental outlook. Money would thus be the fetish of this perversion. To elucidate this thesis it is essential to outline the development of the financial market crisis and the psychological aspects that became apparent in the different phases of the crisis.

The financial market crisis: origin and initial phase

My starting point is the 'global pool of money' (I personalize this for the sake of my argument), always on the lookout for investment opportunities through its investors (Blumberg *et al.* 2009a). Institutional investors such as insurance companies, pension funds, investment funds, hedge funds, or family offices for private wealth management disposed of US$70,000 billion in 2007 (Institutional Investors 2003; Blumberg *et al.* 2009a) and were always on the search for high-yield, low-risk investment opportunities. Government bonds were long regarded as being especially safe, in particular US government bonds. But the low interest level had made US Treasury bonds less interesting and the 'global pool of money' searched for alternative, similarly low-risk investment opportunities. It discovered 'mortgage-backed securities'. Because mortgage loans had thus far been regarded as a safe form of investment, there was an increased demand and new products were developed, namely, collateralized debt obligations (CDOs). Over time, and in the presence of the continuing demand for CDOs, US home-ownership increased, along with a gradual lowering of the initially high demands on the creditworthiness of homebuyers. The last stage of the lowered credit demands was the so-called NINA (no income, no assets) loans; neither an income nor any assets had to be demonstrated to obtain a mortgage loan.

'The state of mind of the system' (Long 2008) is expressed by Warren Buffett from the perspective of today's investors when he says, 'Nothing sedates ration-ality like large doses of effortless money' (Plender 2009). In particular, among banks, mortgage brokers but also homebuyers there was a feeling of continued growth. This was connected with a feeling of invincibility and the impression of having invented the perpetual motion machine for money. 'Everyone' wanted to participate in this endless circus of easy money, while the much talked about and cited 'greed' also played an important role. However, the greed of investment bankers alone does not suffice to explain the psychological and systemic complexities.

During this phase, some market participants nevertheless had an uneasy gut feeling that, in principle, things could not continue like this endlessly. Although this assessment existed, it was drowned out by assumedly rational arguments.

The financial market crisis: phase 2

In about November 2006 the system began to fail. The trigger was falling housing prices, as the loans of more and more overextended borrowers were in default. It nevertheless took until September 2008 for the crisis to reach its height in the United States (Blumberg *et al.* 2009b). Lehman Brothers declared bankruptcy, but the consequences were felt in the area of commercial papers and money market funds, which made the expansion of the crisis to the real economy possible. The bankruptcy of Lehman Brothers had two effects. Because Lehman Brothers was an important issuer of commercial papers, institutional investors received an indication of its imminent bankruptcy; they withdrew $41 billion virtually over-night (Waggoner 2008). As a result, 'the Reserve Funds broke the buck' and gave rise to the further withdrawal of $100 billion from various money market funds over the following two days. Eventually, other financial market fund managers no longer purchased any commercial papers for their funds, corporations could no longer issue commercial papers, and normally unproblematic business transactions and investments had to be cancelled (Blumberg *et al.* 2009b).

The sudden and complete loss of confidence is of particular interest psycho-logically. Although the Lehman Brothers commercial papers represented only 1 or 2 per cent of the reserve fund portfolio, the bankruptcy led to a significant capital loss at the reserve fund, and investors withdrew their money from the money market funds, which had previously been regarded as safe. The extent of the loss of confidence and the huge emerging fear was irrational. The financial market funds no longer trusted the banks, and corporations had difficulties in securing financing.

The financial market crisis: phase 3

When AIG, the largest American insurance corporation, reported being on the brink of collapse one day after the bankruptcy of Lehman Brothers, this was due to another instrument, credit default swaps (CDSs). (The following remarks are based on Egli *et al.* 2009.)

CDSs are securities originally intended to serve as a form of insurance against loan defaults, but can also be used for speculation purposes, because a relatively small investment is expected to bring a high yield. In many instances the bank selling the CDS, in turn, bought the same insurance cover from another bank to hedge itself against risk. This netting led to the development of a complex variously intertwined system of liabilities among banks and comparable institutions, which could no longer be subject to oversight, and cannot today (since a record does not exist). As long as no corporation or bank defaults, this system initially appears to be unproblematic. But when only *one* link in this chain breaks, a downward spiral of unimaginable magnitude is generated.

AIG, like Lehman Brothers, was one of the key players in the market. When Lehman Brothers declared bankruptcy, AIG, a credit insurer of Lehman Brothers, suddenly ran into problems.

The principal difficulty, however, was the lack of transparency in and regulation of this market over the past twenty years. The deregulation of financial markets had become a political catchword prior to the financial crisis.

Two important psychological aspects play a role in the third phase of the crisis. In the forefront of this tightly knit global speculation, i.e. the excessive making of bets, a fascination with gambling and risk taking, accompanied by a loss of a sense of reality, is evident. The gambler's wish for non-regulation involves dodging the rules and results in a loss of confidence by others who can no longer assess the gambler's portfolio risks.

Figure 4.1 summarizes the state of mind of the system at the various different levels.

Hidden behind this complex state of mind is a dynamic process which can, in accordance with Long (2008), be described as perverse. The breeding ground for this development is formed by a narcissistic dynamic at the societal level.

An extended view of perversion

The term 'perversion' is derived from the French *pervers*, which is derived from the Latin *perversus*: turned around, backward, wrong, bad, evil (Kluge 2002). *Pervertere mores* meant in a quite general sense 'directed against customs and morals' (Berner 2002). There is thus – chiefly in the American psychoanalytic literature – a tendency to speak of a perverse attitude towards reality (e.g. Grossman 1993; Wurmser 2002; Arlow 1971; Etchegoyen 1978). Grossman's understanding of the perverse attitude is based on the difference between neurosis and perversion, which was previously defined by Freud: in neurosis the wish is disavowed, disguised or repressed with consideration of the dangers perceived in

Regulatory level	Miscalculation of the risk	No market transparency	Lacking control mechanism	'Wrong' incentive systems	Lacking regulation
Rationalization level	The others behind me? Do not interest me.	It will be alright!?!	Risk? We have to do business!		It has been going well for so many years
Emotional level	Me too... Envy	Invincibility	Greed	Lust with risk and gambling	Pride and arrogance about having achieved so much
Unconscious level			Fear Complexity		

Figure 4.1 Underlying dynamics of a narcissistic society.

reality, while in perversion the perception of reality is altered and the wish is retained (Grossman 1993).

The perverse approach towards reality is therefore not limited to sexual perversions, but constitutes a general attitude towards the denial of reality, diversion, and creation of illusions as a defence against troubling perceptions of at the simultaneous acceptance of reality. This may be understood as the splitting into Yes and No posited by Freud as being paradigmatic for fetishism. Undesirable perceptions and a complex reality are disavowed to avoid cherished fantasies, faith in almightiness, controllability and omnipotence being called into question. Dreams are treated as realities and perceptions as dreams (Wurmser 2002).

Regarding work with a patient, this can mean that the patient may 'look away' when an apt interpretation is offered. Although reality is perceived, it does not have a sufficiently strong influence to have an impact on the cherished beliefs. When reality does not fit, it is denied and disavowed. It may thus well happen that an unpleasant reality is dismissed as a dream or a joke.

The role of the fetish

A component of fetishistic perversions is the use of a non-living fetish to effect a compromise. However, in an extended conception of the perversion, the analyst, for example, may also be understood as the fetish. The patient perceives himself as inadequate and attempts to compensate this inadequacy by means of a fetish. The fetish symbolizes the missing piece, because the patient 'misses the essential piece' (Wurmser 2002).

The fetish serves to distract the fetishist from the unbearable reality of the deficiency. The fetishist initially perceives reality as it is and subsequently denies it, because it is not in accord with his wishful thinking. From Grossman's (1996) point of view the pathology does not consist of the fantasy of the phallic woman, but in the dismissal of reality in order to preserve wishful thinking intact. Dreams are treated as if they were true, and reality is treated as if it were a dream. This approach to reality not only is used in regard to sexual aspects, but can be applied to all types of intrapsychic conflict to dismiss unpleasant realities. The perverse component is that possibly painful perceptions are treated as though they are without significance. It represents a form of dishonesty, a confusion of conscience that permits the individual to act as if reality cannot be distinguished from fantasy (ibid.).

From a Jungian perspective the archetype of the 'invalid' is the symbolic expression of psychopathy, which also includes perversions. It serves as the symbolic representation of 'disablement' (and is not meant to be directed against people with disabilities in the current sense). The 'invalid' lacks something that permits a sense of wholeness. To have at least a temporary experience of wholeness, he employs a 'crutch', which serves as a substitute for the missing piece. The fetish can assume the role of the crutch.

Perversion in this perspective is basically characterized by five features: (1) lack of eros; (2) lack of morals (morals as the attempt of the ego to keep control over the eros); (3) absence of any human development; (4) background depression; and (5) chronic background anxiety (Guggenbühl-Craig 1980). These features contain an important indication of that which also plays a role in non-sexual perversions, the lack of eros and the lack of morals. Both of these will continue to be discussed in the following.

A perverse system

Can these general considerations and characteristics of the perversion of an individual be transferred to a system, a corporation or a society? At this point I would like to follow Long (2008), who poses the following conception. A society can function systemically on the basis of a specific (e.g. narcissistic) dynamic, and thus exerts an influence on the individual and his behaviour. This does not refer, however, to pathologization on the level of the individual, but rather to the state of mind of a system. In particular, the concept of state of mind is an essentially social concept and always needs the other to exist.

Long (2008) develops five significant indicators of a perverse state of mind which she then applies to the analysis of organizations. A comparison of Long's (2008) itemization of the conditions behind perverse systems with the characteristics described by Wurmser (2002) and Grossman (1993) leads to the following general characteristics of perverse system dynamics:

- different splitting mechanisms such as a general disavowal of reality at the simultaneous perception of a troubling reality; this includes the denial of differences;

- dehumanization of relationships and instrumentalization as object;
- shame anxiety;
- compromise formation with the aid of a fetish;
- the taking for real of illusions and fantasies;
- the cyclicity of its effects combined with the difficulty of breaking this cycle.

A general structural deficit, which finds expression in the form of a narcissistic society (Lasch 1979; Long 2008) is required for the development of a perverse system, without which this development would not be possible. Predominant in the psychodynamics of the narcissistic society is the aim of individual maximal self-presentation in the sense of recognition and noticeability by others.

Perversion in the financial market crisis

Each of the factors identified above will be used to explore perversion in the financial market crisis of 2007–8.

Splitting mechanisms

At the centre of a perverse state of mind of the system is the vertical splitting mechanism of disavowal and the concurrent apperception of reality. The perverse state of mind is characterized by a concurrent 'yes' and 'no' attitude to reality. Splitting serves as a defence against a feeling of powerlessness and ignorance that is too anxiety-laden to endure. Reality is too complex to be controllable; the uncontrollability can be perceived and yet not perceived.

The splitting and denial involves all levels of the system. In the first phase of the crisis, when the housing and mortgage markets were continuously rising and more and more CDOs were being sold, the insatiable global financial pool wanted increasing amounts of the 'wonderful', purportedly low-risk and high-interest products. Then, alarm bells should have started to ring – in particular, those of institutional investors, but also those of experienced private investors, who should have realized that a basic rule of investment was being challenged.

But the investors wanted to ignore more than the reality that low risk means low interest. Also denied was the complexity of the instruments. The newly developed structured securities and all of their successors for the private investment sector in the form of certificates constitute highly complex instruments that cannot be fathomed by the use of common sense alone. The bankers themselves no longer understood their own products – in private conversations they are prepared to admit this – but at the start of the crisis there was no mention of complex products; everything appeared to be so simple.

An uneasy feeling, which was repressed, was nevertheless experienced by some bankers; one just did not speak about it. This meant missing the boat. In the discussion of the financial market crisis the words 'greed' and 'envy' are frequently mentioned, but each may serve as a defence against the uncomfortable realization of these denial mechanisms.

Mortgage brokers and mortgage bankers already had an intuitive queasy feeling prior to the collapse. The required credit quality continued to decline and had to decline, because otherwise not enough residential mortgage-backed securities would have been available for bundling, securitization, and sale to the global financial pool. The guidelines changed from 'declared income and declared assets' to 'no income and confirmed assets' to 'no income and no assets'. Ultimately, credit was granted to individuals who had neither assets nor a job. These individuals felt somehow that they had been invited to lie – they call it a sham credit – since declarations of income were not checked, and borrowers felt drawn into disguising the truth (Blumberg *et al.* 2009a: 23).

What becomes apparent here is the denial of reality by both the banks and the borrowers.

In a next stage the sale of bundled mortgages led to their virtual disappearance from the bank balance sheet. Moreover, with the introduction of special entities (special purpose vehicles, SPVs) and the respective guidelines for financial accounting, they vanished – depending on their construction – completely from the balance sheet. It seems there was an unconscious collusion with the financial supervisory authorities, which supports the idea of a denial of rather than a confrontation with reality.

There was a collective state of wanting to participate – to make a lot of money in a short time – and, most importantly, of turning a blind eye. Greed and envy are on the surface the impetus for not wanting to miss out and to participate. Yet behind the greed lies the denial of the uncontrollability of the system, the fear of its complexity, and fear of powerlessness. Participation meant to be part of the system and to maintain the illusion of controllability.

A different splitting mechanism became manifest when the crisis suddenly gained momentum following the bankruptcy of Lehman Brothers, in the difficulties of AIG. The feeling of 'everything is possible' changed literally overnight into 'nothing works any longer'. In splitting, the object is experienced as 'only good' or 'only bad'. The change in perception of the object is found in this sudden, total and completely irrational reversal of the mindset of the system. The wondrous, money-making, wealth-increasing market changed suddenly overnight into a monster that could no longer be trusted, because of the fear of being devoured by it (Blumberg *et al.* 2009b).

An attitude of total mutual distrust emerged among the banks, which no longer wanted to lend money to each other – even though a functioning interbank market works as a sort of lubricant in the system. The corporations also suddenly encountered financing problems since nobody wanted to do business with anyone any more. The financial market, normally highly fluid, became frozen (Blumberg *et al.* 2009b).

This borderline-like splitting effect prevented the perception of reality as a whole, which would have included both the positive and the negative sides of the object. This, in turn, prevented the apperception of one's own fear, powerlessness and helplessness. The described splitting mechanism brings to mind the paranoid-schizoid position of Melanie Klein (e.g. 1946), where the good, helpful object mutates into a destructive one. The mechanism of projective identification becomes effective in the archaic state, so that on a systemic level mutual blaming for the cause of the crisis took place among the banks.

Illusions

Splitting mechanisms underlie the formation of illusions. As a rule, these are illusions of grandeur and omnipotence, perceived as true, while the reality of painful powerlessness and helplessness is avoided. Boundlessness is another of these illusions. Living partially in a fantasy world enables the avoidance of a confrontation with reality. Brokers especially, who made a lot of money, felt like very cool movie stars and were treated as belonging to the rich and wealthy, and had access to expensive clubs (Blumberg et al. 2009a).

To the illusion of grandeur is added the feeling of mastery of the money-making system; the perpetual motion machine of money seemed to have been invented. The wondrous propagation of money seemed to be endless, and everyone profited from it: the construction companies and homebuyers, mortgage brokers and mortgage bankers, commercial and investment bankers, institutional and private investors. It appeared as if this would continue for ever; it had, after all, been going well for many years. This illusion of unending growth and omnipotence is accompanied by the illusion of manageability and control, which prevents the perception of its true opposite, non-manageability and non-control over the complex reality.

Shame-anxiety

Shame always arises from feelings of inadequacy, feelings that one might be weak, defective or deficient. It revolves around the ideal self-image, the ego-ideal that acts as a measure. Shame-anxiety is the fear of experiencing shame or the occurrence of a shameful situation. It is the fear that this experience may be due to one's own fault or carelessness. At the root of shame-anxiety is a lack of self-esteem and self-confidence, because beneath shame-anxiety lies concern with the esteem of one's own person in the social context, and therefore with one's worth in the eyes of others.

The fear behind shame-anxiety is the fear of rejection, withdrawal of love and loss of object; it represents a special form of separation anxiety. The reactions can range from avoidance of the revealing situation to physical inhibition and blocking (Jacoby 1991; Wurmser 2008). The defence mechanism of splitting and illusion formation may be used as a defence against the underlying shame-anxiety.

Comments made during the financial crisis often indicate that an increasingly complex financial world was no longer comprehended, and could not be understood by the majority of bankers or other specialists, let alone investors. During the past two decades a wave of innovation has reshaped the market's work and seemed able to deliver huge benefits for all. But it became so intense that it outran the comprehension of most ordinary bankers and also regulators (Tett 2009).

Today this assessment is also made in private by financiers, but it would have been unthinkable to admit a few years ago that one did not understand the instruments one worked with. It was an unwritten law of the financial markets that this ignorance was neither to be named nor heard. Shame-anxiety may have been at the bottom of the disavowal of ignorance. Among the purportedly omniscient investment bankers this admission would have been akin to an exclusion from the ranks of 'the masters of the universe' – and would have involved a hard-to-bear narcissistic slight. Perverse pride resulting from the illusion of omnipotence and controllability of the system constitutes a further defence mechanism of shame-anxiety (Long 2008).

This shame-anxiety was felt also in executive suites, where nobody paid much attention 'because the risk manager said those instruments were triple-A' (Tett 2009: 9). Such statements demonstrate the rationalization of the inability to understand these products. According to an employee of Standard & Poor's in 2006, a computer already needed an entire weekend to make all the calculations required to determine the risk of a complex CDO (Tett 2009). Such complexity is unlikely to be understood using common sense alone. Shame-anxiety prevents the admission of one's ignorance. This has not changed, even though one of the causes of the financial crisis is known to lie in the complexity of the structured products private investors continue to buy. Derivatives and complex financial instruments are beyond the imagination of most people, including bankers, who act as though they understand, but in fact have only mastered basic mathematics and cannot readily assess the impact.

Dehumanization of relationships and instrumentalization of the other

With the use of splitting mechanisms and illusions, the perception of a difference between the self and the other can be avoided. Boundlessness and absence of difference make the other an extension of the self. The borders between the self and the other are not only not maintained, but destroyed. The basis of this is a narcissistic egocentrism: the pursuit of one's own interest, even to the detriment of the collective good, appears to be legitimate. This dehumanization of relationships, which can be understood as a lack of eros, is continued in the instrumentalization of the other. The other is used and employed merely as an object for the satisfaction of one's own interest. Respectful interaction and mutual giving and taking are not possible, only the use and abuse of others. This abuse is both perceived and denied. It underlies the character of a perpetrator–victim dynamic, which may also be described as the master–servant system cited by Hegel (1807/1988).

In the financial market crisis the instrumentalization of the other was one of the main features of the system and was practised at different levels. The mortgage brokers developed a ruthlessness regarding possible negative consequences of their actions: it was of no importance whether the customer was able to repay the loan or not; what counted was one's own commission. The mortgage bank was only concerned with the number of credits it could bundle and resell. For the commercial bank, which should have thought about the matching maturities of its customer, i.e. the mortgage bank, its own business was more important than default risks. If an uneasy gut feeling appeared, it was drowned out by pseudo-rational arguments such as 'others offer it, so we have to offer it too. This is how we gain market shares' (Blumberg *et al.* 2009a: 26).

As a result of the bundling and securitization, (investment) bankers no longer had a real relationship with the mortgage borrowers. They were merely a number in the spreadsheet. Also, they seem to have lost any feeling of responsibility for their own portfolio and that of their customers. Their own interests, i.e. their own business interests, were more important than those of their customers (Plender 2009). The institutional investors were in a similar situation. They normally invest their assets for and on demand of their investors, but concern for the 'other' behind the assets had long been lost. Also lost was an awareness of for whom the work was being done. One might speak of an 'estrangement of money'.

It appears as though the border between use and abuse is blurred in the perversion (Long 2008). When specific information is used to advantage the bank rather than the customer, is this simply a clever exploitation of the system or does it already represent an abuse of the system? The illusion of boundlessness constitutes another element of the perversion. The instrumentalization was such that existing regulations and control mechanisms were consciously circumvented and last loopholes were identified. Personal gain, therefore, took precedence over losses incurred for the general public, for whose protection these regulations had been developed. In the collaboration within the financial market industry, the other was merely viewed as someone who was either useful for increasing one's wealth, or might possibly prevent one from doing so.

The lack of eros, defined as the main characteristic of psychopathy by Guggenbühl-Craig (1980), can clearly be seen in each of the aspects described. Empathy with and consideration of the other appeared to be left aside in favour of striving for power, dominance and the maximal pursuit of one's own interests. The attitude of 'it-is-not-my-problem-if-the-other-goes-along-with-this' characterized large parts of the system and reveals a lack of eros and morals.

On the whole, this appears to be the expression of a general narcissistic tendency in society where the other is used as an extended self-object, while a genuine relationship with the other is often not achieved. Aspects of this narcissistic structure can be observed in the media (*Germany's Next Topmodel, Big Brother*, talk shows, reality soaps), consumer behaviour (individualization and customizing of products), spirituality (eclectic choice of useful building blocks from different religions) and music (virtuoso musicians are magnified into glamorous superstars), as well in all other areas of life. The illusion of the achievability of superstar status by everyone and the possibility of projective identification appears to compensate for the loss of emotional bonding and relationships in the personal sphere of family and couple as well as in other 'micro-systems' such as communal structures, churches and clubs.

Avoiding perceiving the other and his or her boundaries represents a failure in the ability to differentiate and is generally associated with a limited symbolizing function (Wurmser 2002). The symbolizing function is, however, of crucial importance in the ability to differentiate between the perception of an object as self-object, and therefore as the extended self or as transitional object, and thus a third, symbolizing something else, or as actual object in the sense of the other.

Money as fetish

The role of the fetish has different aspects in perversion. While it serves the pleasurable satisfaction of the sexual drive on the one hand, it may also be understood as an extended self-object. Comparable to the use of the other as object, the fetish serves to stabilize and complete the self. It replaces that which is missing.

In the financial market crisis the fetishistic character of money becomes particularly apparent in CDS speculation. It found expression in the 'casino mentality' with a zest for betting in manifestly deregulated markets. This lust for gambling combined with instrumentalization and illusions of grandeur took on enormous proportions so that the instruments originally intended to serve as insurances had reached ten times the value of the actual underlying corporate bonds.

A broker explained this development: 'Around 2003/2004 I was getting increasingly nervous, because I could see how the CDS market changed from a very legitimate instrument into something *more hot-blooded and interesting*, although it also held much greater dangers' (Blumberg *et al.* 2009b: 41; italics added). It is precisely the term 'hot-blooded' that describes the lust in speculating with CDSs. In my view, CDSs and the CDS market represent the speculative-playful-lust attitude towards money.

However, not only were CDSs used as a fetish, but other investments, and money itself, have assumed more and more of a fetish character. The almost sensual zest for speculation, betting and gambling is immediately apparent in conversations with traders. But it also affects many private investors who speculate on the stock market. In the extended view of perversion, dealing with money and money products may be experienced as a sensation filled with lust. On the level of the system this pleasure has contributed to compensating for a lack of eros and the dehumanization of relationships.

Tucket and Taffler (2008) argue similarly when they come to the conclusion that internet stocks had the function of phantastic objects in the development of the internet bubble.

A fantastic phantastic object is a mental representation of something (or someone) which in an imagined scene fulfils the protagonist's deepest desires to have exactly what she wants exactly when she wants it. We might say that the fantastic phantastic objects allow individuals to feel omnipotent like Aladdin (who owned a lamp which could call a genie); or like the fictional bond trader, Sherman McCoy (who felt himself a Master of the Universe) [in *The Bonfire of the Vanities* (Wolfe 1987)].

(ibid.: 88–9)

Aladdin's wonderful lamp functions like money itself and therefore also bears a certain resemblance to the pond that served as the mirror for Narcissus. The wonderful lamp has to be rubbed for a genie to appear and fulfil the owner's every wish. This is what money will do when it is spent to (hopefully!) fulfil the wish for beauty, prestige, power and influence, control, desire, and also lust.

The projection function of money (Nagel 2008) results from the possibility that it can be changed and exchanged, and thus enables the projection of unconscious wishes, needs, hopes and cravings on money. When the possibilities for projection on the basis of the archetypal qualities of money, which are represented by eros and power, come together with individual experiences and conceptions, the money complex develops (ibid.).

The money complex becomes effective because, as a self-object, money is able to reflect the 'borrowed ego' symbolically and thereby permits the identification with it. This mirroring – which corresponds to the mirroring of the child through the mother – also corresponds symbolically to the mirroring Narcissus experiences when he falls in love with his own mirror image in the pond. The bonding relationships which it was hoped would come into being through the described mirroring are replaced by money. Money is then used for projective identification purposes. With its help, anguish and hurt can be temporarily compensated. The bonding relationship money was to replace has, however, become impossible through the compensatory use of money, leading to a cycle of a lack of emotional relationships, compensation, and a new lack of emotional relationships (ibid.). The vicious circle of money characterizes the mechanism of perversion as a whole.

Cycle

A chain reaction of denial, self-delusion and possibly complicity develops, which leads to further denial, self-delusion and complicity in the sense of a cycle. Because these psychic mechanisms are linked with each other, it becomes difficult to break out of this cycle. One of these mechanisms is the denial of the passing of time; separation is avoided by eternal fusing, resulting in the 'eternal recurrence of the same' (Wurmser 2002: 19, referring to Nietzsche).

The current (non-)discussion of the societal rationale of the financial market crisis shows how difficult it is to break out of this cycle and to become aware of the perverse mechanism. A public debate of the perversion has not yet been initiated; the denial of reality and the splitting mechanisms have still not been discussed. The required review of the financial market regulation is somehow on its way but mostly still awaited.

To prevent any stepping out of this cycle, a scapegoat responsible for the financial crisis had to be found. This was readily achieved: the investment bankers and their greed. The scapegoat mentality in particular shows how rarely the issue of individual responsibility and guilt is broached. Denial, anger and finger-pointing instead of addressing the question of guilt may be understood as the continuance of the defence mechanism (PS/paranoid-schizoid – defensive instead of D/depressive and realistic) (Tuckett and Taffler 2008). From the point of view of perversion, this perverse cycle appears to continue and money as fetish does not seem to have lost its power.

Outlook

What has changed since the outbreak of the crisis? Banks were saved and rescue funds were issued, the bankruptcy law for banks in Germany was adjusted, some kinds of derivative transactions are no longer allowed in Germany, taxes on transactions might be introduced (the meaningfulness of which is disputed intensely), and rules and regulations concerning capital markets are the main focus of supposed necessary changes. The last of these especially seems to be very difficult because of the interconnectivity and interdependency of the globalized financial markets and also because of very different political opinions of the participating nations and their leaders.

Society has been minimally rattled; subjects such as values, morality and responsibility have been in the newspapers and talk shows, and their discussion has become more socially acceptable. But on further scrutiny no comprehensive reflection of the problem has taken place on either an individual or a societal level. The idea that the cause for the crisis could be a state of mind at a systems level has not been discussed; the discussion has stayed on the level of finding scapegoats (the bankers) and changing the rules and regulations regarding the financial and banking system. The insights into the background, especially into the almost unavoidable pull and the dynamics of this perverse state of mind that touches not only the bankers but also 'ordinary people', has been avoided and is probably part of the socio-dynamics.

Since 'money makes the world go round', this reflection should take place at the level of the financial elite, corporate leaders, bankers and entrepreneurs. But since denial of unpleasant interpretations is part of the problem, those who should realize these dynamics to effect some change are the least likely to do so. The insights and necessary changes will rather be avoided.

This leads me to think that maybe only a concrete physical experience, for example having to reduce consumption significantly, to save and to spend less (this seems to be a rather likely economic development in Western countries), can create the suffering necessary to develop a deeper understanding of what the next steps might be.

References

Arlow, J. (1971) 'Character perversion', in *Currents in Psychoanalysis*, 1: 317–36.

Berner, W. (2002) 'Perversion', in W. Mertens (ed.) *Handbuch psychoanalytischer Grundbegriffe*, Stuttgart: Kohlhammer.

Blumberg, A., Davidson, A. and Glass, I. (2009a) 'Die Finanzkrise: Teil 1. Der globale Geldtopf', *NZZ [Neue Züricher Zeitung] Folio*, January: 23–35.

Blumberg, A., Davidson, A. and Glass, I. (2009b) 'Die Finanzkrise: Teil 2. Das Wall-Street Massaker', *NZZ [Neue Züricher Zeitung] Folio*, January: 37–45.

Egli, L., Schenk, T., Schneider, R.U. and Weber, D. (2009) 'Die Finanzkrise: Teil 3. Wie konnte das nur passieren?', *NZZ [Neue Züricher Zeitung] Folio*, January: 47–54.

Etchegoyen, R.H. (1978) 'Some thoughts on transference perversion', *International Journal of Psycho-Analysis*, 59: 45–53.

Fornari Spoto, G. (2003) 'In Benommenheit schwelgen. Die Analyse eines narzisstischen Fetischs', *Jahrbuch der Psychoanalyse*, 46: 29–46.

Goldberg, A. (1998) 'Perversionen aus der Sicht der psychoanalytischen Selbstpsychologie', *Psyche*, 52(8): 709–30.

Grossman, L. (1993) 'The perverse attitude towards reality', *Psychoanalytic Quarterly*, 62: 422–36.

Grossman, L. (1996) ' "Psychic reality" and reality testing in the analysis of perverse defences', *International Journal of Psycho-Analysis*, 77: 509–17.

Guggenbühl-Craig, A. (1980) *Seelenwüsten. Betrachtungen über Eros und Psychopathie*, Zürich: Schweizer Spiegel.

Hegel, G.F.W. (1807/1988) *Die Phänomenologie des Geistes*, Ditzingen, Germany: Reclam.

Institutional Investors (2003) *Institutional Investors Statistical Yearbook 1992–2001*, Paris: Organisation for Economic Co-operation and Development.

Jacoby, M. (1991) *Scham-Angst und Selbstwertgefühl. Ihre Bedeutung in der Psychotherapie*, Düsseldorf: Walter.

Klein, M. (1946) 'Notes on some schizoid mechanism', in J. Mitchell (ed.) (1986) *The Selected Melanie Klein*, New York: Free Press.

Kluge, F. (2002) *Etymologisches Wörterbuch der Deutschen Sprache*, Berlin: de Gruyter.

Lasch, C. (1979) *The Culture of Narcissism: American life in an age of diminishing expectations*, New York: W.W. Norton.

Long, S. (2008) *The Perverse Organisation and Its Deadly Sins*, London: Karnac.

Mentzos, S. (2009) *Lehrbuch der Psychodynamik. Die Funktion der Dysfunktionalität psychischer Störungen*, Göttingen: Vandenhoeck & Ruprecht.

Nagel, C. (2008) 'Geld – Teufelswerk oder Stein der Weisen? Die archetypische Bedeutung des Geldes für Identität, Beruf und Individuation', unpublished thesis, International School for Analytical Psychology, Zürich.

Plender, J. (2009) 'Error-laden machine', *Financial Times*, 3 March: 8.

Tett, G. (2009) 'Lost through destructive creation', *Financial Times*, 9 March. Online, available at: http://tomweston.net/destructivecreation.pdf (retrieved 31 October 2010).

Tuckett, D. and Taffler, R. (2008) 'Phantastic objects and the financial market's sense of reality: a psychoanalytic contribution to the understanding of stock market instability', *International Journal of Psychoanalysis*, 89: 389–412.

Waggoner, J. (2008) 'Reserve Primary money market fund breaks a buck', *USA Today*. Online, available at: www.usatoday.com/money/perfi/basics/2008-09-16-damage_N.htm (retrieved 12 April 2009).

Wolfe, T.J. (1987) *The Bonfire of the Vanities*, New York: Farrar, Straus & Giroux.

Wurmser, L. (2002) 'Ein bedeutendes Stück fehlt. Ein Beitrag zur Psychoanalyse der Charakterperversion', *Jahrbuch der Psychoanalyse*, 44: 11–47.

Wurmser, L. (2008) *Die Masken der Scham. Die Psychoanalyse von Schamaffekten und Schamkonflikten*, Eschborn, Germany: Dietmar Klotz. English translation: *The Mask of Shame*, 1981, Baltimore: Johns Hopkins University Press.

5 Inside the minds of the money minders

Deciphering reflections on money, behaviour and leadership in the financial crisis of 2007–10

Alison Gill and Mannie Sher

Introduction

Our research is directed at the question of why senior, intelligent and respected leaders from all sides of the finance industry failed to prevent a crisis that some had predicted years in advance. We are interested in knowing more about the dynamic influences – personal and global – on the thinking of industry leaders. Here, 'thinking' is considered alongside 'not thinking', the 'inability to think' and 'hatred of thinking'. We therefore created a set of open-ended questions designed to elicit 'thinking'. As we conducted our interviews with about thirty senior figures, we noted our reactions to our interviewees as a way of deepening our understanding of their experiences of the crisis from their roles.

Our hypothesis is that *money, finance* and *capital* serve as 'containers' for hidden individual and social meaning. In our examination we hope to expose the dynamics that contributed to the financial crisis and how they shaped operating paradigms of banks and other financial institutions. Our interview method invited participants to offer free associations and uncensored thoughts in order that we could access deeper levels of understanding of the below-the-surface dynamics of leadership of financial institutions and the financial industry as a whole.

Our perspective in systems psychodynamics (or socioanalysis) focuses on conscious and unconscious relationships between individuals, groups, organizations and society as a whole. The unconscious is perceived not simply as a place in the mind of an individual but as an intricate web of social relations. In this, thinking and feeling are critical aspects of organizational functioning.

We work with the concepts of holism and transference. Holism considers that all parts of all systems affect one another (Tarnas 1991). Transference refers to the displacement of thoughts and feelings from one person or situation onto another person or situation. Countertransference refers to the feelings that the researcher or observer has towards his or her subjects. Both may occur in the relations between research interviewers and their subjects – the observers and the observed. Miller (1990: 170) captures the essence of the transference dynamic in group and organizational work when he states that in the field of human behaviour no conceptual framework is complete without a statement of the role of the observer and his/her relation to the observed.... Consultants collaborate with clients as actors in understanding and perhaps modifying their roles in the organisations.... [Consultants] are integrally part of the process, not outside it.

In this chapter we will examine (1) how opportunities for talking freely enabled our respondents to articulate thoughts that are normally set aside or repressed because of pressures of day-to-day work activity; and (2) how these hitherto unexpressed thoughts aroused, impacted and interacted with our feelings, which enabled us to offer new and testable hypotheses about the collective fantasies and behaviour of the people and institutions charged with stewardship of the economy. We anticipated that our presence in the organization would trigger thoughts in areas of organizational life that Bollas (1989) defines as the 'unthought known' – that is, thoughts that are inchoate and pre-conscious; thoughts that everyone is thinking but will not acknowledge publicly. For example, one chief executive said:

Following the near-collapse of the West's finance industry we have to reorient our thinking. Going for the last million and thinking about the quality of our life and the lives of our customers has to be balanced. Levels of remuneration are not the only things in life.

This thought had been at the back of many people's minds and found its way to conscious expression in public by virtue of our research presence.

In addition, we were concerned that any anxiety and guilt that they might have felt about their roles in the financial crisis would evaporate soon after the crisis passed. We were concerned too that the expectation of a 'bailout', the complacent 'too-big-to-fail' idea and the role of government as lender of last resort would lead to a business-as-usual attitude, and the opportunities for learning from the crisis would be lost.

We designed a list of ten open-ended questions that encouraged our respondents to free-associate rather than feed us the 'company line'. Examples of questions are:

Q.1: The vivid language used in the press over the last twelve months has described 'bankers' and 'city leaders' as 'greedy, stupid and socially useless'. To what extent do these definitions by outsiders, however painful, describe how you as an insider feel about yourself, your organization and your industry? What language, stories and definitions do you and other leaders in the financial industry use when you talk about your work and the role that banking plays in society?

Q.2: If the outsiders' definitions of professionals in the financial industry paint such an extremely negative picture, how do you feel about the potential influencing role of outsiders in future regulatory arrangements? How does the changing nature of banking, finance and regulation impact on your role and your hopes and fears for the future?

Our respondents were chosen because of their roles in different parts of the financial system: banking, insurance, accounting, regulation and civil service.

Through the interviews we found that the experiences of these individuals, their interpretations of what had happened and their understanding of causality, were similar – that is, on the one hand, they felt that they and the finance industry are indispensable to Western liberal democracy, the free market and civilization generally. On the other hand, few were willing to admit the extent of their own participation and collusion in the failings of a system that had privileged them. We think the critical difference here is between how our respondents believe they might have behaved as *individuals* and how they might have acted and achieved collectively. Despite occupying roles with huge authority and powers of control, they absolve themselves individually of accountability; they almost all described events as being outside their control, whereas their places in the system suggested that had they collaborated more effectively across systems and understood more about the nature of systems dynamics, events in the financial industry and their knock-on effects in almost every walk of life would have come more easily within their collective control. On the whole, they tend to ignore the role of rivalry, envy, fear, competition and conflict in relationships between organizations, sectors and systems; they fail to realize how arrogance, regression and narcissism sit alongside the drive for success, identification with community and the desire to live by positive values. This led us to critically assess the nature of leadership failure when systems break down. We believe that in the financial industry, leadership failure is related to the peculiarities of the material they are working with – money and markets – and the context within which they are working – capitalism and globalization – especially because these are such large collective systems that are so very different from individual, small-group and single-organizational dynamics with which they are more familiar.

Our respondents agree that banking – 'oiling the wheels of Western liberal democracy, providing opportunity for growth and dreams' – has changed for ever as a result of the near-meltdown of Western economies. Deregulation and globalization have made clearer the divide between the 'casino' of investment banking and the 'vanilla' of retail banking. The crisis has also, paradoxically, shown their inherent interdependence. The traditional bank manager – the one who 'looked the customer in the eye' and made judgements about reliability and risk – had been lost in efforts to improve the efficiency of high street banking. Technological advances and the desire to reduce costs and increase profit drove out the traditional bank manager who had played a vital role in knowing where to lend money, a role that was underestimated and undervalued by a banking system that had become global. Traditional retail banking business seemed boring, and the new, more lucrative business of investment banking seduced workers by its fast pace and promise of unlimited and accelerated wealth.

When bankers get to that age where they need a bit more money, where they've just got married, bought a house, things start to get tough. They are dealing with aggressive bankers who poach them, offering them lots more money than they are earning and the promise of more. They are putting up with the bad behaviour anyway so they think they may as well go and earn more.

(Senior partner, accounting firm)

Very few grasped the implications of the rapid rise of investment banking with its deep pockets and continued promises of wealth. Nor did they understand the increasingly porous nature of boundaries between retail and investment banking.

My picture of banking has worsened over the years; retail banking I saw as humdrum. But it had a social use. The banker was a person in the community, valued and modest. Technology has changed that; the community element no longer exists. Investment bankers wreak havoc on communities, but have no sense that they are doing this.

(Regulator)

Investment banking incentives were high and risks unforeseen. Investment banking became a gambling business and flourished on the thrill of wins with little thought of loss. Gambling self-sustains with an optimism stoked by the behaviour of leaders of the field.

In a business, money is the lifeblood; people who work in business know its power and importance. In the City, money is an end in itself. In the City there is a dislocation in the amount of money earned and effort. It is a form of curse.

(Non-executive director; regulator)

Risk managers, the leaders, were saying, 'It's OK.' Industry leaders were behaving as if it was acceptable to take high risks. Thus, many people continued to do things they were dubious about. Money seemed to us to be used as a handy symbol because of its ability to contain different and contradictory meanings:

Money isn't motivational to people – it motivates for a very short period. What matters is intellectual challenge, career prospects and being surrounded by other interesting people. Money can however be demotivating, if you discover you are paid less than your peer group. That demotivates and is divisive.

(Banker)

and

It's hard work if you don't have enough money – it's hard to get off the ladder once you're on it. You need more and more money to meet needs you didn't know you had. I pursue the things I like; I have a taste for expensive wine; I have a new car every two years; I have children in public schools – I didn't need these things, but I would find it hard to go back to not being able to have them.

(Banker)

Our reaction to these responses was incredulity that industry players with reputations for superior intelligence and aggressive drive could now be seeking sympathy for mistakes they had made through their lack of foresight and even lack of compassion. Were we ourselves victims of a media flurry to tar all bankers with the same brush as villains? Or were we seeing their genuine vulnerability and stunned disbelief? Were they pulling a fast one on us? We concluded that our interviews were eliciting genuine feelings of shame and remorse, and that in many instances the 'chiefs' actually did not see the crisis coming, and even if they did, they felt helpless. The interviews were becoming cathartic confessionals and we the confessors; it was as if they were waiting for opportunities to unburden, so cornered did they feel by the own sense of shame and failure and by the chorus of hostility that had been evoked from the media, government, shareholders and the public.

In addition to the confessional style of some of our respondents, we also felt the interviews had healing elements in so far as 'thinking' could once more find a place. Many of our respondents commented on the value of the experience of talking. They almost all said the interviews were difficult, they felt stretched, it made them think; some were physically and emotionally distressed by the experience, as was shown in their agitation, stuttering, tears, anger, table thumping, not wanting to end at the appointed time and asking for second interviews.

Our understanding of our respondents' behaviour and our reactions to them is linked to the development of new financial products that created vast new wealth opportunities for so many people in a short time. Everyone got caught up in a manic defence of overbearing omnipotence: 'We have created a new order; all the former rules can be suspended; we have conquered unpredictability and the future is ours. We possess it all' – a virulent form of infantile omnipotence and control of the feeding mother. Immediate and infinite gratification led to the suspension of thinking, even hatred of it, lest the thinking led to a critical re-evaluation of what they were doing, which might require a dramatic re-evaluation of their beliefs in themselves and their powers.

The market as God

Our research respondents believe in the concept of the market as a supreme being – the invisible hand that rewards good behaviour and punishes bad. That is how wealth is created and how grace is received. They also said markets are imperfect, but the best available systems. The market is regarded as an impersonal overriding judge of performance; announcements are made and share prices rise or fall. Nearly 70 per cent of stock is held for less than a second;

performance management is instantaneous. This speed is beyond human comprehension; it distracts and creates a sense of insecurity, causing people to focus on the short term. Instant gratification, not value, becomes the end in itself.

> If disclosure of short-term results focuses behaviour on even more short-termism, it is a vicious cycle. The transaction is valued over the long term and this creates a dreadful lack of trust.
>
> (Non-executive director; banker)

In this 'short-termist' environment, some regulators said they had found themselves 'defending the indefensible'. They observed behaviour known to be excessive, but they were persuaded that this time things were different. Bankers and regulators became captured by mathematics, believing that because they were modelling risk, they could contain it. The regulators were acting with self-delusion. Group mentality had developed and was embraced. People vigorously signed up to the latest idea, saying, 'This time is different.' The regulators said that 'we should not have believed them, but we felt we were up against people's unlimited capacity to persuade themselves otherwise. This clearly happened to us too'.

> Markets are still the best way we have of allocating resources, but they also generate breakdown! Market failure is inherent; regulation only mitigates it. Failure is a given! The problem has become global and the nature of global relationships is not understood. The true underlying problem is that the system had changed, but people hadn't understood that. The need is for individual governments to make changes in regulation, but they can't work fast enough. It is an impossible job. The market system is the best way for wealth creation, but it contains inherently wealth destruction too. There will always be a problem; therefore safety nets have to be provided, like safety deposits schemes, because systems do collapse. Regulation can reduce the amplitude and frequency of crises, but the regulator is in a difficult job because the players are always changing. The market isn't failsafe. In fact, it's designed to fail, but the bankers believe it is failsafe. They have an infinite capacity for self-delusion.
>
> (Regulator)

This 'infinite capacity for self-delusion' played on us, too. Some of the most powerful and celebrated figures in the financial world were talking to us and pouring out their hearts about their blind spots, failures and sense of shame. That filled us with feelings of inverted power – the great confessing to the lowly, grateful for listening to them, revealing their weaknesses as if seeking absolution from guilt. We felt at times as if we were experiencing a form of undifferentiated fusion with some of our respondents, resulting in a destruction of our own thinking capacities and values. We had to work hard to restrain our fantasies of sitting in judgement on our respondents and punishing them. Was this, we wondered, a mirror of a contemptuous judgementalism that some of our respondents themselves projected onto their financial organizations, markets and customers in their pursuit of omnipotent infallibility and self-aggrandizement? We felt we needed to be watchful of our judgemental and haughty attitudes lest they get in the way of our work and undermine our research roles.

Competition, capitalism and globalization

As far back as 1997, senior bankers from the twelve biggest institutions in the world came together, saying, 'We are the heart of the financial system. If we get it wrong, the whole system will suffer.' They were seeking to regulate themselves. In the analysis of the latest crisis, leaders frequently refer to their lack of understanding of the global nature of finance. According to our interviewees, early attempts to create global regulation were flawed because 'the international competitive juices were stronger than the collaborative ones'. The regulators believed that to have a global solution required global cooperation; but authority was not global. The regulators felt powerless. Our interviewees described how national interests superseded the bigger systemic demand. Unable to resolve differences, they dissociated from social reality and distanced themselves from their social obligations. Their proposed self-regulation could not occur because they feared that their own jurisdictions would constrain their ability to compete against those countries not present. Despite numerous attempts, the global finance system remained unregulated.

In our research, we have attempted to assess the contents of people's minds: their thinking, their non-thinking and their hatred of thinking about the financial and banking issues they were involved with on a daily basis. Property as an asset suffered inflated prices around the world in a decade of rising house prices. When prices fell, the financial bubble burst. Sub-prime mortgages in the United States are believed to have been the final straw, but they were not the main cause of the financial meltdown. In conversations with us, our respondents appeared to confirm Goldsmith's (2008) assertions that they inhabited a bubble in which they talked only about their investments. Day-to-day dialogue revolved around investment opportunities. We heard how investment decisions were made solely on 'How much this has gone up in the past?', not 'What is this worth?' Thinking had ceased and greed had overcome fear. They focused exclusively on the upside and ignored the downside. Prudent risk assessment stopped. They say they were disconnected from the true value of what they were selling. Their organizations were over-leveraged and investment bankers borrowed whatever they could in the home mortgages market. Huge mortgages, often as much as 125 per cent the value of the property, or six or seven times earnings, spoke of a system drunk on debt. In the complexity of a financial system driving debt, innovation in finance meant that intelligent individuals who should have known better were maximizing returns primarily to satisfy shareholders, and some banks were borrowing as much as forty times their capital base. Being caught in the crossfire of high leverage was the only means of keeping up with other banks. Certainly, most of our respondents struggle to understand the global, social and systemic nature of the financial crisis. They seldom came up with anything better than headline catch-phrases like 'trust', 'behaviours', 'relationships', 'interdependence', but these could neither help them really understand what had happened to their industry nor lead them to effective solutions.

The interviews produced a sense of responsibility in us. It seemed our respondents were making us feel responsible for them, to provide them with solutions. Should we have been clearer about their responsibilities? Our questions about the systemic nature of finance, about the potential abusive power of groups, resulted in silence, yet they spoke passionately of 'interdependence'. How could there be true interdependence without conversation? This left us confused. Some of our respondents spoke of their fear of litigation, not because of wrongdoing but fear that litigation would expose them as being found wanting. The lonely leader feared 'being found out'. As researchers and organizational consultants, we cannot repair the damage, nor do we seek to judge what happened. Our role is to contribute towards thinking about the role of culture, its strong driving force and how leaders manage the impact of these forces on themselves in their roles.

Despite their many words – and all of them (bankers, regulators, civil servants and lawyers) were articulate – to us they seemed lost. For many, it seems their distress is about their careers ending on a note of appalling indignity, some even facing the prospect of criminal charges; they appeared to be saying that they could not believe that they had been found wanting, caught out by such a catastrophic failure. They seemed unsure how to judge their own part in the failure – unsure as to whether their failure should be judged as personal rather than systemic. To what extent did they understand their roles in choices they made and their accountabilities that could have prevented the failure? All the subgroups had become unconscious players in the dramas of the groups to which they belonged. Everyone seemed at a loss to understand the system beyond their individual part of it. Of course, many do understand and they plead with us to show they do understand, but they claim that from where they stand, especially as regulators, accountants and civil servants, there was little chance of being heard.

Would we be able to hear them? Certainly, 'hearing them' felt as though our response had to be an uncritical acceptance of their helplessness, and collusion in the idea that the crisis was the fault of the bankers. We felt drawn into an 'us and them' split. Reconciling different views of the causes of the crisis was made more difficult because of the way two sides lined up.

Certainly, that was how we, the researchers, often felt about ourselves during interviews – our knowledge of organizational and global systems, behavioural dynamics, and organization and leadership theory had departed from us and we felt sucked into an abyss of inadequacy, feeling that we had lost our own capacity to question, understand or explain. We felt lost in a world of smoke and mirrors, caught in the countertransference of denial, splitting and projection (Long 2008).

Our respondents seemed unable to consider the invisible forces at work; everyone to a greater or lesser extent was involved: the borrowing public, corporate customers, investors, shareholders, regulators, the media, politicians. Seemingly, everyone was persuaded that growth was indefinite, ignoring their own often-quoted advice that whatever goes up, must come down. Together with our interviewees, we struggled to understand the imponderables of culture; the atmosphere and climate of the sector that had engulfed everyone and forced upon them a way of thinking and acting that no one single agency caused or had the power to stop. After many very good years, the 'bubble' had been pricked by mysterious forces that were beyond control of even the 'masters of the universe'. Even as the crisis unfolded, the competitive forces and denial continued.

> The industry was in 'silent complicity'; we were engaged in a 'feat of levitation' that could not go on and on. But it went on and we all believed in it. People knew that eventually the house of cards would fall down. Many CEOs felt, 'we're OK; we will benefit from the catastrophe of others'. Many allowed themselves to feel reassured because the regulator approved of the model of banks not needing much capital. How many said it was about to explode? Why were institutions under pressure to increase their leverage? There was enormous pressure from the institutions. Owners, media, shareholders ... everyone ... None of them said 'stop!'.
>
> (Banker)

Bankers talk a lot but say so very little. We felt drawn to wanting to explain, ask and challenge our interviewees. If 'interdependence', 'collaboration' and 'cooperation' are the hallmark of other disciplines and sectors that have been struggling with these dynamics for decades, why does this seem like a new discovery for bankers, as if they have invented something new? We wanted desperately to be heard – yet the more we leaned forward, looked them in the eye and nodded, the more words would come tumbling out of their mouths. Even our smallest comment or question would result in a stream of consciousness, as if they had thought and thought and thought, but had never drawn conclusions.

The banks, the regulators, the politicians and the auditors knew that banks were running high risks. But risk management in the 1990s and early 2000s moved increasingly towards mathematical modelling and away from human intuition. 'Bubbles' of euphoria (Tuckett and Taffler 2008) get separated from reality; it is a process in which everyone colludes. For Lanchester (2010), capital, capitalists and capitalism are forces enjoined by emotions, some of which are associated with the universal desire to escape reality and be embraced by a warm sense of control and invulnerability that comes from the unrestricted in-flow of goodness (profits, dividends, bonuses) that are not calibrated against the direct input of one's own labour. Other emotions are associated with aggression, daring and challenge that place survival at risk. Normally, the presence of a rational mind with sound ego functioning helps to balance desire with reality and leads to responsible decision making that avoids swings of perception, expectation, mood and behaviour. In economic terms these swings are referred to as 'boom' and 'bust'. When property markets rose, irrational exuberance (Greenspan 1996; Shiller 2005) meant that enormous amounts of money were piling into the mortgage markets. That was good news for capital because mortgages offered a steady stream of set-up fees and repayment money, and it could expect to take part in the increase in house values as property values steadily rose.

We often felt caught in processes of idealization and magical thinking, and sometimes felt that our own insights into unconscious dynamics might be flawed. Here was the answer and it seemed so simple. Our respondents express desired outcomes, but do not address the challenges of how to promote understanding leading to wiser policies and action.

> One needs to be realistic. There will be more pressure to regulate, demonstrate transparency, accountability and effectiveness. That cannot be done without more awareness of, and exposure to, outside interests and influence. Outside influence is necessary otherwise bankers won't be taken seriously. Government, business and civil society must act in concert in making strenuous efforts to enable people to understand and know how the system works, the risks it runs, what it takes to generate value and remain competitive.
>
> (Civil servant)

'Acting in concert' ignores the presence of competition, different levels of power, status and authority. 'Better understandings' is based on a rationalist approach to communications and education; we felt pressure was put on us to collude in ignoring the group basic assumption that sets its face against scientific approaches and defends against the experience of anxiety-arousing knowledge.

We felt at times seduced by the status and apparent knowledge of our civil servant respondents through their closeness to the hub of powerful interconnecting relationships between the banking sector, government and society. Their position at this hub had made them aware of the importance of *collaboration and interdependence* as the most viable way forward for government and society. They spoke eloquently and passionately about these processes. However, as the interviews progressed, we felt the conversations had the quality of a mantra – how everyone and all sectors would benefit if only they would accept the incontrovertible wisdom of *collaboration and interdependence*; yet their statements often sounded too perfect and ignored the negative dynamics of competition and conflict that are inherent and sometimes dominate relationships between organizations, sectors and systems. We were left wondering why so little attention was paid to the presence of omnipotence, regression and narcissism alongside the drive for success, corporate social responsibility, identification with community and other positive values.

Our respondents' positions are too 'either–or' and do not take sufficient account of the presence of the duality of the dynamics – positive and negative – operating simultaneously. We felt pressured to accept their formulae and saw how these drove them towards rigid practices and more theoretical and exhortatory positions.

The driven nature of the speech of our respondents had an obsessive quality. They seemed caught in a balancing act between competing forces in the world of finance – bankers, customers, politicians and regulators – and yet appeared to desperately want to be friends with and liked by all. Their obsessive talk seemed a means of protecting themselves from something they couldn't bring themselves to articulate, namely, the tension between guilt and reparation – their desire to repair the damage that they must have recognized had been part of their lives for many years. Now, with the crisis, it seemed their rationalizations were no longer holding up and no longer holding them up. We wondered about their evangelical speech. Was it a case of them losing faith, or had they already lost faith in themselves and their work, and were now regressing to a faith that had earlier sustained them? Belief in capitalism, in the free market and in deregulation had been shown to be illusory, creating benefits for a few at the expense of the many. Was that the reason, we wondered, why some were now preaching a universal loving faith that incorporated everyone, as if by doing this they hoped to be taking banking back to its pristine days of doing things only for social good? We had the impression they were bitter and feeling deceived by their profession, their systems, their colleagues after a lifetime of devoted work 'lubricating society', and now it had all come undone and they have no answers.

Bankers everywhere are driven to reduce or even eliminate risk in their investments. Previously, this was done on a basis of trust that developed via interpersonal relationships between lender and borrower. To the relief of bankers and regulators, mathematicians and economists produced all-encompassing mathematical models that dispensed with the time-consuming and subjective assessment skills of bank managers in assessing risk. With new mathematical models it was possible to correlate the apparently uncorrelatable, and this opened up the field to new financial products such as sub-prime loans as a source of collateralized debt obligations (CDOs). These products were spread throughout the global financial system, unsupervised and largely invisible to even well-informed investors.

> Bankers believed this time it's different because we are modelling. Bankers were captured by mathematics – the 'quants'.... But they failed to price risk in their products and that is the bottom of every problem. 'Quants' – those mathematical geniuses who persuaded banks of their quantification models – said they could price risk and they were wrong! People were prepared to be convinced that risk could be calculated and this led to the abandonment of caution. The longer things seemed to be going well, the more inclined they were to believe. People's behaviour fed the feel good-factor. There was unconscious collusion between the users of the system and suppliers of the system. The crisis had to happen. Credit card users and bankers and markets shared the unconscious fantasy – triumph of hope over experience.
>
> (Regulator)

We were incredulous at the naivety of our respondents who held tenaciously to the view that because risk had been fully accounted for, the financial crisis was an accident – an unconnected series of events that finally pushed the system over the edge. We felt that we were being asked to sympathize with the victims of an accident, possibly in order to avoid the public's opprobrium towards them as abusers. In almost the same breath, while pushing the 'accident' idea, respondents would say the collapse of Lehman Brothers was through bad decision making; that banking regulators, through Basel II, deliberately allowed banks to lend without sufficient capital; for example, Northern Rock, Alliance & Leicester and Bradford & Bingley in the United Kingdom had all eagerly adopted Basel II. We were asked to believe that there was no villainy at play, there were no power games, that the markets are not driven by selfish behaviour, that there are no wealth gaps, no injustice. Few of our interviewees even admitted that people had suffered in the crisis. Many of our interviewees had been ordinary people who had made good. They had achieved well-off statuses. They could not, it seems, live with the idea that their gain may have caused losses to others. The story seems to be rationalized thus: things have turned out for the best.

The dance of false confidence

Most of our banker respondents answered our questions confidently and self-assuredly. We would have liked to see a little more critical doubt in their answers, but their replies were about giving it straight: 'This is how it is and I don't expect to be questioned.' The masters know the rules of the game and seem only slightly bewildered by the resultant mess and were quick to pin the blame elsewhere – 'the supervisors stopped supervising and the managers stopped managing' – but there were no answers as to why. The analytics, they say, were appealing, subjectivity was lost, and numbers and models reigned supreme.

> We need to define the sort of system we want and the behaviours we want. We got too complicated; management got focused on analytics, not management. Regulation got focused on analytics, not supervision. Supervision stopped; everyone was looking at the numbers. In the past, supervisors came to see us; they looked us in the eye and judged whether what we were saying stacked up. These were informal and subjective judgements. This has been lost. The regulators too got focused on models and analytics; they stopped talking and listening. We got obsessed with numbers and quality of algorithms; we stopped being human beings.
>
> (Senior executive, banking)

What was not being 'human beings' defending against? Seeking risk-free perfection? Avoiding the ordinariness of work and inevitability of financial cycles? 'Understanding' and preparing for the cycles had been rejected as processes; growth was made concrete. Our respondents were torn between their intellect and their emotions. They were in touch with feelings mainly when describing the feelings of others. They were good at analysing them, but could not as easily apply those same emotions to themselves. They were defended and remote and it was hard sometimes to warm towards them.

In the countertransference, sometimes it felt easy to have a slight sense of triumph over our respondents – when the great bankers, who come alive with a complex puzzle, said the interviews with us were 'stretching and tough' and 'exhausting' because they were unable to answer some of our questions, or to look into themselves to find an answer; others seemed to have a straightforward 'bat back' response devoid of thought – 'it's about who people are'.

We found it difficult at times to record all their words. Their monotone, rapid flow of words made listening and full exploration difficult. We tried, but the volume and speed with which their thoughts were verbalized made it difficult. We were presented with contradictions; for example:

- It is not easy to self-diagnose, but we are the best people to work out what went wrong and what to do about it.
- We are the right people to resolve problems, but outsiders are better at seeing issues.
- We have the brains to sort this out, if only we could get ourselves to sit in the same room together.
- Actually, we are powerless to change this, because bankers are all 'self-interested and conflicted'.
- I can't fault the interventions and cooperation at a global level, but it has been politically motivated.

Interdependence

Interdependence of financial institutions is an issue thought about deeply since the financial crisis. Events had forced our respondents to change their perceptions of themselves and the world they moved in. Their role relationships with government, regulators, investors, customers and society have forcibly come under scrutiny. They are troubled by the behaviour of the more powerful players in the financial industry and the impact this has on their organizations. Most are thoughtful people, aware of the need to act in socially responsible ways and of the role the financial services industry plays in the 'ecosystem'. But they are ignorant of the dynamics needed to achieve symbiosis – cooperative, mutually beneficial relationships between people and groups – that should, they believe, form part of their thinking and their values. They realize that unrestrained growth compromises the interconnectedness of financial systems where everything is interlinked.

As a result of the crisis, and reinforced by our interviews, some respondents are open to considering the weaknesses in financial systems. They are open to the idea that their organizations may have been responsible for inflicting hurt and damage. Bankers and regulators alike agreed on establishing relationships with customers, rather than seeing them as units of transactions, encouraging them to spend responsibly within their means; using money as a vehicle for developing and maintaining a standard of living, not offering unrealistic fantasies of unlimited wealth.

In others, another type of reaction is noticeable. Anger and disappointment are tempered by cultural norms of pragmatism and dealing in facts. Respondents who understand well the nature of relationships across society and globally are realistic in their evaluations of what had happened. They were stunned by the events and wished they had better ways of understanding their predicaments. In spite of their desire to know more, their limited understanding of structures and dynamics of interconnected systems of the financial industry is not as helpful as they would have liked to think. Equally, they found it hard to believe that the strength and power of the financial industry could derail the economy, but their commitment to the 'ecosystem' is strong, as are their values and beliefs in being helpful in developing people and business to achieve what they want. It seems that these respondents are unconsciously frightened of their own aggression and the power of their industry to do harm. Fear of this aggression is expressed by projecting it onto other parts of the financial system, such as those in government, whom they describe as the real spoilers who over-regulate and chase intelligent and motivated people away. Banks, they insist, are nothing more than 'intermediaries' between capital and commerce.

Senior people in all branches of the financial services say they value the principles of interdependence and are committed to the social values of funding infrastructure and building new communities (Hudson 2009: 3). Public and private funding must work together, they say, but they do not readily know how. All agree that bankers and regulators and politicians must work together and break out of their closed mindsets, but few can articulate a way to make this truly happen. They would have to overcome the difficulties of listening to others, just as we struggled to listen to them. Even government organizations that are meant to represent and manage competing interests in society have become very technical and exclude other views. Regulators and civil servants describe how their prejudice against 'greedy' bankers has changed with increased acquaintance, and they realize that bankers could be a force for good. Through talking in depth with bankers, some of our own stereotypical views of bankers' narrow focus, high intelligence and greed altered, and generalizations and bias surrendered. Our respondents said that contempt easily pervades their system, where 'experts look down on others who do not understand economics or financial products the way they do'. Stakeholders interacting with one another in financial services see things primarily from their own group's perspective alone. This makes change difficult as people become more dissociated from social reality and social obligation.

Conclusion

On the whole, our research demonstrates that bankers, regulators, shareholders, politicians and civil servants have a good grasp of the seeming overt issues that led to good and bad behaviour in the financial crisis. They clearly recognize that fraudulent behaviour by individuals should not go unpunished, but they are unable to comprehend how the invisible forces of culture drove a particular type of behaviour that underpinned the crisis. Behaviours that are driven by culture present a paradox to them; on the one hand, they recognize and associate competition, rivalry and pace of business transaction as positive forces very much at the root of their successes. On the other hand, they realize that these cultural norms may have played a far greater role in the crisis than they are able to understand. It is hard for the finance masters to believe that there are forces impacting on them over which they have little or no knowledge or control. Consequently, our respondents feel they should not be tainted with guilt about their involvement in the financial crisis, as the general culture of high risk and high leverage and high debt were the causes in which everyone participated. Were they fraudulent or just found wanting? To what extent should they be held accountable for the powerful but impersonal forces that drive culture? Who should pay for the crisis? If you are part of the banking inner circle, you do not expect to have to pay for the crisis. Retail banking, blue-collar workers and public servants are paying for and being punished through loss of their jobs and homes for the crisis the investment bankers and leaders of the global finance system had created but from which they had managed to distance themselves.

Individual accountability versus systemic accountability seems not to have been truly understood. Judgement was displaced, so guilt and anger are objectified and distanced and projected into 'the market'. Leaders in financial services talk about 'the market' in a way similar to clergy speaking about God.

Our respondents overall wished to be fair, refusing to make generalizations or judge bankers or high earners simply because the bankers could not comprehend the large impersonal global and cultural forces playing on the system. As people living by rules, regulators and accountants are shocked by the descent into chaos. Those who were members of faiths were appalled at their unconscious collusion or self-justifying rationalizations leading to their participation in 'sinful practices'. All were 'unnerved' and sought reassurance of a 'society being robust' enough for things to right themselves again naturally. They could not face or deal with their helplessness to understand and put right wrongs they had wrought. They despaired of more regulation as the answer; the principles of self-regulation by people who were good, upright and conscientious, they say, should be followed because at all costs their self-image must be maintained; they must not be found wanting. Guilt is a difficult emotion to acknowledge. It is easier to find fault and blame others.

Our respondents stress the importance of *collaboration and interdependence* as the most viable way forward for government and society, but on the whole they seemed unable to consider that rivalry, envy, fear, greed, competition and conflict – the dark side of human functioning – had played a significant role in people taking up their roles in the financial meltdown, and how ignorant they really are of human psychological and ecological systems and complex, large and impersonal organizations. The balance between the positive forces of optimism, humanitarianism and hope and the negative forces of competition, rivalry, envy and greed had been distorted to such an extent that they had actually been redefined and glossed over as all positive in their own right. Little regard is given to how the forces of irrationality had inverted the meaning of language and had distorted and perverted reality.

The financial crisis has forced a paradigm shift in an understanding of interconnectedness and how it plays out between retail and investment banking; between governments globally; between government and the financial sector; between financial services and the media; and between the lender and the borrower. The illusion of separateness is no longer sustainable. Some of our respondents – the senior partners in accountancy firms, the regulators and those bankers who acknowledged they were found wanting – were open to this as a concept. However, it is the wealthiest, the investment bankers, the ultimate judges of the economy, who have the furthest to go. Those who benefit the most and those who know the most, have the most to unlearn and relearn.

References

Bollas, C. (1989) *Forces of Destiny*, London: Free Association Books.

Goldsmith, M. (2008) 'The madness of crowds, past and present: Charles Mackay's classic volume on speculative bubbles, published 167 years ago, sheds much light on the delusions of mass greed', *Bloomberg Business Week*, 16 December.

Greenspan, A. (1996) 'The challenge of central banking in a democratic society', speech at the Annual Dinner and Francis Boyer Lecture of The American Enterprise Institute for Public Policy Research, Washington, DC, 5 December.

Hudson, L.J. (2009) *The Enabling State: Collaborating for success*, London: Foreign and Commonwealth Office. Online, available at: www.fco.gov.uk/resources/en/pdf/pdf9/enabling-state-v3 (retrieved 23 November 2011).

Lanchester, J. (2009) *Whoops! Why everyone owes everyone and no one can pay*, London: Allen Lane.

Long, S. (2008) *The Perverse Organisation and Its Deadly Sins*, London: Karnac.

Miller, E.J. (1990) 'Experiential learning in groups I: The development of the "Leicester" model', in E. Trist and H. Murray (eds) *The Social Engagement of Social Science: A Tavistock anthology*, London: Free Association Books.

Shiller, R. (2005) *Irrational Exuberance*, Princeton, NJ: Princeton University Press.

Tarnas, R. (1991) *The Passion of the Western Mind*, Reading, UK: Pimlico.

Tuckett, D. and Taffler, R. (2008) 'Phantastic objects and the financial market's sense of reality: a psychoanalytic contribution to the understanding of stock market instability', *International Journal of Psychoanalysis*, 89: 389–412.

6 The attempted murder of money and time

Addressing the global systemic banking crisis

Richard Morgan-Jones

Introduction and synopsis

Money and time feel like increasingly scarce resources. The link between them is at risk of being killed off. This has been increasingly so since the international banking credit crisis, beginning in autumn 2007, that left enterprises, large and small, short of underpinning finance to secure future trading. In order to understand some of the dynamics of the world system of trade and the financial investment and capital markets that sustain it, this chapter seeks to explore the challenge to the global financial system of the relationship between money and time, a relationship in which each is in need of the other for both to have meaning.

It will be suggested that this pivotal relationship has been 'attacked' by speculators in the global financial markets and the derivative shadow banking system in a way that destroys the reliability and meaningfulness of the everyday workings of investor capitalism. Furthermore, it will be suggested that such speculative trading using so-called real-time trading in instantaneous capital market exchange attempts to nullify and 'kill off' the time-based meanings of money as a boundaried form of exchange alongside limited social and global resources.

This chapter seeks to explore in two sections the crisis in creating a sustainable system of financial exchange in relation to time. The first section attempts to provide a number of examples that illustrate the way the global financial exchange institutions attack the relationship between money and time.[1] The second provides a reflective framework from a psychoanalytic perspective. Time is personalized by being experienced as *duration* with a present, made meaningful in relation to a past and a future. The attack on duration typifies a dynamic outlined in the group and social dynamics of *incohesion*, described by Earl Hopper (2003). To explore the failure of the emotional and social container for such social systems, the chapter unpacks the internalized *dead mother* described by André Green.

Part 1: the attempted murder of time and its meaning in financial trading

The corporate murder of the body clock

Anna, in her twenties, loves her job in the head office of one of the largest City of London investment banking houses. She loves responding to demands to digest complex pieces of information about financial markets, products or companies. This uses her considerable gifts for languages, which enables her to be a valuable resource to her bank for the emerging Far Eastern markets in Delhi and Shanghai across different time zones. At the same time as loving her work, she also hates the timescales that are demanded of her. The norm in her team is never to leave the office before the boss, who typically stays until 8 or 9 p.m. and often demands that a report be on his desk by 7 a.m. A few times, her mobile phone has notified her at home after 12 midnight that an email was awaiting her attention, and twice a taxi was sent to take her to work in the middle of the night. There are enough similar stories from the City to confirm the invasion of private lives 'owned' by the firm. She describes it as an experience of having her body clock assaulted and at times killed off completely under the weight of the 24/7 global money market to which her investment bank seeks to be responsive. She is paid well, but not given the larger bonuses that traders attract to reward their profits for the firm. However, she is, in consequence, seeking a move to another centre where the work ethic is not so demanding, as she is feeling deprived of sleep, overstressed and unable to find the means to relax and recover in her time off.

In a literal and physical way, this employee has the skin of her individual time zone assaulted. This example indicates the way the 24/7 timescale gets under the skin of an individual and leaves them struggling to remain effective and creative in a demanding and responsible job.

The denial of the meaning of time in longer-term investments

Paul is a trader who works in one of the largest capital exchange companies in the City of London. His task is to provide brokerage between large institutional fundholders, including governments, pension funds and investment banks, on an international scale. By providing an independent and confidential deal-broking service, his team, indeed his organization, provides anonymity to buyers and sellers in order to promote the efficiency of a market seeking the right pricing level for quoted investments and financial instruments. Although there is some down time for building information, research and forging relationships with colleagues and clients, most of his trading work is conducted at a frenetic pace. He describes it as like playing tennis with a dozen balls coming at you at the same time from different directions. On the trading floor, instantaneous information bombards the senses: the television news on a large trading floor screen, shifting prices on his desk screen, a series of averages, ratios and volumes on a

*second desk screen and a white board with information 'runners' listing yet
further data.*

*The stated aim of this modus operandi is to be able to take advantage of
available prices at the best rate and trade them instantaneously across the world
in what is described as 'real time'. To achieve this, the trader's eyes flicker
across the team colleagues around him, who gesture and yell like a bunch of
bookies at a race track, indicating the movement of prices and deals across their
market sector in order to secure the best deal of the moment. He describes his
state of mind as 'in full flow', hardly conscious of the detail essential to respond
intuitively to the mood of the movements in figures. All this while he is speaking
via a long corded telephone to clients doing trades, selecting across a range of
eight to a dozen voices accessed by buttons on his line-switching desktop. He
regards his considerable salary and six-figure bonus by results as just reward
for the honed intuitive skills that will leave him burned out within five years.*

A key hypothesis in this chapter is that the attempt to make such trading systems efficient in the name of balancing the price between buyers and sellers at
any given moment has key unintended consequences. One consequence is that
any awareness of the ownership or nature of the investments being traded in so-
called real time nevertheless denies and nullifies – we might say 'murders' – the
reality of the time-related meanings of the monetary investments. Mortgages on
property, whether commercial or business, afford a householder or an entrepreneur a trustworthy source of funding that can be paid off over a period of years
as regular income allows. A pension fund represents the investment of years of
life savings in order to provide for income in retirement. Government bonds represent the investment in a government's future over a period of time based on
ability to repay in the future. As the recent crisis in oversold sub-prime mortgages in the United States has revealed, where unreliable investors have not been
screened then the meaning of the investment shifts. It becomes perverted from
its emphasis on trusted investment to a system for meeting the pay-related targets
of traders in the property market and an opportunity for larger return or profit for
large amalgamated funds and investment banks.

This relates to a second unintended consequence that decouples time and
money. The principle argued by free-market economists who encourage a large
and deregulated financial sector is that the unimpeded and complex flow of
capital investments globally facilitates accurate levels in market pricing. They
argue that just as people seek the shortest queue at the supermarket checkout to
save time, so free markets serve the efficient throughput of goods. The equal
sharing of information supposedly facilitates market efficiency. This argument is
based on the premise that purchasers behave rationally and in their own self-
interest. This is the argument behind the idea that greed serves a common good.

Such an argument ignores two points. One is that people do not always
behave rationally. Loyalty and the need for security can skew best price. The
second is that the pace of market exchange is determined in some measure by
traders attempting to secure a maximum volume of trades to meet profit. This is
enhanced by the dynamic of group solidarity in traders swapping deals with each

other that is a feature of financial market life. In short, it can be described using the casino analogy of the *croupier's take*, where the greater the number of bets, the greater the percentage for the trader. But if trading is skewed, what about the ownership of a trading joint stock company?

Merger and acquisition: the oligopoly of the financial sector

The invention of competitive markets as a means of enabling efficient exchange has become one of the most innovative ways of enabling buyers and sellers to meet in a single environment and use a similar means of exchanging goods and supplies. This is true whether of a small produce market, a price comparison website or an inter-bank trading floor. Each facility exchanges information that gives access between buyers and sellers and at the same time moderates price through the regulating mechanisms of supply and demand. Scarcity increases desirability and price; choice and availability reduce both. Such open trading has proved a far more efficient way of regulating supply, demand and price than the command economies attempted by the centralized regimes of former communist states.

The argument is made that the same thing applies to financial markets, where shareholders can trade their holdings in quoted equities and so regulate price in a free market. Yet that argument ignores the potential role of the market shaping itself to its own advantage by distorting price through aggressive investment.

> *In 2009 Kraft, the American cheese manufacturer and distributor, mounted an aggressive and successful campaign to buy up shares to purchase the 186-year-old established UK chocolate manufacturer Cadburys. After a long and bitter resistance to the takeover, Cadburys capitulated, but only after the bias of speculative trading by London hedge funds seeking to offset losses following the credit crisis. It is they, as recent 'carpet-bagging' owners of 40 per cent shareholding alongside pension fund managers, who were more interested in stimulating share price through a hostile takeover bid than were long-term shareholders, including employees. Apart from hedge funds, winners included the large bonuses given to incoming and out-going directors who had sealed the deal along with the banks and legal advisers in the City. Meanwhile, the UK government also lost considerable tax revenues by ownership moving to the United States. This was despite calls from the prime minister, Gordon Brown, and the business secretary, Lord (Peter) Mandelson, to reduce the scale of the financial sector while ignoring pleas from the trade union Unite to only allow long-term share-holders to vote on the sale of a company.*
> (Information source: *Guardian* newspaper, London, 20 January 2010)

This not untypical merger story describes how short-term institutional investors, aided and abetted by the banks and financial services advisers, have the power to affect the economic and political future and decision making. This ignores the meaning of time-honoured investments over a longer period signifying trust and commitment to the complex interrelationships of stakeholders, including staff, investors, customers and brand identity.

The argument in this section points to how the unregulated market monopoly of investment banking and hedge funds nullifies the true meaning of time in the long term, preferring instead short-term investment practices to accelerate mergers and acquisitions that 'murder' the time-related meanings of investment. Efficiency trumps sustainability. Jinette de Gooijer (2009) uses the idea of corporate murder to understand the experience of staff made irrelevant or redundant in the process of corporate mergers and acquisitions. This chapter argues that victims include reliable employment for local communities enjoyed down the generations; a solid national firm with an international reputation; and a principled framework for protecting the interests of long-term investors and regulating short-term speculators. Each of these 'murder victims' links the interdependence of money and time, in both labour and investment.

But if that is true of the 24/7 culture of global banking staff, the bundled trading of depersonalized capital investments, and the world of speculation in mergers and acquisitions, I will now turn to the cornerstone of what heralded the great credit crash and financial crisis that ended the first decade of the twenty-first century.

Futures, derivatives, swaps: managing risk or avoiding knowledge of it?[2]

Futures

Agricultural trading to secure the guarantee of an advance price for a future harvest first appears in rudimentary form on clay tablets from Mesopotamia dating from 1750 BC (Tett 2009: 11). In 1849 the Chicago Board of Trade established the modern equivalent of traded futures and options on agricultural commodities. Securing an option on a price for a future harvest provided reliable cash flow for farm labourer wages, equipment and seed. Wheat farmers would, in a more cautious and fearful approach to risk, hedge against the low prices that would follow the excess supply of a bumper crop. Speculators would take on this risk, gambling that the yield would be low and the price high so that they could profit by the difference between the price they guaranteed the farmers and the eventual market price. Emotionally, the management of risk lay in the balance of fear and greed.

Derivatives and the shadow banking system

In the 1970s, electronic technology for trading brought in derivatives to the financial markets creating the so-called *shadow banking system*. Derivatives are essentially contracts that are bought and sold whose value *derives* from commodities, bonds, equities or currencies. The idea of such trading is to insure against risk and hedge an investment by securing payment if its price should fall or fail in the future. As Tett describes it, 'At the heart of the business is a dance with *time*' (2009: 10).

Housing mortgage as the reliable currency for derivatives

In the 1980s, securing capital backing for housing mortgage loans was developed through the creation of mortgage bond markets where investors would hope to see the value of bonds increase in relation to rising house prices and so produce a better return than merely investing savings in a building society. Large Wall Street banks pioneered such bond markets and charged high fees for bundling and selling such securitized bonds. This world of high risk, high reward, high bonuses is vividly portrayed in Michael Lewis's description of the ruthless, manic, male-dominated competitive world of Salomon Brothers investment bank in *Liar's Poker* (1990).

Tett's book (2009) credits the development of creative risk management using derivatives to the team at J.P. Morgan investment bank in New York. Their Broad Index Secured Trust Offering (BISTRO) created the predecessor of collateralized debt obligations (CDOs), which bundled together investments in a portfolio at different levels of risk with correspondingly different levels of return. Mortgage bonds could thus be seen as the secure element within a portfolio that could not fail to increase in value as the housing market was promised to rise. Within these instruments, less reliable debts could be concealed.

Tett comments, '[C]omplexity makes the world of derivatives opaque, which serves bankers' interests just fine. Opacity reduces scrutiny and confers power on the few with the ability to pierce the veil' (2009: 10). She also suggests that '[t]he crucial thing about derivatives was that they could do two things: help investors *reduce* risk or create a good deal *more* risk. Everything depended on how they were used, on the motives and skills of those who traded them' (ibid.: 14).

Swaps that increase virtual capital

One of the key aims of the design of such investments was to increase the flow of capital within the market, thereby increasing the traders' percentage take in profits. A further financial instrument was the credit default swap. Banks that could find parties with complementary needs in clients, one to insure the risk of a loan being unpaid and the other to gamble that it would be paid, could engineer a swap. The banks would take large fees from both parties without any capital being provided to secure the trade. This provided capital backing for risks. International banking agreements secured by the Basel accord required regulation of liquidity such that a fixed proportion of available assets could be paid by the bank if claimed by customers.[3]

By using derivatives and swaps it was possible to provide a complex structure of insurances against future possible risks. This bypassed the Basel requirements because investments that were insured against a future default in payment did not appear on the bank's balance sheet. By trading in promised payments in the face of defaults, and swapping them as a means of trading, banks could receive vast fees without the apparent risk of having to provide a percentage of capital funds in liquid and available form. Fees, profits and bonuses boomed.

Overselling leading to unregulated meltdown

What Tett's book reveals is that the move towards what she describes as the 'industrialisation' of these forms of trading shocked even the original founders of the idea at J.P. Morgan. True estimation of value at risk went out of the window as naive belief in the ever-extending rise in house prices and ever-increasing available capital for mortgages increased sales of mortgaged housing to people whose capacity to pay was never examined. As Tett puts it, 'Because the bank was securitizing its mortgages with off-balance-sheet vehicles, it did not need to hold a large volume of capital reserves ... and it could extend about three times more mortgages per unit of capital' (2009: 229). The crash in the housing market through defaulted mortgages heralded economic meltdown across the world in the autumn of 2007.

In the United Kingdom, emulation of the US system of raising capital for mortgages on the capital bond markets using complex new derivatives was developed, among others, by the regional, and traditionally conservative, Northern Rock bank. When on 13 September 2007 BBC business editor Robert Peston reported that the bank had sought emergency funding from the Bank of England, and that

> although the bank remains profitable, the fact that it has had to go cap in hand to the Bank is the most tangible sign that the crisis in financial markets is spilling over into businesses that touch most of our lives.
>
> (Quoted in Tett 2009: 228)

The night of Peston's report led to the bank's website crashing as people tried to withdraw savings, and the next morning there were queues of anxious people wanting their investments back, causing a panic run on the bank.

The history of financial bubble and bust

There has been a huge literature and comment on the causes of the crash, of which the description above is but one element, albeit a key element. In surveying 'eight centuries of financial folly', Reinhart and Rogoff (2009) provide detailed econometric analysis of financial crises in banking down the centuries under the evocative title *This Time Is Different*. In the most recent example of such a crisis, they suggest that the belief that 'this time it is different' was based on the notion that central banks had at long last learned how to manage inflationary risk. All they had to do was to resist raising interest rates when asset prices spiked and to cut interest rates to prop up falling prices.[4] However, the promise that inflation had at last been beaten only appeared to be proved by the boom in the financial markets. At the same time, artificial boosting of available funds for capital investment also caused the economies of the Western world to boom, while at the same time making them vulnerable to a crash. This myth of future investor security, they conclude, was oversold. The phantasy that all the regulation that was needed lay in control of inflation proved a false god. As they put it,

> Technology has changed, the height of humans has changed, and fashions have changed. Yet the ability of governments and investors to delude themselves, giving rise to periodic bouts of euphoria that usually end in tears, seems to have remained a constant…. We have come full circle to the concept of financial fragility in economies with massive indebtedness. All too often, periods of heavy borrowing can take place in a bubble and last for a surprisingly long time. But highly leveraged economies, particularly those in which continual rollover of short-term debt is sustained only by confidence in relatively illiquid assets, seldom survive forever, particularly if leverage continues to grow unchecked…. Encouragingly, history does point to warning signs that policy makers can look at to assess risk – if only they do not become too drunk with their credit bubble-fueled success and say, as their predecessors have for centuries, 'This time is different.'
>
> (ibid.: 292)

The dynamics of such a blinded culture has developed complex financial instruments that use short trading of longer-term investments to murder the meaning of the labour, investment savings and timescale on which money and promises are exchanged, let alone the concealed plunder of planetary resources without regulation or taxation. As the global credit crisis has illustrated, this has exported failure to manage risk from the investment banks, governments and regulators into the body politic, who as taxpayers now have to bail out the banks or fear collapse of the financial system of currency exchange, let alone the burden on the planetary ecosystem.

Conclusion to part 1

Having described the attack on the crucial link between money and time as interdependent meaning systems, this chapter now turns to explore possible psychodynamics that might inform what underlies such aggressive destructiveness.

Part 2: dynamics of incohesion

The group dynamics of incohesion in the financial sector and murder
of the meaning of money and time in depersonalized investment

In exploring some of the key group and cultural psychodynamics at work in the financial markets, I want to develop the work of psychoanalyst Wilfred Bion. In describing a theory of group and social dynamics, he described three *basic assumptions* around which people form *cohesion* in groups. These three types of group dynamics were suggested by groups that were bonded by emotions held in common around three kinds of patterns of emotion described as *dependency*, *pairing* and *fight–flight* (Bion 1961).

This basic assumption theory was initially developed in two directions. First, Pierre Turquet (1974, 1975) described some groups as bound by a rigid sense of *one-ness* that defied differentiation of any kind and attacked any comers, from inside or outside the group, who manifested difference of any kind. Second, Gordon Lawrence *et al.* (2000) described other groups that developed a shared basic assumption around the narcissistic values of *me-ness*, whereby the group defied any notion of there being a group at all that might make demands on an individual's independent entitlement (Morgan-Jones 2010).

It is possible to describe the boundary phenomenon of these groups by suggesting that in the first, *one-ness*, there is an aggressive attack on the boundary and right to exist of any other possible grouping, while the second, *me-ness*, is characterized by an attack on the right of the group itself to exist and make demands on its members. In consequence, both sorts of group have a tendency to recycle violations of individual members and of whole groups by denying the possibility of an ecosystem of interdependent groups and organizations that is at the heart of democratic and economic systems.

It was this feature of the way such groups were shaped by incoherent, traumatized and traumatizing forces that led Earl Hopper (2003) to describe them as a shared basic assumption based on an *incoherence*, either *aggregated* or *massified*, that attacked systems of meaning and common sense. Examples of such systems dynamics can be seen in the extremities of racism that carries no tolerance for the skin and identity that mark out other, and different, racial groups. It is illustrated vividly in the transgenerational transmission of trauma described in extreme nationalistic tribalism, such as in the Balkan wars, by Vamik Volkan (2010). It can also be seen in the single-minded idealization of the free market that demands extremes of market efficiency from all involved with business and finance in order to maximize efficiency at the price of sustainability. As we have seen already, this violates the right of investors, pension holders and employees to protect their long-term time-based interests.

Groups and social institutions depend upon a fabric of meaning, reliability and trust in order to function. Within the dynamics of *incohesion* that have been illustrated above, reliability fails and attacks the very fabric or skin that holds the body of social and financial institutions together. It is like an immune-suppressant disease. I have elsewhere suggested that *incohesion* dynamics provide descriptions not just of *basic assumption activity* but of something more primitive for being instinctually physical, psychological and social, all three at the same time. For this dimension Bion used the term the *protomental matrix*, describing it by saying, 'what is physical and what is mental cannot be distinguished', and from it basic assumptions are formed (Bion 1961: 154; Morgan-Jones 2010). My hypothesis is that such dynamics recycle trauma by attacking the skin or boundary that holds a group together. In doing this they attack the container and the fabric of time and space within which a group exists and, along with it, a history and sense of continuity and *duration*[5] that might carry hope and trust into the future.

My evidence for this hypothesis is that the perceptive and innovative descriptions of *one-ness* and *me-ness*, as well as Hopper's description of *incohesion* dynamics, all involve the violating of defences. *One-ness* attacks the skin of other groups, while *me-ness* attacks the group identity of any group that might make demands on an individual. I have suggested therefore that these are shameless violating attacks on the very boundary or skin of a group and the right for it to have a coherent identity, let alone a voice that it might embody (Morgan-Jones and Torres 2009; Morgan-Jones 2010). My hypothesis is that the investment banks and exchanges have rigged the market with the collusion of governments globally. In consequence, it is ordinary borrowing and saving citizens and enterprises who have had their trust shamelessly violated and their right to voice a protest and seek redress undermined.

I now wish to go deeper into the analysis of denial of time that links past, present and future in taking up but one aspect of time in psychoanalysis that Sievers (2009) mentions, namely in the work of André Green on the *dead mother*.[6]

The dead mother and the murder of time

In describing the attack and violation of the social and institutional fabric of money and time and the relation between them, it is worth asking the question, what is it that attacks so powerfully such vital institutional life in global society? What is it that has undermined the capacity of global finance and international banks to be able to provide a secured and sustainable future?

A central dynamic of risk for investment banks is in carrying fear and greed on behalf of the body politic (Dixon and Morgan-Jones 2010). On the one hand there is the fear that they will take dangerous risks in the name of greed for greater profits for the bonuses of employees, for shareholders and taxpayers. Each and every one of these stakeholders has colluded in encouraging them to do this by denying the need for regulation. On the other hand there is the fear that may paralyse them, preventing them from taking any risks at all. These twin dangers form a balancing act that, as we have seen from the first part of this chapter, has put the world at risk, fuelled by greed and blind to the possibility of realistic fears.

A further hypothesis that, I propose, should be thought about is that this has been an attempt to deny the realities of the limitations of resources of time, money and the securing of natural resources that the link between them represents. Failure to see this has resulted in a spiral of frenzied feeding without regard for the future resources of the planet or their destructive pollution, including the resources of clean air and water. There has been a denial of these losses and risks and an almost unconscious wilfulness in refusing to acknowledge the destruction of meaning systems to hold the hope of a future in place.

In psychoanalytic thinking it is the role of the mother to provide for life and a sense of continuity in life, both literally and symbolically. This is epitomized by Winnicott's description (1965) of the importance of the mother, who regulates and provides a safe but stimulating background for the growing child. The opposite is a dead and deadening mother that is implicit and deeply related to what has been described above as the uncontained dynamics of *incohesion*. In describing the internalized *dead mother*, Green asserts that this is

> an imago which has been constituted in the child's mind, following maternal depression, brutally transforming a living object, a source of vitality for the child, into a distant figure, toneless and practically inanimate.... Thus, the dead mother, contrary to what one might think, is a mother who remains alive but who is, so to speak, psychically dead in the eyes of the young child in her care.
>
> (1986: 170)

What seems to follow is a sense of a maternal death that is never-ending, an absence that is always present, revealed in the sense of being haunted by a ghost that can never be banished as it has become a primary object for the self and its 'most enduring aspect' (Gerson 2009: 1347).

In an evocative paper entitled 'From the ignorance of time to the murder of time. From the murder of time to the misrecognition of temporality in psychoanalysis', Green (2009) argues that the task of psychoanalysis is not to recover memory. Rather is it to reconstruct, or indeed to construct for the first time, the significance of time and history in an historical experience that has been emptied and killed off in order to survive the trauma of impingement and neglect. This trauma, Green suggests, in turn creates a dynamic of unsatisfiable greed for a phantasy that cannot exist and cannot be mourned. These are the conditions for profound melancholia. As Green puts it, such dynamics create 'the impression of acting, not in the manner of the unconscious outside-time, but in the manner of anti-time, that is to say, a murder of time' (ibid.: 14).

In this sense I am suggesting that the social dynamics underlying the credit crisis can be understood as an expression of an emotionally dead and deadening maternal object in society.

In linking these ideas to the cultural and transgenerational experience of recycled trauma for survivors in Holocaust families, Gerson develops the idea of humankind as like a *dead mother*, 'so absorbed with its own losses, fears and needs that it remains silent and unmoved by the plight of the victim' (2009: 1347). It could be argued that the world has allowed the banking and financial trading industry to cruelly create a world where we have become victims of our own greed. On the global front, Stapley (2006) and others have linked the rapid changes in world culture shaped by worldwide trade, communications and finance as a traumatizing 'loss of a way of life', creating new sources of emotional terror that are yet to be contained. Psychoanalysis suggests that such traumas, such experiences of emotional overload become repeated and recycled as projective identifications and transmitted down generations in a way that creates a violent splitting process between those haunted by an unarticulated sense of deadness with loss of meaning and those manically asserting a rational approach to life where all can be contained within a striving for financialized and commodified dominance of meanings, values and relationships (see Volkan 2010).

Economist John Kenneth Galbraith has introduced his notion of the economics of everyday fraud occurring in social exploitation. He writes:

> Some of this fraud derives from traditional economics and its teaching and some from the ritual views of economic life. These can strongly support individual and group interest, particularly, as might be expected, that of the more fortunate, articulate and politically prominent in the larger community, and can achieve the respectability and authority of everyday knowledge. This is not the contrivance of any individual or group but represents the natural, even righteous view of what best serves personal or larger interest.
>
> (2004: 4–5)

What the financial sector appears to have created is a world where people with mortgage loans, access to work, savings and pensions are rendered voiceless in having their identity and right to protect themselves stripped away. They are made fools of by greedy banking institutions, with the collusion of governments chasing 'fool's gold'. They are silenced by opaque sales techniques and attempted economic efficiency that idealizes capital trading above lifelong emotional and socially based identities that give meaning to life. The investment and trading banks have failed to provide a dependable container for the task of carrying fear and greed on behalf of the global community, instead creating a social dynamic based on exporting anxiety and the consequences of shameless attacks on the skin and boundary that holds together human endeavour, which is at risk of being rendered incoherent.

Conclusion

The current political and economic tasks facing the world are huge. This chapter has sought to provide an analysis of a central dimension of these issues from a psychoanalytic and socioanalytic perspective. It has described aspects of the ways the relation between time and money has been killed off by the culture of unregulated global speculation in the shadow banking system that has threatened to derail systems of monetary exchange and has impoverished many individuals, communities and enterprises. It provides a framework for exploring how sustainable economic activity needs protection, rather than being denuded by excessive speculation.

Notes

1 These examples and analysis draw upon interviews with individuals from global investment organizations from the City of London, along with researched and media reports of the unregulated development of shadow banking and derivative trading markets.
2 Gillian Tett (2009), a Cambridge social anthropologist working for the *Financial Times*, has produced a journalistic account of the characters who developed the complexity of new derivative financial instruments in the capital investment markets that brought about their own downfall. In providing a history and time-line for these instruments of financial trading I draw largely on her research.
3 It is worth noting that although the new September 2010 version of capital requirements for banks (Basel III) has increased the capital backing required to avoid the need to bail out banks, there is no agreement to regulate derivative trading as yet.
4 This was known as the 'Greenspan put', named after the chair of the US federal bank and well-known monetarist economist.
5 French philosopher Henri Bergson coined the idea of reality being *intuited* by a sense of *duration*, which appears to have been a source of Wilfred Bion's emphasis on the idea of 'coming into being' accessed by *psychoanalytic intuition*.
6 Sievers (2009) has also provided a rich and deep survey of the range of approaches to understanding time in psychoanalysis as applicable to organizations.

References

Bion, W.R. (1961) *Experiences in Groups and Other Papers*, London: Routledge.
de Gooijer, J. (2009) *The Murder in Merger: A systems psychodynamic exploration of a corporate merger*, London: Karnac.
Dixon, K. and Morgan-Jones, R.J. (2010) 'Financial bodies called to account: corporate risks of carrying fear and greed on behalf of the body politic', in R.J. Morgan-Jones, *The Body of the Organisation and Its Health*, London: Karnac.
Galbraith, J.K. (2004) *The Economics of Innocent Fraud: Truth for our time*, London: Penguin Books.
Gerson, S. (2009) 'When the third is dead: memory, mourning, and witnessing in the aftermath of the Holocaust', *International Journal of Psychoanalysis*, 6: 1341–57.
Green, A. (1986) *On Private Madness*, London: Hogarth.
Green, A. (2009) 'From the ignorance of time to the murder of time. From the murder of time to the misrecognition of temporality in psychoanalysis', in L.G. Fiorini and J. Canestri (eds) *The Experience of Time: Psychoanalytic perspectives*, London: Karnac.
Hopper, E. (2003) *Traumatic Experience in the Unconscious Life of Groups*, London: Jessica Kingsley.
Lawrence, W.G., Bain, A. and Gould, L.J. (2000) 'The fifth basic assumption', in W.G. Lawrence, *Tongued with Fire*, London: Karnac.
Lewis, M. (1990) *Liar's Poker*, London: Penguin Books.
Morgan-Jones, R.J. (2010) *The Body of the Organisation and Its Health*, London: Karnac.

Morgan-Jones, R.J. and Torres, N. (2009) 'Under the skin of the organisation: violation and shamelessness – searching for a model to explore protomental dynamics', paper presented at ISPSO Symposium 'Differences at Work: Towards Integration and Containment', Toledo, 26–28 June.

Reinhart, C.M. and Rogoff, K.S. (2009) *This Time Is Different: Eight centuries of financial folly*, Princeton, NJ: Princeton University Press.

Sievers, B. (2009) '"Pushing the past backwards in front of oneself": a socio-analytic perspective on the relatedness of past, present, and future in contemporary organizations', *Organisational and Social Dynamics*, 9(1): 21–42.

Stapley, L.F. (2006) *Globalization and Terrorism: Death of a way of life*, London: Karnac.

Tett, G. (2009). *Fool's Gold: How unrestrained greed corrupted a dream, shattered global markets and unleashed a catastrophe*, London: Little, Brown.

Turquet, P. (1974) 'Leadership: the individual in the group', in G.S. Gabbard, J.J. Hartman and R.D. Mann (eds) *Analysis of Groups*, San Francisco: Jossey-Bass.

Turquet, P. (1975) 'Threats to identity in the large group', in L. Kreeger (ed.) *The Large Group: Dynamics and therapy*, London: Constable.

Volkan, V.D. (2010) 'Psychoanalysis and international relationships: large-group identity, traumas, at the hand of the "other", and transgenerational transmission of trauma', in H. Brunning and M. Perini (eds) *Psychoanalytic Perspectives on a Turbulent World*, London: Karnac.

Winnicott, D.W. (1965) *The Maturational Processes and the Facilitating Environment: Studies in the theory of emotional development*, London: Hogarth Press and the Institute of Psycho-Analysis.

Part II
Finances

7 Towards a socioanalysis of the current financial crisis

Burkard Sievers

I do not think that anybody can tell me that there is not going to be another financial blowup of some kind. I hope we don't have another big one – at least in my lifetime.

(P.A. Volcker, quoted in Cassidy 2010: 30)

Introduction

What first appeared as a financial crisis limited to US banks in the autumn of 2008 soon spread and began to threaten national economies around the world. The collapse of banks, the dramatic increase in unemployment rates, the critical state of the entire automobile industry, the decrease in national GNPs in 2008 and 2009, and other factors have forced us to face a changed world. And although some economies seem to have improved, no one is able to predict with any certainty the length and impact of the economic crisis.

Though at present, the summer of 2010, the crisis is still reverberating (for example, the unemployment rate in the United States is up to 10 per cent and anxiety about another recession is virulent), for many the crisis has been consigned to the past. Big banks are not only doing business as usual but, because of state support and low interest rates, are producing profits that exceed those before the crisis. While some believe that the recession – at least from a mere technical perspective – has come to an end and the world economy has been rescued from the abyss into which it threatened to fall (Pauly *et al.* 2009: 81), others, like the Nobel laureate Paul Krugman, are convinced that we still are 'living in a dark age of macroeconomics' (Dizikes 2010), 'caught in a situation more than a little reminiscent of the mid-1930s' (ibid.).

To date, the predominant public discourse on the financial crisis and its aftermath appears to have been limited to a political and economic one. While the perception of the crisis was catastrophic, a focus was on finding the appropriate choice of financial and economic means to diffuse the damage, to encourage banks to offer credit both to one another and to their customers, to boost production and consumption, and to bail out financial and economic enterprises that threatened to collapse without government support. Meanwhile, as the attempt to formulate international financial regulations appears doomed to fail, the US and

EU governments see salvation in national regulations. Not least, the European Union is preoccupied with finding appropriate financial means to solve the euro crisis, which was precipitated by Greece and looks likely to spread to other European countries, notably the so-called PIIGS (*sic!*), i.e. Portugal, Ireland, Italy, Greece and Spain.

Despite various ongoing attempts to reduce or prevent future global disasters, we are permanently encouraged to believe that the present capitalist system and its free markets must and will survive. The idea that we must radically alter our quest for affluence owing to the foreseeable dramatic if not catastrophic changes in our ecosystem (e.g. Case and Gosling 2010) is not widely held. Serious concern that capitalism, as such, may ultimately lead to the death of freedom and what we regard as democracy and humanity is either broadly ignored or derided as a pipe dream (or nightmare) of those people who never get it right.

In the media, the discourse regarding the crisis and its outcome has been primarily restricted to financial and economic facts and explanations, the apportioning of blame on apparently responsible parties, and the analysis of appropriate measures to prevent the very worst. The insight, however, that the financial crisis – like all bubbles and busts of financial markets – 'was essentially psychological in origin' (Shiller 2008: 24) is not broadly shared, either in the media or in most of the literature, although it is gaining traction. In our attempt at a deeper understanding of the sub-prime crisis from a socioanalytic perspective, we thus are in a sense, broadly 'handicapped ... by economists' understanding of human beings' (Bain 2009: 1).

Robert Shiller (2008: 43–4, 55, 57, 62), professor of economics at Yale University, explains the extent to which the crisis originated from contagious collective thinking that is similar to an epidemic. This collective thinking was coined by a whole range of unalterable assumptions: that the exorbitant increase in house prices and the real estate boom would never end; that the financial market was based on economic rationality; that one could rely on financial experts as well as rating agencies (ibid.: 69). Only when the bubble of speculation began to burst in 2007 did it become obvious to what extent this collective thinking was based on unchecked assumptions and was, to a high degree, irrational. One is reminded of Bion's (1959: 189) view of basic assumptions as having 'the characteristics of defensive reactions to psychotic anxiety'.

While bankers on occasion contemptuously refer to financial instruments as being quite simple and easy for anyone to understand, the financial system appears from the outside as magical financial engineering. However, the financial industry as a whole seems to a large extent based on a form of magic thinking understood in socioanalytic terms as manic defences. Such manic defences can also be detected in the state's response to the current crisis.

As Winnicott (1935: 132) states, the manic defence embodies 'omnipotent manipulation or control and contemptuous devaluation'. Among other things, the manic defence is characterized by 'denial of inner reality, a flight to external reality from inner reality, holding the people of the inner reality in "suspended animation", denial of the sensation of depression ... by specifically opposite sensations' (ibid.: 132). Rycroft (1972: 86) adds the tendency towards 'identification with objects from whom a sense of power can be borrowed'.

Towards a socioanalysis of the current financial crisis

Although it would be fascinating to look at the historical, economic and political background and development of the present financial crisis in more detail, I shall restrain myself here and will refer instead to some of the phenomena, to various dynamics and to critical episodes of the crisis in this attempt to contribute possible answers to the question of how the crisis can be perceived and understood from a socioanalytic perspective.

I am working with the double assumption that any attempt at understanding the crisis from a socioanalytic perspective should go beyond the obvious 'facts and figures' to the development of hypotheses about the various unconscious dynamics that contributed to its escalation, and that any adequate socioanalytic attempt at understanding this crisis and its underlying unconscious dynamics would be more than any one socioanalytic scholar could manage. My main intent is thus not to suggest a comprehensive socioanalysis of the crisis. Instead, I will examine some existing socioanalytic approaches and theories, and attempt to articulate how they may contribute towards an understanding of global finances and the current crisis in particular. Thus, the previous work of scholars may offer possible directions for thinking about what currently appears to be unthinkable and unknown.

Based on the assumption that both the socioanalysis of the financial industry and its markets and that of the current crisis in particular are yet to be written, my idea here is to attempt a kind of preface for a venture at understanding. Hence, the following selection of psychoanalytic and socioanalytic approaches and theories is subjective; it does not claim to be complete. In large part, I will stay faithful to the original voices of the authors presented.

These approaches fall into the following categories: Manic-Depressive – Illusion/Disillusion; Narcissistic Processes and Corporate Decay; Toxicity, Miasma and the Inconsolable Organization; Corruption and Perversion; Unconscious Phantasy Relationships; States of Mind and Unconscious Group Functioning; and Social Psychosis.

Manic-depressive – illusion/disillusion

Psychoanalytic attempts at understanding a financial and economic crisis, its reactions and effects, appear to be practically non-existent until the 1990s. The only source I have found is an article by W. Béran Wolfe (1932) on the Great Depression. Making the questionable assumption that 'nations react to calamity exactly as individuals' (ibid.: 209), Wolfe offers the thesis that 'any national disaster is likely to produce national reactions comparable to those generated by the breakdown of a romantic life-formula in an adolescent confronted with his first frustration by reality' (ibid.: 209). Although Wolfe's limited perspective refers to a nation as a collective of individuals, most of the neurotic reactions towards the crisis that he describes broadly – for example, perceiving the depression as 'normal', denial of hopelessness, 'frantic search for new magical formulas', 'cult of devil-chasing and scapegoat-baiting' (ibid.: 211), and suicide – mirror contemporary reactions to the present situation.

Douglas Kirsner (1990), through whom I became aware of Wolfe's article, appears to be the first contemporary scholar who explicitly elaborates some of the psychoanalytic aspects of a recent financial crisis, namely, the stock market crash of 1987. While the financial world before the crash was based on the illusion of unlimited growth of the share market on the part of 'bankers, brokers and freelance financial geniuses' (Galbraith 1987: 65), Kirsner takes the view that

> the crash of 1987 was viewed by many as a pestilence visited upon us from outside the system.... This was achieved through an inappropriate conviction that the economic system was intrinsically sound, through a defensive disavowal of economic reality and a splitting of the economic system into good and evil, where the evil was seen as coming from outside while the good was viewed as intrinsic.... In fact the potential for the crash was often denied and fear of a crash was regarded as irrational.
>
> (1990: 34–5)

Even when the crash came, it was initially denied and the technocratic myth was confirmed by many, with the view that 'everything could be manipulated and controlled by the right interventions' (ibid.: 41). And as it continued,

> many people were involved with a manic denial of reality in which they refused to accept that there were some fundamental transformations in the market, with enormous consequences for the world economy.... The zeitgeist of the market had been that of disavowal.... The stock market crash inflicted a large narcissistic blow to delusions of omnipotence, together with an attendant refusal to face the unnamed terrors on unknown situations. The reaction of many is not a depressive anxiety which can experience impotence and ignorance and thereby possibly repair any emotional damage. There is, rather, a denial of the external reality of loss, powerlessness and uncertainty, and a replacement with an even more omniscient and omnipotent phantasy that yes, we can foretell the future in general and control it.
>
> (ibid.: 43, 48)

Narcissistic processes and corporate decay

Howard Schwartz (1990a, b) offers the concept of corporate decay using the theory of the organizational ideal. Corporate decay is related to, if not an outcome of, narcissistic processes on the side of organizational role-holders. His chosen organization for analysis, General Motors, is of particular relevance, as it filed for bankruptcy protection on 1 June 2009.

Schwartz's central thesis is that organizational role-holders tend to buy into a dramatized 'fantasy about the organization's perfection' (1990a: 1), which is

> the return to narcissism, in which the organization and its highest particip-
> ants are seen as the center of a loving world. Since the return to narcissism
> is impossible, orienting the organization to the dramatization of this fantasy
> means that the organization loses touch with reality. The result is organiza-
> tional decay – a condition of systemic ineffectiveness.... Organizational
> decay may be compared with the consequences of hubris.
>
> (ibid.: 1)

The notion and theory of the ego-ideal, which Schwartz applies to organizations, can increase our understanding of the function of money – both in general and in the present context. This is illustrated by Wolfenstein. He states:

> Money is the measure of the man. This implies that psychical values are
> akin to commodities. This commoditization of the inner world extends to
> the ego itself. Money, that is to say, takes up residence in the super-ego or
> ego-ideal. The super-ego is monetized. The ego, which is judged by and
> measures itself against the super-ego, is thus commoditized. Dimensions of
> selfhood that are not commoditized – that can not be measured by money –
> are alienated and devalued.
>
> (1993: 302)

Money appears to have taken up residence in the ego-ideal of the financial market.

Toxicity, miasma and the inconsolable organization

In several of his writings, Mark Stein has focused on the (mis)use of money and capital in corporations and capital management. Though these articles are important sources for a socioanalysis of finances and financial disasters, in the present context of the global financial crisis I will pay special attention to his more recent paper on 'toxicity' (M. Stein 2008).

Stein does not explicitly refer to money or finances in this paper, yet it is the notion of toxicity itself that offers a direct link to the financial crisis and its after-math, in so far as it may contribute to a better conceptualization and understand-ing of what have broadly become known as 'toxic assets'. It is reasonable to assume that the toxicity ascribed in a metaphorical sense to assets in the aftermath of the bank crisis is not limited to these assets themselves but refers to financial institutions and the financial market at large; toxicity may even have tainted wide areas of the economy. The fear of contagion has led to widespread loss of trust and thus caused enormous regression in both financial and economic activities.

Yiannis Gabriel's (2008a, b) concept of 'organizational miasma' provides a further leading perspective on toxicity in systemic contexts. Gabriel (2008a: 52) analyses some of the inevitable burdens that organizations place on their members but also some of the surplus privations and sufferings that many of them inflict.... [He] develops a theory of organizational miasma, a concept that describes a contagious state of pollution, material, psychological and spiritual, that affects all who work in particular organizations. [Gabriel] ... delineates the fundamentals of organizational miasma, as a theoretical concept describing and explaining numerous processes of certain organizations. These include a paralysis of resistance, an experience of pollution and uncleanliness, and feelings of worthlessness and corruption.

Howard F. Stein's (2007) notion of the 'inconsolable organization' throws further light on the unconscious dynamics of the financial crisis and its impact on many organizations. Drawing on Gabriel's work on miasma, Howard F. Stein (2008: 91) proposes 'the new metaphor and concept of an "inconsolable organization"' that refers to 'a state of affect paralysis in the face of massive, often sustained, loss that cannot be mourned' (ibid.). He elaborates the thesis that 'when organizational loss goes unacknowledged, and mourning is proscribed, inconsolable grief and miasma follow' (ibid.).

Corruption and perversion

Corruption is an increasingly hot topic in both organizational practice and the discourse of organization theory. Though it seems at first sight that the phenomenon of organizational corruption might play only a minor role in the financial crisis and its aftermath, some of the socioanalytic literature on corruption may be relevant for the present analysis.

Jane Chapman (2003) explores the relatedness of task hatred and task corruption in organizations. Task hatred may emerge from avoidance of the organization's primary task. Task corruption happens if 'the change in the nature of the task ... [is] destructively motivated, whether at the conscious or the unconscious level' (ibid.: 46).

What Chapman describes as 'task corruption by simulation' appears relevant in the present context. Task simulation

is where the system or individual adopts the appearance of task engagement precisely in order to avoid task engagement.... The corruption derives from the destructive intent: not only is real task killed off and system energies devoted to the appearance of the tasks being done, but task values are subverted and task power becomes abusive. Simulating organisations, i.e. those which behave as if they are a system engaged in a real task in order to avoid becoming a system engaged in a real task, are characterised by poor morale, low system energy, high levels of politicking, questionable ethics, and high levels of conflict.

(2003: 46–7)

Task corruption by simulation is of special relevance to the major changes banks have gone through during the financial boom that preceded the financial crisis. Traditionally, commercial banks were committed to the role of 'monetary' inter-mediates to their customers by helping them make deposits and take loans to pursue their personal interests as either consumers or producers, while modestly profiting themselves. Meanwhile, however, many banks gave only the appear-ance of undertaking their original task. A new, unacknowledged primary task emerged – that is, to make as much money as possible and to 'own' it for the sake of megalomaniac prestige and power as a financial institution on the world market. To the extent that banks began gambling in the international casino of finance, they betrayed not only most of their customers but also their original primary task and thus were in danger of becoming corrupt organizations.

Susan Long (2008a), in *The Perverse Organisation*, illustrates how corrup-tion may often be a bedfellow of perversion: 'Perverse dynamics eventually lead to corrupt behaviours within the system' (ibid.: 2). 'Organised corporate corrup-tion is a conscious manifestation, the iceberg tip of an unconscious perverse societal structure and dynamic. Corruption builds on an underlying social fabric of perversity' (ibid.: 3).

Though this concept was developed before the financial crisis reached its height in the September 2008 collapse of Lehman Brothers, the concept of the perverse organization makes an important contribution to the understanding of the blindness about organizational risk grounded 'in the collective emotional life of people in organisations' (Long 2008b). Long's emphasis

> is on perversity displayed by the organisation as such, rather than simply by its leaders, or other members, even though they may embody and manifest perverse primary symptoms to the extent that they at times engage in corrupt or criminal behaviours. What is explored is a group and organisation dynamic, more deeply embedded than conscious corruption. Within the per-verse structure some roles become required to take up corrupt positions. They become part and parcel of the way things work. The person may condemn certain practices, but the role requires them. Tensions between person and role may mean that the person in role acts as they would not while in other roles. Such tensions may lead to the dynamics of perversity.
>
> (Long 2008a: book jacket)

Although Long focuses on the 'narrow' frame of organizations and corpora-tions in particular, one may extend beyond this frame by exploring the extent to which perversion is ingrained in the financial world – and thus in the capitalist system at large – and how this global perversion can be perceived and under-stood in order to extend the range of our thinking as well as our concern and responsibility. Needless to say, this will make us more aware of the helplessness, powerlessness and despair to which this exploration may inevitably lead.

Unconscious phantasy relationships, states of mind and unconscious group functioning

In contrast to the theoretical and rational explanations of behavioral economics in situations of decision making, uncertainty and time pressure, Richard Taffler and David Tuckett propose 'an interdisciplinary set of theories presently labeled emotional finance' (Tavistock Policy Seminars 2008). With this new paradigm, the authors emphasize

> the key role of the emotions as drivers of investor[s'] behaviour.... It aims to provide an understanding of financial market behaviour and investment processes by formally recognising the role unconscious needs and fears play in all investment activity.... One core insight is that thoughts create feelings, and that feelings create thoughts.
>
> (Taffler and Tuckett 2007: 18)

In their article 'Phantastic objects and the financial market's sense of reality', Tuckett and Taffler (2008) focus primarily on the internet bubble between 1995 and 2000. Whereas internet stocks had at first been phantastic objects, they later became reviled, 'stigmatized and felt to be a massive liability' (ibid.: 403) when the stock market dramatically crashed in April 2000.

> In the crash, investors suffer the return of the repressed. Knowledge that their investments were based on very risky assumptions had always been there; but such doubts were unconscious while an idealized love affair was in progress. Investors became conscious of the knowledge and feelings hitherto split off, including perhaps the anxiety stirred by their previous activities. They were now forced to own the experience of risk and to notice facts that had always been there.... The phantastic object was now an unconscious persecutory object.
>
> (ibid.: 403–4)

Social psychosis

In my paper ' "Your money or your life?" Psychotic implications of the pension fund system: towards a socio-analysis of the financial services revolution' (Sievers 2003), I focused on the psychotic thinking and dynamic underlying pension funds systems and shareholder value optimization. My conceptualization of psychosis comes from W. Gordon Lawrence (2000: 4–5), who regards psychosis in general as

> the process whereby humans defend themselves from understanding the meaning and significance of reality, because they regard such knowing as painful. To do this, they use aspects of their mental functioning to destroy, in various degrees, the very process of thinking that would put them in touch with reality.

Jack Welch, former CEO of General Electric, was once one of the biggest pro-
moters – if not 'the father' – of the 'shareholder value' movement. Although he
has since recanted and declared it to be a 'dump idea' (Guerrera 2009), pension
funds are still playing a significant role in the financial market. They have – both
as actors and as 'victims' or 'casualties' – been heavily involved in the present
crisis and its aftermath, not least with the result that millions fear for their pensions and hence their futures.

The working hypothesis of my paper was that

> the pension fund system, because of its inherent defenses against persecu-
> tory and depressive anxieties, is based on psychotic dynamics. Participation
> in the pension fund system encourages a psychotic dynamic; the expected
> pension after retirement is seen to protect one from a 'miserable' way of
> life, from deprivation, from annihilation and feelings of dependency, grati-
> tude, love, and guilt. As people increasingly strive for an affluent retirement,
> commoditized money nurtures the illusion that the more money one accu-
> mulates the more certain death will be kept away. It further [is] … argued
> that the psychotic dynamic inherent in the pension funds system is not
> limited to those who invest in the funds, but further finds an expression or
> 'resonance' in the organizations that manage the funds and their respective
> role holders. Money paid into a pension scheme serves – in addition to its
> 'pecuniary' function – as a 'conductor' of psychotic anxieties. As a con-
> sequence, pension funds have become the main players in a kind of global
> marshalling yard where underlying anxieties are transferred and shifted in
> various ways. Loaded with their customers' expectations and anxieties about
> adequate pensions after retirement, pension fund organizations tend to main-
> tain and spread a globalized collusion of psychotic thinking.
>
> (Sievers 2003: 187)

My current thoughts are based on the working hypothesis that the thinking of
various actors in the real estate and financial markets has been, to a high degree,
psychotic – and to some extent still is. This hypothesis comes from the assumption that it is not so much individual persons or their actions through which the
'reality' of organizations and markets is coined, but instead through the thinking
of role-holders in their respective contexts and organizations, for example house-
buyers, employees of banks, insurance companies, private equity firms, hedge
and pension funds, economists, and politicians.

The decisions of homebuyers, investment and commercial banks, real estate
agencies, hedge funds, etc. during the real estate market boom were based on the
unshakeable assumption that this boom – unlike all previous ones, such as the
1987 stock market crash and the 'dotcom' boom and bust of 1995–2000 –
appeared to be the very first in the history of humankind that would last indefinitely. The unshakeable belief that real estate prices would permanently increase
was based, in part, on the limited available land for development and the
expected increase in population and economic development in the United States

(Shiller 2008: 69). This has proved to be a myth. The belief that it would go on indefinitely is, however, typical of almost every boom – as long as it continues and is based on an illusion, which, as Freud (1927: 31) indicates, exists 'when a wish-fulfilment is a prominent factor in its motivation, and in doing so we disregard its relations to reality, just as the illusion itself sets no store by verification'.

Such thinking in the financial world was underpinned by a collectively shared manic defence – a psychotic process by which countless role-holders unconsciously were impelled to mobilize their personal manic parts beyond such mobilization in other role and systemic contexts. Here I confine myself to a few examples:

- Many governments – first and foremost the Bush one in the United States – emphasized vehemently at the beginning of the financial crisis that this crisis would not lead to catastrophic consequences. The fact that the public was repeatedly reassured that a disaster like the Great Depression of 1929 would not recur possibly had a calming effect on some but, concurrently, made high levels of anxiety and apprehension more obvious. Many banks reacted similarly long before they ultimately became aware of their losses.
- The frantic pace of reaction by some national governments to the bursting of the financial bubble appears to be more an expression of manic defence against immense helplessness and anxiety than of thinking and reflection.
- The nationalization of banks and their takeover by their countries can be understood more as a manic defence than as an alleged strategy to 'conquer' (and better run) them.
- The astronomical cost of credit securities and buyouts as well as the economic stimulus programmes applied by some governments – without any estimate of the medium- and long-term consequences for national budgets and future generations, not to mention the question of how these national deficits could ever be reduced – is further evidence for my assumption.
- The fact that some banks were bailed out and thus rescued by their governments mirrors a degree of state intervention unknown in the capitalist world since World War II. It 'implies something about the fact that we might have imperceptibly and globally entered into a new and unchartered phase of capitalism when the prevailing economic system has in effect become a "State-Assisted Capitalism"' (H. Brunning, private email communication, 14 May 2009). The state has emerged as the only reliable container not only for the free-floating toxic debenture bonds but also for the anxiety and the despair concomitant with them. At present, it is not known what these temporary solutions will stimulate in citizens and in the world globally (ibid.) – and for our perception of the future of democracy.
- The unswerving conviction that the present financial crisis was caused by disturbances within the system, without taking into account the possibility of a systemic crisis of capitalism itself (Wade 2008: 39; Žižek 2008: 10), seems to indicate a denial of reality.

• Last but not least, the media and the literature on the financial crisis seem to neglect the fact that 'a house of one's own' or 'one's home' is just not a commodity but, first and foremost, a 'phantastic object' (Tuckett and Taffler 2008), a 'symbol for life and death, freedom and dependency' (Hirsch 2006; cf. Bourdieu 2005). This neglect is surprising, since the Bush government, especially since 9/11, intensively propagated national programmes to encourage people – minorities in particular – to purchase their own homes. When the bust hit, hundreds of thousands of American homebuyers realized they could not repay their sub-prime mortgages and feared eviction from their homes. Thus, a long-cherished (and long-propagated) dream became a nightmare, and countless people became despairingly aware that what they were seduced to take on as reality was actually an illusion. The endless despair and the trauma of countless home buyers – not to mention the growing number of unemployed people – are rarely acknowledged in the financial discourse; their fate, if it is considered at all, is most likely seen as 'collateral damage', a term for civilians killed in the Iraq War.

Considering the financial crisis and its aftermath from the perspective chosen here, there is ample evidence to suggest that vast parts of the world and its economy are in a globalized collusion of psychotic thinking and thus in a state of 'psychosis unlimited'.

A brief synopsis – and some concluding considerations

Despite my choice of the six approaches sketched above being limited (and selective), it becomes obvious that there is already quite a body of psychodynamic and socioanalytic theory that may be of further help in developing an understanding of some of the unconscious dynamics of the financial world and the current financial crisis in particular.

In retrospect, it appears to me that the map drawn here leaves many open questions that have not yet been raised and which are still in search of thinkers. These open questions concern, above all, a deeper socioanalysis of the contemporary predominance of the financial world, both in the economy at large and in our lives, our 'images of man' and our worldviews.

It seems that socioanalytic contributions explicitly dealing with the unconscious dynamics of capitalism are scarce, if not non-existent, in the field of the psychoanalytic study of organizations. Despite the discontents we may have with capitalism, it appears that we have made peace with it. Even the hardened ex-communist powers like Russia and China are busily building capitalist systems of their own. We all profit and suffer without making a deeper attempt to illuminate the implications of our discontents. Like 'the main stream of the psychoanalytic movement', we broadly appear 'to accept capitalist society, equating it with civilization itself' as Hansen (1956) once stated, drawing on Marcuse's (1955) *Eros and Civilization*.

Not only were many – if not most – role-holders in the financial industry unable to calculate the risk of their transactions, much less to understand the instruments and products they were dealing with, many prominent economists, academics and politicians (according, for example, to Heinsohn 2009) seemingly ignored their own 'not-knowing' regarding the foundations of economic theory how the market actually works and how it is constituted: 'The politics of economics in the crisis resemble emergency surgery without any knowledge of anatomy. We still deceive ourselves about the basics of interest, money and market' (ibid.).

Apparently there is much to be done in order to better understand the world in 'the time of financial crisis'. In doing so, a capacity for 'not-understanding', or not rushing to understanding, may be a virtue rather than an indication of incompetence. As Gotthold Ephraim Lessing (1772, 4. act, 7. appearance), a German poet at the time of the Enlightenment, states in his 'bourgeois tragedy' *Emilia Galotti*, 'He who does not lose his mind over certain things does not have a mind to lose.'

In concluding, I want to sketch at least two of the many open questions to be further elaborated in the present context: risk management and the function of the financial industry in contemporary societies and the world.

Despite the fact that risk is of manifold relevance to the financial crisis, we broadly seem to have left the notion of risk and risk management to the experts (and supposed acrobats) in the global financial world. Instead of conceptualizing and further elaborating 'risk in depth and at large', we tend to extrapolate and project it into the future, the outer world and the financial one in particular (for example, cf. Hirschhorn 1999; Pelzer 2009; Pelzer and Case 2007; M. Stein 2003; and see Chapters 11 and 21, by Pelzer and Hirschhorn respectively, in this volume).

Another question worth exploring is whether and, if so, to what extent the financial system as a societal or global subsystem is at present serving as a kind of container (and a 'scapegoat' or cover story) for various other virulent issues and broadly neglected problems, on the level both of societies and of the world at large, including fundamentalism and the 'war on terror', the increasing scarcity of natural resources, the North–South divide, widespread famine, and our increasing inability to understand the world in which we live – to mention just a few. The financial world seems at present to be the most obvious domain in which psychotic thinking as an expression of the 'normality of madness' can most easily be hidden behind the 'rationality' of the market.

To the extent that we and the world at large seem unconcerned with such not-knowing and lack a willingness to understand, the financial crisis and the world of finance in general thus may serve as a container for the toxicity in the world at large and – one might assume – in ourselves, which we, for understandable reasons, do not want to face.

References

Bain, A. (2009) 'The economic crisis as manic depression: a few thoughts', Online, available at: www.acsa.net.au/articles/The%20Economic%20Crisis%20as%20Manic%20Depression.pdf (retrieved 9 May 2009).

Bion, W.R. (1959) *Experiences in Groups*, New York: Basic Books.

Bourdieu, P. (2005) *The Social Structures of the Economy*, Cambridge: Polity Press.

Case, P. and Gosling, J. (2010) 'Leading through the veil: seeing to the other side of catastrophe', paper presented at the Standing Conference on Organizational Symbolism (SCOS), Symposium, 'Vision', Lille.

Cassidy, J. (2010) 'The Volcker Rule: Obama's economic adviser and his battles over the financial-reform bill', *New Yorker*, 26 July: 25–30.

Chapman, J. (2003) 'Hatred and the corruption of task', *Organisational and Social Dynamics*, 3(1): 40–60. First published (1999) in *Socio-Analysis*, 1(2): 127–50.

Dizikes, P. (2010) 'Nobel laureate Krugman: "Dark age of macroeconomics" is upon us', *MIT News Office*, 10 February. Online, available at: http://web.mit.edu/newsoffice/2010/krugman-event.html (retrieved 10 February 2010).

Freud, S. (1927) 'The future of an illusion', in *The Standard Edition of the Complete Psychological Works of Sigmund Freud*, vol. 11, London: Hogarth Press.

Gabriel, Y. (2008a) 'Organizational miasma, purification and cleansing', in A. Ahlers-Niemann, U. Beumer, R. Redding Mersky and B. Sievers (eds) *Organisationslandschaften. Sozioanalytische Gedanken und Interventionen zur normalen Verrücktheit in Organisationen/The Normal Madness in Organizations: Socioanalytic Thoughts and Interventions*, Bergisch-Gladbach, Germany: Verlag Andreas Kohlhage.

Gabriel, Y. (2008b) 'Oedipus in the land of organizational darkness: preliminary considerations on organizational miasma', in M. Kostera (ed.), *Organizational Epics and Sagas: Tales of Organizations*, Basingstoke, UK: Palgrave.

Galbraith, J.K. (1987) 'The 1929 parallel', *Atlantic Monthly*, January: 62–6.

Guerrera, F. (2009) 'Welch rues short-term "obsession"', *Financial Times*, 12 May. Online, available at: http://us.ft.com/ftgateway/superpage.ft?news_id=fto031220091430053057 (retrieved 11 May 2009).

Hansen, J. (1956) 'A psychoanalyst looks for a sane society', *Fourth International*, 17(2): 65–9. Online, available at: www.marxists.org/archive/hansen/1956/xx/psych.htm (retrieved 18 May 2009).

Heinsohn, G. (2009) 'Die nächste Blase schwillt schon an', *Frankfurter Allgemeine Zeitung*, 20 May, 116: 31.

Hirsch, M. (2006) *Das Haus. Symbol für Leben und Tod, Freiheit und Abhängigkeit*, Giessen, Germany: Psychosozial-Verlag.

Hirschhorn, L. (1999) 'The primary risk', *Human Relations*, 52(1): 5–23. Reprinted in B. Sievers (ed.) *Psychoanalytic Studies of Organizations: Contributions from the International Society for the Psychoanalytic Study of Organizations (ISPSO) 1983–2008*, London: Karnac, 2009.

Kirsner, D. (1990) 'Illusion and the stock market crash: some psychoanalytic aspects', *Free Associations*, 19: 31–58.

Lawrence, W.G. (2000) 'Thinking refracted', in *Tongued with Fire: Groups in experience*, London: Karnac.

Lessing, G.E. (1772/2008) *Lessing's Emilia Galotti*, BiblioLife.

Long, S. (2008a) *The Perverse Organisation and Its Deadly Sins*, London: Karnac.

Long, S. (2008b). 'The perverse organisation and its deadly sins', Online, available at: www.karnacbooks.com/AuthorBlog.asp?BID=69 (retrieved 14 May 2009).

Marcuse, H. (1955) *Eros and Civilization: A philosophical inquiry into Freud*, Boston: Bacon Press.

Pauly, C., Reuter, W., Schmitz, G.P., Schulz, T., Steingart, G. and Wagner, W. (2009) 'Wahnsinn 2.0.', *Der Spiegel*, 48, 72–83. Online, available at: www.spiegel.de/spiegel/print/d-67871661.html (retrieved 25 February 2010).

Pelzer, P. (2009) 'The displaced world of risk: risk management as alienated risk (perception?)', *Society and Business Review*, 4(1): 26–36.

Pelzer, P. and Case, P. (2007) 'The displaced world of risk management: covert enchantment in a calculative world', in M. Kostera (ed.) *Mythical Inspirations and Storytelling for Organizational Realities*, Basingstoke, UK: Palgrave.

Rycroft, C. (1972) *A Critical Dictionary of Psychoanalysis*, Harmondsworth, UK: Penguin Books.

Schwartz, H.S. (1990a) 'Narcissism project and corporate decay: the case of General Motors'. Online, available at: www.sba.oakland.edu/faculty/schwartz/GMDecay.htm (retrieved 17 December 2008).

Schwartz, H.S. (1990b) *Narcissistic Process and Corporate Decay: The theory of the organization ideal*, New York: New York University Press.

Shiller, R.S. (2008) *The Subprime Solution: How today's global financial crisis happened, and what to do about it*, Princeton, NJ: Princeton University Press.

Sievers, B. (2003) ' "Your money or your life?" Psychotic implications of the pension fund system: towards a socio-analysis of the financial services revolution', *Human Relations*, 56(2): 187–210.

Stein, H.F. (2007) 'The inconsolable organization: toward a theory of organizational and cultural change', *Psychoanalysis, Culture and Society*, 12: 349–68.

Stein, H.F. (2008) 'Traumatic change and the inconsolable organization', in A. Ahlers-Niemann, U. Beumer, R. Redding Mersky and B. Sievers (eds) *Organisationslandschaften. Sozioanalytische Gedanken und Interventionen zur normalen Verrücktheit in Organisationen/The Normal Madness in Organizations: Socioanalytic Thoughts and Interventions*, Bergisch-Gladbach, Germany: Verlag Andreas Kohlhage.

Stein, M. (2003) 'Unbounded irrationality: risk and organizational narcissism at long term capital management', *Human Relations*, 56(5): 523–40.

Stein, M. (2008) 'Toxicity and the unconscious experience of the body at the employee–customer interface', *Organization Studies*, 28: 1223–41.

Taffler, R. and Tuckett, D. (2007) 'Emotional finance: understanding what drives investors', *Professional Investor*, Autumn: 18–20.

Tavistock Policy Seminars (2008) 'Markets, meaning and madness', London: The Tavistock and Portman NHS Foundation Trust, 20 November. Online, available at: www.hero.ac.uk/uk/business/archives/2008/when_markets_go_mad_Jun.cfm (retrieved 11 May 2009).

Tuckett, D. and Taffler, R. (2008) 'Phantastic objects and the financial market's sense of reality: a psychoanalytic contribution to the understanding of stock market instability', *International Journal of Psychoanalysis*, 89: 389–412.

Wade, R. (2008) 'Systembeben. Neue Steuerungsinstrumente für die Weltwirtschat sind erforderlich', *Lettre International*, 83, Winter: 35–40.

Winnicott, D.W. (1935/1975) 'The manic defence', in *Through Paediatrics to Psychoanalysis*, London: Hogarth Press.

Wolfe, W.B. (1932) 'Psycho-analyzing the Depression', *Forum and Century*, 87(4): 209–14.

Wolfenstein, E.V. (1993) *Psychoanalytic-Marxism: Groundwork*; London: Free Association; New York: Guilford Press.

Žižek, S. (2008) 'Hoffnungszeichen. Doch die eigentliche Auseinandersetzung beginnt nach dem Sieg Obamas', *Lettre International*, 83, Winter: 7–10.

8 Sense-making stories and evaluative cultures of fund managers
Evidence from Istanbul

Emre Tarim

Introduction

This chapter discusses research on how fund managers cope with the uncertainty of the past, present and future of markets and their investments by observation and narration of contents available on scopic market screens (Knorr Cetina and Preda 2007). I will argue that 'evaluative cultures' in both the public and the private spheres help shape the narratives used to make sense of market information on the scopic market screens.

Background

The advances in communication technologies, digitization of marketplaces and increased globalization of finance capital have led to a dramatic increase in the speed and amount of data/information and fund flows across markets (Sassen 2005). Scopic market screens as described by Knorr Cetina and Preda (2007) are multiple computer screens that are powered by proprietary software and fed by numerous data vendors and market organizations all around the globe. These technological devices record, store and retrieve data/information and fund flows that roam the global financial system. The forms of representation on scopic market screens are information narratives, alphanumeric symbols and graphs denoting price, quantity, volume, and so on. The novelty of scopic market screens is that they allow investors to participate in these flows through observation and interpretation acts, and trading moves without the necessity of being in an actual marketplace and physically interacting with buyers and sellers.

The digitization of markets and the introduction of scopic market screens has therefore meant that marketplaces have gone through a process of anonymization, streaming, and consequent withering of social networks, which used to be major sources of information and data for market participants (Knorr Cetina and Preda 2007: 127–9). In a context like this, the streaming mode in financial markets is increasingly 'scientized and technologized' (Mackenzie 2005: 556) because theoretical and technical tools integrated into scopic market screens allow measurement and calculation of market-related phenomena such as price, risk, volatility, value and return on a global scale. This new scientized, technologized and digitized marketplace can be considered as accommodating numerous 'evaluative cultures' that are constituted by a 'shared set of beliefs, practices, ways of calculating, and technical systems … [that have] some coherence and some continuity over time' (Mackenzie 2009a: 3–4). Moreover, it is not uncommon to observe frequent concurrent use of more than one evaluative culture on this new plane of risk and return calculations, such as 'chartism' and 'fundamental value analysis' (Smith 1998). These are mostly in the public domain as regards their paradigmatic principles and practical applications, but there are also proprietary and private evaluation models of financial organizations that are closed to the wider investor community (Beunza and Stark 2005). All in all, these evaluation cultures and their specific calculation tools are significantly reliant on recording, storage and retrieval of an ever-increasing range of data/information and fund flows by scopic market screens. They are also reliant on integration and channelling of these flows or 'simple datums' into the evaluation cultures' calculation tools and sense-making frames in order for investors to be able to consistently and continuously convert them into 'higher datums', namely, 'interpretation/evaluation/judgment' (Sassen 2005: 27). Continuous observation of scopic market screens with 'intensity and preparedness' (Knorr Cetina and Preda 2007: 131), and with the guidance of evaluative cultures, allows investors to cope with a 'bewildering array of [financial] products and of price data that change second by second' (Mackenzie 2009b: 13). Observation with intensity and preparedness provides a crucial incentive for investors, namely the minimizing of losses and maximizing of returns on their investments.

In the following, I explore evaluative cultures that are present in an asset management company (AMC)[1] and operative in futures, bonds and equity markets of the Istanbul Stock Exchange (ISE) and inter-bank currency market. The evidence presented here comes from the dealing room of the AMC, where five fund managers are responsible for managing around fifteen different financial products that have direct or underlying investments in these markets. Observing and recording trading room events and conversations, and informal discussions and formal interviews with the fund managers, constitute the methods of exploration of evaluative cultures. Narratives of the fund managers collected through these methods are analysed as manifestations of paradigmatic and vernacular market knowledge that inform the evaluative cultures that market actors generate and adapt. The analysis therefore focuses on *in-situ* narratives, or what I call the 'momentary stories', their 'causal and temporal structures' and the universe of actors and objects. Some of these aspects are quantified in Table 8.1 (p. 111). This is followed by an attempt to delineate the outlines of two seemingly distinct evaluative cultures that surround fixed-income and equity-based financial products respectively and to place these cultures within the larger market culture explored in the ISE. The delineation is informed by the analysis of *in-situ* narratives as well as ethnographic observations of the ISE's intermediaries and investor types, and discussions with the fund managers in the AMC.

Role of narratives in the ISE

As part of a larger ethnographic exploration of the ISE equity market between 2007 and 2009, I spent twenty working days in April and May 2008 in the AMC. My other field observations in the ISE consisted of four- to six-week stays in four brokerage houses (all but one in non-participant observation), one month-long spell of participant observation in the CNBC-e studios, and a two-week internship programme in the ISE headquarters. For the ISE's ethnography, I concentrate on two topics, namely sense-making narratives *in-situ* and narratives of education, entertainment and legitimation told in and exchanged between market organizations and the media (Tarim 2009). This chapter's focus is on sense-making narratives generated by the fund managers working for the AMC and how these narratives help reduce uncertainty about the past, present and future of the investments made by fund managers. Their sense-making and trading activities during the observation period constitute the evidence for description of evaluative cultures present in the AMC as well as for the coordinates of these evaluative cultures within the larger market culture of the ISE.

The asset management company

The AMC is a mid-size asset management company, one of twenty-three such companies operating with a Turkish Capital Markets Board (CMB) licence. It had approximately US$110 million under its management during the time of my observations. The AMC manages nine different mutual funds issued by its parent company, six pension funds owned by a local branch of a global insurance company, and private assets of several dozen individual investors. There are five male Turkish managers in the trading room, each with an average of fifteen years' experience in the leading companies of the fund management industry in Turkey. Three of them manage the funds that have most weight in equities, and the remaining two managers look after the funds that have greatest weight in fixed-income securities. Each manager is connected to the markets he invests in, and follows them via scopic market screens provided by local and global data vendor companies. The managers also use proprietary monitoring programs that measure each fund's performance on a real-time basis.

Because each fund managed by the AMC has an investment charter regulated by the CMB, the managers operate within the rules and objectives stated in the charter. The most significant of these is the benchmark rule by which a fund has to carry a certain percentage of its total investment in a predetermined security class. For instance, if the fund managed is an 'A type' fund, the weight of Turkish equities in the fund's total value cannot be lower than 25 per cent of the overall fund value. However, none of these funds are index or benchmark replicators, so the fund managers try to beat the relevant returns on indexes in which they invest, no matter how minuscule their positive performance may be, owing to fund charters and CMB directives. Another significant aspect of these restrictions is that the managers cannot take higher risks by short-selling in spot securities, use of leverage, or violating the charter benchmark rules. Although they invest in different securities, owing to the restrictive and rather conservative fund management rules one common investment strategy used by the fund managers is anticipating the short-term and mid-term trajectories of indexes in general and certain securities in particular. This is important, because on such anticipation the managers can change the weight of security class or single securities within the fund product to beat the index or benchmark in question, or have smaller losses compared with the relevant benchmarks. Each manager therefore keeps a careful eye on the flows as represented on the scopic market screens as well as on the real-time performance of their funds vis-à-vis these flows. With small tweaks in fund compositions during market hours, the managers strive to beat the index or benchmark returns (or losses).

Sense making and storytelling in financial markets

Compared with production market organizations and the modality of such flows therein (White 2000), the element of surprise and uncertainty in information/data and fund flows as well as the latter's breadth in and out of financial market organizations is more frequent, owing to the aforementioned digitization and scientization process. This undermines the limited cognitive capacity of market actors in processing information/data (Mackenzie 2009b: 13–14) and problematizes the neoclassical axiom of information/data as unproblematic signals generating rational Bayesian reactions among fully rational market actors (De Bondt 2005: 165). Even if market actors develop heuristics or cognitive schemes over time to filter the relevant bits of information/data flows and ways of connecting them to explain the past and present, and predict the future, qualitative and quantitative aspects of the filtered flows in scopic market systems such as quantity, volume, volatility, content, and so on, and reactions of other market actors to these flows, may carry elements of surprise and uncertainty. The feature of a multitude of real-time information/data and fund flows and their multidimensionality in financial markets therefore encourages real-time sense-making commentary and trading responses by market actors operating in scopic markets. This occurs almost as if they are players and commentators in several virtual sports games simultaneously, facing surprise and uncertainty 'produced in an ordered and orderly fashion' (Preda 2009: 1–5) owing to constitutive rules and roles that help sustain stable and orderly market places (Abolafia 1998).

There is a power in storytelling in sense making and decision making under such circumstances. This comes from the fact that storying is a sense-making effort that puts events and actions of actors in non-random sequences beyond mere chronology, and attributes meaning to their acts. This is in accordance with their contributions to surprises and uncertainties related to risk and return performances of present and prospective investments. This mode of explanation is embedded in time and place and is in stark contrast with paradigmatic or categorical ways of knowing and explaining. The latter achieve sense making by demonstrating an event or action as a manifestation of universal law or theory (Polkinghorne 1988: 21). Storytelling therefore allows narrative imagination to transform actors and objects into actants capable of acting and being acted on without limitations of any fixed property or character (Greimas and Courtes 1982: 5, cited in Czarniawska 2004: 80). This is conducive to the generation of locally coherent and relevant vernacular knowledge about actants, especially investor mass, whose intentions remain intelligible only through proxy data/ information because of the anonymity of digitized markets. Generation of narrative knowledge improves the explanatory and predictive power of more stable sense-making frames within market organizations such as cognitive schemas, scripts for action, paradigmatic theories and evaluative cultures. In a reverse manner, storytelling before scopic market screens in the above commentary-making manner invokes these more stable frames as connective logics and carries the contours of evaluative cultures in them (Weick 1995: 128).

Capturing momentary stories in the AMC

During my stay in the trading room of the AMC, I was given a desk situated next to Manager Y (equity) and allowed to take notes and record room conversations. I also had informal discussions and an interview with all the managers during and after market hours about their investment strategies and use of the scopic screens. Because each manager was bound by fund charter rules, there was little collective tinkering about investment strategies. Collective cognition activities were thus limited to reactions towards news and market events flowing on the screens, and to discussions about the short- to mid-term future trajectory of the markets and securities the managers observed and/or invested in.

From detailed descriptions of trading room events and discussions over fifteen intense observation days, I captured sense-making narratives that I call 'momentary stories'. In my ethnography of the ISE, I use the following operational definition of momentary stories: momentary stories are verbal and/or written discourses of more than one sentence that are produced in front of scopic market screens by market actors who use the logics of cause–effect, correlation, similarity (to past experiences) and randomness (lack of other logics). These logics connect screen-visible events and actions or proxies that actors believe represent anonymized events and actions. Storytelling as such is done to come up with higher datums or interpretation beyond simple sensory description. These stories are about explaining the past and present state of the market (and its investment-related components) and/or predicting its future trajectory.

Emplotment types and sources of information used in constructing momentary stories

The logics of cause–effect, correlation, and similarity and randomness are 'emplotment types' devised for classifying sense-making narratives collected during the field observation. These emplotment types correspond to heuristics or rules of thumb that market actors seem to be repeatedly invoking to make connections among events and actions to make sense of information/data and/or news stories they notice on the screen. These rules of thumb are generated by continuous observation and narration of market screens by market actors in a manner that is explained in the previous section regarding generation and retrieval of narrative knowledge and explanation in organizational sense making. Cause–effect logic is the most widely invoked emplotment tool in storytelling (Tilly 2006). The other logics devised in this study, such as 'correlation', are derived from the cause–effect logic in order to register ontological nuances in financial markets such as co-movement of market indexes and its manifestations in the evaluative cultures explored.

Contra-logic narratives also occur. They are important in exploring evaluative cultures in two ways. First, they intimate emotional disappointment or a sarcastic attitude in the face of epistemic failure of evaluative cultures. Second, expression of these emotions usually takes the form of describing what is wrong with the state of the market and hence occasionally stating what market ontology entails should under the given circumstances.

In regards to classification of knowledge and information source types such as paradigmatic, vernacular, private and public, this typology is devised by studying standard textbooks on finance and economy, observing the scopic market screens and publicly available information/data flowing through them, and, last but not least, being in dialogue with my informants about the nature of their sense-making and investment activities and my understanding of the collected data and its significance for my research. The latter is essential for ensuring the validity of ethnographic research, as the bulk of data used in ethnographic research is generated by informants' routine activities and their explanations to the researcher (Gold 1997). Table 8.1 presents frequency of momentary stories and momentary story-like narratives (under the logic of observation) captured in the AMC in accordance with the definition above. The momentary story-like narratives are what Gabriel (2000: 25) calls proto-stories, stories with 'a rudimentary plot'. In Table 8.1 the logic of 'observation' refers to narratives without a single strong logic explicitly connecting the observed events and actions or their proxies on the market screen.

Findings

In this section, first, the contra-logic and randomness stories are presented. These narratives intimate the managers' paradigmatic and narrative knowledge about the markets by explaining what is 'wrong' with the markets observed. After this, a summary of most frequently used actants in narratives and their properties as attributed by the managers are presented. This is followed by a note on the nature of narrative imagination at work in correlation and cause–effect stories and in the use of private and paradigmatic knowledge. As will be explained in detail in the discussion section, these story examples and descriptive statistics about actants point to two seemingly distinct evaluative cultures among equity

Table 8.1 Momentary and proto-momentary stories

	Cause–effect	Correlation	Observation	Randomness	Similarity	Total	Proxy data use	Direct news – private knowledge	Self-narrative	Past	Past and present	Present	Present and future	Future	Past, present, and future
D-1	8[1]	2[2]	3	—	—	13	12	2 – 2	6	1	2	3	2	—	5
D-2	4	—	1	—	—	5	4	1 – 0	1	—	1	1	—	1	2
D-3	6	—	8	—	—	14	13	3 – 0	5	—	2	7	3	1	1
D-4	3	—	6	—	—	9	7	3 – 0	5	1	2	3	3	—	—
D-5	5	—	8	—	—	13	10	2 – 2	3	1	1	7	2	—	2
D-6	4	—	3	—	—	7	5	0 – 1	2	—	1	—	4	1	1
D-7	3[4]	2[3]	5	—	—	10	8	3 – 0	6	—	4	3	2	1	—
D-8	4[5]	1	10	1	—	16	13	7 – 0	6	3	3	6	3	—	1
D-9	6[6]	—	8	—	1	15	12	5 – 3	3	—	7	5	1	—	2
D-10	15	1[7]	7	—	1[8]	24	23	14 – 0	3	1	11	6	2	—	4
D-11	2[9]	—	2	—	—	4	4	1 – 1	1	—	1	2	1	—	—
D-12	3	2[10]	4	—	—	9	5	2 – 2	4	—	1	8	—	—	1
D-13	7	—	3	2	—	12	11	2 – 1	5	1	2	3	3	2	1
D-14	2	—	7	1	—	10	7	2 – 1	5	—	2	7	1	—	—
D-15	10[11]	1	14	1	—	26	19	10 – 3	10	2	6	7	7	—	4
Total	82	9	89	5	2	187	153	57 – 16	65	10	46	68	34	6	23

fund and fixed-income fund managers. The fixed-income managers, on the one hand, seem to have more faith in, and act according to their paradigmatic knowledge about, economics and finance in their narrative interpretations. In contrast, the equity managers seem to be more market oriented with the help of their vernacular knowledge about the ISE, investor profiles, as well as what goes on in other markets as they observe through scopic screens.

What is wrong with the markets?

The superscripts in Table 8.1 are single instances of the following 'contra-logic narratives':

1   Contra-cause–effect: Manager W (fixed-income) laments the positive stock markets in the United States despite the hike in the interest rates: 'Their interest rates are at 3 per cent, the six-month bills from 2.6, and still they are buying the stocks. I don't get it, what bullshit, they announce losses, and still they get the stocks, look at the DAX, 1.3 per cent up, why, what is the reason?'

2   Contra-correlation: Manager Z (equity) observes the stagnation in the ISE despite the recent upbeat performance of the US and European stock markets: 'Well, what will we do now? The outside has been going up for a few days and here it does not move an inch.'

3   Contra-correlation: Manager Z: 'The US has opened positive but why the hell are they selling here!'

4   Contra-cause–effect: Manager W: 'Oops, look at the Dow, still positive, I can't get it, it is around 12,900 and they are still buying it. If it was around 12,300, I could understand' (chart-based expectation and contra-realization).

5   Contra-cause–effect: Manager Y after observing some specific sells in several securities and the overall sales in the ISE (despite positive expectations about the US first-quarter GDP announcement) adds, 'What kind of a herd is this, they are selling without a reason!'

6   Contra-cause–effect: Manager W tells Manager T (fixed-income) that 'one of my contacts in Xbank sold TL 700 million worth of two different bonds for Ybank, though he did not disclose the buyers because there were many'. Manager T does not believe it, as he does not see any significant change on his scopic market screen. Manager W says the trade was completed over the counter. Manager T then explodes, 'Then why the hell don't they buy dollars with it!'

7   Contra-correlation (cause–effect): Manager Y and Manager X (equity) chat about the positive markets abroad and then observe the negative index in the ISE. They attribute it to the initial public offering (IPO) of Turkish Telekom (TT). (The assumption in the room was that investors were selling shares and US dollars – a popular hard currency among Turkish savers to free up capital for the TT IPO. The fixed-income managers W and T anticipated that once the IPO was completed, the dollar would recover.)

8   Contra-similarity: Manager W observes several figures concerning US employment to be released at 15:30 (Turkish time). Despite the better than expected 'ex-agriculture' employment data, other employment data came worse than expected. However, the market reaction in the United States was positive: 'What the f***? The data is minus and they are still buying it like hell. A couple of months ago, the Dow was 13,200 and with a minus figure in the same data, it just collapsed here and there, and now it is minus again and they are buying it like hell!' Manager Y: 'It is due to the charts.' Manager Y and X are quite content with the rises in the stock markets; X says, 'Now the mood is different'. Manager W stands up at his desk: 'F*** the mood ... look at the fundamentals ... I never used to swear so much ... I'm resigning.' He leaves the room.

9   Contra-cause–effect: Manager Z hears an interview with a company official on CNBC-e and notices a small price hike in the company share. After listening to the interview for a few seconds, he rules out a connection, confirmed by Manager X.

10   Contra-correlation: Manager W: 'Bond is down, the stock market is down, but then why the f*** is the dollar down...'

11   Contra-cause–effect: Manager W makes the following remarks after the TT IPO is completed and the company is floated on the ISE: 'The TT is over, we said after that the dollar would be up, and that did not materialize either, f*** it.'

As can be seen in the above sense-making narratives that observe contra-logics, the managers get rather uneasy when the dominant emplotment logics do not seem to work. Apart from the eleven instances of contra-logics, six of which were invoked by the fixed-income managers, randomness was invoked five times, four of these times by the fixed-income managers. Randomness also refers to narrative reactions to apparent failure of one of the logics in explaining the situation on the scopic market screen. This (lack of) logic has nothing to do with the imagery of randomness espoused in the finance theory. Randomness brings strong negative emotions in the managers, owing to their inability to make sense of the market:

Day 8: Right after the better than expected US 2008 Q1 GDP release, Manager W remarks the following: 'They are shorting everything, the dollar is down, the ISE is down, the futures is down, everything is down, it does not make any sense, there must be something peculiar to the ISE...'

Day 13: (1) Manager W jokes, 'It is a queer market, it can go either way.' (2) Manager T comments on the US dollar hitting TL 1.24, then says, 'I don't get it!' his face is in his hands.

Day 14: During a discussion with Manager W at his desk, he makes the following remark: 'You are not here at the right time if you wanted to learn about the effects of data releases, they don't mean a lot, people's reactions are mixed [not categorical], correlations between securities seem to be lost, this is not a good time, markets turn around back big time and you can lose.'

Day 15: Manager X laments the unpredictability of the markets: 'This market is a f***ed up market; you do something, it falls; you wait, it goes up; you don't know what it is, a weird market, I have never seen anything this boring...'

While the contra-logics and randomness reveal themselves in the above jittery, disappointed or sarcastic statements, they are aberrations within the dominant vernacular and paradigmatic modes of sense making among the fund managers.

Actants and their narrative properties

When it comes to the totality of meaning created and represented via these narratives, certain actants feature frequently in the managers' narratives. These are 'the market', 'here', 'the ISE', 'the TurkDex', the 'bond market', 'the Dow [Jones]', 'the DAX [Deutscher Aktien IndeX]', 'the NASDAQ', 'abroad', 'Euro markets', 'rate', 'price', 'US data', 'the Philadelphia Fed Manufacturing Index', 'Q1 US GDP', 'US trade figures', 'the US Consumer Confidence Index', the 'ISM Manufacturing Survey', 'dollar', names of brokerage houses operating in the ISE, code name of shares, 'inflation', 'growth', 'the Fed [Federal Reserve]', 'rate cut', 'the [Turkish] Central Bank', 'the ECB [European Central Bank]', 'LIBOR [the London Interbank Offered Rate]', global company names such as 'AT&T', 'Barclays', 'CITI', 'Lehman', 'they', 'f***ing people', 'pimps', 'small investors', 'bastards', 'foreigners', 'aggressive guys', 'momentum traders'-investor 'types' in the ISE and in global markets', 'Emre the researcher',[2] 'charts', 'resistance point'.

These actants are usually given neutral agency if they are non-human actants such as the Dow, the DAX, LIBOR, and so on. Such agencies draw on paradigmatic and vernacular knowledge about their indirect and direct effects on the Turkish financial markets and hence the funds under management. It should be noted that only in twenty narratives did the managers resort to universal paradigmatic knowledge about the economy and financial markets to explain events and actions. Moreover, more than a third of these narratives were spoken by the fixed-income managers. On the other hand, although correlation among markets, securities, and macroeconomic phenomena is invoked only eleven times in the momentary stories, in twenty momentary stories that have cause–effect as their logic, the causes stem from news and market events from abroad, and the effects are (to be) observed in the Turkish financial markets.

Anonymous actors made intentional and purposeful

If actants are human, then the attribution of unity, motive, blame and credit as tropes of meaning-makers within stories (Gabriel 2000: 36–7) are frequently used to explain past and present events or justify the predictions made about the future. These explanations and predictions stem from characters and attributes of human actants in question. They are generated either on the spot, drawing on available proxy data, or from continuous market observation and experience that take the form of stable cognitive frames, or by a combination of both. In sixty-nine narratives, otherwise anonymous investors are attributed the unity and motive to (have) act(ed) in ways that conform to specific readings of proxy data (fifty-three narratives) or existing beliefs about investors (sixteen narratives). The attribution of unity and motive is not confined to human actors. Intermediary organizations are also attributed unity and motive despite the fact that they are serving hundreds of retail and institutional investors. There are sixteen narratives in which these organizations are construed to be acting as unitary actors with motive.

Narrative imagination at work

The aforementioned momentary stories that establish one-way correlation (cause) between markets and news events abroad and the Turkish markets and events (as effect – thirty-one stories as such out of ninety-one cause–effect and correlation stories) do so without any test of statistical significance. Although the managers can retrieve time series data on their market screens about various markets among which they believe there are correlative or cause–effect relationships, they are satisfied with observing the scopic market screen and confirming these 'logical' relationships by narrative imagination.

   In a similar vein, only sixteen narratives benefit from use of private knowledge or information in their emplotment. By private knowledge or information, I mean vernacular knowledge acquired through managers' experience and networks in the market which is not available outside these networks. This relatively insignificant use of private knowledge gathered through experience and networks, plus merely twenty narratives that rely on paradigmatic knowledge, also attests to the importance of narrative imagination in making sense of flows observed on the scopic screens. Narrative imagination is therefore crucial in sense making in front of the scopic screens and generating narrative knowledge about the scopic markets in which the managers operate.

Discussion of the evaluative cultures in the AMC

As described, 'evaluative culture' is composed of a set of beliefs, practices, ways of calculating and technical systems that have some coherence and continuity over time. In the case of the fund managers, the practice of calculating and monitoring the fund performances as well as determination of the magnitude of tweaks to outperform the relevant benchmarks were achieved by proprietary software tools integrated into the scopic market system. They allowed the fund managers to have a quantified view of how their funds were coping with the information/data and fund flows without having to do manual calculations.

The labour time freed by the technical systems of calculation and monitoring therefore reverted to the observation of scopic screens with intensity and preparedness.

This observation mode was especially overt among the three equity managers, as their funds were composed of thirty-plus shares and a small minority of fixed-income products. It entailed flicking between different parts of the market screen. These parts represented the market components that were believed to affect the value of returns and risks on the securities within the funds. Because of the variety and breadth of information/data incorporated into their sense-making activity, the equity managers' bodily practice of observation consisted of minimum bodily movement, constant eye movements and small tilts of the head to focus their visual attention on a certain part of the screen, and constant contact with their computer mouse to shift through screen interfaces and log buy–sell orders into the remote-access trading system.

The fixed-income managers, by comparison, seemed to have more free time to pass by playing arcade games on their computers or snoozing at their tables. This was possible because their funds were composed of lesser numbers of components in fixed-income and equity products, and currencies. Because the fixed-income market in Turkey is dominated by government bonds issued in Turkish lira and other currencies, the equity managers' focus was on the macroeconomic and political news flows from Turkey and abroad. Particular attention was paid to inflation, consumption and production data from abroad and Turkey which might have an effect on currency parities as well as central banks' interest rate policies. However, announcements of information/data on these aspects happened at relatively longer intervals. Similarly, the benchmark products and actual securities in fund products had longer maturity periods. Therefore, the fixed-income managers were relatively less screen oriented and more macro-economy and politics focused at national and global levels. Consequently, only around 30 per cent of the captured narratives were initiated and/or told by the fixed-income managers. However, more than a third of the narratives that had paradigmatic knowledge from economics and finance as the source of explanation were generated by the fixed-income managers.

In fact, I might have heard fewer stories from the fixed-income managers had it not been for the volatility and macroeconomic uncertainty in the United States and developed-country economies and financial markets during the time of observations in 2008. This period was several months before the Lehman Brothers collapse and the unravelling of the global financial system. April–May 2008 for the fund managers was therefore a period of heightened uncertainty due to negative and positive information/data flows from the developed economies and financial markets. The uncertainty was exacerbated by mixed reactions from the global and Turkish investment communities alike, as evidenced in the contra-logic and randomness stories presented previously. The equity managers were initially rather optimistic about the future of the markets. This was because their observation activities and cognitive models seemed to be wider in scope and more accommodating towards investor sentiment as observed by the magnitude and power of fund flows abroad and in the ISE. The equity managers sometimes ignored negative news when they were contradicted by positive stock market moves before and after the news announcements. Such contra-moves benefited the well-exposed equity funds. However, towards the end of the observation period equity managers became quite upset after acting according to the anticipated and confirmed major negative news flows from the United States and the global economy, which were contradicted by resilient stock markets abroad and in Turkey.

This brings the chapter to the final point of discussion about the evaluative cultures explored in the trading room, namely the shared beliefs about the place of the ISE and the Turkish economy in the grand scheme of the global economy and financial markets. In the cognitive models of both types of managers, the markets and the economies they invest in are peripheral to the major centres of the global economy and finance. In total, more than 30 per cent of the narratives take the events (to be) observed in a set of developed economies and markets (mainly the United States and to a lesser extent Germany) as either direct or implied causes of financial market performance (to be) observed in the ISE and Turkish currency markets. This belief in a cause–effect relationship and its sense-making and decision-making outcomes within the fund managers' performance is a phenomenon of the past five to seven years according to them and the findings of my ethnographic observations among domestic retail investors and their intermediaries (Tarim 2010).

In a nutshell, the period following the 2000/1 economic and financial crisis in Turkey has been a time of positive structural transformation in the Turkish economy, which has attracted a more dedicated global institutional investor profile to the Turkish markets compared to that in the 1990s. The crushing dominance of 'the foreigners' in the ISE equity market in relation to portfolio values coupled with their lack of weight in the trading volumes has meant that domestic retail, and to a smaller extent domestic institutional investors, have provided the bulk of the liquidity in the ISE. The modality of this liquidity provision has been predominantly in line with short-term investments or speculative trading based on information/data and fund flows in and out of not only the ISE but also the developed markets. Justifications for this sense-making and trading mode among Turkish investors and the fund managers alike invariably invoke the phrases 'globalization of the ISE' and 'the foreigners are here'. The fund managers do pay attention to their paradigmatic knowledge about the economy and financial markets. Yet it is largely their vernacular knowledge about the globalization phenomenon that shapes their observation and sense-making protocols. This is especially pronounced among the equity managers seeking to be able to better cope with the Turkish financial markets' dynamics stemming from global and national investors' sentiments and habits.

Conclusion

Evaluative cultures in financial markets take shape over time by continuous observation, practice, and making sense of experiences within marketplaces with the assistance of technical systems and narrative imagination. The digitization and scientization of marketplaces, coupled with cross-border portfolio investments among developed and emerging markets, have paved the way for an ever-increasingly quantified and seemingly integrated plane of global financial markets. The evaluative cultures of the fund managers explored in this chapter attest to this phenomenon from the perspective of peripheral market actors, albeit there exist distinctions among them due to the local market regulations and the paradigmatic and vernacular nature of the financial products managed.

Notes

1 The AMC is a pseudonym for the organization studied.
2 I was turned into an actant in constant jokes about the fall in the US dollar. Managers T and W, who invest in US dollars, future contracts and securities nominated in US dollars, were quite hurt by the fall in the US dollar during my observation period. So, I was attributed blame and credit for the volatility of the US dollar, depending on my presence or absence in the room. On day 14 I was asked by Manager T, as a joke, not to enter the room because the US dollar/Turkish lira parity had risen to 1.27 in my absence!

References

Abolafia, M. (1998) 'Markets as cultures: an ethnographic approach', in M. Callon (ed.) *The Law of the Market*, Oxford: Blackwell.
Beunza, D. and Stark, D. (2005) 'How to recognize opportunities: heterarchical search in a trading room', in K. Knorr Cetina and A. Preda (eds) *The Sociology of Financial Markets*, Oxford: Oxford University Press.
Czarniawska, B. (2004) *Narratives in Social Science Research*, London: Sage.
De Bondt, W. (2005) 'The values and beliefs of European investors', in K. Knorr Cetina and A. Preda (eds) *The Sociology of Financial Markets*, Oxford: Oxford University Press.
Gabriel, Y. (2000) *Storytelling in Organizations: Facts, fictions, and fantasies*, Oxford: Oxford University Press.
Gold, R.L. (1997) 'The ethnographic method in sociology', *Qualitative Inquiry*, 3: 388–402.
Knorr Cetina, K. and Preda, A. (2007) 'The temporalization of financial markets: from network to flow', *Theory, Culture, and Society*, 24: 116–38.
Mackenzie, D. (2005) 'Opening the black boxes of global finance,' *Review of International Political Economy*, 12: 555–76.
Mackenzie, D. (2009a) 'The credit crisis as a problem in the sociology of knowledge', working paper, November 2009. Online, available at: www.sps.ed.ac.uk/__data/assets/pdf_file/0019/36082/CrisisRevised.pdf (retrieved 1 September 2010).
Mackenzie, D. (2009b) *Material Markets: How economic agents are constructed*, Oxford: Oxford University Press.

Polkinghorne, D.E. (1988) *Narrative Knowing and the Human Sciences*, Albany: State University of New York Press.

Preda, A. (2009) *Information, Knowledge, and Economic Life: An introduction to the sociology of markets*, Oxford: Oxford University Press.

Sassen, S. (2005) 'The embeddedness of electronic markets: the case of global capital markets', in K. Knorr Cetina and A. Preda (eds) *The Sociology of Financial Markets*, Oxford: Oxford University Press.

Smith, C.W. (1998) *Success and Survival on Wall Street: Understanding the mind of the market*, Lanham, MD: Rowman & Littlefield.

Tarim, E. (2009) 'Tilly's technical accounts and standard stories explored in financial markets: the case of the Istanbul Stock Exchange', *Sociological Research Online*, 14. Online, available at: www.socresonline.org.uk/14/5/21.html (retrieved 2 November 2010).

Tarim, E. (2010) 'Two waves of globalization in the Istanbul Stock Exchange since 1985 and the evolution of the domestic retail investor', *Competition and Change*, 14(3–4): 343–62.

Tilly, C. (2006) *Why? What happens when people give reasons ... and why*, Princeton, NJ: Princeton University Press.

Weick, K.E. (1995) *Sensemaking in Organizations*, London: Sage.

White, H. (2000) 'Modelling discourse in and around markets', *Poetics*, 27: 117–35.

9 What, me worry?

Deregulation and its discontents: accurate reality testing reveals flaws to deregulation

Seth Allcorn and Howard F. Stein

This chapter aims at understanding the current financial crisis in the United States and around the world. We ask, and attempt to answer, two questions: (1) how could the chairman of the Federal Reserve, Alan Greenspan, and countless others maintain for so long faith in a political ideology – deregulation – that had created so many negative outcomes since the 1980s; and (2) how could the ideology of deregulation so completely ignore the foibles of human nature that so often generate illogical, unrealistic and irrational outcomes such as Enron, WorldCom and Tyco – financial catastrophes and mismanagement that led to the 2002 Sarbanes–Oxley legislation?

Stated differently, why did so many government officials and politicians believe for so long that deregulation as a national policy would work? By extension, how could the reality it has created – massive problems – be so completely obliterated for over three decades? This chapter offers answers to these questions. We will develop the thought that three decades of poor risk management and 'mistakes' were unconsciously motivated by a fantasy-driven 'unreality principle'.

We begin by reviewing recent testimony by two government officials, then discuss the history of deregulation over several decades, and finally offer psychodynamically informed insight into what happened. We conclude by offering ideas for avoiding the blind embrace of misguided political and economic ideologies in the future.

Greenspan and Cox testimonials

In his testimony before the US Congress on 24 October 2008, Greenspan said that '[t]he whole intellectual edifice of modern risk management collapsed.... Those of us who have looked to the self-interest of lending institutions to protect shareholders' equity, myself especially, are in a state of shocked disbelief' (Suburban Energy Management Project 2008). Representative Henry Waxman asked Greenspan, 'Where do you think you made a mistake?' Greenspan replied:

> I made a mistake in presuming that the self interest of organizations, specifically banks and others, was such that they were best capable of protecting

their own shareholders and the equity in the firms. It's been my experience ... that the loan officers of those institutions knew far more about the risks involved and the people to whom they lent money than I saw in even our best regulators at the Fed were capable of doing. So the problem here is something that looked to build on a solid edifice, and indeed a critical pillar to market competition and free markets did break down. That shocked me.... When the facts change, I will change.

(ibid.)

At issue is the reality that the facts had long changed, but had been ignored. Note: as long ago as 1996, Alan Greenspan spoke of 'irrational exuberance' in response to the boundless enthusiasm of the tech bubble and the accompanying denial of economic reality, that the bubble would eventually burst. Clearly, there was some appreciation that a policy like deregulation, if blindly pursued as an end itself, was not immune to irrationality and human nature.

Consider a second example: Security and Exchange Commission chairman Christopher Cox's October 2008 roundtable discussion further attests to this failure of accurate reality testing. 'In October, Cox appeared at a roundtable that the agency was hosting at its Washington, D.C., headquarters. He delivered a tough, grim message: The federal government had failed taxpayers by not regulating the swaps market.' 'The regulatory black hole for credit-default swaps [a credit default swap (CDS) is a swap contract in which the buyer of the CDS makes a series of payments to the seller and, in exchange, receives a payoff if a credit instrument – typically a bond or loan – goes into default (fails to pay)] is one of the most significant issues we are confronting in the current crisis,' Cox said, 'and it requires immediate legislative action'. He continued:

The over-the-counter credit-default swaps market has drawn the world's major financial institutions and others into a tangled web of interconnections where the failure of any one institution might jeopardize the entire financial system. This is an unacceptable situation for a free-market economy.

(Dennis 2009)

Once again, the question is how the 'unacceptable' was acceptable, *for three decades*. The history of unregulated credit default swaps (CDSs) illustrates the fantastic fantasy-based dream-like nature of financial decision making, especially if one takes into account American International Group's (AIG) not setting aside reserves to cover the unregulated CDS instruments it insured. What, from the viewpoint of reality, is unacceptable became acceptable and preferred because it corresponded to the widespread belief that unfettered business practices invariably create wealth and prosperity supported by *no limits* to credit. Reality and information to the contrary did not matter.

To understand how this played out at the corporate level, consider Porter Stansberry (2008), who writes that

[a]lthough AIG's credit default swaps (CDS) were really insurance contracts, they weren't regulated. That meant AIG didn't have to put up any
capital as collateral on its swaps, as long as it maintained a 'triple A' credit
rating. There was no real capital cost to selling these swaps; there was *no
limit* [emphasis added]. And thanks to what's called 'mark-to-market'
accounting [a practice Enron aggressively pursued], AIG could book the
profit from a five-year credit default swap as soon as the contract was sold,
based on the expected default rate.

AIG's now infamous failure created a worldwide solvency threat.

The U.S. government took control of American International Group Inc.,
providing it a bailout to prevent the bankruptcy of the nation's biggest
insurer and the worst financial collapse in history. AIG's failure was not an
option due to its size and the dependence of the world-wide financial industry upon it.

(Son and Holm 2008)

Robert O'Harrow Jr and Brady Dennis, *Washington Post* staff writers, provide
insights into AIG's failure in their three-part article 'The beautiful machine'. The
following portion appeared on 1 January 2009:

AIG, once the largest and most profitable insurance company in the world,
failed last year, prompting a federal intervention because of its exposure to
credit-default swaps (CDSs) that help investors hedge their bets, thus
improving the liquidity and efficiency of financial markets. But, when sold
as insurance for shaky underlying assets CDSs increase systemic risk. AIG
sold $80 billion worth of subprime-related credit-default swaps on Wall
Street between 1998 and 2005.... Loss of their AAA rating prompted the
posting of additional collateral to back up its CDSs. When the company
could not come up with enough cash, the Federal Reserve and the Treasury
had to step in to avoid a credit-default swaps collapse that would bring the
world economy down.... In hindsight, it is clear that government regulation
was lacking regarding the CDS boom.

(O'Harrow and Dennis 2009)

Does this make any sense? We suggest it makes sense only within a context of
the fantasy-like altered reality of Wall Street and an unquestioned ideology of
deregulation.

The reality of deregulation

The lack of regulation in the United States has a long history dating back to the
Sherman Antitrust Act of 1890 and its subsequent enforcement by Theodore
Roosevelt and William Taft early in the twentieth century. The recent history of

deregulation, whether current or dating back thirty years, is similar except that with time the social and economic damage have increased.

In sum, thus far the statement by Greenspan about banks and others protecting their own shareholders and the equity in the firms leads us to reflect upon how a mistaken belief like this continues to exist in the face of abundant evidence to the contrary. We now underscore the profound nature of Greenspan's revelations with a brief overview of one of the worst examples of the undesirable outcomes of deregulation: the savings and loan fiasco that arose on President Reagan's watch.

The 1980s savings and loan deregulation scandal

In a CNN Money.com interview of 14 May 2008, billionaire George Soros said:

> Since the 1980s, the global financial system has been dominated by an ideo-logy I call market fundamentalism – the idea that markets are perfect and regulations are always flawed. But markets aren't perfect. Left to their own devices, they always go to extremes of euphoria or despair. The Federal Reserve and other regulators should recognize this, since they've had to bail out the markets in crisis after crisis since the 1980s.

The 1980s savings and loan scandal was the largest theft in the history of the world at that time and illustrates the doctrine of 'market fundamentalism'. How? Deregulation eased restrictions, permitting owners to lend to themselves. The government bailout cost the taxpayers around $1.4 trillion.

Wade Frazier (2008) notes, 'Deregulation was the buzzword of the Ronald Reagan administration, and "getting government off the public's back".' Ironically, the American public has never paid more dearly than it did during Reagan's deregulation. Many transactions during the S&L scandal were plainly fraudulent. One strategy was selling property back and forth to each other, raising the price each time.

Only recently has it been recognized that deregulation is a *problem*; since the early 1980s it has been seen as a vast cultural *solution*. As William Kleinknecht (2009) argues in his book *The Man Who Sold the World: Ronald Reagan and the betrayal of Main Street America*, the Reagan administration dismantled eight decades of social reform, replacing protection of workers with protection of corporate leaders.

Reflections

How can outcomes like these be explained? Gitlow describes how lobbying and political pressure compromised regulators such as the Securities and Exchange Commission:

> Lobbyists for special interest groups would contact relevant Congressmen and Senators. Their aides would contact Commission staff. If desired results

were not forthcoming, the contacts would go to higher levels of officialdom, and eventually could involve threats or reprisals against Commission budgets.

(2005: 106)

For instance, five senators (the Keating Five) – Alan Cranston (Democrat, California), Dennis DeConcini (Democrat, Arizona), John Glenn (Democrat, Ohio), John McCain (Republican, Arizona) and Donald W. Riegle (Democrat, Michigan) – were accused of improperly intervening in 1987 on behalf of Charles H. Keating Jr, chairman of the Lincoln Savings and Loan Association, which was the target of a regulatory investigation by the Federal Home Loan Bank Board (FHLBB). The FHLBB subsequently backed off taking action against Lincoln. Charles Keating, when asked if massive lobbying efforts had influenced the government officials, responded, 'I certainly hope so' (CBS News 2008).

An additional critical contributing factor is the constant search for new ways of doing business on Wall Street. This search led to the exploiting of loopholes, gaps and regulatory voids. Once these new methods are developed, they are steadfastly defended by the lobbying Gitlow describes.

Gitlow also notes that investor interests are not served by these outcomes:

Protection [of investors] becomes necessary when chief executives, possessors of unbridled power, become obsessed with greed, and exercise the power over their managerial lieutenants, directors, accountants, attorneys, securities dealers, bankers, financial analysts, and regulators so that all become complicit in the consequences of 'cooking the corporate books'.

(2005: 131)

The American individualist myth of 'bad apples' or 'lone wolves' needs to include deviant *group* processes in order to understand the 'success' of deregulation.

What is surprising, even shocking, is the fact that this financial and ethical debacle involved a breakdown of an elaborate structure of law, professional codes of conduct, and regulatory agencies that had grown up in the wake of the earlier stock market collapse of 1929, and the Great Depression that followed.

(ibid.)

The outcome of this unregulated market led to the extinction of many large investment banking companies or their transformation into other types of banking. Examples of these failures are Bear Stearns, Lehman Brothers, Goldman Sachs and Merrill Lynch. Many other financial institutions have been bailed out, such as Fannie Mae and Freddie Mack, Citigroup and Bank of America.

Deregulation can easily be shown to have generated many failures. How can a prominent advocate of deregulation say, 'I made a mistake in presuming that the self interest of organizations, specifically banks and others, was such that they were best capable of protecting their own shareholders and the equity in the firms', when there existed an overwhelming amount of evidence to the contrary (Suburban Energy Management Project 2008)? How can an ideology of deregulation and market fundamentalism continue to be embraced by a major political party?

Ideology and the failure to accurately test reality: the unreality principle

We begin to answer the question of why Greenspan and others continued to believe in deregulation, by exploring the unconscious and seductive elements of the ideology that led to the failure to accurately test reality. Consider the following interchange between Chairman Waxman and Alan Greenspan:

CHAIRMAN WAXMAN: You found a flaw in the reality...

FORMER CHAIRMAN GREENSPAN: In the model that I conceive of the critical function and structure of how the world works.

CHAIRMAN WAXMAN: In other words, you found that your view of the world – your ideology – was not right, that it was wanting.

FORMER CHAIRMAN GREENSPAN: Precisely. That's precisely the reason I was shocked, because I've been going for forty years or more with very considerable evidence that the model was working exceptionally well.

(Suburban Energy Management Project 2008)

It is convenient enough to focus on Greenspan's testimony and the painful vulnerability and disillusionment that lie within. He and his shocking realization may be regarded as signifying a larger and more problematic aspect of the global collapse. But individual focus is only part of the picture. Individual leaders are always part of groups. A large political party has unquestioningly maintained this ideological perspective for decades. Likewise, the American public and private enterprise seldom questioned the perversities generated by the implicit incentive of 'anything goes'. Was it really working so well for forty years, as Greenspan testifies? Also to be appreciated is that beyond American society, the institutions and societies of many other countries tacitly consented to support an alternative reality. If 'anything goes' and everyone is at the moment benefiting perhaps in greedy ways, why look a gift horse in the mouth? And, according to the rationalist-objectivist ideology that has long dominated economics, 'no limits' deregulation is desirable and realistic!

However, on a cautionary note, former chairman Greenspan notes:

Remember what an ideology is – a conceptual framework for the way people deal with reality. Everyone has one. You have to, to exist you need an ideology. The question is whether it is accurate or not. And what I am saying to you is yes, I found a flaw – I don't know how significant or permanent it is, but I have been very distressed by that fact.

(Suburban Energy Management Project 2008)

Beneath ideology: deregulation and the failure to consider human nature

We now focus on our second question: how could this ideology ignore the foibles of human nature? How could individual proclivities that include arrogance, aggression, greed and psychological defenses be overlooked? The darker side of human nature was ignored, largely owing to the power of wish and fear. Corporate excess speaks to the darker side. Likewise, the phenomenon of people buying houses they could not afford tellingly 'speaks' to unconscious processes of unbridled wishes. The widespread slogan 'No Limits', together with AIG's 'enabling' policies, attests to the work of greed and other unconscious dynamics. It is as if an entire cultural era bought into Ayn Rand's steely philosophy of 'objectivism' and business school belief that people look out rationally and realistically for their own enlightened self-interest. The result is that what is true about human motivation was suppressed, and what is false was elevated into sacred economic dogma. Ideological convictions about 'objective' economic decision making served to mask how profoundly 'subjective' (unconscious) such choices are.

Throughout this period, imperial CEOs and executives were well paid to crush opposition to their absolute authority.

We suggest that a picture emerges of a profound psychological 'fit' between historical context, cultural ethos, corporate identity, organizational group process, and the darker side of executive personalities. Only a cultural historical, political and organizational climate of deregulation and 'no limits' to ambition could have made a home for these leaders. The boundless narcissism and aggressive policies of corporate exploitative leaders was in part fueled by identification and unconscious collusion from employees, managers, shareholders and those numerous professionals supposedly responsible for keeping the ethical rudder of the organization on a straight course. Everyone was getting rich. Why worry?

Many, or most, 'mistakes' are unconsciously driven, by individuals or groups. When we hear somebody say or write that he or she was surprised to hear something from someone, we back up to wonder what that person expected or even needed the other person to say, and why. So when Greenspan says that bank loan officers 'knew far more' (a part of the fantasy; if lacking they could have been fired) than the Fed regulators, we would want to know why the bank officers were unable to act on that knowledge. Why were they driven to lend over and over again to people who were poor credit risks? Something unconscious drove the willingness to override reality and indulge in long-term risky behavior. What drove the denial of the riskiness embodied in the ideology of deregulation?

Ideology from a psychological and social perspective

To answer our second question we must first ask: what is ideology for? What functions does it serve? Why is it so compelling? Christopher Bollas (1992) reminds us that those who embrace an ideology maintain the conviction of its certainty via mental mechanisms aimed at eliminating all opposition. The ideo-logical mind ceases to be complex. Attention becomes overly focused and excludes all that is not contained in the ideology. Dogmatic certainty is the result. All opposition to it is edited out. Life and thought become streamlined, simplified and largely externally directed by incorporating the ideology into one's self-identity, creating self-direction. The rigid, closed nature of ideological thinking stifles heretical reflection because it is the unconscious function of ideo-logy to prevent reflection. This dynamic contributed to the reign of deregulation for decades.

The trouble is that ideology is not merely a cognitive map or conceptual model. Rather, it is a form of thought in which individuals and groups have deep emotional investments consistent with Bion's (1977) notion of valence. By its nature, ideology is not held provisionally. Those who are emotionally invested in it defend ideology as more precious than life itself – as evidenced by the last lines in the above Greenspan testimony. Most people, including organizational scholars and researchers, assume either that ideology is a cognitive/affective system that is a 'final cause' and requires no further explanation, or, in the Marxist tradition, is simply a reflection and rationalization of economic interests and power relations. Through much research dating as far back as Erich Fromm's pioneering *Escape from Freedom* (1941; see also Koenigsberg 1975), it has become clear that ideology rests in part upon unconscious fantasy and affect symptomatic of the 'unreality principle' that connotes an attitude towards the world oblivious to reality overriding reality through the free reign of fantasy, wish and unconscious processes.

The way ideology 'works' psychodynamically poses a paradox. On the one hand, in embracing an ideology one submits to cognitive and affective constric-tion. On the other hand, ideology promotes the projective construction of reality (individually and in a group), promoting unlimited exercise of the pleasure prin-ciple and/or the death instinct. Put differently, one can be imaginatively bound-less within the boundaries of ideology that sets one free from the confines of accurate reality testing. As a result, culturally dominant ideologies such as the free market, laissez-faire and deregulation are not only about 'themselves' but about something else that everyone knows but cannot (yet) put into words. Herein resides the 'stuff' of dreams and fantasies and the plausibility of an eco-nomic ideology not well grounded in accurate reality testing. Thus, political and economic ideologies turn out to be akin to the shared 'day residue' and 'manifest content' of dreams, creating the task of cultural dream interpretation (see Stein 1994) and the elucidation of the 'dream work' behind the socially shared dream (ideology).

The unreality principle: individual and group dynamics

James Glass's book *Psychosis and Power* (1995) links psychosis, ideology and public life. He writes, 'Power driven by delusion is vicious and sadistic, and delusion is no stranger to political actors and movements' (ibid.: 14). He argues that while individuals and groups may contain reality-oriented elements, under the pressure of anxiety and regression rigid black-and-white thinking that does not tolerate ambiguity emerges. When this is combined with paranoia, a real sense of threat arises. Glass addresses the paradox of unconscious inner emptiness and conscious outer arrogance: 'the core self feels empty, depleted, dry; barren; its appearance in adaptation may simulate aliveness, but the core experiences itself as dead' (ibid.: 185). Delusion, which symbolizes the death of knowledge and accurate reality testing, arises where 'existence is understood secretly in … terms of unreality, deadness, lack of being' (ibid.).

Finally, Glass situates ideology as a cognitive-affective solution to deep regression, inner emptiness and the flight from reality.

> A political ideology … that finds itself mired in closed systems of thought, in cultlike behavior, in racist and unyielding concepts of reality replays what on an infantile-developmental level might be understood as the paranoid/ schizoid position and its immersion in omnipotent power.
>
> (1995: 187)

Political and ideological formulations based on these dynamics are in flight from the external world with its competing demands. Political and economic ideologies that become massive sociocultural defenses form the basis of the unreality principle.

R.D. Hinshelwood (2009) has argued, similarly to Glass (1985, 1995), that in *destructive* social groups (such as those found in the recent history of the United States, we would add), certain ideas become overvalued as ideologies. It is the psychological function of ideological thought to overvalue certain ideas and at the same time radically devalue and exclude others. In turn, there is a blurring of boundaries between self and ideology: person is equated with idea. One does not merely have the idea, one embodies it. Destructive groups narrow and destroy thought. The group ideal, as embodied in the ideology, attempts to repair wounded narcissism. (For a study of how 'willful ignorance' undergirds and fuels ideology in the history of religion, see Carse 2008.)

Similarly, Gordon Lawrence writes that psychosis in general is

> the process whereby humans defend themselves from understanding the meaning and significance of reality, because they regard such knowledge as painful. To do this, they use aspects of their mental functioning to destroy, in various degrees, the very process of thinking that would put them in touch with reality.
>
> (2000: 4–5)

Individuals and organizational and cultural dynamics may share this outcome. The flight from distressing experience grounded in unreality becomes preferred, even required, over recognition and acceptance of reality (Burkard Sievers, email, 28 July 2009). Susan Long (2008) similarly notes that a perverse state of mind may acknowledge reality but also simultaneously deny it, leading to a state of fixed ideation and fantasy that protects against the pain of an awareness of reality and at the same time its denial. How, then, can reality bending of this nature be achieved?

The experience of unreality consists of an unbridled exercise of the pleasure principle and/or the repetition compulsion (in the service of mastering trauma and loss, or the death instinct). In groups, it finds expression in unconsciously driven 'basic assumptions' overwhelming and replacing reality-oriented 'work', or harnessing 'work' to the enactment of basic assumptions (dependency, fight/flight, revitalization, fusion into oneness, etc.; Bion 1959; Turquet 1974). Political and economic ideologies can serve as massive sociocultural defenses that uphold the unreality principle. These closed systems of thought (ideologies) keep the feelings of emptiness, weakness, separation and annihilation at bay. Political and economic ideologies leave no room for doubt but also *no room for critical or reflecting thinking*. Adherents to ideology do not learn from experience. Unconsciously driven ideology shapes experience. Tom Main (1985: 59) writes, '[S]ome meetings never develop reality-tested relations but remain gripped by an immovable collusive system with contributions and responses so dominated by mutual projective fantasies that good reality-testing is impossible and a general retreat into narcissistic mental models blocks all progress.'

Another perspective that sheds light on adherence to an ideology is Turquet's basic assumption of oneness. Oneness arises in groups 'when members seek to join in a powerful union with an omnipotent force, unobtainably high, to surrender self for passive participation, and thereby to feel existence, well-being, and wholeness' (1974: 357). The group embraces a cause or system of beliefs outside itself that serves to direct its worldview, how it interprets reality and responses to that interpretation.

The unreality principle leads us to conclude that ideology contains at its core strong emotion filled unconscious identifications with its precepts and subtext. People selectively embrace ideologies because they resonate with the self, creating highly personalized meaning for the ideology. Ideology and self are unconsciously merged and thereafter not readily known to oneself and others, or easily articulated. The ideology is right because it feels right – end of discussion. Evidence to the contrary is avoided (selective attention) or, if recognized, disposed of via denial, intellectualization and rationalization. The ideologically driven failures discussed here do not serve as cautionary tales. With reality mastered, the distressing experience of anxiety is avoided, allowing good feelings to emerge. Typical rationalizations may include assertion that the problems attributed to the ideology arose because of defects in implementation or that the failures are not attributable to the ideology or were already occurring when the ideology was implemented. For Greenspan – and, to his credit, he does recognize a flaw – he continues to hedge the reality of this knowledge by saying he does not know how significant or permanent the flaw is – whereas the flaw is in reality driven by human nature.

In a recent and timely article, David Tuckett and Richard Taffler (2008) explore how economic (stock market) decision making is heavily influenced (overdetermined) by fantasy, unreality, groupthink (Janis 1971), unconscious basic assumption thinking (Bion 1977) and the ignoring of emotions, while it is consciously governed by a presumably rational ideology of utility-maximizing behaviors. Investing is approached with repression of risk, and conscious thought affixed upon short-term reward in the risk/reward equation. Obsession with short-term reward in turn rests upon unconscious wish for and belief in a bountiful 'phantastic object' (Tuckett and Taffler 2008: 396–7), one that fulfills one's fantasies of omnipotence. We thus arrive at the fusion of protectively constructed reality, strong unconscious emotionally driven identification, fantasies and psychological defenses in support of this closed system of thinking and feeling that enables and enhances blindly adhered to ideology.

There are additional perspectives that provide insight into how rigid beliefs in the ideology of deregulation that ignore human nature and unconscious individual and group processes paradoxically make greed a societal good, and the absence of rules, regulations and limits a form of economic but disastrous freedom.

Compulsive repetition

It is a truism that those who do not learn from experience are doomed to repeat it. We should consider that repetition compulsion figures in somewhere in the recurrent pattern of regulation, deregulation and re-regulation including the subprime mortgage problem that started a worldwide recession. Each time a scandal arises due to non-regulation and deregulation, some people or institutions failed and/or were punished. Correcting legislation may have been enacted (e.g. Great Depression legislation and the Sarbanes–Oxley Act of 2002). Legislatures resolved to never let this kind of excess happen again, but regulating the darker side of human nature is not possible. 'Greed runs through the entire documentary [CNBC's documentary *House of Cards*]. Even Allan [*sic*] Greenspan at the end admitted that what happened will happen again at some point, and there is nothing anyone can do about it, because it's human nature to be greedy, bottom line' (Kroll 2009). Culturally as well as economically, we were unable to 'learn from experience' (Bion 1977), recreating avoidable error. So, we have to ask why the three decades of group/cultural sabotage and self-destruction were allowed to occur despite many disastrous outcomes.

Government is bad

Why have Americans so long resisted relying on regulating the economy? In part, Levine (2004) argues we have long harbored the fantasy of 'bad government' = 'big government', projecting onto government our inner bad objects, combating them 'in' the government, and perceiving ourselves as helpless victims at the hands of all-powerful oppressors. For Ronald Reagan, government was the problem. Big government takes our hard-earned money as taxes and limits and restricts what we can do, entangling small and large business in costly operating mandates.

In this psychodynamic view, the American ideology of 'freedom' is insepar-able from the experience of having 'oppressors' to overthrow – even if they are our own. Distressing propensities and desires are projected onto 'big govern-ment' and the battle against one's own impulses and internal objects is waged through an attack on the government. The world is thus simplified, as Bollas (1992) notes: We are good. Government is bad.

Autonomy versus submission

Americans have been quite ambivalent about autonomy and submission to authority. Americans ideologically prize inner-directedness, but, as David Riesman long ago (1953) wrote in *The Lonely Crowd*, Americans practice other-direction (currently called being 'a team player' – submitting to group author-ity). We think that we should be able to trust inner-direction (deregulation), but instead go wild and need to be reined in by outer-direction (re-regulation). We want to trust ourselves but prove that we cannot be trusted. We blame 'big gov-ernment' for 'interfering', but need 'Big Brother' to 'interfere' to set us straight again.

For Ronald Reagan, big government had to be slain. President Reagan essen-tially endorsed an oedipal revolt that had long lingered in policymaking. Amer-ica, ostensibly the land of opportunity, became a land of no-limits opportunism, unleashing greed and the darker side of human nature upon financial sector and economy.

Corporate 'groupthink', greed is good, and the post-9/11 ethos of 'Shop till you drop'

By now it should be clear that, in addition to timeless, universal unconscious process that opposes government regulation (greed, oedipal revolt), there are others that are more specific to the era from Ronald Reagan's presidency through the present. Attention to language provides an important clue. We argue that what Fed chairman Greenspan termed 'irrational exuberance' should be taken at its word in understanding deregulation and the utter failure of oversight.

The triumph of 'irrational exuberance' was accomplished via group process in organizations and between organizations. Individual corporate executives did not accomplish their high-flying sleight of hand alone. There was abundant silent, tacit and open complicity (enablement) that supported their increasingly bold fin-ancial activities. As Abraham Gitlow (2005) shows, the supposed gatekeepers of corporate integrity – including auditors, legal advisors, financial analysts, invest-ment bankers and regulatory bodies – all turned a blind eye to corporate fraud. The decision-making bodies of countless corporations engaged in what Irving Janis (1971) called 'groupthink', the mobilization of unwavering consensus and absolute loyalty to the leadership as the price of group membership.

Unchecked executive corporate greed and self-interest are in part a derivative of human nature and in part the outcome of 1980s 'Reaganomics'. Post-9/11 in the United States, an additional contribution was made. Shortly after the calamity, President George W. Bush admonished Americans to go out and shop, to prove to the Muslim terrorists that Americans were not afraid. The motto 'Shop till you drop' became a theme in the American ethos in the years that followed the attacks. Financially, this took the form of 'cheap, easy credit' (Personal News Network 2008). Bush helped initiate, direct and prolong the 'credit-fueled consumer binge' (Bacevich 2008: B03). In particular, Bush promoted home-ownership at almost any cost to the integrity of the finance industry. Manic housing purchases and consumer consumption propped up the US economy during most of the Bush presidency. This amounted to a counter-phobic hurtling into further cultural deregulation!

Solutions

What realistic solutions are possible that are not founded on magical thinking – that is, that are not part of the problem? Part of a dawning recognition of the reality of the past three decades consists in awakening from the cultural trance in which we have been so invested. It is a making of the largely unconscious conscious, and in the process gaining the hope of shaping a future that does not repeat the past. Further, as Gitlow writes,

> We should have learned that the solution lies in encouraging and stimulating a willingness to speak to that power when it moves in the wrong directions. But that is a devilishly difficult outcome to achieve, because power is the ability to inflict pain, and pain is a huge deterrent to challenging power.
>
> (2005: 131)

'Speaking truth to power' (Kennedy and Adams 2007) carries with it the risk of disclosing the organizational secret that everyone knows but cannot acknowledge. The organizational whistle-blower is bullied and often fired.

In order to move on, we must first accept the magnitude of the losses and grieve for them, including ultimately the trauma of a near-depression (an economic 9/11) and, for many, the loss of the country's values to an ideology of no limits. We must retrieve those thoughts and feelings we have dissociated and projected onto others to reduce the attendant anxiety these defenses introduce, thus reducing regressive tendencies and psychological defensiveness that contribute to unreality. To be liberated from the past, we must first be able to acknowledge that it happened and that we all are in some measure responsible for 'it' happening.

References

Bacevich, A. (2008) 'He told us to go shopping. Now the bill is due', 3 October, B03. Online, available at: www.washingtonpost.com/wp-dyn/article/2008/10/03/AR20088 100301977_pf.html (retrieved 24 February 2009).

Bion, W.R. (1959) *Experiences in Groups*, New York: Basic Books.

Bion, W.R. (1977) *Learning from Experience*, in *Seven Servants: Four Works by Wilfred R. Bion*, New York: Jason Aronson.

Bollas, C. (1992) *Being a Character: Psychoanalysis and self experience*, New York: Hill & Wang.

Carse, J. (2008) *The Religious Case against Belief*, New York: Penguin.

CBS News (2008) 'Keating scandal haunts McCain', 24 March. Online, available at: www.cbsnews.com/stories/2008/03/24/politics/main3964240.shtml?source=RSSattr=P olitics_3964240 (retrieved 4 August 2010).

Dennis, B. (2009) 'A meek ending for mighty unit that gutted AIG', *Washington Post*, 21 February. Online, available at: www.washingtonpost.com/wp-dyn/content/art-icle/2009/02/20/AR2009022003304_pf.html (retrieved 29 February 2009).

Frazier, W. (2008) 'The savings and loan scandal and public accounting', *The Home Page of Wade Frazier*, December. Online, available at: www.ahealedplanet.net/savings. htm#doomed (retrieved 30 December 2008).

Fromm, E. (1941) *Escape from Freedom*, New York: Farrar & Rinehart.

Gitlow, A. (2005) *Corruption in Corporate America: Who is responsible? Who will protect the public interest?*, Lanham, MD: University Press of America.

Glass, J.M. (1985) *Delusions: Internal dimensions of political life*, Chicago: University of Chicago Press.

Glass, J.M. (1995) *Psychosis and Power*, Ithaca, NY: Cornell University Press.

Hinshelwood, R.D. (2009) 'Ideology and identity: a psychoanalytic investigation of a social phenomenon', *Psychoanalysis, Culture and Society*, 14: 131–48.

Janis, I. (1971) 'Groupthink', *Psychology Today*, 5(6): 43–4, 46, 74–6.

Kennedy, K. and Adams, E. (2007) *Speak Truth to Power: Human rights defenders who are changing our world*, Brooklyn, NY: Umbrage Editions.

Kleinknecht, W. (2009) 'Reagan brought America to ruin', *Oklahoma Observer*, 25 February: 18. Online, available at: www.okobserver.net/wp-content/uploads/2009/02/ 22509observer.pdf.

Koenigsberg, R. (1975) *Hitler's Ideology: A study in psychoanalytic sociology*, New York: Library of Social Sciences.

Kroll, J. (2009) 'House of cards', ActiveRain, 16 February. Online, available at: http:// activerain.com/blogsview/936215/house-of-cards (retrieved 5 May 2009).

Lawrence, W.G. (2000) 'Thinking refracted', in *Tongued with Fire: Groups in experi-ence*, London: Karnac.

Levine, D. (2004) *Attack on Government: Fear, distrust, and hatred in public life*, Char-lottesville, VA: Pitchstone.

Long, S. (2008) *The Perverse Organisation and Its Deadly Sins*, London: Karnac.

Main, T. (1985) 'Some pyschodynamics of large groups', in A. Colman and M. Geller (eds) *Group Relations Reader 2*, Washington, DC: A.K. Rice Institute.

O'Harrow, R. and Dennis, B. (2008) 'The beautiful machine', *Washington Post*, 31 December. Online, available at: www.washingtonpost.com/wp-dyn/content/article/ 2008/12/31/AR2008123102771_pf.html (retrieved 3 January 2009).

Personal News Network (24 September 2008) 'El Qaeda, not Wall Street is to blame', Isabar.pnn.com. Online, available at: http://isabar.pnn.com/articles/show/24816-el-qaeda-not-wall-street-is-to-blame (retrieved 14 February 2009).

Riesman, D. (1953) *The Lonely Crowd*, New Haven, CT: Yale University Press.

Son, H. and Holm, E. (2008) 'Fed takes control of AIG with $85 billion bailout', *Bloomb-erg*, 17 September. Online, available at: www.bloomberg.com/apps/news?pid=206010 87&sid=a6QAz6YiyRAI&refer=home (retrieved 31 January 2009).

Soros, G. (2008) 'Soros: global investing's godfather', *CNNMoney.com*, 14 May. Online, available at: http://money.cnn.com/2008/05/12/pf/soros_interview.moneymag/index. htm?postversion=2008051404 (retrieved 20 April 2009).

Stansberry, P. (2008) 'How AIG's collapse began a global run on the banks', *Daily-Wealth*, 7 October. Online, available at: www.dailywealth.com/archive/2008/oct/2008_oct_04.asp (retrieved 24 March 2009).

Stein, H. (1994) *The Dream of Culture*, New York: Psyche Press.

Suburban Energy Management Project (2008) 'Federal regulators' role in financial markets: house hearing on the 2008 global financial crisis', *Suburban Energy Management Project*, 4 November. Online, available at: www.semp.us/publications/biot_reader.php?BiotID=552 (retrieved 30 December 2008).

Tuckett, D. and Taffler, R. (2008) 'Phantastic objects and the financial market's sense of reality: A psychoanalytic contribution to the understanding of stock market instability', *International Journal of Psychoanalysis*, 89: 389–412.

Turquet, P. (1974) 'Leadership: the individual and the group', in A. Coleman and M. Geller (eds) *Analysis of Groups*, San Francisco: Jossey-Bass.

10 The failure of risk management in the financial industry

The organization in the mind of financial leaders

Byron Woollen

The industry let the growth and complexity in the new instruments outstrip their economic and social utility as well as the operational capacity to manage them.
(Lloyd Blankfein, CEO Goldman Sachs, 'Goldman Chief Admits Banks Lost Control', *Financial Times*, 9 September 2009)

For those interested in the organizational and psychodynamic aspects of the 2008 financial crisis, Blankfein's statement merits close attention. One year after the collapse of Lehman Brothers, Blankfein suggests that the financial industry as a whole was severely compromised by organizations that had neither an appropriate appreciation of the complexity of investment risk, nor the operational rigor to manage it. What is not explicit in Blankfein's comment, that which is left for us to interpret, is an understanding of what motivated the leadership of these organizations to ignore both the irrational quality of their pursuit and the limitations of their organizations. What would motivate those at the top of their industry to 'let' themselves take risks that led to such an extraordinary failure? Greed and power have served as quick answers and have fueled a populist backlash against the financial industry. But a more descriptive analysis of the systemic dysfunction and leadership of these financial institutions is called for.

Two cases are borrowed from the author's work consulting to Wall Street over the past decade (banks, hedge funds, endowments and insurers) to illustrate a structural deficiency that has become endemic to this industry. The issue presents in three forms:

1   The leadership of many banks and funds is, for reasons that will be described, psychologically vulnerable to fantasies that distract them from the reality of the markets in which they work.
2   Financial institutions are often led, managed and resourced in a way that compromises the necessary integration among complementary functions. The disciplined interchange between the investment and control (operations/ administration) functions that is essential to appropriately understand and manage the complexity of contemporary investment risk is undermined by a

systemic conflict between these areas. This is a conflict that is either exacerbated or controlled by organizational culture.

3   Management of risk is generally appointed to a specific role or process (increasingly to software-based algorithms) rather than being contained by developing a culture that allows all organizational members who participate in the system of investing to participate.

Given the destructive potential of these issues for the financial industry and well beyond, how do we understand the pervasiveness of such organizational failures? What insights can we offer about how the role of leader in financial organizations plays on the psychology of those who take the role? And what models are available as object lessons for how this organizational dynamic might be better managed to produce more resilient organizations? These are questions grappled with here. Both the cases offered in this review are of large money management firms, but there are other examples cited based on turmoil in the banking and insurance industries. In all cases, the analysis applies for any business in which profit is realized purely from the leverage of capital.

What can money tell us about desire?

An investment professional's work plays at the margin between hard analysis and magic. Good investors anchor their bets on reasoned judgments based in research and modeling, but in all cases they are hoping that their thesis predicts events in the future. When successful, their investments render profits and the analyst feels the thrill of turning an idea into money. The emotional stimulation of this practice is played down in the industry, but in less guarded moments the thrill realized shows itself. As one successful portfolio manager told me, 'We turn straw into gold.' Evoking the magical dwarf of fairy tales reveals the excited pleasure that comes when one is able to 'create' money, like the childhood fantasy of finding treasure and from it gaining all the associated rewards of power, acquisition and potential. And, as in the story of Rumpelstiltskin, the limits of desire dissolve further with each successful transformation of something with no monetary value (an idea) into greater wealth. The acquisition of money is different from that of other objects because money is abstract and can mutate endlessly into other forms (objects, services, influence or power). Its accumulation destabilizes our understanding of what we need by stimulating the potentially limitless quality of our appetite. Most importantly, money is used to create more money, and no matter how vast the profit, our appetite for more expands to accommodate. In his essay 'Money mad', Adam Phillips describes money as that which

> always promises something other than itself – it is only, as we say, worth what it can buy – it seems to protect us, as promises do, from the fear of there being nothing and no one that we want. Nothing around that

makes appetite – or its derivatives, faith, hope, curiosity – worth having. Not desiring is far more daunting a prospect than the availability of what one desires.

(2005: 154)

For those in the financial world for whom the numbers describing profit drift towards abstraction, where many investment leaders realize personal wealth that overwhelms their ability to spend it, money can become something else: a fetish that defies limits and multiplies desire. Compared to the Kleinian description of voracious greed aimed at aggressive dominance through destruction (Klein 1975), Phillips suggests that money's tendency to perpetuate the unconscious fantasy of infinite appetite – without any particular object (reality) towards which it is aimed – may be even more disruptive than greed to the ability to form and maintain productive relationships, including one's relationship to reality. Where greed is a solution to control the unobtainable object, the protean fetish of money protects us from the depressive oblivion that waits should we ever exhaust our desire.

As an example, take Charles Prince III's now infamous comment 'When the music stops, in terms of liquidity, things will be complicated. But as long as the music is playing, you've got to get up and dance. We're still dancing' (Kaufman 2007). This is rife with suggestions that the leader of one of the world's largest financial institutions was inexplicably cavalier about risks that his company was taking – 'things will be complicated'. His metaphor evokes the game of 'musical chairs' in which participants are thrilled by the complete lack of control of knowing when the music will stop and accept that all participants but one will be 'done in' by the surprise. But how could the CEO of such an institution tolerate participation in this game unless he believed that he was, as Phillips suggests, 'protected' by the magical promises inherent in great wealth?

In contrast, the leader of an investment group (the second case offered here) was able to guide his firm through the same crisis with no significant loss. We can acknowledge the greater degrees of complexity involved in leading an enormous global financial institution. But no matter the size of the institution, the chief executive's mandate is always that he (or she) uses his authority to enforce the containment of risk – that he has an appropriate and realistic fear about the potential threats to his enterprise. In Prince's case, his sense of accountability became confused as he felt compelled to move to outside forces (the 'music' in his terms) for fear of missing out on what he acknowledges to be short-term gains. The leader of the investment group, on the other hand, was able to maintain a clearer sense of his accountability by recognizing that the fear of missing out on a rally is 'greed, not fear'.

The investment organization in the mind

If those leading financial institutions are vulnerable to fantasies that soothe their fears of limitation and absence, then an attunement to limitation – an important guide for any leader – is inherently antagonistic. Distinguishing between different types of fear is instructive. The healthy fear of loss should fuel risk aversion, while the fear of missing out on a perceived opportunity (speculation) fuels the desire for more – a desire that clouds attention to risk. We could anticipate that the leaders who suffer from the latter type of fear would suffer from a distorted psychic representation of the organization; that the organization in the mind of these leaders would reflect both the unconscious belief about the power of money and a primitive hostility to limitation. More than an imbalance, there would be a conflict between the way that the investing (profit-making) and control (cost) entities were represented in the minds of these leaders. To confirm this hypothesis, we should look for evidence of degraded structures, authority and accountability in the control functions of these firms, while investment functions and roles are subject to forms of collective idealization.

The structure of the investment organization has always depended on the interplay between the minority who make the investments (analysts, traders) and the distinctly less powerful, though larger, group that see to it that investments are managed appropriately. With the increased complexity of the financial world, the need for greater transparency and collaboration between these functions has become more pronounced. With the advent of more interrelated markets (e.g. housing and securities) and investment instruments like derivatives, swaps and structured investment vehicles (SIVs), investment risk can no longer be fully contained only by those analyzing and making the investments. Given the bespoke quality and lack of transparency inherent in some of these products, those working in the control functions of the financial industry (valuation, technology, settlement, accounting, legal, tax, etc.) must keep pace with the increasingly exotic nature of the investments if the risks that they pose are to be managed.

Blankfein's critique of his industry (Jenkins 2009) states plainly that this level of collaboration has not been successful. These businesses found themselves in crisis, in part, because their capacity for control through operational rigor did not keep pace with the demands made by the investments. This is all the more puzzling given that the imbalance cannot be due to a lack of financial resources at the disposal of these companies, nor can it be blamed on a shortage of intellectual or technical ability that could have been applied. At a superficial level, the diminished controls are due to neglect. At a deeper level, the inability of some leaders to attend to the full organization is evidence of a more hostile enactment against those entities that demand attention to reality testing and control. Rather than allowing realities (including their embodiment in organizational functions) to modify the experience of pleasure, they are ignored or denigrated in an effort to keep alive an unfettered relationship with desire. A flagrant example of this is the starkly irrational disregard for risk in the case of AIG. The company sold hundreds of billions of dollars of insurance in the form of credit default swaps, without any attention – in fact an active disregard for – the necessary capital reserves required for insurance calls (Taibbi 2009; Lewis 2010; Lowenstein 2010).

In contrast, there were financial leaders who not only were able to balance the ideas of reward *and* risk in their own minds, but also saw to it that the organizations they led were shaped to manage both. As described in *Fool's Gold*, Gillian Tett's excellent account of the derivatives trade at J.P. Morgan Chase, Jamie Dimon saw his bank through financial turmoil by consistently empowering not only the profit makers but also the control functions. Tett describes a powerful symbolic statement by Dimon, who on his first trip to London as CEO left the investment bankers of the City of London waiting for hours while he first visited the IT department in the suburbs. Dimon raised the compensation for those working in risk management to the point where traders moved to work in the area, and he fought an overly 'siloed' culture by having a special dining room built so that managing directors from different areas would meet and talk 'eye to eye' (Tett 2009: 114).

My own experience, both in financial organizations that have successfully managed the balance of risk and reward and in those that have not, supports this hypothesis and suggests that there are specific challenges that are too often underestimated by financial leaders. The lack of personal insight into the effects of money on one's unconscious life is an obvious issue that can be, but too often is not, addressed by leaders. At the more concrete level of organizational structures and processes, the necessary level of collaboration calls on leaders to be mindful of several things:

- Those working in financial operations must be motivated and offered resources to tolerate a process of constant adaptation if they are to be able to process new forms of investment in a way that mitigates risk for the organization.
- Just as technology and models change frequently for analysts, so do the processes and systems within the non-investment functions antiquate quickly, calling for fresh resources to upgrade.
- The asymmetrical power relationship between analyst and control functions is challenging to manage. Control functions must be provided with sufficient authority and respect so that they may reasonably be expected to raise issues with investment professionals that may influence their practices.
- Tolerance for mistakes in the investment and non-investment areas is also asymmetrical. An investor who profits on every investment is guilty of being overly conservative and not taking enough risk. For those in operations, even minor mistakes are often conflated with failure, owing to their potential to only erode profit. If the internal response to mistakes is not appropriately managed within non-investment functions, those working there will quickly develop a culture that is antithetical to learning and change.

When these issues are not appropriately addressed, investment organizations are susceptible to being inadequately developed. The result then replicates within the company the compromised organization as held in the mind of the leader.

Two cultures form: the culture of the analyst, in which investor professionals are overly credited with the complete success of the firm and are not asked to consider their part in a larger system; and the culture of control, in which employees take on a passive stance vis-à-vis the counterparts who invest. At its worst, the culture of 'back office' fosters a demeaned control environment with resulting high turnover, diminished morale and employees passively retreating from their roles. It is an organizational schism that allows the investment leader to perpetuate the expansion of desire by unconsciously degrading internal functions that might otherwise keep important limits in mind.

The following case describes a well-reputed investment group that found itself surprised and unprepared for the turmoil produced during the credit crisis of 2008. My involvement with the firm followed on the heels of its beginning a major restructuring of the operation and risk functions.[1]

Cummings Capital

Coming from a large hedge fund in the Midwest, Roy took over as CEO of Cummings Capital following the departure of the previous leader, David, who held the position for just under two decades. During David's tenure, Cummings had multiplied its assets under management many times, leaving the firm with a sterling reputation in the industry.

Believing that he had time to get settled before he made any significant changes to the firm's strategy, Roy immersed himself in better understanding the firm's portfolio of investments. The day-to-day work progressed well, but Roy's research into the investments left him with a growing sense of unease. Like many funds, Cummings had realized strong returns by leveraging its assets. Liquidity was also challenged by a large number of illiquid investments in other funds. All of this combined to create a situation in which if Cummings needed capital, there was little that could be quickly liquidated. Added to this, Roy became increasingly unsettled by the difficulty he had getting clear data about the state of the portfolio. The risk team working under him was slow to produce the information that he requested and much of what he reviewed came to him in a series of antiquated and confusing reports. As Roy hoped to gain confidence from meetings with his chief risk officer, he found instead that his concerns about the funds' lack of liquidity only escalated. The risk officer seemed strangely detached and less than fully responsive to Roy's concerns.

Roy began to move certain positions out of the Cummings portfolio and slowly invest in assets that offered greater liquidity should it be needed. Then, in September of that year, Lehman Brothers collapsed and Roy lost the time that he had counted on to shift the risk profile of his portfolio. Within a month, a significant portion of the Cummings AUM (assets under management) had disappeared. Assets in the portfolio shrank and several funds that had been invested in either lost money or folded.

Working to salvage the fund, Roy immersed himself in his organization. He continued to have difficulty gaining clear information about the status of investments and risk profiles. The difficulty was exacerbated by an operations function working with inappropriate and antiquated systems that were challenged when it came to tracking the complexity of the firm's portfolio at the speed that was necessary to keep up with shifts in the markets. The managers in this area were stressed and often ineffective at getting better results from a staff that seemed largely disassociated from the sense of crisis that was pervasive among the analysts. Some in the investing teams damned the people working in operations, and operational staff resisted changing their methods. When questioned about why a process or report was being executed in a way that rendered sub-par results, operational managers and staff would often resist a deeper involvement in problem solving, displaying a vague confusion about why past processes would not suffice to meet future needs.

Following the period of crisis and with a restructuring of the operations already under way, I was hired by Roy to conduct an organizational assessment. In particular, he wanted insight into the causes for what he perceived as an operational group that was dangerously uninterested in coordinating to produce the level of reporting and feedback that the investment professionals needed to manage investment risk. After interviewing nearly a third of the company, I offered the following insight.

During the years under the previous leadership, David had expertly managed the investing group's success. His directives to the investors were clear, and when they were successful, he rewarded them handsomely. He was not tyrannical, but when a portfolio manager failed to meet the benchmarks for success, he was replaced. The analysts accepted this arrangement and admired their leader's firm control and clear accountability. But his leadership of Cummings as a resilient business was more qualified. The state of the organization following his departure revealed that the culture at Cummings was too singularly focused on the success and power of its investment leaders. In this environment, responsibility for managing investment risk was neither sufficiently shared throughout the organization nor appropriately monitored by the firm's board. The leader of the previous operations group (the chief operating officer, COO) was universally recognized as ineffective and had never successfully advocated for his people. As a result, systems and technology had fallen far behind the state of the art, no management or talent development was offered and process improvement was only initiated following operational failures and the occasional harsh feedback from the investment function. Change was generally reactive, slow and insufficient.

The control functions at Cummings deteriorated because those working there had accepted the heroic, nearly infallible image of the previous CEO. Unwittingly, David had promoted this attitude by fully authorizing only those on the investment side and simultaneously engendering a passive complacency within operations. His unspoken pact was that if they would not create management and organizational development challenges for him, then he would ask the minimum of them in return. Over time, the control function became inadequate to its task and the attitude of the investment teams towards those processing their investments ranged from indifferent to disdainful.

From Roy's point of view, there were issues with some of the investments that he inherited, but, more importantly, the complexity of the overall portfolio, and the interplay between certain assets held, could not be fully appreciated and adjusted, given the information provided by Cumming's control functions.

Diminished authority and control

In the Cummings case, the leader's unconscious hostility towards the recognition of critical limits was made manifest in the organization he led. This occurred through promoting an idealization of the role of investor (he-who-would-always-bring-in-more-money) by fostering a culture of passivity and deterioration within the control functions, by allowing the investing functions to perpetuate a contemptuous devaluation of their colleagues in operations and by keeping in place a weak COO who was never given the authority to do what the organization needed of him. Contrary to what one might imagine, the atmosphere for those in operations during David's tenure was not felt to be oppressive. In fact, at the time of my interviews, people were terrifically nostalgic about those days. Those in operations (but, interestingly, never those in the investing function) described the company as feeling like a 'family'. The analogy carries positive associations of comfort, security and protection, but when these qualities reach an extreme by evoking 'family', it is rarely good for a business. Businesses count on employees having sufficient commitment and protection to allow them to focus on their work, but they also must tolerate straight talk, challenge, conflict, change, competition, personal risk and prioritizing the mission of the organization over the feeling of comfort. A business like Cummings need not promote an ethic of ruthlessness to succeed, but it must have a leader who appreciates the need to exert his or her authority for the good of the firm. It needs someone who challenges the workforce, who sets high expectations for learning and improvement and who will move a person out of a role or out of the company when the circumstances call for it. The fact that David proved so competent at driving his authority among the investors but withheld this same degree of influence on operations suggests that his negligence was, at some level, motivated, rather than due to a lack of ability or will.

If we're tempted to think of Cummings as an anomaly, we only need consider the stories of the multibillion-euro losses blamed on SocGen trader Jerome Kerviel in 2008 (Clark and Jolly 2008), the collapse of Barings Bank following the rogue trading of Nick Leeson (Stevenson 1995), the demise of Amaranth Advisors following Brian Hunter's $6 billion loss on natural gas investments (Anderson 2006), or Joseph Cassano, who sold nearly half a trillion dollars worth of credit default swaps (CDSs) for AIG (Taibbi 2009) without that company holding even a fraction of that amount on hand. In each case, subsequent investigations proved that these 'rogue' investors were working within systems that either ignored or failed to have in place the appropriate controls to monitor risk or, in some cases, even to adequately monitor trading activity. In each case, the potential of the investing function was idealized and those managing control were denied the necessary authority and resources they needed to fulfill their role.

As further evidence of the hostile enactment against limitation, in several cases (Cassano at AIG being the most recent) there were incidents in which brave internal watchdogs attempted to raise concerns about investing practices and were angrily shut down by the more powerful above them (Taibbi 2009).

Leadership practice in an integrated financial organization

How, then, does the leader of such an organization avoid the dangerous organizational pitfalls described above? What practices offer a better prognosis and the potential for leaders to navigate the intense psychological pressures they come under when serving in this role? The following case describes a leader who has successfully shepherded his firm through the recent financial upheavals by instilling in employees his own awareness that attention to the potential for loss deserves as much attention as the focus on reaping rewards.

His advantage to date is due to a disciplined adherence to three principles:

* An investor who does not monitor his or her own potential for greed will never appropriately attend to the inherent risks of his investment. Setting a personal or organizational standard for the greatest profit possible only incites the taking of counterproductive risks when investing.
* Long-term orientation. Striving for short-term gains fuels the sort of speculative investment that ignores important risks.
* Rather than focus on profit, emphasize excellence in execution. This can serve as a cultural standard for the entire organization and help ensure that all functions meet expectations.

Frost enterprise

Nat had served as CEO of Frost Enterprise since its inception. Although he started with relatively modest assets under management, Nat achieved steady returns by sticking to an investment strategy that prioritized excellence in execution, managing risk as aggressively as he managed returns, and holding all of his analysts to a standard of absolute intellectual integrity when it came to betting on various assets. As an organizational leader, Nat took it as a given that those supporting the investment functions needed to meet the same level of performance as he demanded from his investment analysts. He hired Sal, the COO, to whom he gave complete authority over operations and who had an equal seat among the senior partners in the investment area. Sal's job was to ensure that his capacity for control kept pace with the growing size and complexity of AUM.

Over time, Nat's patience and discipline resulted in his firm growing and attracting capital from those who were impressed by Frost Enterprise's ability to avoid the financial landmines that diminished other investment groups. I was asked to consult to the firm to help rethink organizational design and processes so as to better address the company's expansion.

One of my first impressions of the firm was of the consistency of the organizational culture. The values made explicit by Nat's attitude towards investing were known throughout the organization. A junior accountant would be able to speak to what Nat prioritized and what behaviors he would not abide. Mutual respect was not only mouthed as an organizational priority but demonstrated daily in the interactions among people and the environments in which they worked. For example, in contrast to my experience in most firms, where the operational areas are decidedly less well appointed and resourced than the floors and rooms occupied by the investors, Frost's operational areas mirrored the comforts enjoyed by those in its investing function. No one was in any doubt that the control functions held equal power to the investors; they were handsomely paid and given voice in company decisions.

While Frost passed through the credit crisis relatively unscathed, the continued growth of the firm and the greater complexity of the investment opportunities (derivatives, CDSs, structured products) stressed the organization. Many more hires were made in the operational area and the demands on these employees grew exponentially as they were required to work through and offer feedback to the analysts on the intricacies of the portfolio. During this time, friction between investing and operations emerged in a more serious fashion than heretofore, as those in operations – living up to the ethos of sharing in the monitoring and management of risk – dutifully pushed back against certain investment practices. The concern on the operational end was that without the appropriate planning and adjustments made beforehand, these highly complex investments could overwhelm their ability to maintain systems and reporting that would clearly define risk for the enterprise. The analysts, who had historically counted on Frost's operational capacity to manage any investment they made, found it unsettling that their ambition might be curbed. Nat found himself needing to respond to some analysts who questioned whether he was going to let 'the tail wag the dog' and to operational managers who felt strongly that the risk-averse culture of the firm might be compromised. Sal supported Nat by continuing to build the organization that the investors needed, but his feedback to Nat about the potential risks of complex investments in an environment of rapid growth was consistent.

Sophisticated in his appreciation of organizational behavior, Nat was aware that the firm's culture might change for the worse if those in the control functions began retreating from their roles in reaction to the anxiety being held by their area. In response, he, Sal and I designed an offsite workshop that brought the heads of investing together with the heads of the operational units. The goal was to foster a deeper appreciation of each side's changing responsibilities and for Nat to drive home the message that Frost would continue to be a single business in which every role was necessary, appropriately authorized and resourced. The offsite culminated in the formation of a new committee, reporting to Nat and Sal, comprising two senior investors and two senior operational managers.

The committee's mission was to bring to the surface issues that might compromise efficiency, collaboration and the culture at large.

Within the first year of its existence, the committee members offered a thoughtful critique of the way those in leadership – specifically Nat, Sal and the management committee – were now holding their roles. They reported that with the rapid growth of the firm, authority and accountability had become diffuse in the larger organization, resulting in confusion around priorities. One result of this confusion was that certain operational areas were taking a protectionist posture that confounded collaboration. Nat and Sal took the committee's report seriously and made changes to the management committee's agenda so that discrepancies in operational strategy could be brought to the surface, resolved and corrected through the firm. Nat also made it clear that while investing would always be the engine that drove the enterprise, he needed senior operational managers to work through any idealization of the investors that might inhibit their responding aggressively when they saw risks to the firm.

One of Nat's great advantages as an investment professional was his awareness of the potentially corrosive effects that money has on judgment. He spoke and wrote often about the potential for the pursuit of great profit to blind people to the more advised approach of weighing risk against return. Nat understood a variation of what Phillips described: that the protean potential of money can engender a sense of magical protection from the unpredictable – or even predictable – calamities that trigger loss. Part of Nat's mission as chief executive had been to put in place rigorous hiring and development practices that acculturated his analysts to tolerate the experience of missing out on the possibility to gain more profit when the potential risks suggested greater prudence; to become comfortable, over years of supervised practice, with saying 'no' to opportunities – especially when the markets and Frost's competitors tempted them to bend their investment philosophy for an opportunity that seemed extraordinary. Part of the ethos of investing imparted by Nat to his analysts was that they must learn to monitor the emotional disturbance that is inevitable, as they work in an industry that would radically transform their material lives.

The ability to realize strong profit defines power within these financial organizations, and consequently the power relationship between analysts and those in operations is never equal. While the personal wealth of those in operations at Frost could never compare with that of their colleagues in the investing function, the distribution of profits to employees contributed to an unproductive psychological effect that was challenging to manage. For the senior managers in the operations areas, the investors' acumen resulted in their lives and the lives of their families being materially changed to a degree that most had never dreamed of. This, combined with the stature of these investment professionals locally and in the financial world, made these managers and staff vulnerable to abandoning a realistic assessment of their colleagues in favor of unproductive idealization. It took the experience of the investing/operations committee, formed following the offsite, to recognize through their own process the degree to which those in operations often took an overly deferential posture in relation to their colleagues in the trading room. By passing on the committee's experience in presentations to other senior leaders, a process was begun in which operational leaders were asked directly by Nat to rethink the way that they took their roles in relation to their investor colleagues.

A consciousness about money's influence on the psychology of individuals in the firm was a defining advantage for Frost Enterprise compared to competing firms like Cummings. In contrast to Frost, the leadership at Cummings perpetuated an unproductive dependency on their CEO. David became comfortable as a patriarchal figure and mistook complacency for an environment of strong morale where, to his relief, few complained. Unwittingly, he fostered a patriarchal culture that stimulated a regressed sense of well-being in which the father provided abundance and managed risks to the family. For their part, operational staff contented themselves with the daily execution of tasks and gave little thought to questioning or improving their process.

A culture of risk management

The leadership of the organizations described here is noted for contributing significantly to whether or not each financial firm was able to anticipate and adapt to changes in markets. Both leaders share the quality of swaying the organizational culture with a charisma that bonded people to their mission and contributed the basic assumption posture (Bion 1961) taken by the firm as a whole. During profitable, less challenging years it was easy for both firms to fall into a position of dependency on the nearly magical figure who oversaw the process of creating wealth for all employees. In David's case, the leader and his followers colluded to build an organization that perpetuated that dependency and strangled opportunities in the system for information to flow up and correct investment practices. In the other case, the equally charismatic leader, Nat, used his influence to build an ethos of suspicion in which it was assumed that things no one had ever anticipated might emerge and threaten the business. The depressive position (Klein 1975) fostered by Nat was one in which he regularly spoke of the potential vulnerability of the firm and the need to remain vigilant to the loss that could be inflicted from unanticipated change. To monitor for the unexpected, he made it clear that he needed a system-wide adherence to identifying internal obstacles that might stifle communication about investment risk. By focusing on excellence of practice as a means to realize an end of investment success, he promoted an idea of the organization with which employees eagerly identified. For most of his followers, Nat's idea of Frost became an idealized object that, once internalized, bolstered their personal sense of meaning and so became a part of an identity that they fervently defended.

In both cases, the investment firm's culture was seeded by the values of its top leader, and in the end it is the cultural imperatives that define the organizational response to risk. Just as the manufacturing and building industries have shown that safety (a different form of risk management) is best contained when it is managed at all points in the system by a cultural adherence to specific values

(Simon and Leik 1999), so is investment risk best managed by a conscious cultural dedication across the organization. To rely on policies, software programs or a specific role (chief risk officer) is to try to contain the anxiety within a bureaucratic matrix rather than through the necessary relationships that must be constantly renegotiated to keep collaboration fresh (Hirschhorn 1988). Those businesses that hope to avoid the dislocation of functions described by Blankfein (Jenkins 2009) will only do so by mutual engagement – by adjusting organizational structures so that participants have the opportunity to review, learn and feed critical information to leadership. But there are also larger systemic issues at work.

The competition among investment professionals within an organization and among financial institutions is pitched to such a degree that change will call for extreme discipline at both an industry and a societal level. The psychic pressure on CEOs to resist the fear of 'missing out' is formidable in an environment where peers gain from short-term, risky investments. Consider the current phenomenon of pension funds 'doubling down' with high-risk investments in an attempt to recoup losses while the fallout from the credit crisis continues. Even in the wake of the financial crisis, those who might attempt to lead from a position of greater organizational discipline would likely be fired from many public companies for failure to feed the money-mad fantasies of their boards and investors. For similar reasons, the prospect of successful government regulation seems unlikely in the near future. It would call for politicians and appointed officials to dampen the potential for short-term economic growth at times when such growth involves too much risk to the system; to recognize when the public's desire is being enflamed by opportunities that belie realistic social and economic utility. Imagine, for instance, Alan Greenspan having removed the punchbowl from the party by pushing up interest rates at a time when banks, funds and homebuyers were drunk with the leverage provided by cheap money. Our broader system suffers the same reluctance to authorize and resource those bodies that would better inform and check businesses that, left to their own, will continue to dance to the music, convinced that someone else will be left without a chair when the music stops.

Note

1 The names of organizations and individuals in both cases described here have been changed to protect confidentiality.

References

Anderson, J. (2006) 'Betting on the weather and taking a cold bath', *New York Times*, 29 September.

Bion, W. (1961) *Experience in Groups and Other Papers*, New York: Routledge.

Clark, N. and Jolly, D. (2008) 'Fraud costs bank 7.1 billion', *New York Times*, 5 January.

Hirschhorn, L. (1988) *The Workplace Within: Psychodynamics of organizational life*, Cambridge, MA: MIT Press.

Jenkins, P. (2009) 'Goldman chief admits banks lost control', *Financial Times*, 9 September.

Kaufman, H. (2007) 'The dangers of the liquidity boom', *Financial Times*, 30 July.

Klein, M. (1975) *Envy and Gratitude*, New York: Free Press.

Lewis, M. (2010) *The Big Short: Inside the doomsday machine*, New York: W.W. Norton.

Lowenstein, R. (2010) *The End of Wall Street*, New York: Penguin.

Phillips, A. (2005) *Going Sane*, New York: HarperCollins.

Simon, S. and Leik, M. (1999) 'Implementing culture change at GE: breaking the safety barrier', *Professional Safety*, 44(3): 20–6.

Stevenson, R. (1995) 'The collapse of Barings: the overview', *New York Times*, 28 February.

Taibbi, M. (2009) 'The big takeover', *Rolling Stone*, issue 1075, 19 March.

Tett, G. (2009) *Fool's Gold: How unrestrained greed corrupted a dream, shattered global markets and unleashed a catastrophe*, London: Little, Brown.

11 Risk as present futures

An elaboration on risk and fear

Peter Pelzer

> We have no future because our present is too volatile. We have only risk man-
> agement. The spinning of the given moment's scenarios. Pattern recognition.
>
> (William Gibson 2003)

Working on the topic of risk and trying to understand what risk actually is,
increasingly leads to bewilderment. There seems to be neither a coherent definition nor a common understanding of what risk is beyond a vague everyday
understanding that it is a consequence of a decision, or an action, or the processes of an industrial plant. Different views have developed. On the theoretical
level, it makes a huge difference when looking at risk from an economic (Knight
1921/1946), psychological (Slovic 1987; Kahnemann and Tversky 1984), sociological (Beck 1986, 2007), cultural (Douglas 2003), mathematical (MacKenzie
2003a), statistical (Hacking 1975) or philosophical (Sloterdijk 2006) point of
view. The conclusions partly overlap; partly they contradict each other. All this
provides for a good discussion about a complex, controversial topic. The variety
of approaches on risk clearly demonstrates that it is a relevant and fascinating
topic that can and should be researched from many different angles. The angle
chosen here is that of the connection between risk and fear – fear that has to be
contained and disguised by tools such as probability, statistics and risk management. That risk management includes inherent risks itself – for example, autistic
qualities – is seen as a worrying phenomenon. The basic assumption is that risk
makes future present, and turns future's uncertainty into order, but this assumption may fail risk's meaning.

Risk is a very timely topic. The securitisation of debt, namely of mortgages,
was at the centre of the global financial crisis of 2008 (Cloke 2009; Mian and
Sufi 2008) leaving a lot of questions unaddressed. Researching the global financial crisis with socioanalytic methods in order to achieve an understanding
beyond the obvious facts and figures (Sievers 2010) will help to overcome the
fundamental handicap, as Bain (2009) addresses economists' understanding of
human beings. This chapter is about futures and options, risk and fear; in short,
'risk as present future(s)' tries to contribute to this endeavour.

Risk is a modern invention

The future is unwritten.

(Joe Strummer[1])

Risk is a modern idea. Despite the fact that people in older cultures took action that we nowadays would immediately call risky, such as setting sail for unknown places, the concept of risk only became possible when it replaced the concept of fate. Luhmann (1991) claims that ancient advanced civilizations developed different concepts for dealing with analogous problems and therefore did not need a term like 'risk'. Of course, uncertainty about the future has always been a topic. Divination was a common solution. According to Tedlock, for instance, 'Divination is a way of exploring the unknown in order to elicit answers (that is, oracles) to questions beyond the range of ordinary human understanding' (2001: 189).

Divination could not guarantee reliable knowledge and certainty, but at least it provided a decision that did not anger the gods. A profound change must have taken place to allow the introduction of the concept of risk. Angry about the public view of globalization and its coverage in the media, Peter Sloterdijk (2006) develops a view of globalization and its consequences from a philosophical point of view. His hypothesis is that we can quite reliably date the beginning and end of the growth of globalization. The beginning is marked by Columbus's discovery of America; the end can be set to the end of World War II.

He argues that today we live in a globalized world – that is, the process of globalization has been completed – and have to face the consequences that we, the Europeans, began with our journeys over the oceans. Sloterdijk turns the lesson that other cultures prove the European conviction of an immutable local order of things to be contingent, to the insight that this is not the loss of the centre but the loss of periphery. Nothing can be kept at a distance any more. The local is not the centre of the world; such a centre does not exist.

To leave the local involves the uncertainty of return. It is precisely this that marks the difference: a physical return of the person also means the return of goods and what was found or traded abroad. Manning a ship is a serious investment, so the return on investment becomes a crucial factor. Borrowing, investing in equipment and setting sail for discoveries is a race for dubious opportunities in opaque distant markets. Discoveries, claims Sloterdijk (2006: 78), are just a special form of investment. Emerging capitalism required a different method of dealing with uncertainty, with the possibilities of loss of goods as a result of shipwrecks – that is, the inability to obtain a return on investment and to repay credit. The new behaviour is about taking risk and at the same time about dealing with the risk; diversifying it by inviting others to share the monetary consequences of the risk and the potential profit. Ideas of risk and insurance require a different mindset from that involved in fate. It places humans as architects of their own future rather than as dependent on the whims of gods.

Discoveries aim at the unknown; something to find behind the horizon. They include the vision of that which cannot be seen from the point of departure. The restructuring of European thought about action to include risk explains the somehow surprising, almost mysteriously successful offensive power of the generations of seventeenth-century discoverers and the beginnings of imperialism. The readiness to take risks is fuelled by the obligation and compulsion to gain profits to pay off credits. Going to sea always needed luck for survival, but now it introduced different opportunities. It became possible to calculate successes and failures; gains and losses. And it needed planning – in other words, a turn to the future: a 'futurization' of governmental, entrepreneurial and epistemic action. Taking risk became the central aspect of modernity. Probabilistic calculation to evaluate the chances of making the future predictable, increasingly developed and used in the unfolding risk culture, was a move 'against the gods' (Bernstein 1996). Risk management is unthinkable when fate is the predominant conception of the future.

Time is money: money is time

The replacement of fate by risk was possible only in the context of other developments. A closer look at the link between risk, time and money is necessary. Risk is about the evaluation of possible future events. Their consequences can be expressed in terms of money. Wherever risk is expressed as a probability of future events, its background is in the economic calculation of return on investment – that is, the return in the form of capital/money. 'Time is money' is a well-known statement of the fact that wasting time also means losing money. Putting the relationship between time and money into an equation means also that the reverse holds true: money is time. Someone with a liquidity problem may buy time in the form of a credit to put his or her company back on its feet. In other words: it is possible to buy the future.

Time and money are continuous and divisible. In principle, they are infinite. Time is measured against the idea of eternity. With the loss of the perspective of eternity in modern times, life time can be seen as dangerously scarce. But what is the advantage of converting time and money; what is their exchange value?

Money, we might say replaced God in the human relationship to time and eternity. I will argue here that a theological fixation was removed in favour of a monetary fixation. The failure to provide proof of God's existence at the time of the development of ideas of a globalized return on investment contributed to the replacing of the idea of God with the more mundane idea of a symbolic global exchangeability, i.e. money. The precondition for this was that money became a token or symbol instead of a material possession. The money in circulation became an ideal coin valued as a fixed weight of gold or silver by a state bank. Holding the coins in circulation gave the right to exchange them for the amount of gold defined by the state bank. With this move – that is, systematically attaching a sign to current money different from its manifest value – money was changed into a commodity (Rotman 1987: 25).

Beyond the pragmatic dimension owed to emerging capitalism, money serves as a radical counter-image to time in one crucially important respect. Following a Heideggerian argument, Hörisch (1996: 159–60) argues that the experience of time finds its ultimate intensification in death. Humans are mortal. Death marks one's 'very own', non-referential, irreconcilable, certain and undecided possibility of Being. The very own possibility – this is irreplaceably my death; the non-referential possibility – it can only be experienced as the end of every reference of communication; the irreconcilable possibility – it is impossible to talk about my own death in the future perfect tense: 'I will have been dead' is just a grammatical construction; the certain but undecided possibility – death is certain, the date is not (*mors certa, hora incerta*); the possibility: death cannot be experienced in life.

Money is the counter-principle at every single point. It is not an inescapable, individually unique fact but the social medium per se. It is made to move from one purse or account to another. It has universal reference concerning things, dates, and natural and legal persons. It is reconcilable; one can talk in the future perfect tense: I will have experienced the expiry date of my life insurance. It is uncertain because it can be changed into anything; it is indifferent. It is very decided concerning exchange rates, expiry dates and legal liabilities. Finally, it is not a subject but a medium. Hörisch concludes that the fascinating aspect of money's relationship to time is that 'money has killed death; but the dead remain. There seems to be a power which is wealthier, more potent and more liquid than death' (1996: 160).[2]

Both resources – time and money – are scarce and have the highest value placed on them. Eternity, which was discontinued (*sic!*) with the negation of a god, is revitalized by money as the means to keep time liquid and infinite. Scarce money can counteract scarce time on several levels. In favour of meta-temporal money, we invest time; gaining money motivates the loss of time; money accumulates past and passing time; money is virtually eternal; wealth survives the mortal who owns it. Money cannot die. In short, time is money because the meta-temporal medium of money makes it possible to rule time (Hörisch 1996: 168).

With the doubt about God's existence and the profound challenge by capitalistic moves to replace him by money, a serious second doubt follows. The belief in God justified the prospect of eternity. In this belief, there is something beyond death. Life, which can no longer be sure about eternal prospects, must be deeply annoyed by its threatening scarcity. This scarcity is emphasized, as it can only be preserved by its sale in work (Hörisch 1996).

Probability

> You can only predict things after they have happened.
>
> (Eugène Ionescu[3])

Despite the fact that risk has been around for several centuries, we have still not achieved a widely accepted definition. There is a vague understanding in everyday life connecting it to uncertainty, to unexpected outcomes, which makes the usage uncontested. Risk and uncertainty are not fate any more, so why not try to calculate it?

The roots of the attempts to gain control of uncertain outcomes were, perhaps not surprisingly, in the context of gambling (Hacking 1975). It involved the possibility both of winning and of losing. The question is how to calculate the probability of an event combined with the magnitude of the gains or losses at stake. The idea of risk is neutral. Since the beginnings of mathematical calculations around this idea, an 'avalanche of numbers' (Hacking 1990) has been raised, accumulated, created, calculated as the basis of scientific knowledge, transforming the nature of evidence, of knowledge and of authority. Probability theory has provided a modern way of thinking. However, 'the taming of chance' (Hacking 1990) includes a by-product. Numbers generated in masses (Pelzer 2007) and ordered capture patterns of the past, with serious shortcomings for prediction of future developments:

> [P]robability is the expression of an assumed pre-existing order which rests on the idea of the expected and the certain, i.e. the recurrence of what is already known.... [P]robability is a form of prediction or prior awareness which defends the system against the strange and the unknown; the system is therefore incapable of dealing with information that is non-probabilistic and unpremeditated.
>
> (Cooper 1987: 397)

If we take Cooper's remark on probability seriously, it is applicable to the term for which probability serves as an expression, i.e. risk. Given this, then risk is an expression of an assumed pre-existence that rests on an idea of the expected, though not the certain. We know what to expect when we designate something as a risk. It is either what we intend to achieve, the success, or it is what we intend to avoid, the failure. Both can be described, although their dimensions are not usually known.

In considering the future, we try to make sense of what we know. Risk is an attempt to make sense of what might happen in the future. Sensemaking is included in the making of risk. Weick (1995) insists on hindsight for the problem of sensemaking. Although Weick might well wince at this elaboration,[4] I see his description of uncertainty as containing a valuable insight for the character of risk. People try to find out whether their assumptions regarding the present are correct by looking for new information:

> Faced with news as an outcome, people ask, what history might have generated this outcome and what should I do presuming that the history I have constructed is plausible? Uncertainty about the actual future is replaced by more certainty about the present, which itself was an actual future just a short time ago. The greater certainty about the meaning of the present news is created because the people reconstruct a history that serves as a plausible explanation how it got here.
>
> (ibid.: 96)

Using probability statistics means the telling of a story about the past to inform us about how the past got here, into the present. This is a form of retrospective sensemaking to gain the possibility of making sense of the future, assuming that we can tell how it will be if the path we identified from the past to the present will continue as identified to the present. An organization's capability for sense-making in the face of uncertainty about the future (ibid.: 97) is a precondition for risk management.

Futures and options: putting future into the plural and contingency

Fate was singular; something written in the book of life, fixed and not possible to influence. Risk opens the future; provides for the consciousness of options. Things may be different in the future, depending on a present decision. Future is also contingent – that is, things may turn out to be different than expected. No fate means 'no guaranteed outcome'. Not only do we *not know* the future, but the future itself is not determined. There are products within international financial markets that have incorporated this consideration so deeply and self-evidently that they can serve as vivid examples. They are widely used, immensely influential in current business life and they create anxiety and public discussion. Articles like 'Stop the international speculators!' (Schmidt 2007) and comparisons with locust plagues (Pelzer 2009) are part of the public reaction. The construction and peculiarities of these markets, including the attitudes and behaviours of traders, are increasingly in the focus of research (e.g. Lilley and Lightfoot 2006; MacKenzie 2003b; Knorr Cetina and Bruegger 2002). Since their research, risk has become more than a very interesting research object. The gigantic losses of the markets since 2008 originate in the securitization of debt, namely of mortgages (Cloke 2009; Mian and Sufi 2008). The infamous CDOs (collateralized debt obligations) and CDSs (credit default swaps) can be seen as more sophisticated forms of those derivatives which in this chapter are taken as an example for dealing with the future and bear this connection in their name: futures and options. The terms 'security' and 'securitization' turned out to be euphemistic (Koslowski 2009): the securitized papers were by no means made more secure; on the contrary, the whole process became less transparent. Risk, as it turned out, was not eliminated.

Any discussion about the excesses of the market of derivatives during the crisis must be informed by the knowledge that these financial instruments were initially introduced to manage the risks involved in volatile markets. To manage risk means to transfer the risk of a party not willing to accept it as part of their own business, to a party who is willing to bear the risk against a premium. Banks traditionally performed this function and were the agents between parties. Taking over the risk from one party immediately triggers the search for matching opposite risks. One risk involved for production companies lies in the instability of prices on their supply as well as on their sales side. The latter also includes risks concerning currency rates in international trade. Instruments invented for transferring the risk are called futures. Futures are contracts in which one side contracts to buy and one side to sell a given quantity of an asset at a set price on a given future date. The seller achieves certainty about the price of his (or her) goods on a given date in the future irrespective of the actual price on that day. He is willing to accept what he considers might be a premium and to forfeit the chance of getting more if the price rises accordingly. He also gains the certainty of not losing money if the price falls below the agreed level. An option is a contract that gives the right but not the obligation to buy or sell an asset at a given price on a given date in the future. The value of the option is dependent on the asset (the underlying) named in the contract. These financial instruments can be traded without delivery of the underlying commodity – that is, they have a value of their own, which nevertheless is dependent on another asset: they are derivative.

Derivatives are about the price of 'underlying commodities' in the future, hence their name: futures. The other form is about the choice to buy/sell or not to buy/sell, with a fixed price – an option. The remarkable fact about these financial instruments is how easily self-evident future is put into a plural and how easily it is combined with the general contingency of the future and the ability to have choice, i.e. buy and sell options. Trading futures also means that they depend on decisions – which leads us directly back to risk.

Money copes with contingency. Future is fundamentally uncertain. If money replaces God, a functional equivalent is needed for God's function of acting as the reassuring instance that guarantees that whatever will be, will be good, because it is in God's hands. The equivalent is the idea of having enough money at one's disposal to be able to react to future contingencies, i.e. future needs or threats. In the form of capital, money has the task of transforming indeterminable complexity into certain complexity. Money is used to maintain options as options (Deutschmann 1999) and put 'future' into the plural.

Autism: a challenge of certainties

The world of figures and numbers is fascinating and helpful in many respects. They help to measure and compare, to quantify and judge the resulting quantities; to benchmark and to create hierarchies; to control and to manage. With their help it becomes possible to measure what it makes sense to quantify. But this is just a tiny part of reality. Expanding the importance of numbers incorporates its own dangers. Numbers seduce:

> Numbers give certainty. They are a system of order which is understandable without inferring emotions. It is possible to hierarchize, parallelize, draw conclusions. And they provide a pleasure because it is possible to recognize how something works in the easiest way. Numbers have always easily made friends with me.
>
> Numbers are a presentation of the world which is, due to its concentrated pureness, addictive.

I'm quite sure that people who operate a lot with numbers slowly lose the capacity to perceive emotions and be able to empathize with others. The mind sorts itself into a completely different direction.

(Lau 2004: 110)

This quotation is taken from an article about the author Axel Brauns. While these remarks do not sound very special – any restricted view of the world has its own limitations and consequences for the topic researched – but, in combination with the author's background, they provide another dimension. Axel Brauns is autistic and in his book *Buntschatten und Fledermäuse* (Brauns 2002) he describes his slow journey out of it. What he describes as the effect of numbers is the experience of an autist's retreat into a perfect world. Lau (2004) concludes that juggling with figures is often reported as a special ability among autists, but also that for them, this represents not a talent but a handicap. Autism was first defined as removal from reality, together with a relative or complete predominance of the inner world. Autists perceive the world in details, often very precise, but they have mostly lost the ability to put them into a whole picture.

Numbers can act as addiction. The concentrated pureness they convey can seduce one into taking them for a representation of the whole of reality. Numbers protect by providing a phantasy of certainty, but there is a price to pay for this certainty. Numbers, for example in the form of market research figures, do not prevent a flop; rating does not prevent banks from suffering losses, but may provide a justification for the investment. However, the most important protection provided by numbers is hidden. Those who live in a world of numbers are distanced, not reachable by the scurry of a reality made of dust, sweat, shouting and singing, fragrance and stench, flowers and compost; in short, by real life. The altars of the goddess of certainty are filled with exact numbers fed by analyses of the finest grading. Everything murmurs perfection. Hidden are the relics, because death is the only perfect state of humans. No uncertainty; no change any more (Seibt 2004: 105).

The phobic reflex: risk and fear

Rosa names the basic fear of modernity as 'slipping slopes' (2005: 190). We have the impression of standing on slipping slopes – that is, of livimg in a world of increasing contingencies where not acting, not deciding immediately, creates the fear of being left behind. Humans act within a condition of permanent and multidimensional change and increasing contingencies. This renders not deciding impossible. Those who do not move lose options for the future (Rosa 2005), or constantly face a new quality of risk.

The perception of risk is always influenced by the level of fear triggered by the future's uncertainty. Living on slipping slopes in the accelerated globalized world means less security and less reliable order at the same time. Everything moves independently, and apparently without any chance of being influenced by the individual. Warburg interprets culture and religion as treatments of fear. Humans find themselves in a chaotic world in which anything capable of independent movement causes reactive fear: the phobic reflex (Gombrich 1970/1981). The relationship between risk, time and money, embedded as it is in religious and cultural considerations, as argued above, can also be interpreted as a reaction to the phobic reflex. Numbers take the place of representing risk and as a hidden function, also representing fear.

The entrepreneur and manager C.P. Seibt describes the role of numbers in organizations provocatively: 'With numbers people in the economy inform themselves. By belief in numbers people construct themselves artificial realities' (2004: 104). There is nothing wrong in quantifying those things which can be measured meaningfully, so long as it is recognized that they represent just a tiny part of reality. Beyond that, numbers create an artificial reality not supported by the reality so described (Kalthoff 2007). Artificial realities need a belief system, at least a solid motivation to embrace them instead of reality: 'The gods of the believers in numbers are self protection, certainty, control, power. And above all the highest goddess stands in solitary splendour: fear' (Seibt 2004: 105). Fear, or the phobic reflex, is part of everyday life.

The rare confession by an insider that fear is at centre stage in business life, and naming it the highest goddess, as Seibt (2004) does, opens the view that much behaviour and many decisions are related to fear. Risk avoidance means avoiding nightmares coming true. Risk management appears to deal with these fears, although hidden under the cover of rational calculation. Recent psychological research demonstrates the importance of affect and identifies two modes of thinking for risk: 'risk as analysis and risk as feelings' (Slovic *et al.* 2004; Loewenstein *et al.* 2001). Risk as analysis is the familiar mode of risk management: analytic, logical, reason-oriented encoding of reality in abstract symbols, words and numbers, oriented towards delayed action. One source for casting doubt on the privileged position the rational model has is the failure of invariance. Kahneman and Tversky (1984) found inconsistent choices when the same problem appears in different frames. Describing the same problem with different calculations, the first expressing the gains, the second the losses, changes the preference. The avoidance of losses is preferred, even if the basic figures are the same. If decision making were rational, one would expect the preference to be the same. 'The moral of these results is disturbing. Invariance is normatively essential (what we should do), intuitively compelling, and psychologically unfeasible' (ibid.: 346).

Describing the difference as two modes of thinking (the experiential and the analytic system) makes the hierarchy between feeling and rationality, with rationality preferred as the more advanced mode of thinking, questionable. The analytic system works by established rules of logic and evidence. This is the realm of probabilities. The experiential system represents reality with images, metaphors and narratives to which affective feelings have become attached (Slovic *et al.* 2004: 316). The worrying outcome of such research is that although the experiential system has helped humans to survive by quickly assessing situations, for instance regarding wild animals or poisonous food, it may, although still helping us in reaching decisions, also mislead us. As demonstrated implicitly by Kahneman and Tversky (1984), the experiential system can be manipulated by simply reformulating a decision situation: numbers can deceive (Gigerenzer 2002). It is also subject to inherent biases of magnitude (small changes in the environment seem to be emphasized at the cost of larger changes further away), or because of its visceral nature (e.g. hunger, thirst, sexual desire, emotions, pain, craving for drugs have hedonic impact and a powerful effect on behaviour). Slovic *et al.*'s conclusion is clear:

> We cannot assume that an intelligent person can understand the meaning of and properly act upon even the simplest of numbers such as amounts of money or numbers of lives at risk, not to mention more esoteric measures or statistics pertaining to risk, unless these numbers are infused with affect.
>
> (2004: 321)

Freud struggled for quite some time in his analysis of the potential of pathology of normal subjects and the phenomenon of suppressed fear. He finally concluded that basic fear is the result of the comparatively early birth of humans. Born in a vulnerable state of organic helplessness, the human baby has a need for a protective environment. The result is a biological fixation on the mother, whose care and help are so essential that any sign of her disappearance is the paradigmatic case of danger. From then on, any feeling of remaining without the loved object is the signal for a similar fear. The result is that environmental dangers cause significant fears and the value of an object able to protect against such dangers is enormously increased (Honneth 2006: 39).

What Axel Honneth (2006) develops from Freud's writing points to a more mature handling of the phobic reflex, or the fear of failure. Starting from the insight about the early creation of vulnerability and the fear of loss of the protecting environment, he argues that Freud develops a thesis on how to gain freedom of will. This can never be a spontaneous realization that all our longings and wishes are expressions of our own will. On the contrary, to gain a sense of agency requires a long, arduous, painful process of working through and remembering in which we try to appropriate the previously separated elements of our will against insistent repression and resistance. As the reason for repression is fear, we have to succeed in accepting this fear as an integral part of our personality. To the extent to which we are successful, we are able to cleanse our will of influences and elements that we cannot understand as our own will. 'The relationship of a human to herself, so Freud's superb insight could be summarized, consists in the process of self-appropriation of one's own will by the affective confession of fear' (ibid.: 46–7).

Risk is order

Future's grammatical form is the singular. Living in the present, we expect a future to come – something that is not yet present, to become present and immediately turn into past. We are perfectly aware of the fact that it may turn out to be different from what we expect. Nonetheless, these expectations of future events will be transformed into a presence, a very concrete one, the one we will experience. In a way, there is one future waiting for us, one which we do not know about now, that does not exist now, but it will be the one we will experience. But this future is not certain. It is always in the process of being shaped and constantly changed by concrete decisions, interpretations of these decisions and reactions by others, a changing environment, etc. Everything is permanently in flow, emerging, complex, hard to predict, contingent – precisely (*sic!*) uncertain. The uncertainty is a result of the fact that we do not know which of the futures we can imagine is the one to come. However, this image, as self-evident as it may appear, still carries a pre-modern grounding. It seems as if fate still is a fundamental for thinking about future. Fate was in the singular, something written in the book of life, fixed and not capable of being influenced. Risk opens the future, provides the consciousness for options. Things may be different in the future, depending on a present decision. Future is also contingent – that is, things may turn out to be different than expected. No fate means no guaranteed outcome. Not only do we do not know the future, but the future itself is not determined. The future is unwritten – remains to be written. We are making the future.

Future in organizations, though, seems to be a clear, linear structure developing on the time arrow from past over to present. It can be seen as a trajectory. Risk is concerned with a movement across a space, something thrown from one position to another, as the Latin etymology indicates for a trajectory: *trans*=across, *jacere*=to throw. Höpfl (2000: 21) argues as an effect of the ordinary that which I would find appropriate for risk, too:

> It is the language of pro-jection, of moving forwards and of indicating a future arrival position or state, or re-jection of the throwing out of those things or people incompatible with the pro-jection, it is the language of abjection and the de-jection of things thrown away. So when organisations declare specific objectives, outcomes, points of arrival and so forth, they throw forward an ordering into future time.

Future is an unprotected environment into which planning is directed, the decision is performed; the aim of a project is set. Anything 'Other' is eradicated in this process. Risk is concerned with the possibility of different outcomes; that the trajectory is left and the objective failed in order (*sic!*) to prevent it, to eradicate the possibility of failure, variation or difference. Different outcomes are the realization of risk, which is seen as a failure of risk management.

This chapter is an elaboration of the consequences of the replacement of God by money – of fate by risk – of a generalized return – from distant voyages, discoveries or, in short, through investment. Risk is the form of considering possible futures, evaluating them and acting accordingly. Risk, as it is seen here, is not just an expression of uncertainty, of what may go wrong, but the so-called rational expression of dealing with an unknown future made known in the present as artificial, produced reality. Risk is, according to the somewhat unexpected and slightly disturbing insight, order. Risk orders future by making it present. Risk is containment of the threatening future by ordering it.

Risk management by numbers, then, misses the central aspect. Because future is open, contingent, and because probability extrapolates only the known, risk calculation cannot represent fear of the unknown. In a way, we are still at sea with the attitude of early anonymous investors behind the discoverers. We calculate the amount of money to be replaced for the economic loss, not for the sailors' lives. It is money which replaced eternity. And with realizing this, it becomes clear that risk is open for the influences of culture, power, feelings and scientific interest. It may be attached to virtually any topic as a means to form, influence and manipulate opinions and options.

Thinking of risk as part of the process of self-appropriation of one's own will by the affective confession of fear, as Honneth (2006) interpreted Freud, is the challenge we face when money is the medium that supplies a cover for a realization of risks in times which no longer ask for a cover of metaphysical claims (Hörisch 1996: 172). Risk may enable us to deal with the future in the double meaning of the word: risk may handle the future, and it may make a deal by buying a future. The world is contingent, but therefore it offers options. And it offers futures to choose from – which is much more than the financial markets have on offer.

Notes

1 This is the title of a 2007 film, directed by Julian Temple, about the life of Joe Strummer, singer and songwriter of The Clash.
2 Quotations from German originals are translated by the author.
3 Quoted in Rockett (1999).
4 To paraphrase Weick's own suspicion of his use of an argument by Stinchcombe (Weick 1995: 96).

References

Bain, A. (2009) 'The economic crisis as manic depression: a few thoughts', Online, available at: www.acsa.net.au/articles/The%20Economic%20Crisis%20as%20Manic%20Depression.pdf (retrieved 25 January 2010).
Beck, U. (1986) *Risikogesellschaft. Auf dem Weg in eine andere Moderne*, Frankfurt am Main: Suhrkamp. English translation: *Risk Society: Towards a new modernity*, London: Sage, 1992.
Beck, U. (2007) *Weltrisikogesellschaft*, Frankfurt am Main: Suhrkamp. English translation: *World at Risk*, Cambridge: Polity Press, 2009.
Bernstein, P.L. (1996) *Against the Gods: The remarkable story of risk*, New York: John Wiley.

Brauns, A. (2002) *Buntschatten und Fledermäuse*, Munich: Goldmann.

Cloke, J. (2009) 'An economic wonderland: derivative castles built on sand', *Critical Perspectives on International Business*, 5: 107–19.

Cooper, R. (1987) 'Information, communication and organization: a post-structural revision', *Journal of Mind and Behavior*, 8: 395–416.

Deutschmann, C. (1999) *Die Verheißung des absoluten Reichtums. Zur religiösen Natur des Kapitalismus*, Frankfurt am Main: Campus.

Douglas, M. (2003) *Risk and Blame*, collected works vol. 12, London: Routledge.

Gibson, W. (2003) *Pattern Recognition*, New York: C.P. Putnam.

Gigerenzer, G. (2002) *Calculating Risks: How to know when numbers deceive you*, New York: Simon & Schuster.

Gombrich, E.H. (1970/1981) *Aby Warburg. Eine intellektuelle Biographie*, Frankfurt am Main: Europäische Verlagsanstalt.

Hacking, I. (1975) *The Emergence of Probability: A philosophical study of early ideas about probability, induction and statistical inference*, Cambridge: Cambridge University Press.

Hacking, I. (1990) *The Taming of Chance*, Cambridge: Cambridge University Press.

Honneth, A. (2006) 'Aneignung von Freiheit. Freuds Konzeption der individuellen Selbstbeziehung', *WestEnd: Neue Zeitschrift für Sozialforschung*, 2: 32–48.

Höpfl, H. (2000) 'On being moved', *Studies in Culture, Organizations and Societies*, 6: 15–34.

Hörisch, J. (1996) *Kopf oder Zahl. Die Poesie des Geldes*, Frankfurt am Main: Suhrkamp.

Kahneman, D. and Tversky, A. (1984) 'Choices, values, and frames', *American Psychologist*, 39(4): 341–50.

Kalthoff, H. (2007) 'Ökonomisches Rechnen. Zur Konstitution bankwirtschaftlicher Objekte und Investitionen', in A. Mennicken and H. Vollmer (eds) *Zahlenwerk. Kalkulation, Organisation und Gesellschaft*, Wiesbaden: VS Verlag für Sozialwissenschaften.

Knight, F.H. (1921/1940) *Risk, Uncertainty and Profit*, London: London School of Economics, series of reprints of scarce tracts in economic and political science 16, 5th impression, Boston: Houghton Mifflin.

Knorr Cetina, K. and Bruegger, U. (2002) 'Traders' engagement with markets: a post-social relationship', *Theory, Culture and Society*, 19: 161–85.

Koslowski, P. (2009) 'Spekulation: Wette oder Glücksspiel?'; *Frankfurter Allgemeine Zeitung*, 246, 23 October: 12.

Lau, P. (2004) 'Weit draußen', *brand eins*, 2: 106–11.

Lilley, S. and Lightfoot, G. (2006) 'Trading narratives', *Organization*, 13: 369–91.

Loewenstein, G.F., Weber, E.U., Hsee, C.K. and Welch, N. (2001) 'Risk as feelings', *Psychological Bulletin*, 127:267–86.

Luhmann, N. (1991) *Soziologie des Risikos*, Berlin: Walter de Gruyter. English translation *Risk: A sociological theory*, Berlin: de Gruyter, 2005.

MacKenzie, D. (2003a) 'An equation and its worlds: bricolage, exemplars, disunity and performativity in financial economics', *Social Studies of Science*, 33: 831–68.

MacKenzie, D. (2003b) 'Long-term capital management and the sociology of arbitrage', *Economy and Society*, 32: 349–80.

Mian, A.R. and Sufi, A. (2008) 'The consequences of mortgage credit expansion: evidence from the U.S. mortgage default crisis', Online, available at: http://papers.ssrn.com/sol3/papers.cfm?abstract_id=1072304 (retrieved 29 November 2009).

Pelzer, P. (2007) 'The futility of excess, or: the displaced world of rules and regulations', *Culture and Organization*, 13: 157–69.

Pelzer, P. (2009) 'The displaced world of risk: risk management as alienated risk (perception?)', *Society and Business Review*, 4: 26–36.

Rockett, J.P. (1999): 'Definitions are not what they seem', *Risk Management: An International Journal*, 1: 37–47.

Rosa, H. (2005) *Beschleunigung. Die Veränderung der Zeitstruktur in der Moderne*, Frankfurt am Main: Suhrkamp.

Rotman, B. (1987) *Signifying Nothing: The semiotics of zero*, Stanford, CA: Stanford University Press.

Schmidt, H. (2007) 'Beaufsichtigt die neuen Großspekulanten!' *Die Zeit*, 6, 1 February: 21–3.

Seibt, C.P. (2004) 'Wer sich nicht glaubt, glaubt an Zahlen', *brand eins*, 2: 104–5.

Sievers, B. (2010) 'Beneath the financial crisis', in H. Brunning and M. Perini (eds) *The Psychoanalytic Perspective on the Turbulent World*, London: Karnac.

Sloterdijk, P. (2006) *Im Weltinnenraum des Kapitals*, Frankfurt am Main: Suhrkamp.

Slovic, P. (1987) 'Perceptions of risk', *Science*, 236: 280–85.

Slovic, P., Finicane, M.L., Peters, E. and MacGregor, D.G. (2004) 'Risk as analysis and risk as feeling: some thoughts about affect, reason, risk, and rationality', *Risk Analysis*, 24: 311–22.

Tedlock, B. (2001) 'Divination as a way of knowing: embodiment, visualisation, narrative, and interpretation', *Folklore*, 112: 189–97.

Weick, K.E. (1995) *Sensemaking in Organizations*, Thousand Oaks, CA: Sage.

12 Trading opportunities and risks

Conflicting methods of coordination in investment banks[1]

Jesper Blomberg, Hans Kjellberg and Karin Winroth

Introduction

While shares arguably are central objects in the financial industries, our empirical work suggests that there is no one single identity for these objects (see Winroth *et al.* 2010). Rather, shares are regularly qualified (Callon *et al.* 2002) as exchange objects on markets, as investment objects in portfolios, as knowledge objects in analyses, etc. That is, the identity of a share varies with the situation in which it is enacted. With the rise of investment banks in the financial industries (see Morrison and Wilhelm 2007), several such alternative versions of shares are actively being produced by experts working within the same organization, e.g. stockbrokers, stock traders and analysts. While these expert groups thus construct different share identities, they are typically able to cooperate and coordinate their various activities involving shares. In this sense, shares can be seen to work as boundary objects (Star and Griesemer 1989), being 'plastic enough to adapt to local needs and constraints ... yet robust enough to maintain a common identity across sites' (ibid.: 393).

Over the past decade, risk management has emerged as a separate area of activity within investment banking. Based on an ongoing ethnographic study of Swedish investment banks at work, we study efforts to coordinate practices between this new occupational group and (stock) traders, one of the more established occupational groups within investment banking. These groups are interesting since the coordination of their respective practices seems to be particularly problematic and controversial. Traders tend to either forcefully ignore risk managers or complain about the hassles they cause for them as they go about their business. Risk managers, on the other hand, complain about the difficulties of conveying to traders an understanding of the importance of carefully assessing risks. In the light of the recent financial turmoil, this situation becomes particularly topical, as various interest groups now promote risk management as an important solution in preventing future crises (e.g. Institute of International Finance 2008).

While considerable attention has been given to both financial risk management (Power 2004, 2005a, b; Kalthoff 2005) and trading (Abolafia 1996; Knorr Cetina and Bruegger 2002a, b; Fenton-O'Creevy *et al.* 2004; Zaloom 2006), this chapter focuses on the interaction between risk management and trading practices. It seeks to contribute to our understanding of the practical construction of a risk culture within one of the more important types of organization in the financial industries.

We approach this problem by describing how stock traders construct share identities based on external (market) influences and trading opportunities, and how risk managers translate shares into the currency of risk. While shares work as boundary objects that allow for flexible coordination between traders and other experts, such as analysts and brokers, risk managers opt for another coordinating principle, that of *methods standardization* (Star and Griesemer 1989). We trace the difficulties of achieving coordination between traders and risk managers (including compliance and alignment with the current legal frameworks) to *interferences* between these two alternative approaches to coordination (Mol 2002). In short, we ask: (how) do the worlds of traders and risk analysts meet? If they do, then what frictions or conflicts arise in the encounters between these worlds, and how are these frictions or conflicts handled?

Five sections follow this introduction. In the first, we outline how different viewpoints and practices within investment banks may be coordinated through boundary objects and methods standardization. In the second section we introduce the reader to investment banking before contrasting the practices of stock traders and risk managers in the third section. In the fourth section we discuss how their respective approaches to coordination are linked to different organizational models and how they interfere with each other. In the final section we present our main conclusions.

Coordinating practices through boundary objects and methods standardization

Work in the financial markets is multifaceted and performed by a diverse set of actors, including (stock) exchanges, investment banks, institutional investors, publicly listed corporations, regulatory agencies, financial news media, etc. The emergence of new occupational groups and organizational types over the past thirty years suggests that the division of labour in the sector is increasing. In short, the machinery of global finance is becoming increasingly sophisticated. One important development in this respect has been the rise of the modern investment bank as a central type of organization within the financial industries (see Morrison and Wilhelm 2007).

Within investment banks, several expert groups, including stockbrokers, stock traders and analysts, work side by side at tasks that are highly interdependent. The growing importance of risk managers over the past twenty years further adds to this organizational complexity. However, previous research has focused primarily on the practices of individual expert groups (e.g. Abolafia 1996; Blomberg 2004; Fenton-O'Creevy *et al.* 2004; Knorr Cetina and Bruegger 2002a). In one such study, Beunza and Stark (2005) characterize the form of organization found in trading rooms as heterarchical, because of the minimal hierarchy and considerable organizational heterogeneity that it exhibits. Our research interest lies in further exploring how the practices of these diverse groups of experts are coordinated.

In a much-celebrated article, Star and Griesemer (1989) addressed this issue in the context of scientific work, an area similarly characterized by heterogeneity of actors and activities. Drawing on the sociology of translation (Callon 1986; Latour 1986, 1987), they introduced the concept of *boundary objects* as an analytical tool for addressing how cooperation and coordination between different social worlds may be possible without these worlds sharing a single view of the object or phenomenon they engage with (Star and Griesemer 1989). A boundary object must therefore be weakly structured in common sense – rendering various readings of it possible – while being capable of becoming strongly structured in specific settings – being understood as something precise in the various 'worlds' within which it is being used.

In our previous work we have found the notion of boundary objects to offer a plausible account of how coordination is achieved between some of the professional groups found working within investment banks (Winroth *et al.* 2010). Specifically, we have studied traders, brokers and analysts, who all actively work with shares. These expert groups construct qualitatively different share identities in terms of their constitutive associations (what goes into the identity construction), the potential uses of the share (e.g. to generate commission fees, to provide a topic for discussion with clients) and what the share represents (e.g. a going concern, an investment opportunity). Despite these different identities, the shares retain a common denominator, allowing them to move into and out of the respective 'expert worlds' without too much difficulty and so contribute to coordinating the experts' activities. When we turned our attention to the increasingly important area of risk management, however, the notion of shares as boundary objects seemed to lose much of its analytic power. Risk managers showed only marginal interest in the identity of shares, and instead sought to coordinate their activities with other occupational groups in a much more explicit manner.

This prompted us to turn to the second coordination tool proposed by Star and Griesemer: methods standardization. Methods standardization involves formulating and disseminating a precise set of instructions focusing on how to do certain things (Star and Griesemer 1989: 407). In the next section we examine how traders and risk managers employ these two coordination tools in their efforts to interact with other occupational groups within the investment bank.

Introducing investment banking practice

Investment banking is an international phenomenon. Over the past twenty years, Swedish investment banks, first established in Sweden during the 1990s, have grown increasingly similar to their US- or London-based competitors. Today, the Swedish investment banks in our study exhibit much the same structures, dynamics and concerns as their US and British competitors (as described by Eccles and Crane 1988; Hayward and Boeker 1998; Zaloom 2006).

Investment banks are primarily active in three lines of business. First, they mediate transactions on the stock exchange in a line of business called 'equities' or 'securities'. This operation primarily concerns the secondary markets for shares – that is, the stock markets, which are described by summary statements such as 'S&P Retakes 1200'; 'Dow up 143.22' in the business press, on the news, etc. The second line of business is called 'banking' or 'corporate banking', and consists in providing expert advice to owners and managers of public corporations on corporate financial matters, including mergers and acquisitions (M&As) and initial public offerings (IPOs). The third line of business is called 'asset management' and involves giving advice on investments to clients managing larger assets.

Our focus is on the equities line of business, within which three expert groups perform relatively specialized tasks. *Traders* buy and sell financial products. They typically specialize in a certain type of security product, such as shares, bonds, currencies, derivatives, which are exchanged on specific product markets maintained by stock exchanges. *Brokers* (or 'sales') maintain contacts with 'retail' clients, i.e. investors who wish to buy or sell securities. Their task is to generate orders for the traders. In their sales work, brokers make use of sector and company analyses performed by the in-house analysts. These *analysts* (sometimes called 'research') gather information about industries and companies, including customers and suppliers, technological developments, general economic conditions, etc. This information is translated into official recommendations to buy or sell.

In recent years, *risk managers* have become increasingly important to the equities line of business. Among other things, risk managers establish risk assessment procedures to ensure that the banks' positions (their house investments) comply with current regulatory frameworks. The role of the risk managers has been formalized into a specific risk management function, and the number of risk managers employed has grown. This growing importance of risk management has also introduced new coordination issues, as reflected in the following two statements by a stock trader and a risk manager:

> Well, in a way there are no risks. Of course you have to take positions when your clients sell their risks to you, otherwise you have no credibility, but as long as you take proper measures ... charge what it costs and take good collaterals, there are no real risks.

> (Trader)

> We have a four-line defence system. Each line is designed to take care of 100 per cent of the risks we are exposed to. We know what happens if we don't take this seriously, both from our own history and from the famous American examples. The attitude that there are no risks, or that you need not control for them as long as you make good money, can break any major investment bank.

> (Risk control manager)

There is a significant difference between the two expert groups not only in how they perceive risk but also in how they relate to other groups within the investment bank.

Securities trading and risk management

Stock traders: chasing a moving target

In recent years, several studies have analysed the work of traders, their personalities and their understanding of a global virtual market (e.g. Abolafia 1996; Knorr Cetina and Bruegger 2002a; Hasselström 2004; Fenton-O'Creevy *et al.* 2004; Zaloom 2006). Prior to the automation of stock exchanges, trading was usually performed by stockbrokers working on the exchange floors, shouting out their 'desires and intentions to buy or sell' (Baker 1984: 789). Automation meant that the process of matching orders to buy and sell, determine market prices and allocate shares was computerized (Muniesa 2004). As a result, the typical site for market activity (buying and selling) changed from the physical market floor to the in-house trading desk at a brokerage firm or investment bank. Brokering and trading activities were also increasingly separated and performed by specialists.

Stock traders broadly perform three types of activities: cash trading, market making and proprietary trading. *Cash trading* involves executing customer orders to buy and sell shares. Since the price for a security varies over the course of the trading day, the trader has to set a price at which the customer is offered the chance to buy or sell the security. This is also called *market making*. As traders are generally trusted to know what the 'right' price is for the securities they specialize in, some of them are given the task of trading for the house, an activity known as *proprietary trading*. That is, they buy and sell securities on behalf of the investment bank itself. As was noted by Fenton-O'Creevy *et al.* (2004), these three trading activities often overlap, with one person performing more than one type of trading.

Traders spend a lot of time trying to understand 'the market'. The market, they explain, depends on information, whether substantiated or not. Information about changes in various product markets, about world politics, about expected changes in the supply of or demand for raw materials, about changes in interest rates, etc. To traders, there is typically no limit in principle concerning the things that might affect 'the market'. As a consequence, they describe trading as an activity embedded in an information universe (see also Knorr Cetina and Bruegger 2002a). Although each specific market is delimited in terms both of what can be traded there and of who is authorized to trade, what affects those markets is much less specific. Indeed, it has been suggested that the defining characteristic of financial markets is their lack of objectivity and completeness of being (ibid.). It is not surprising, then, that traders suggest that the market is impossible to grasp solely by means of logical thinking. One of our interviewees put it in the following way:

> The financial market is like a creature. So many things are involved in how it moves; you cannot judge it only by analysis; you need a feeling for it. The moves depend on so many events and various flows. The market is just like a wild animal.
>
> (Head of trader group)

The reliance on flows of information means that the traders constantly re-enact their markets as part of their efforts to comprehend and act in a momentary world. What took place fifteen minutes ago is water under the bridge. So, how do traders relate to the continuously changing universe they confront? Previous studies suggest that traders need to know both 'how the world works' and 'how to work the [financial] world' (Willman *et al.* 2001). Accordingly, traders may use highly abstract financial theories to understand the markets, and to communicate with others about instruments on the markets. In addition, however, they also need to know how this understanding can be put to practical use, since the 'real world' does not always act in accordance with theory. For this, practical experience, intuition and 'a feeling for the market', sometimes referred to as 'the psychology of traders', become important complements.

> You can't learn this from books. You can learn from theory how to value an option, how to value a share, but that does not necessarily need to be true. There are no rules in this world; there are no absolute truths.
>
> (Trader)

Consequently, to comprehend the markets you need to predict how other traders and other important players will act and react when prices change. Therefore, reading the signs of change and stability becomes crucial. However, without clear rules on how to play the markets, traders develop their own clues for predicting future changes. One trader described this as 'scanning the world':

> You start the day by reading papers – to update yourself, see if anything has happened in the world during the night, politically or in the market. And then this continues throughout the day; the working day never really ends. Me – I'm rather graphics oriented. I check graphs of indexes on prices, specific shares and currencies. I have my criteria I check every morning. And then you hopefully have read about everything, there is a continuous flow of news and rumours. You throw ideas around with the other traders in the room, but also with others, traders in the market, customers. You continuously try to create an image of what is happening.
>
> (Trader)

In the trading room, rumours indicating possible changes in the market are spread and discussed throughout the day. Being in a trading room, then, is to be in a position where information continually comes your way. Since your colleagues at the desk are experts on different markets, the buzz in the room is put forward as crucial and very useful. Moreover, international news channels are shown on screens in the room, giving traders the possibility of updating themselves on the latest global news. As trading in oil, gold and other natural resources is closely related to political relations between countries and regions, such news itself becomes of great interest and may directly affect the market. A particularly interesting piece of information, likely to affect the traders' assessments of shares, concerns the future.

> A lot revolves around expectations in our job – what people expect will happen. We use the expression 'the market prices in' what is going to happen. If you expect an economic recovery in, say, about a year, then the market is ahead when for instance calculating risks.... But it is never given what is going to happen, even if you have all the parameters.
>
> (Trader)

Apparent in our interviews with traders is their focus on 'the market', making shares first and foremost a commodity. Whether traders trade for the bank or a customer, they typically pay no attention to the possibilities of exercising ownership rights. At most, a particular share is a short-term, passive investment. That is to say, traders rarely think of shares as products in the way investors, analysts or brokers do. Instead, shares are continuously enacted as goods, as objects ready to be exchanged with little or no preparation. A critical task for a stock trader is to qualify the share with a specific price. To them, the market price of a commodity comes across as the result of some "'magic formula', and is expected to represent all relevant information about an asset (Fenton-O'Creevy *et al.* 2004). Since new information is constantly being made available, traders expect considerable price changes to occur.

Risk managers: setting up defences from the sidelines

The risk control managers are responsible for the investment bank's risk control system. They try to identify, assess and monitor the various risks that the investment bank is exposed to at each point in time. The objective of risk management in the early 'noughties' was primarily said to be the elimination of unnecessary operational risks, whereas investment banks currently emphasize compliance with legal requirements to safeguard the functioning of the financial system and protect individual investors. In response to the financial crisis, the investment banks in our study made considerable efforts to strengthen their risk control procedures during 2009.

The character of investment banking exposes investment banks to considerable financial risks, i.e. probabilities of incurring losses.[2] Risk managers distinguish between three types of risks, which are also recognized in the regulatory frameworks: credit risk, market risk and operational risk.[3] As far as stock trading is concerned, the most important risk is market risk, although operational risks are always present.

Our customers control most of our trading activities. The fundamental logic is that the customer wants to be relieved from risk. Then the trader says, 'OK, we will buy that risk from you' – and then he tries to do a good deal on the risk–reward relation. To be perceived as a serious house, and to be able to do good business, we have to be able to take quite large positions. But – and this is *the* question – how big positions should the individual trader be allowed to take?

(Risk manager)

To handle these risks, risk managers set up a risk control system. In a three-line defence system the first line consists of the individual risk owners (a share trader taking a position for the investment bank), a designated product risk controller (the securities risk manager) and the manager for that specific business area (the head of securities). The risk owner is responsible for the risk he or she takes in a specific deal; they cannot legitimately blame somebody else, or the system. And although their responsibility does not extend to the actual losses incurred, they may well be fired for trading beyond their limits. The head of securities is responsible for keeping the department's total risk exposure aligned with the bank's risk policies. The risk manager assists the head of securities in guiding and controlling the individual traders.

The second line of defence consists of the banks' central risk manager groups. These groups are led by the chief risk officers and consist of central risk managers for each major type of risk (market, credit and operational risk). This line is concerned with the architectural aspects of risk rather than individual or group responsibilities and conduct. They define the different types of risk, determine how to measure them, design risk reports and formulate risk policies. The risk managers continuously assess whether the risks that the bank is exposed to are measured properly and whether there are risks that escape the current system. Operational risk is of special interest in this respect:

For market and credit risk we have several well-researched and well-functioning models that we apply. Operational risk is a fuzzier concept, newer and harder to get a grip on. Currently we have a special team dedicated to looking into operational risk and how we should deal with that.

(Risk manager)

The third line of defence is built into the trading system itself – that is, into the more or less automated IT system that, in the best of all worlds, monitors the risks produced by the bank's activities and ensures that they are within the limits set by the bank's risk policies. For instance, if a trader tries to take a position (i.e. buy a certain number of shares at a certain price for the bank) producing a risk beyond his or her risk limit, the system prevents the trade from being executed. The risk managers are the architects, developers and maintenance crew for this defence system, but they also act as communicators between top management and risk takers. At the Stockholm office of one of the investment banks in our study, three risk managers are physically located in the middle of the large trading room. There they help, guide and control the ongoing activities. In short, risk managers try to translate the board's appetite for risk into policies, instructions and limits that the traders can understand, and the customer needs indicated by the traders' requests to take positions into messages that the board can understand. In this respect, risk managers have a typical middle management function.

> If a trader says, 'We need to do 10,000 futures in this', it is my task to translate that request into risk, or rather to ask, 'What is the worst that can happen if we do this? A really black, bad day, how much can we lose on this?' Then I go to the board and explain, 'The traders want to do this. If everything goes against us, we will lose this. Are we prepared to take this risk?'
>
> (Risk manager)

This mediating role is also reflected in the risk managers' perception of themselves as 'selling' the risk system to the experts and managers. If this communication breaks down, the traders will start to look for loopholes, seeking out actions 'below the radar'. 'We have to weed out the bad behaviours and bad attitudes. We need a 100 per cent risk-proof culture and in good times that doesn't come by itself' (Risk manager).

While risk managers thus put considerable weight on achieving compliance with routines and procedures, they also acknowledge a trade-off between detailed and rudimentary risk monitoring and control. They stress that investment banking is performed by human beings and that these humans enact rules as well as new ways of working. The more complex the system, risk managers argue, the less it will work when somebody is doing something that does not fit the definitions, models and assumptions. Thus, it is not self-evident that the more specific the system, the better it is. Instead, the bank tries to keep a balance between specific monitoring and control and more general and robust risk measurements.

> When we talk to traders, we try to explain the risk model as consisting of five moving parts: price ... which you could hedge ... volatility, interest rate, future dividends and time. But even this borders on being too complex. So we simplify even further – and this is a good example of the practically useful stuff: we have made a two-dimensional model focusing on the two most important parameters: price and volatility. We draw that diagram and illustrate to the traders where they should be ... how they must compensate increased risk in one dimension in terms of the other.
>
> (Chief risk officer)

This view has its corollary among traders, who perceive the prospect of a very specific system with a myriad of risk limits as moving focus away from actual trading. Thus, traders prefer a system with a few robust parameters that they can keep in mind while trading. To cater to these demands, the risk managers seek to design a system capable of keeping the traders within a designated 'risk box' while still allowing them to carry out fast, efficient and innovative trading.

> There is a classic conflict within finance, between the entrepreneurially driven and the rule-lovers. It is within the regulations, how one relates to ethics and risk, but also in the attitude towards risk assumed by the financial supervisory authority. This regulatory system tends to inhibit our friends the entrepreneurs.
>
> (Chief executive officer)

But what constitutes a good balance between control and innovative trading? During our first interviews, in 2005, the scales clearly favoured innovative trading as compared to the more recent interviews conducted after the autumn of 2008. For now, increased control appears to be gaining ground, but the work of controlling for risks and achieving compliance with set routines is a never-ending task.

Discussion: coordinating investment banking practices

Traders and the share as a boundary object

Trading practices revolve around 'the market' and the information universe in which it is embedded. While traders' daily practices testify to the centrality of knowledge, reflected in expressions such as 'scanning the world', they de-emphasize the use of analytical capacities. Rather, they describe their work as emotionally intense, lacking absolute truths and requiring the development of a 'feeling for the market'. As part of this work, traders enact shares as objects of exchange to be compared with other such objects. As such, the shares are shifted about by external developments, including changes in interest rates, prices of raw materials, global political events, etc. In themselves, shares are relatively empty; traders are interested in share prices, paying little attention to the corporations behind the shares.

This share identity differs considerably from those constructed by the other experts working in securities. The analysts routinely construct the share as a stable investment object filled to the brim with knowledge content, including sophisticated calculations, sociality in the form of top managers and their strategies, and materiality in terms of production facilities, etc. The broker's version of the share is not as focused on knowledge content, but depends more on rhetoric and its relation to the investment portfolios and policies of specific clients (i.e. investors). Despite these differences in share identities, traders are able to routinely and continuously interact with analysts and brokers in the very core activities of handling shares. A sort of arm's-length distance is upheld between the experts, with the share acting as a buffer capable of absorbing differences in local practices. This provides traders with a certain amount of freedom to act based on their reading of 'the market' and developing their own trading strategies.

In terms of the methods employed by the expert groups that engage with shares, there are distinct differences. Traders scan the world, listen and contribute to the buzz of the trading room, and interact with the trading system, placing orders to buy and sell specific numbers of specific shares. In contrast, stockbrokers are salespeople who primarily talk to clients, making recommendations and trying to interest them in specific deals while taking their portfolios and investment strategies into account. Analysts, finally, are researchers who engage in thorough analyses of specific corporations using detailed analytical models to support their work of assessing the value of a share. All three groups engage with shares in their own specific way. Even among traders themselves there is no common method; traders are instead encouraged to be creative and to develop their own approaches to trading.

Risk managers and the standardization of methods

There are aspects of the practices of risk managers that resemble both those of analysts and those of traders. An important part of risk managers' practice is concerned with knowledge objects, and they employ relatively detailed models in their efforts to understand these objects. In this sense, risk managers are epistemically oriented, just as analysts are; both groups try to make sense of a complex phenomenon by applying elaborate models. On the other hand, risk managers are similar to traders in that they are not particularly interested in the internal dynamic of shares but rather in the risks they involve for the investment bank. In this sense, a risk manager's view of shares resembles that of a trader, who is also interested in one particular share quality. But while traders are interested in prices, risk managers are interested in risks.

There is an important difference, however, between the risk managers and the other occupational groups – a difference that can be sensed already in their formal label of 'managers'. As was noted by Beunza and Stark (2005), trading rooms can be described as heterarchies, characterized by minimal hierarchy and considerable organizational heterogeneity. The practices of risk managers, however, are not entirely aligned with this organizational model. In contrast to analysts, who offer their analyses of specific shares to clients, brokers and traders more or less as topics for conversation, expecting there to be other views, risk managers are less flexible concerning how others respond to their work. Compared with the brokers' recommendations and conversations with clients, the contrast is even clearer. Risk managers are concerned with the spread of their way of approaching the knowledge object, which essentially involves translating shares and other financial products into the currency of risk. Other actors within the investment bank are encouraged to do the same, and in this respect the shares are prevented from performing as boundary objects between risk managers and other occupational groups. This can be seen in the efforts to establish procedures for handling risk, including the introduction of various limits as safety valves in the trading system. We suggest that these activities are examples of methods standardization as discussed by Star and Griesemer (1989).

By educating, promoting and literally imposing their methods for measuring and calculating risk, and requiring others to adjust their actions accordingly, risk managers interfere directly with trading practice. The use of terms such as 'compliance' and 'alignment' to discuss the results of their efforts further underscores the ambition to standardize methods; such terms are completely nonsensical when coordination is achieved via boundary objects. Being aware that their efforts do restrict the traders' abilities to freely engage in trade, risk managers seek to make their methods as simple as possible to reduce the amount of detail control (and at the same time increase compliance).

Coordinating the use of coordinating tools

In the model proposed by Star and Griesemer (1989), boundary objects and methods standardization are viewed as complementary tools for achieving coordination. On the basis of our empirical material, we suggest that they may rather be competing, at least under certain circumstances. That is to say, the use of methods standardization may prevent the use of a certain boundary object to achieve coordination.

Through their recourse to methods standardization, risk managers could be said to introduce hierarchical control ambitions into the heterarchical mode of organizing characteristic of trading rooms. The reported challenge of striking a balance between rules and entrepreneurship within investment banks reflects the tension between these two forms of organizing. Despite the import attributed to protecting the interests of clients and owners, then, investment banks do not seem to be prepared to abandon heterarchy altogether. The flexible and plastic coordination achieved by using the share as a boundary object allows the different expert groups to engage in their respective practices as part of a 'heterarchical organization' like an investment bank. Risk managers' attempt to coordinate through methods standardization is not as flexible. As a result, we see a hierarchical control system being implemented in parallel to the heterarchical practices of the expert groups working in equities.

The consequences of these parallel systems are not easy to assess. An upbeat assessment would be to argue that they complement each other; that the risk management system provides a much-needed counterweight to the profit-promoting system of bonuses based on trading results – adding a brake pedal to the powerful accelerator pedal, if you will. An alternative reading of the complementarity thesis would be to argue that the risk management system simply buffers the traders from external pressures to comply with regulations and directives – that the talk of striking a balance between control ambitions and entrepreneurial activity reveals that risk management is mostly window dressing. We opt for a third assessment, which is based on a questioning of the prospects of successfully maintaining two parallel systems within the investment bank. As we have tried to show, the practices related to coordination through boundary objects and methods standardization interfere with each other. The organizational friction that these interferences generate, we suggest, is productive; it provides a reminder of the multiple objectives and values that investment banking serves, and must seek to align. From this perspective, further improving communication between risk managers and traders is not necessarily a good thing. The more specific consequences that these interferences have, however, remain to be further investigated.

Conclusions

Our study has shown how the growth of risk management introduces a different type of coordinating tool into investment banking. By relying on methods standardization as opposed to coordination through boundary objects, risk management carries with it a hierarchical mode of organizing that stands in sharp relief to the heterarchical organizing characteristic of expert groups active in the equities line of business of investment banks. This coordinating tool lacks the flexibility and plasticity that we observe the share to have as a boundary object between expert groups. The practices associated with these parallel systems of coordination are not completely decoupled but interfere with each other, creating varying degrees of friction within the investment bank. This friction, we suggest, is productive in highlighting the diverse values that the financial industries are called on to produce.

In summary, we draw three main conclusions. First, boundary objects are practical, useful tools for coordinating heterarchical organizations. Second, as coordinating tools, methods standardization and boundary objects may interfere with each other, potentially creating organizational tensions and conflicts. Third, such tensions and conflicts are neither good nor bad in principle; their quality depends on the yardstick employed, for example whether we are concerned with the internal work organization of investment banks or the external consequences of investment banking.

Notes

1 We would like to thank the Bank of Sweden Tercentenary Foundation for financial support (research project P2006-0797:1).
2 Within the financial sector, risk is commonly defined as the standard deviation of the return on total investment and degree of uncertainty of return on an asset.
3 *Credit risk* concerns whether or not the issuer of a bond (the debtor or borrower) can pay back at the settled date of maturity. This probability affects the price of the bond. *Market risk* concerns the value of a specific security and how it is affected by changes in a number of risk factors, including stock prices, interest rates, foreign exchange rates and commodity prices. *Operational risk* relates to the conduct of business within an investment bank and includes legal risks (e.g. of fraud, or lack of compliance with routines), the probability of human errors, IT-system risks, etc.

References

Abolafia, M.Y. (1996) *Making Markets: Opportunism and restraint on Wall Street*, Cambridge, MA: Harvard University Press.

Baker, W.E. (1984) 'The social structure of a national securities market', *American Journal of Sociology*, 89: 775–811.

Beunza, D. and Stark, D. (2005) 'How to recognize opportunities: heterarchical search in a trading room', in K. Knorr Cetina and A. Preda (eds) *The Sociology of Financial Markets*, Oxford: Oxford University Press.

Blomberg, J. (2004) 'Appreciating stock-broking: constructing conceptions to make sense of performance', *Journal of Management Studies*, 41: 155–80.

Callon, M. (1986) 'Some elements of a sociology of translation: domestication of the scallops and the fishermen of St-Brieuc Bay', in J. Law (ed.) *Power, Action and Belief: A new sociology of knowledge*, London: Routledge & Kegan Paul.

Callon, M., Méadel, C. and Rabeharisoa, V. (2002) 'The economy of qualities', *Economy and Society*, 31: 194–217.

Eccles, R.G. and Crane, D.B. (1988) *Doing Deals: Investment banks at work*, Boston: Harvard Business School Press.

Fenton-O'Creevy, M., Nicholson, N., Soane, E. and Willman, P. (2004) *Traders: Risks, decisions, and management in financial markets*, Oxford: Oxford University Press.

Hasselström, A. (2004) 'Modes of knowing: the fashioning of financial market knowledge', in C. Garsten and M. Lindh de Montoya (eds) *Market Matters: Exploring cultural processes in the global marketplace*, Basingstoke, UK: Palgrave Macmillan.

Hayward, M.L.A. and Boeker, W. (1998) 'Power and conflicts of interest in professional firms: evidence from investment banking', *Administrative Science Quarterly*, 43: 1–22.

Institute of International Finance (2008) *Interim Report of the IIF Committee on Market Best Practices*, Washington, DC: IIF.

Kalthoff, H. (2005) 'Practices of calculation: economic representations and risk management', *Theory, Culture and Society*, 22(2): 69–97.

Knorr Cetina, K. and Bruegger, U. (2002a) 'Traders' engagement with markets: a post-social relationship', *Theory, Culture and Society*, 19(5–6): 161–85.

Knorr Cetina, K. and Bruegger, U. (2002b) 'Global microstructures: the virtual societies of financial markets', *American Journal of Sociology*, 107: 905–50.

Latour, B. (1986) 'The powers of association', in J. Law (ed.) *Power, Action and Belief: A new sociology of knowledge*, London: Routledge & Kegan Paul.

Latour, B. (1987) *Science in Action: How to follow scientists and engineers through society*, Cambridge, MA: Harvard University Press.

Mol, A. (2002) *The Body Multiple: Ontology in medical practice*, Durham, NC: Duke University Press.

Morrison, A.D. and Wilhelm, W.J. Jr (2007) *Investment Banking: Institutions, politics, and law*, Oxford: Oxford University Press.

Muniesa, F. (2004) 'Assemblage of a market mechanism', *Journal of the Center for Information Studies*, 5(3): 11–19.

Power, M. (2004) 'The risk management of everything', *Journal of Risk Finance*, 5(3): 58–65.

Power, M. (2005a) 'Enterprise risk management and the organization of uncertainty in financial institutions', in K. Knorr Cetina and A. Preda (eds) *The Sociology of Financial Markets*, Oxford: Oxford University Press.

Power, M. (2005b) 'The invention of operational risk', *Review of International Political Economy*, 12: 577–99.

Star, S.L. and Griesemer, J.R. (1989) 'Institutional ecology, "translations" and boundary objects: amateurs and professionals in Berkeley's Museum of Vertebrate Zoology, 1907–1939', *Social Studies of Science*, 19: 387–420.

Willman, P., Fenton-O'Creevy, M., Nicholson, N. and Soane, E. (2001) 'Knowing the risks: theory and practice in financial market trading', *Human Relations*, 54: 887–910.

Winroth, K., Blomberg, J. and Kjellberg, H. (2010) 'Enacting overlapping markets', *Journal of Cultural Economy*, 3: 3–18.

Zaloom, C. (2006) *Out of the Pits: Traders and technology from Chicago to London*, Chicago: University of Chicago Press.

13 Roles, risks and complexity

An exploration of the triangle institutional investors, executive boards and supervisory boards in the Netherlands

Erik van de Loo and Angelien Kemna

Introduction

The recent crisis in financial markets has triggered questions about the actual and perceived role of shareholders. In public debate, they have been criticized for a one-sided financial, overly risky and short-term orientation. In this context, Eumedion, an interest group representing institutional investors in the Netherlands and Europe in particular, has initiated an independent qualitative survey.[1] It asked for an exploration of the roles defined in the law and relevant Dutch corporate governance codes for the management and supervisory boards of listed companies and shareholders on the one hand, and the perceived roles of these participants on the other. From April to October 2009 we organized in-depth interviews and round-table discussions with representatives of management boards (current and former CEOs), supervisory boards, the Dutch central bank, regulatory authorities of Dutch financial markets, private and institutional investors, and experts or scholars on corporate governance, company law and investment and asset management. The survey and the report (Kemna and Van de Loo 2009) are the result of an interdisciplinary approach exploring aspects of the experience, perception and behaviour of the various participants in their respective roles in the context of the Dutch financial system. As such, it is the fruit of an interdisciplinary approach combining insights, perspectives and frameworks from the domains of corporate governance, financial markets and asset management with those from leadership, group and systems psychodynamics (Gould *et al.* 2001). In this chapter we will focus on changes in the perceptions, experiences and behaviours of key players in their roles as member of the managing board, supervisory director or investor, as the case may be. We will explore how these key players experience and understand their own as well as the corresponding roles of other key players. Organizational role analysis (Borwick 2006) has been a leading framework in the conduct and analysis of the interviews. Organizational role analysis differentiates between the *defined role* (the formal definition and characteristics of the role), the *described role* (the actual experience and behaviour of the person in the role) and the *systemic role* (how the role fits the system and makes the system work). Individual experiences and behaviours of individuals in their roles typically reflect significant characteristics of the system or organization. After the presentation of the various roles and their inter-relatedness, we will frame the systems complexity in terms of multiparty and interorganizational collaboration (Prins 2006, 2010; Neumann 2010). The enormous complexity of the financial system makes it also increasingly volatile and unpredictable. The risks seem insufficiently contained, as the recent series of financial crises reveal. A serious question is how to address these risks related to the primary task in a constructive way instead of avoiding them by unconscious collective defensive routines (Miller 1993; Hirschhorn 1999). We will conclude this chapter with a few recommendations about how even a small and relatively simple set of behavioural steps might improve the relationships among this trian-gle of institutional investors, members of the management board and supervisory directors.

From simple to complex: governance change in the financial and economic system

The findings of our study can best be described by placing them in the perspect-ive of the events of the past ten years (e.g. Fentrop 2002). A complete historical analysis is not intended here, only that which pertains to the roles and relation-ships between the participants who are involved in managing Dutch listed com-panies. Until the internet/accounting fraud crisis around 2000 and 2001, which triggered a strong focus on regulation and control, the management of a listed company had a relatively simple social system, with three key actors or particip-ants: the management or executive board, the supervisory board and the institu-tional investors. The most characteristic behaviours as they were at that time are set out in the following subsections.

Management board

The management board was the dominant player among the three participants. Its main characteristic was as a collegial body, with the chairman as its tempo-rary steward. The board was jointly responsible for the strategy of the company and felt to be the owner of the company. The management board was in control in terms of strategy and steering the company and did not feel the slightest need for supervision from either supervisory directors or shareholders. Because of anti-takeover measures, management board members felt relatively protected against potential hostile action by competitors or shareholders.

Supervisory board

The supervisory board was a somewhat reticent player, consisting of former members of management boards from the 'old boy' network. It functioned as a sounding board for strategy and placed its own networks at the disposal of the management board of the company. Its specific knowledge of the sector was not great in general, but this was compensated for by appointing former members of the management board of the company itself as supervisory directors. The supervisory board functioned as an advisory council in terms of role and behaviour. Both the management board and the supervisory board were satisfied with this situation. They each knew precisely what they could and could not expect from one another. There was a minimal relationship between the supervisory board and institutional investors.

Institutional investors

The institutional investors were somewhat passive players and consisted mostly of Dutch insurers, pension funds and major asset managers. The pension fund and asset managers did not really feel engaged with the company as shareholders; their interests were too small. For years, asset managers had been investing worldwide, and pension funds were also permitted to invest in shares outside the Netherlands. They were increasingly phasing out assets in Dutch shares. Only the insurers, who had accumulated interests in Dutch shares because of the tax exemption for 5 per cent participating interests, felt empathically engaged with the strategy of the company. They maintained an intensive dialogue with the company's management board. Power was ultimately in the hands of the management board, and this was generally accepted in the Dutch situation at that time.

The characteristics of this relatively simple system are as follows:

- few players with one dominant player (the management board);
- few rules (legal/governance) and protection for the company against hostile takeover and shareholder involvement;
- simple investment objectives (tax-related/prudential), mainly focused on the long term;
- familiar behaviour, because only minor change in the roles and relationships occurred.

Changes in roles of existing participants

Relationships changed greatly after the internet/accounting fraud crisis. The reasons for the changes include the following: new legislation and regulations, partly as a consequence of the accounting scandals; stricter external regulatory authorities; and globalization and the accompanying increase in Anglo-Saxon influence.[2]

Management board

First, the management board lost its position as the dominant player, owing to the increased power of supervisory directors, shareholders and external regulatory authorities. Second, the collegial management board came under pressure because of the increased influence of the Anglo-Saxon model. This has led to the emergence of the CEO as the dominant player in the management board, which has changed the roles and dynamics within the management board and represents a new reality and challenge for the supervisory board in its responsibility of selecting and supporting leadership, and evaluating its functioning. It has fuelled the narcissism of CEOs, resulting in an increase of 'Sun King' behaviour (Cools 2005; Kets de Vries 2009). Finally, companies have been affected by the radical changes in their shareholder groups, a decrease in the interests of Dutch institutional investors, an increase in the interests of Anglo-Saxon institutional investors and a greater spread of shareholders with smaller stakes.

Our interviews indicate that the climate in which the management boards are operating has changed. CEOs feel that supervisory directors are less focused on corporate strategy and that they understand they must accept the more supervisory and controlling nature of their involvement. Nevertheless, requests from supervisory directors for extra information are mostly met with distrust. The CEOs believe that supervisory directors are overly pressured by shareholders, who in the CEOs' opinion are only interested in governance issues and little concerned with company strategy. The degree of trust between members of the managing board and supervisory directors is a decisive factor in whether one will contact the other in case of concerns, questions or doubts. It is feared that 'opening up' might mean a negative backlash towards managing board members.

Most fund managers were not and are not taken seriously, as it is felt that their focus is too limited and not linked to corporate strategy. They are felt to be more of a nuisance than a support. At the same time, the CEO is confronted with all kinds of corporate governance questions by a separate corporate governance team from the institutional investor. On top of that, codes, legislation and regulations regarding dealing with price-sensitive information prohibit the kind of dialogue that potentially could improve this situation.

As a consequence, the CEO is in danger of no longer feeling like the owner of the company and is consequently more inclined to pursue his or her own short-term interests. In this context, one can speak about the 'ownerless company', where no one person feels like the owner of the company or represents the interests of the company's stakeholders.

Supervisory board

The supervisory board has also been confronted with a series of significant changes. As a consequence of the internet/accounting fraud crisis, new codes of governance have shifted more responsibilities, power and related expectations to the supervisory board. Its members have to supervise and are held accountable for the result. One might argue that the risk of failure as a company (not having the right strategy, not having the capacity to implement the strategy, not being in control of key risks, etc.) has been shifted towards the supervisory board. The supervisory directors feel pressured by more demanding shareholders, whose influence also has grown. All of this has become more apparent as a result of an Anglo-Saxon shift in the shareholders' group.

As a result of the pressure exerted by politicians, the media, interest groups and shareholders, the whole supervisory board focuses almost grimly on supervision and is confronted with an influx of information placed at its disposal by the management board. Its members are aware of liability and personal reputation risks.

It is widely acknowledged that the key factor in the functioning of the supervisory board in relation to management is not so much the structure (a one-tier versus a two-tier board) but the quality of and the trust in the relationships and collaboration. The preconditions required for this are absent in many cases: the supervisory board is often too large and it meets too infrequently and for too short a time. Moreover, members seldom or never meet separately from the management board. Furthermore, a lack of sector knowledge has been identified and the evaluation of the board's own effectiveness falls short, at both individual and team level. This is completely in line with the loud appeal for drastic improvements to be made to the effectiveness of non-executive boards (Conger and Lawler 2009; Conger 2009).

Finally, the relationship of the supervisory board with all stakeholders, and with the institutional investors in particular, involves the CEO alone. It is unusual and mostly regarded as undesirable for a supervisory board to conduct a dialogue with individual stakeholders separately from the CEO. This means that the supervisory board does not have a sufficiently clear picture of what these relationships actually are, and signals are not picked up soon enough, particularly when problems already exist. In the absence of a direct relationship of its own with shareholders, the supervisory board then has little choice but to support its own CEO. The risk that conflicts will polarize and become practically insoluble increases as a consequence.

Institutional investors

Institutional investors have acquired more influence as a result of the introduction of the new code of governance. In addition, more possibilities have arisen as many companies have abolished their anti-takeover measures. Institutional investors have needed to become familiar with the new set of Dutch governance rules. Eumedion has supported its members in monitoring the maintenance of and compliance with these new rules. Many institutional investors have set up their own governance teams, operating separately from the fund managers, who often do not even know how the governance teams are going to vote at the AGM (general shareholder meeting). Not only does this lead to frustration on the part of the managing board and supervisory directors of the company, but such duplication of each other's work also leads to internal friction for the institutional investors themselves.

In addition, the arrival of active Anglo-Saxon institutional investors who are mostly focused on the short term has influenced the behaviour of the Dutch institutional investors. Since these Anglo-Saxon institutional investors were able to show high short-term profits, the originally long-term institutional investors were forced by their clients and the media to achieve comparable returns. As a result, little remains of the long-term institutional investor with a good knowledge of long-term value creation at a company. They do not have the mindset of owners and are not incentivized as such by their end clients. They are more 'share owners' than 'share holders'. With concepts like modern portfolio theory and diversification, they try to beat the benchmark by short-term buying and selling. This has increased the distance between them and the companies in which they invest. Their mutual understanding has deteriorated even more as a result, and the strict enforcement of the law on price-sensitive information is only driving the parties further apart. The only serious contact between supervisory board and institutional investors occurs in times of conflict, which is a situation that does not generally lead to prolonged and sustainable relationships.

Finally, the commercial pressure experienced by institutional investors to generate short-term performance for the end clients is further reinforced by other forces. First, the financial assessment framework of the Dutch central bank, the prudential regulatory authority, incentivizes pension funds to invest for the short term. Second, members of the management boards of listed companies are also oriented towards the short term, because their bonuses are based on short-term share price results. And, last but not least, the attention of the media is mainly focused on short-term returns on investments.

Arrival of new players

The end of the internet bubble and the worldwide accounting scandals meant that the hitherto relatively calm environment surrounding Dutch listed companies became a focus of keen public interest. Measures had to be taken. The participants at the Dutch listed companies have continued to be subject to tighter control by the public, the regulatory authorities and the interest groups.

Politicians and media

Politicians and media played a role in this period by intermittently giving populist and caricatured descriptions of the participants, describing ruthless shareholders whose sole aim is short-term profit and who have no interest in long-term strategy and commitment; sleeping supervisory directors who neither understand what shareholders want nor are able to keep management board and CEO in check; 'Sun King' CEOs with no consideration for the company and its stakeholders, whose aim is their personal glory and their own well-filled wallets; and finally, regulatory authorities who allowed all of this to go on for far too long and did not take firm enough action.

A simplified presentation of the situation creates a high risk that solutions will be sought in terms of a quick fix in a sub-area, with no comprehension of the consequences this will have for all participants. Exaggerated trust is placed on one individual in response to this change, however, and there is an unrealistic expectation that things will soon be better as a result.

Regulatory authorities

As previously stated, the Dutch central bank and the authority financial markets have recently entered the field more firmly, significantly impacting the interrelationships between the various participants. Out of fear of insider trading and non-compliance with the new codes of governance, management boards have decided on more distant investor relations contact. Less consultation takes place with major shareholders on important issues. As a result, they are also unable to share really important information, or doubts concerning strategy. Furthermore, there is pressure from the VEB, the Dutch investors' association, because small investors are at a disadvantage if institutional investors receive more information than they do.

In addition, there is also unfamiliarity with the acting-in-concert rules, as a result of which institutional investors are reticent about contacting each other. Collaborating with other institutional investors, in certain circumstances, can actually give rise to an obligation for parties to give notification of a substantial interest in the event of a notification threshold being exceeded, or to issue a public offer for all shares in the company in the event that the collective interest is at least 30 per cent. The criteria for meeting the definition of acting in concert lead to a lack of clarity. There is a fear of becoming publicly discredited if another party alleges that a rule has not been complied with, with all potential reputational consequences. Institutional investors may become more reticent, therefore, about consulting with each other and collaboration in and outside AGMs.

Complexity, interdependence and lack of trust

Our interviews have made it clear that players' views of each other's role behaviour have become harsher in recent years. The increased mutual tensions between players can be better understood through the many changes in the playing field of the Dutch listed companies described above. In the course of a few years, a simple social system has evolved in a complex social system with the following characteristics:

- increased number of players without one or a few being dominant;
- many rules, with more emphasis on legal and governance issues and less protection of the company;
- a multiplicity of investment objectives due to new participants and the influence of prudential supervision (financial assessment framework), as a result of which a short-term focus has become much more marked;
- unfamiliarity with and incomprehension of one's own roles and those of others, because the changes in roles and relationships have been rapid.

The survey reveals the consequences of the rapid change from a relatively simple to a highly complex social system. With all these new players in the field and with existing players in new roles, both the defined and the described roles of the various participants have changed and are changing. It is very clear how complex is the way in which all the roles are interlinked and, as a result, how a change in one role potentially impacts all other roles and the functioning of the system at large. The role of the regulatory agencies is one of the striking examples. During the interviews with individual participants we were impressed by how much they were still struggling to understand and define their own actual and desired role, as well as the roles of others in the financial field. It could be concluded that too little time has passed between the introduction of the new code and legislation in response to the internet/accounting fraud crisis and the credit crisis to actually allow all the changes to be assimilated. Or worse, the new legislation constrains and eliminates the shared reflective space that various actors require in order to understand and adapt to one another's roles.

All parties involved acknowledge that trust and good interpersonal relationships are crucial in order to make the system work, both within and between the various key role-holders and interest groups. Trust is critical to be able to survive in a world full of interdependencies, where one's fate is deeply co-determined by others whose behaviour one cannot control. It is helpful here to differentiate between various types of trust in order to be more precise about the kind of trust that is needed. Lewicki and Bunker (1996) describe three types: (1) *calculated or deterrence-based trust* (calculating that it is in one's own best interest to collaborate; not trusting others might be very detrimental); (2) *knowledge-based trust* (knowing the others sufficiently well to make it possible to anticipate their behaviour); and (3) *identification-based trust* (identification with the other's desires and intentions). The changes in the roles and the role relationships described in this chapter have decreased the understanding and the predictability of role-related behaviour within the financial system. Attempts to master the complexity of the system and to control aspects of it have actually, and unintentionally, undermined universal laws of establishing and maintaining trust in organizations – for example, attempts such as regulating fairness around the sharing of price-sensitive information. What we describe here is not so much about striving for empathic, affection- and identification-based trust, which is a precondition for lasting personal relationships. On the contrary, calculated and knowledge-based trust are critical and often provide a sufficient base for effective collaboration in the organizational and political context. In negotiations and conflict handling, for example, one might have situations where parties hate one another but are ready and willing to trust in order to achieve results (Raiffa 2002). They have calculated that there is no other way to resolve the issues. Trust becomes a reflection of the acceptance of the reality of being (inter)dependent.

Not trusting, not accepting the (inter)dependencies and complexities creates dissatisfaction and negative stress for those performing the various roles (as we observed in our survey), and it undermines the effective functioning of the system at large.

Multi-party collaboration

The complexity of the present system can also be described as a 'multi-party' problem (Prins 2006, 2010). The key factor in a multi-party situation is the combined action of a number of parties, each with a distinctive role and interest. No single party is able to solve the problem alone or to force a sustainable solution. They have to rely on each other and are dependent on each other for finding a good solution. The behaviour and attitude of an individual party can, however, strongly influence the whole. Increasing numbers of problems can be characterized as multi-party problems. Multi-party situations can be characterized as high risk, volatile, unpredictable and fragile. One issue of one party, one incident, one bad surprise may potentially derail and destroy the multi-party collaboration.

Moreover, most multi-party problems are also of a multi-issue nature. This is also the case in the financial system, where there are a multitude of interlinked issues, with the involvement of a multitude of different parties. The challenge is to work constructively with this multi-issue and multi-party reality. Although the study of multi-party situations is still in its early stages, a number of relevant complexities and pitfalls nevertheless have already been identified. For the purposes of our survey, this analysis offers a framework within which recommendations can be placed. A multi-party situation comprises four distinct forms of complexity (Vansina and Tailleu 1997):

1   *Strategic complexity.* Not only are the parties occupied with searching for and gauging their own strategies and roles, but also they do not yet know, understand or believe the strategy of the others. They are better able to decide on their own strategies if the aims of the other parties are known. Another complication here is that the parties have to collaborate with others whose interests do not always run parallel to their own, or with others whom they can sometimes regard or encounter as opponents.

Experience teaches that a multi-party situation benefits hugely if all the parties involved have an idea of, and respect for, the interests of all the others, while recognizing a common overarching interest at the same time. They all have to endeavour to do as much justice as possible to the separate and the common interests. If this is not what they want, or if they are unsuccessful in the attempt, either a deadlock will develop (the cooperation fails, a crisis occurs), or a solution with winners and losers is forced through on the basis of power.

Unclear and confused strategies often are a reflection of the nature of the complexity of the situation. A multi-party strategy typically emerges over a period of time; it cannot be clear from the beginning. One could say here: 'welcome to reality'. Take, for example, the global survey by Felton and Fritz (2005), taking in more than 1,000 board directors. More than 75 per cent of the directors indicated that they wanted to spend more time on risk and strategy – not surprisingly, as more than a quarter indicated that they have no or only limited understanding of their company strategy. More than half admitted having little or no understanding of the key initiatives to secure the long-term future of the company.

2   *Informational complexity.* An abundance of information is available on parties, themes and problems. How much of this is relevant? How do you know that you know sufficiently well what you must know? How do you know what you do not yet know? How do you know how well you have to weigh up what you know?

3   *Procedural complexity.* The parties have to deal with each other but have no unequivocal authority relationship. They do not constitute a formal organization together and no rules have therefore been specified initially with regard to decision making, conflict management, exchange of information, whether or not to exclude parties, etc. It is considered crucial for a multi-party system to organize itself promptly.

The manner in which agreement is reached on the required method of organizing and operating is certainly as decisive for the effectiveness of the method as the final organizational structure itself. The parties must perceive the decision-making process about rules, roles and interests to be fair and just (Van der Heyden and Limberg 2007). Parties have a tendency to answer fairness with fairness in complex situations, while perceived unfairness generally elicits hostility and obstruction.

4   *Socio-emotional complexity.* Tension and emotion often build up rapidly in an unclear situation in which the individual and collective interests are great. Parties can feel unappreciated, for example, or accused, subordinated or excluded in an instant. How effectively do parties deal with this? The enormous complexity and the frequently deficient organization and addressing of this make multi-party collaborations exceptionally fragile, since a single incident can have a huge destabilizing effect within a short time. People should be prepared for this in terms of communication, organization and conflict resolution.

Collaboration involves conscious and unconscious processes, rational and irrational dimensions, which many leaders and decision makers deal with clumsily and inexpertly (van de Loo 2007), with all the attendant consequences, which also occur in financial and stock markets (Tuckett and Taffler 2008).

When parties and actors within a social system feel threatened by a complexity that is beyond them, they have a natural tendency to reduce the complexity. Classic examples are the formation of premature sub-coalitions; the exclusion of one or more parties, or the levelling of accusations against them; or the simple denial of the situation. Parties who cannot cope well with the lack of clarity resort to what are known as social defences (Miller 1993; Hirschhorn 1999), which are strategies that are collectively and unconsciously applied as protection against the cumulative anxiety. There is apparently an inability to collectively recognize the difficulty and the risk. In most cases the focus then comes to lie unilaterally on a sub-question (e.g. excessive remuneration, the introduction of a code), or unrealistically high expectations apply to a number of individuals who are considered to have the ability and the obligation to save the integrity of the system as a whole.

The primary task of an organization or group is considered to be whatever task needs to be performed in order for it to survive. One might state, for example, that the primary task of a supervisory board is to monitor the overall strategy and the quality and effectiveness of the leadership of the company, while an institutional investor might define his or her primary task as making a fair return on investments in order to sustain long-term relationships with his or her end clients. But these formulations exclude the interdependent nature of the context they are operating in. If one operates in a multi-party reality, this needs to be reflected in the primary task. Sustainable survival incorporates elements of cross- and interorganizational collaboration (Neumann 2010).

Recommendations

On the basis of the complexity of the social system described in this chapter, we can make a few recommendations. How can participants individually and in their collaborative action deal more wisely and more effectively with the increased complexity? To this end, we point out four important aspects that are essential to the successful implementation of any recommendation:

1   *Awareness*: all participants should become and continue to be aware of the complexity. This means to see their own role, task and behaviour in the context of the greater whole in interaction with others. Technical proposals, adjustments to roles, rules and codes should also be considered carefully in terms of their (potential) effect in the system as a whole. Integral, well-thought-out and gradual change produces the greatest chance of success in this respect.

2   *Multidisciplinary approach*: the complexity outlined requires an approach that uses a combination of legal, investment-specific, tax-related, prudential, political, economic, socio-psychological and ethical perspectives. Behaviour and perception are essential components in this process. Representatives of these diverse disciplines must endeavour to achieve practicable solutions more collectively than has been the case until now.

3   *Differentiation*: the complexity should be reduced where possible by, for example, more and better differentiation of roles (Borwick 2006), tasks and rules, type of investor (Coyne and Witter 2002), type and size of company, and by different roles within one party, as for example with the supervisory board (e.g. Conger and Lawler 2009; Conger 2009).

4   *Training and study*: creating the right time and space to understand one's own role and the roles of others. This means paying attention to the behavioural translation in order to really be able to deal with rules, roles and structures devised. The parties must take the time to become accustomed to the rules, to learn to discuss role conflicts and to adjust behaviour and roles accordingly. This will help in addressing issues of behaviour, trust and

communication in the correct manner. There is important work to be done here, both within the various participants (management board, supervisory board, institutional investor, regulatory authority) and between participants. This requires, among other things, a rethinking of training processes and other ways of evaluating the quality and effectiveness of players and roles. Cooperation does not materialize out of thin air (Hansen 2009).

In line with this approach, we have elsewhere formulated a series of behavioural recommendations that are intended to improve the present system in small steps and can be implemented almost immediately (Kemna and van de Loo 2009). Fully acknowledging the huge complexity and interdependencies of the financial system, we are aware that effective interventions for system change typically have their focus one or two levels below overall system level (Coleman 1990). Ideally, they impact the rules of interaction between parts of the system.

An example may be of use here. Most friction occurs in the relation to shareholders and at the AGM in particular. The AGM is an annual meeting at which formal business must be settled and where corporate governance issues are discussed. This formal nature is not really compatible with an open discussion of how things stand as regards company strategy and risk management, for example. Yet it is precisely this kind of discussion that shareholders need in order to arrive at a better understanding of the company in which they have invested. It is advisable in this light to hold a number of meetings for all shareholders every year at which substantive themes such as strategy and risk management can be dealt with in greater depth. Even if not all shareholders can or wish to attend, this additional clarification of crucial subjects may still relieve some of the pressure on the AGM and help to create a better understanding and relationship.

This relates to one of our central findings, which applies to all participants: the financial playing field has changed strongly in a short period of time and has evolved into a complex social system. Roles, motivations and behaviours of the various players, as well as their relationships and interdependencies, are unclear and insufficiently discussed by these players. Describing and discussing these patterns has, in the context of our survey, created insights and potentially decreases the often tense relationships among participants.

Notes

This chapter is a shortened and elaborated report of our original study (Kemna and van de Loo 2009).

1 For quantitative research among institutional investors, please refer to a study carried out at the request of the Monitoring Committee (see Monitoring Commissie Corporate Governance Code 2008).
2 Also see the recent study by Boot (2009), in which he deals extensively with the causes and consequences of what he calls the uprooted company.

References

Boot, A.W.A. (2009) *De ontwortelde onderneming. Ondernemingen overgeleverd aan financiers?*, Assen, the Netherlands: Van Gorcum.

Borwick, I. (2006) 'Organizational role analysis: managing strategic change in business settings', in J. Newton, S. Long and B. Sievers (eds) *Coaching in Depth: The organizational role analysis approach*, London: Karnac.

Coleman, J.S. (1990) *Foundations of Social Theory*, Cambridge, MA: The Belknap Press of Harvard University Press.

Conger, J.A. (ed.) (2009) *Boardroom Realities: Building leaders across your board*, San Francisco: Jossey-Bass.

Conger, J.A. and Lawler, E.E. III (2009) 'Sharing leadership on corporate boards: a critical requirement for teamwork at the top', *Organizational Dynamics*, 38: 183–91.

Cools, K. (2005) *Controle is goed vertrouwen nog beter*, Assen, the Netherlands: Van Gorcum.

Coyne, K.P. and Witter, J.W. (2002) 'Taking the mystery out of investor behavior', *Harvard Business Review*, 80: 68–78.

Felton, R.F. and Fritz, P.K. (2005) 'The view from the boardroom', *McKinsey Quarterly*, special edition 'Value and Performance', March: 49–61.

Fentrop, P. (2002) *A History of Corporate Governance, 1602–2002*, Amsterdam: Prometheus.

Gould, L., Stapley, L.F. and Stein, M. (eds) *The Systems Psychodynamics of Organizations*, London: Karnac.

Hansen, M. (2009) *Collaboration: How leaders avoid the traps, create unity and reap big results*, Boston: Harvard Business Press.

Hirschhorn, L. (1999) 'The primary risk', *Human Relations*, 52: 5–23.

Kemna, A. and van de Loo, E. (2009) 'Role of institutional investors in relation to management boards and supervisory directors: a triangular survey', Online, available at: www.eumedion.nl/page/downloads/Kemna_Van_De_Loo_Report_FINAL_-_English.pdf (retrieved 29 October 2010).

Kets de Vries, M.F.R. (2009) *Reflections on Character and Leadership*, Chichester, UK: John Wiley.

Lewicki, R.J. and Bunker, B.B. (1996) 'Developing and maintaining trust in working relationships', in R.M. Kramer and T.R. Tyler (eds) *Trust in Organizations*, Thousand Oaks, CA: Sage.

Miller, E. (1993) *From Dependency to Autonomy: Studies in organization and change*, London: Free Association Books.

Monitoring Commissie Corporate Governance Code (2008) 'Rapport over de evaluatie en actualisering van de Nederlandse corporate governance code'. Online, available at: http://commissiecorporategovernance.nl/page/downloads/review_rapport_0107.pdf (retrieved 29 October 2010).

Neumann, J.E. (2010) 'How integrating organizational theory with systems psychodynamics can matter in practice: a commentary on critical challenges and dynamics in multiparty collaboration', *Journal of Applied Behavioral Science*, 46: 313–21.

Prins, S. (2006) 'The systems psychodynamics of collaborative work: issues in direction setting of the process', dissertation, Leuven: Catholic University Leuven.

Prins, S. (2010) 'From competition to collaboration: critical challenges and dynamics in multiparty collaboration', *Journal of Applied Behavioral Science*, 46: 281–312.

Raiffa, H. (2002) *Negotiation Analysis: The science and art of collaborative decision making*, Cambridge, MA: The Belknap Press of Harvard University Press.

Tuckett, D. and Taffler, R. (2008) 'Phantastic objects and the financial market's sense of reality: a psychoanalytic contribution to the understanding of stock market instability', *International Journal of Psychoanalysis*, 89: 389–412.

van de Loo, E. (2007) 'Bewuste en onbewuste processen van samenwerken', *Management en Organisatie*, 61: 219–27.

Van der Heyden, L. and Limberg, T. (2007) 'Why fairness matters', *International Commerce Review*, 7: 93–101.

Vansina, L. and Tailleu, T. (1997) 'Diversity in collaborative task-systems', *European Journal of Work and Organizational Psychology*, 6: 183–99.

14 When profit seeking trumps safety

The risks and opportunities of liminality in commercial aviation in post-9/11 America

Amy L. Fraher

This chapter contributes to an understanding of the socioanalytic aspects of finance in contemporary society by examining the complicated interrelatedness of money and safety within the US commercial aviation industry. Its thesis is that the airline industry's fixation on financial bottom lines and increasing profit has diminished safety priorities, causing a shift in pilot demographics from a stable, high-skilled, homogeneous work group to a less experienced, undisciplined, liminal group. This shift has led airlines to rely increasingly on individuals' professionalism and personal discipline to ensure safe flight operations, compensating for containment shortfalls in the system. Yet a series of accidents provides evidence that aviation industry leaders' lack of attention to this demographic shift and failure to contain the emerging liminal state has contributed to the development of a perverse culture, with troubling ramifications for air safety.

Finance

While many commercial airlines would like the public to believe that the terrorist attacks of 11 September 2001 caused the post-9/11 downturn, informed insiders considered the aviation industry overdue for an adjustment. The events of 11 September simply provided the struggling airline industry with a popularly accepted excuse to downsize, while eliciting sympathy as one of the most visible images of America's struggle against terrorism. As if through a clever magic trick, industry leaders distracted the public by blaming the slump on terrorists, war, SARS (severe acute respiratory syndrome), economic recession, greedy employees, aggressive labor groups and frugal consumers while airline executives, bankruptcy lawyers and economic consultants made millions of dollars.

Take United Airlines, for example. At one point the world's largest international air carrier, United spent nearly three years in bankruptcy protection, a luxury not available to its international competitors. When it emerged from bankruptcy in 2006, executives dealt 400 managers in for 10 million shares, or 8 percent of the total company, worth an estimated $115 million on top of their annual salaries. Meanwhile, CEO Glenn F. Tilton received a $600,000 salary in addition to $4.5 million in benefits, over $15 million in stock options and restricted shares, and a $3 million signing bonus – a total compensation package of $23.8 million for 2006 alone (Bailey 2007; Morgenson 2006: B1). All this while employees were furloughed (laid off), wage and benefits slashed, and consumers increasingly denied the most basic of flight amenities.

United spokesperson Jean Medina defended this compensation as 'appropriate to enable United to attract and retain top performers' whose compensation is 'tied to future performance of United's stock' (Morgenson 2006: B1). Others are not so convinced. Executive pay expert Brain Foley notes that 'players don't seem to discipline themselves as much as they should', 'external forces aren't executing any braking power', and bankruptcy 'courts don't seem to hold people as accountable as they should' (ibid.).

This laissez-faire approach by government regulators can be traced back to the US Airline Deregulation Act of 1978, signed by President Jimmy Carter in order to disband the Civil Aeronautics Board, allowing airlines to compete over routes, schedules and fares in a free market. Although a leaner, more competitive aviation industry emerged, the government nonetheless remained intimately involved. The post-9/11 bankruptcy filings of US Airways, Delta, Northwest and United Airlines are particularly emblematic of the industry's reliance on government interventions to stay solvent, even during this 'deregulated' period. Among the largest bankruptcies in US history, these private companies left taxpayers footing the bill for their managerial inefficiencies, with little regard for workers' interests. For instance, when legacy carriers United and US Airways emerged from bankruptcy, $9.7 billion was shifted to the government-backed Pension Benefit Guarantee Corporation, causing employees to lose a staggering $5.3 billion of the retirement benefits they earned. The pension plans of Delta and Northwest have been similarly underfunded by a combined $16.3 billion. If these airlines terminate their plans, employees will lose over $5 billion in earned benefits (US GAO 2005b).

Another managerial strategy to offset the impact of skyrocketing fuel prices, low-frill competitors' cheaper cost overhead, and post-bankruptcy airlines' leaner workforce was to consider merging. Although mergers are not unusual in US aviation industry history, so many air carriers considered merging in the post-9/11 period that Congress commissioned a study to review the process. Each merger offers unique advantages, but typically airlines cut costs through downsizing their fleet, furloughing employees and eliminating operational redundancies while increasing revenue by restructuring debt, renegotiating aircraft leases, and expanding networks to serve more city-pair markets, building customer loyalty.

Yet airline mergers are unsettling for employees, who routinely lose money, benefits, control over their schedules, sometimes even their jobs, with little time to prepare or adjust. And because pilot seniority establishes the order for promotion, aircraft assignment, work schedules and pay, disputes over the integration of seniority lists can be particularly contentious. US Airways' and America West's pilot unions, for example, have yet to agree on the terms of their seniority list integration requiring the companies, which merged over five years ago, to still run largely separate flight operations as labor unions battle it out in court.

Safety

Many airlines' struggles to stay solvent in the post-9/11 period originated with decisions made during the initial phase of deregulation when intense competition and unfettered expansion required the extensive purchase of new airplanes and record hiring of employees at industry-leading pay rates. Between 1985 and 1988 alone, nearly 30,000 commercial pilots were hired in the United States. To contextualize this, consider the fact that there are only about 70,000 pilots currently employed in the commercial airline industry in America.

In 1989, *Future Aviation Professionals of America* estimated that US airlines would hire another 32,000 pilots by 2000, and the Federal Aviation Administration (FAA) estimated that airline fleets would increase by 25 percent, or nearly 4,200 additional commercial aircraft (*New York Times* 1987). This rapid aviation industry expansion exhausted the available labor supply and put younger, less experienced pilots eager to embark on a lucrative career path in the cockpit of nearly every air carrier. As Captain Vern Laursen, vice president of flight training at TWA, cautioned, by 1999 'every airline in the country will have 30-year-old captains' (Lavin 1989).

Contributing to the pilot shortage was the mandatory retirement of large numbers of experienced Vietnam-era pilots at age 60, competitive bonuses paid to keep military pilots in the service, and the high cost of civilian flight training. To overcome this pilot paucity, airport flight schools developed accelerated training programs while airlines simultaneously reduced previous standards for age, vision, height and weight, and flight experience. This meant that by the late 1980s a pilot with no college diploma or operational experience, a few months of ground training, and as little as 250 flight hours logged via flight instruction, sightseeing tours or banner tows in small single-engine airplanes could be at the controls of a complex commercial flight in challenging environmental conditions. Particularly disconcerting is how these inexperienced copilots not only represented a safety risk but placed an inordinate amount of pressure on the captain – who may not have had a great deal of experience either – to instruct and mentor while simultaneously performing his or her own duties. Yet it is all perfectly legal by FAA regulations.

The impact of these demographic changes became evident almost immediately.

Case 1: Continental Airlines Flight 1713, 1987

In 1987, Continental Airlines Flight 1713 was delayed leaving Denver's Stapleton Airport by almost two hours, owing to snow, fog, freezing temperatures and reduced visibility. Once cleared, the airplane deiced and awaited takeoff clearance for nearly another half-hour as snow continued to fall. The takeoff roll was initially uneventful until the first officer, flying the aircraft, over-rotated on liftoff, stalling the jet, which impacted the runway and rolled inverted, killing 28 of the 82 occupants on board.

Both pilots were inexperienced in their crew positions and unaccustomed to their required duties during cold-weather operations. The 43-year-old captain had just 166 total hours in the DC-9, of which only 33 were as captain. The 26-year-old first officer had been hired by Continental Airlines just four months before the accident and had only 36 DC-9 flight hours. He was assigned the accident flight, only his second as a Continental copilot, because he had not flown in nearly a month and needed to gain proficiency.

Yet unbeknownst to the captain, the first officer had a documented history of poor performance and problems during training. A previous employer described him as 'tense and unable to cope with deviations from the routine'. At Continental, his flight instructor also voiced concerns: 'Completely lost control of the airplane'; 'Pitch control jerky'; 'Altitude control when pressure is on is somewhat sloppy'; and 'Airspeed control generally way out of limits'. All these refer to piloting deficiencies that became a factor during the accident flight (NTSB 1987: 10–11).

Predictably, the National Transportation Safety Board (NTSB) determined that the probable cause of the accident was 'pilot error'. Yet in its final report it included an unusual systemic indictment (NTSB 1987: 38):

> The rapid growth of the aviation industry at a time when fewer experienced pilots are in the workforce has reduced the opportunity for a pilot to accumulate experience before progressing to a position of greater responsibility. This loss of 'seasoning' has led to the assignment of pilots who may not be operationally mature to positions previously occupied by highly experienced pilots.

Although specific ways to address these deficiencies were not offered, the NTSB (1987) suggested that 'the time has come for the FAA to establish and the industry to accept' operational safeguards to compensate for this 'loss of seasoning'. Yet no such industry response was forthcoming. Why?

Case 2: GP Express Airlines Flight 861, 1992

In 1992 a second fatal accident occurred involving unseasoned airline pilots new to their flight deck roles and over their heads in a challenging situation. GP Express Airlines Flight 861, a Beech C-99, hit the ground, killing three people, when the inexperienced crew lost situational awareness while maneuvering in clouds. It was the 29-year-old captain's first day as an airline pilot and his 24-year-old co-pilot's second month. Both had logged a large percentage of their flight experience in small single-engine airplanes with minimal actual instrument experience in clouds (NTSB 1993a).

One unusual company cost-saving strategy central in this accident was GP Express's policy to provide only one aeronautical approach chart to each crew. During this accident the chart was held by the first officer. As pressure built, the new captain became disoriented, overwhelmed and increasingly reliant on the first officer's erroneous flight guidance. Yet without a chart for verification, the captain had no way to identify the copilot's mistakes or reorient himself.

Approximately three minutes prior to impact, the first officer joked sarcastically about the captain's obvious task saturation: 'Didn't realize that you're going to get this much on your first day did ya?' 'Well, it's all kind of ganged up here on me a little fast', the captain confessed (NTSB 1993a: 5).

Two minutes later, the captain discussed executing a 'missed approach' – akin to going around for another try. But the first officer persuaded him to continue landing. They crashed one minute later.

Case 3: Scenic Air Tours Flight 22, 1992

A third fatal accident caused by organizational failures and a young pilot who lacked 'seasoning' involved a commercial sightseeing company in Hawaii in 1992. The 26-year-old captain had been employed by Scenic Air Tours for about eight months prior to the accident and took off in a 1957 Beech-18 on the 'Volcano Special' sightseeing tour. Although the flight was not certified for instrument conditions, the captain entered the clouds over Mount Haleakala and became disoriented, colliding with the rising terrain and killing all nine people on board (NTSB 1993b).

Particularly disturbing was the post-accident discovery that the young captain, eager to advance his commercial career, falsified his employment application, stating that he had accumulated 3,200 flight hours when in fact he only had about 1,600, well below Scenic Air Tours' 2,500 minimum. Over the previous four years he had worked for at least nine different aviation employers, five of whom dismissed him for causes such as 'below standard work', 'failure to report for duty', 'poor training performance' and 'misrepresentation of qualifications' (NTSB 1993b: 14). Yet this information was not made available to Scenic Air Tours.

In the ten years prior to this disaster, the NTSB investigated twelve sightseeing company accidents that resulted in ninety-six fatalities, of which six crashes were caused when, as in the case of the Scenic Air crash, a fully functioning aircraft was mistakenly flown into the ground. These commonalities prompted more questions about safety, training and oversight in the aviation industry – in particular, the FAA's failure to require that commercial operators conduct a substantive background screening of pilots before employment. In at least three accident investigations between 1987 and 1992, the NTSB urged the FAA to require aviation employers to screen pilots more thoroughly. Yet the FAA dismissed these recommendations, believing that the benefits of these requirements would not outweigh the cost of promulgating and enforcing the new regulations (NTSB 1993b: 39).

Case 4: GP Express Proficiency Checkflight, 1993

A fourth fatal crash involving young pilots quickly working their way up the commercial aviation ranks occurred in 1993 on a dark Nebraska night. The official purpose of this flight was for a company check airman, age 28, to administer an FAA proficiency check to another check airman, age 29, both captains at GP Express Airlines. Yet it emerged that the actual goal of the flight was a midnight opportunity for the two young pilots, known to be good friends who liked to joke around, to conduct unauthorized aerobatic maneuvers in their fifteen-seat turboprop (NTSB 1994).

The flight started with the accident pilot asking the check airman if he was 'up for a "vertical thing"' on takeoff as he radioed company ground personnel at the airport to 'look out the window' and watch (NTSB 1994: 12). Once airborne, they continued with other stunts, including a lethal aileron roll maneuver which, moments prior to ground impact, both pilots confessed never attempting before. Post-crash investigation revealed that the required FAA paperwork was already complete and in the company mailbox. Clearly, the pilots never intended to conduct a proper FAA check ride. Based on this evidence, the NTSB determined that both pilots violated company policies, FAA regulations and the tenants of prudent airmanship, and cited GP Express's failure to establish a safety culture committed to pilot professionalism (NTSB 1994).

Safety implications

Evaluating the commonalities between these accidents reveals some compelling systemic similarities highlighting industry-wide problems with professionalism, pilot training, FAA oversight and the ways airlines screen and hire new employees, schedule inexperienced crews and measure competency in this new generation of pilots. Six of the seven accident pilots were less than 30 years old, had acquired experience flying small single-engine airplanes and were hired between 1987 and 1991, the rapid post-deregulation expansion period, with minimal flight time. Progressing quickly up the commercial ranks, more than half of these young pilots found themselves in the captain's seat within months of initial employment, just as TWA training Captain Laursen had cautioned against. Four of the accident pilots crashed within their first eight months of employment, one on his very first day as an airline pilot. And almost half had a documented history of serious performance problems with previous aviation employers which was never communicated to new employers. These examples of basic skill deficiencies, both technical and teamwork, become particularly alarming at the commercial pilot level because, as Captain Larry Rockliff, vice president of training at Airbus, observed, 'Once you're already in the profession' employed as a airline pilot 'and simply transferring or transitioning from one aircraft type to the next, it's very, very late to be teaching basic skills that were missed' (NTSB 2004: 239).

These aviation industry accident trends did not go unnoticed. Safety analysts predicted that even if accident rates remained constant, the anticipated 3–4 percent annual industry growth would result in a near-doubling of US air crashes by the turn of the twenty-first century. In global terms, this meant an airline crash every week worldwide by 2015 (Gore 1996). This information, among other sobering insights, caused the FAA to slowly awaken to the daunting challenge it faced: how to enforce aviation safety during the rapid industry expansion caused by deregulation. It conceded that it was having difficulty keeping up: the average time to produce a new regulation, even one with urgent safety consequences, was three to four years. Motivated lobbyists often drove the rate of industry change through select projects. Important innovations were often undermined by overly conservative financial concerns. And safety changes, such as those recommended by NTSB accident reports, were often rejected simply because the odds of another mishap occurring was so remote it could not justify the costs.

Prompted by these concerns as well as the mysterious mid-air explosion of TWA Flight 800, the in-flight fire on board ValuJet Flight 592, and the corresponding 340 fatalities, President Bill Clinton created the White House Commission on Aviation Safety and Security led by Vice President Al Gore in 1996. The commission recommended a reengineering of the FAA's regulatory and certification programs with the goal of reducing aviation accidents by a 'factor of five within a decade'. Stuart Matthews, president of Flight Safety Foundation, succinctly noted that 'the FAA was simply never created to deal with the environment that has been produced by deregulation of the air transport industry' (Gore 1996: 1.1). Although that observation was made almost fifteen years ago, little has changed in the regulatory oversight of airline pilots, in large part because of cost (Fraher 2011). Even with all this evidence, finance continues to trump safety in commercial aviation.

These concerns attracted attention from labor unions as well. In 2009 the Air Line Pilots Association (ALPA), the world's largest pilots' union, released a white paper entitled *Producing a Professional Airline Pilot*, which discussed how the fallout from 9/11 significantly changed the business model at most major air carriers. This new approach encouraged companies to cut costs by parking larger airliners and furloughing more experienced, and therefore more expensive, employees – the 'seasoned' pilots the industry lacked – shifting over 50 percent of the nation's flying to commuter affiliates to save money. The strategy has proven to be especially profitable, increasing major airlines' virtual network while reducing overhead costs. A Delta 737-300, for instance, requires eighty-one passengers to break even but Delta's commuter partner Comair only requires twenty-one passengers on a regional jet on a similar route (US DOT 1998). And an average Delta pilot earns about $120,000 per year while a Comair pilot averages $36,000.

For years, strong unions like ALPA controlled this outsourcing through contract negotiations and the threat of job action. But after 9/11, with most contracts voided by bankruptcy judges, and labor unions in fear for their survival, airline management was free to negotiate anew, and regional airlines jumped at the chance to expand service, further fragmenting the industry.

Case 5: Colgan Air, 2009

Prioritizing short-term financial gains over other, long-term interests continues to come at a high cost. Consider Continental Connection Flight 3407, operated by Colgan Air, which crashed five miles from its destination in 2009, killing all forty-nine on board and one person on the ground. As in the previously discussed accidents, both the captain and the first officer had limited operational experience flying their complex aircraft in icing conditions, had trained in accelerated civilian flight programs logging a large percentage of flight time in small single-engine airplanes, and found themselves over their heads in a challenging situation made progressively worse by their own inexperience (NTSB 2009a).

On approach for landing in Buffalo, the captain, flying the aircraft in icing conditions, allowed the airplane's speed to become dangerously slow. This caused activation of a stall warning device called a 'stick shaker' which turned off the autopilot and vibrated the control yoke indicating impending stall, as designed. Although the airplane was in no imminent danger, the captain, concerned by the icing, startled by the warning and confused by the autopilot disconnection, panicked, slowing further and ultimately losing control of the aircraft. The NTSB (2009a) concluded that it was the captain's inappropriate nose-up inputs that caused the airplane's wing to stall, not the icing conditions. If he had responded properly, the airplane would have likely recovered sufficient airspeed and avoided ground impact (ibid.: 82).

The cockpit voice recorder revealed that both pilots were not properly monitoring the aircraft instruments, distracted instead by non-essential communications such as commuting, applying to major airlines, changing aircraft, upgrading and the copilot's annual gross salary of $15,800. This lack of situational awareness was compounded by fatigue as both pilots, yawning repeatedly throughout the flight, had apparently commuted to Newark the night before, sleeping in the flight crew lounge purportedly to save money (NTSB 2009a).

Although the 47-year-old captain had two years of captain experience and over 3,000 flight hours, he only had 109 flight hours in the accident aircraft. He was hired in 2005 with just 618 hours, 250 of which were accumulated in a pay-for-training program called Gulfstream Training Academy in Florida. Aspiring pilots enter the seven-month program with as little as 200 flight hours and no college degree, and for $32,000 students receive accelerated training as a regional airline copilot. After completion, most pilots, like the accident captain, have enough flight time to land an entry-level job at one of the many US commuter airlines. Yet questions remain about the quality of this preparation for the fast-paced, challenging environment that lies ahead for them.

For instance, the accident captain's training records showed that although he successfully completed the Gulfstream program, he had several documented areas of difficulty with aircraft control. And prior to attending the academy, he had failed three FAA check rides, and then later, at Colgan, his Airline Transport Pilot certificate – all requiring remedial training before he subsequently passed (NTSB 2009a: 10).

The 24-year-old copilot had been hired a year before the accident with about 1,600 flight hours accrued through two years of part-time flight instructing in Arizona. By her own admission, 'all of that [flight time] in Phoenix' was of little help preparing her for an airline career. 'I had more actual [instrument] time on my first day' at Colgan Air 'than I did in the sixteen hundred hours I had [before I was hired]', she joked on the day of the crash (NTSB 2009a: 291). Eager to make more money but clearly uneasy about her lack of operational experience, she shared, 'I really wouldn't mind going through a winter in the northeast before I have to upgrade to captain.' And in an eerie case of foreshadowing about five minutes before the crash, she shared, 'Back in Phoenix, if I'd "seen this much ice", I'd "thought oh my gosh, we were going to crash". I would have "freaked out"' (ibid.: 278). 'I've never seen icing conditions. I've never deiced ... I've never experienced any of that' (ibid.: 291).

The FAA's 'call to action'

The Colgan Air crash so shocked America that Congress convened a hearing and the FAA hosted twelve regional meetings investigating pilot training and qualifications, crew fatigue and safety standards. Four key areas emerged as needing improvement: (1) air carrier management responsibilities for crew education and support; (2) professional standards and flight discipline; (3) training standards and performance; and (4) mentoring relationships between mainline carriers and their regional partners (FAA 2010: 5). The report identified several concerns for airline managers such as 'the importance of a safety culture'; pilot scheduling and 'fatigue concerns'; the 'need to pay a "living wage"'; and 'the need for better screening of pilots' rather than '"cookie-cutter" solutions solely based on flight time' (ibid.: 19).

Encouragingly, the FAA (2010: 22) noted that '[t]he single defining theme' which emerged after the Colgan Air accident 'was that a focus on quality, not just quantity' is essential. While total flight time measurement 'can be an indicator of a pilot's proficiency and suitability' for airline operations, 'quality of training and quality of experience are far more important in determining an individual's readiness to operate in the air carrier environment'. What seems to be universally recognized is that 'a generational "paradigm shift" in the pilot population' is occurring, involving 'a fundamental shift in experience, expectations, and work practices' which requires corresponding training and managerial changes. However, there is no consensus on what those changes should include. Yet the concept of liminality may help bring this complex situation into clearer view.

Liminality: a useful descriptive concept

Liminality is a useful descriptive concept here because, rather than blaming individuals, liminality highlights the socioanalytic factors and resultant containment shortfalls of the system as a whole. Derived from the Latin word for threshold, *limen*, the word 'liminal' was first applied by French anthropologist Arnold van Gennep to describe 'rites of passage', a term that denotes changes in 'place, state, social position and age', a transition period 'betwixt and between' different roles (Turner 1969: 94–5).

Several recent case studies have productively examined work performance through a lens of liminality and provide a way to comprehend the impact of this transitional state (Elmes and Barry 1999; Garsten 1999; Tempest *et al.* 2007). Two of these studies focused on the Mount Everest climbing disaster which killed eight people in 1996. Until fairly recently, Mount Everest remained the preserve of the world's most elite mountaineers, who passed death-defying rites of passage under apprenticeship to senior climbers on smaller mountains in order to learn the culture, norms and rules of their profession. Then, in 1985, a wealthy businessman named Dick Bass forever changed the field by climbing the highest peak on each continent, suggesting, 'anyone can climb if they have enough money and training' (Elmes and Barry 1999: 168).

Over the next decade, large numbers of commercial climbing companies emerged, charging clients upwards of $70,000 to ascend mountains like Everest. As a result, high-skilled experienced climbers with internalized norms and rules of their field with respect for the mountain and with Sherpas as partners gave way to liminal, less-skilled, undisciplined client-climbers with little knowledge of the field or respect for cultural norms and a higher potential for denial, rationalization, self-aggrandizement and entitlement (Elmes and Barry 1999: 179).

These changes had an impact on teamwork and the workload of team leaders in risky ways. Inexperienced, liminal mountaineers in ambiguous roles as both customer and climbing team member created particular management challenges. Driven by personal ambitions, inexperienced client-climbers had little desire to coalesce as a team, and could easily stretch beyond their personal competencies, with dire consequences for the entire group. These factors combined to cause 'a shift in the work-group cultures of high-altitude climbing teams, from more collaborative, high-learning, intentional group cultures to more regressive, low-learning, dependent group cultures' where competition for customers increased team leader pressure to get clients to the top (Elmes and Barry 1999: 165–6). In 1996 this dependency dynamic resulted in organizational overreach, team breakdown and death on top of Everest, evidencing that 'there are genuine limits to management practice in the contexts of liminality' (Tempest *et al.* 2007: 1040). This suggests that 'managers need to find ways to temper their drive to succeed with an awareness of and reflection upon the restrictions that businesses face in such settings' (ibid.).

There are parallels between the findings in the Mount Everest liminality studies and aviation culture today. Like mountaineers decades ago, previous generations of commercial pilots learned the culture, norms and rules of their field through years of apprenticeship under other pilots, usually in the military. As accelerated airport training academies emerged, new pilots now had the opportunity to 'pay for training', essentially buying a flight deck seat after only a few months without necessarily learning the important lessons for survival, just like

Everest client-climbers. In both cases a tacit industry assumption remains that although they often lack the background, education and operational experience of previous workgroups, these liminal workers are nonetheless savvy enough to know their limits and will not endanger others. Obviously, this is not always true.

Trapped 'betwixt and between', aspiring pilots are eager to land air carrier jobs, log airline flight time and upgrade to captain as soon as possible, in the hope of advancing their aviation careers. In fact, the need to earn a livable wage, often to pay back high-interest flight training loans, demands this transition. Yet eager but inexperienced pilots can easily find themselves over their heads in challenging situations without the requisite skill set to survive. Meanwhile, weak regulations, financial pressures, employee turnover and fragmented networks make commuter airlines, often the first rung of the civilian pilot's career ladder, the least able to provide the apprenticeship these fledgling airline pilots need. Airline managers' fixation on financial bottom lines and lack of attention to pilots' liminal state fostered a regressive culture that Tempest *et al.*'s (2007) liminality study cautioned against. The loss of containment once provided by corporate culture, strong labor unions, supportive management, clear contracts, fair work rules, established seniority lists and defined career paths that included significant operational experience has resulted in pilots' development of defenses to compensate for containment shortfalls. As Sir Edmund Hillary noted, mountaineering 'used to be a team effort. Nowadays, it's much too "everybody-for-himself". That can get you killed' (cited in Elmes and Barry 1999: 175). The same could be said for aviation.

Evidence of liminality in aviation today

The lack of containment in this liminal environment makes it particularly difficult for airline employees to concentrate on job performance at work. Take, for example, the Northwest Airline pilots who, out of radio contact for an hour, overflew their Minneapolis destination by 150 miles in October 2009 with 147 passengers on board. After investigating the incident, the NTSB reported, 'The crew stated they were in a heated discussion over airline policy and they lost situational awareness' (CNN 2009a).

That same week a Delta Air Lines crew also lost situational awareness when they landed their 767 with 194 passengers on a taxiway at their hub airport, Atlanta-Hartsfield International, instead of their assigned runway (CNN 2009b). Just months before these two incidents, Delta had acquired Northwest through merger, creating what one airline analyst called the 'tsunami of airline consolidations' (AP 2006).The deal nearly fell through when a standoff emerged between the 7,000 Delta and 5,000 Northwest pilots' unions, each wanting greater seniority for their labor group.

In another post-9/11 labor-related incident, United Airlines was forced to cancel a flight in 2008 when the captain announced to passengers that 'he was too upset to fly' after a dispute with another employee about wearing his hat.

The pilots' union had urged pilots to remove their hats in protest at a managerial decision setting aside yet another $130 million in stock in an executive incentive plan while cutting routes, parking planes and laying off employees. It was a sign 'to show management' that pilots were 'serious about regaining what was stripped' from employees 'during bankruptcy' (Yu 2008: 3B).

Even the 'hero' pilots who landed their crippled Airbus on the Hudson River in 2009, Captain 'Sully' Sullenberger and First Officer Jeff Skiles, found themselves pondering the impact of airline mergers on the morning of their fateful accident (NTSB 2009b).

'Wonder how the Northwest and Delta pilots "are getting on"', Skiles remarked as a Northwest jet taxied behind them during engine start.

'I wonder about that too', Captain Sullenberger responded, 'I have no idea ... hopefully better than we and [America] West do.'

'Be hard to do worse.'

'Yeah ... Well I hadn't heard much about it lately but I can't imagine it'd be any better', Sullenberger replied (NTSB 2009b: 22).

Although technically a violation of the FAA's sterile cockpit rules, these types of conversations are common on the flight deck of nearly every airline today as pilots struggle to cope with the drastic changes that have befallen their profession and the ensuing liminal state. Even once aggressive labor groups now shy away from confronting airline management, fearing repercussions. Take the Airline Mechanics Fraternal Association strike at Northwest Airlines in 2005 when 4,400 mechanics and aircraft cleaners walked off the job, angry about the company's demand for $176 million in wage and benefit concession and a 53 percent loss of jobs. In an unprecedented reaction pilots, flight attendants and other labor groups refused to strike in sympathy, afraid for their own jobs (Maynard 2005).

The chaotic state of the post-9/11 aviation industry generated such widespread concern in Congress that the Government Accountability Office (GAO) was tasked to investigate the implications of airline bankruptcies, mergers, loss of pension plans, high fuel prices and even re-regulating the struggling industry. One study claimed that 'the airline bankruptcy process is well developed and understood', even discussing the liquidation of employee pension plans and offering examples of the significant loss of benefits senior airline employees will experience when they retire. Yet it nonetheless claimed that there was 'no evidence' that bankruptcy 'harms the industry' (US GAO 2005b: 19, 27). Another report noted that '[t]he historically high number of airline bankruptcies and liquidations is a reflection of the industry's inherent instability' (US GAO 2005a: 20). However, it did not investigate the implications of this instability and lack of containment for employees. In fact, not one of the government's reports discussed the impact of this tumultuous liminal climate of outsourcing, mergers, downsizing, furloughs and changing work rules on teamwork, employee job performance or safety.

Yet Captain Sullenberger (2009) made the connection between airlines' fixation on the financial bottom line and its impact on employee performance and safety while testifying to Congress. Voicing experienced pilots' concerns, he noted that aviation employees 'have been hit by an economic tsunami'. The 'terms of our employment have changed dramatically' and the managerial decisions placing 'less experienced and less skilled' pilots on flight decks today will have 'negative consequences to the flying public – and to our country'. As a result, 'I am worried that the airline piloting profession will not be able to continue to attract the best and the brightest', which is 'vital to safe air travel and our country's economy and security'. It is time for airlines to 'refocus their attention – and their resources – on the recruitment and retention of highly experienced and well-trained pilots', making that 'a priority that is at least equal to their financial bottom line'.

ALPA (2009: 1) was even more pointed in its criticism, observing that unless significant changes are made in 'today's archaic regulations', airlines will continue 'to hire low-experience pilots into the right seat of high-speed, complex, swept-wing jet aircraft in what amounts to on-the-job training with paying passengers on board'.

Concluding thoughts

It seems clear that as US airlines became increasingly fixated on maximizing profits in the post-9/11 period by outsourcing flying to regional carriers and furloughing experienced pilots, a shift occurred on America's flight decks from stable, high-skilled, homogeneous teams to less experienced, undisciplined, liminal groups, a change that directly resulted in at least one accident and the death of fifty people. With all this evidence, what remains curious is why airline executives, government regulators and the flying public persist in their apathy. To understand this disregard, Long's (2008: 68) model of 'perverse greed' provides insight.

Like so many other American corporations today, exploitative airline executives repeatedly obtained multimillion-dollar pay packages for themselves at the expense of the workers in their charge. To accomplish this, they engaged government agencies, labor unions, boards, stockholders and bankruptcy judges as accomplices, convincing them that their strategies were best for the long-term viability of their companies. Meanwhile, passengers' search for cheap tickets, made even easier by internet websites, allowed consumers to lock in the lowest price while turning a blind eye to the risks, assuming that government regulators would monitor aviation safety. Yet overburdened regulators, tasked with the conflicting mission to both promote aviation and regulate safety, exercised little control.

A systemic fantasy emerged in the post-9/11 period that airlines can be lucrative for executives, self-managing for regulators and risk-free for passengers with no impact on employees or safety. In a sense, greed linked executives, regulators and passengers in a fantasy of 'goodness' as they colluded to avoid seeing reality: the growing systemic risk created by their 'perverse greed' and its impact on pilots' liminal state. It was only after an accident like the Colgan Air one that anyone began to ask questions – too little, too late.

The concept of liminality, then, allows us to perceive how contemporary conditions in US commercial aviation have created a situation of both heightened risk and increased opportunity (Garsten 1999). The risks have been well documented in this chapter. As both Captain Sullenberger and the ALPA report have underscored, the time is ripe for a transformation of the system of aviation. Whether we take advantage of this opportunity to press for the necessary changes and reprioritize safety over finance remains to be seen.

References

Air Line Pilots Association (ALPA) (2009) *Producing a Professional Airline Pilot*, Washington, DC: ALPA.

Associated Press (AP) (2006) 'United and Continental in merger talks', *New York Times*, 13 December.

Bailey, J. (2007) 'News analysis: the cycle turns, and airline shares have fans again', *New York Times*, 3 April.

CNN (29 2009a) 'Airliner crew flies 150 miles past airport', 29 October.

CNN (2009b) 'FAA probes plane's landing on Atlanta Airport's taxiway', 21 October.

Elmes, M. and Barry, D. (1999) 'Deliverance, denial, and the death zone', *Journal of Applied Behavioral Science*, 35(2): 163–87.

Federal Aviation Administration (FAA) (2010) *Answering the Call to Action on Airline Safety and Pilot Training*, Washington, DC: FAA.

Fraher, A.L. (2011) *Thinking Through Crisis: Improving teamwork and leadership in high-risk fields*, New York: Cambridge University Press.

Garsten, C. (1999) 'Betwixt and between: temporary employees as liminal subjects in flexible organizations', *Organization Studies*, 20(4): 601–17.

Gore, A. (1996) *White House Commission on Aviation Safety and Security: Final report*.

Lavin, C.H. (1989) 'Pilots scarce, airlines see 30-year-olds as captains', *New York Times*, 11 January.

Long, S. (2008) *The Perverse Organisation and Its Deadly Sins*, London: Karnac.

Maynard, M. (2005) 'Well-laid plan kept Northwest flying in strike', *New York Times*, 22 August.

Morgenson, G. (2006) 'Gee bankruptcy never looked so good', *New York Times*, 15 January.

National Transportation Safety Board (NTSB) (1987) *Continental Airlines Flight 1713* (NTSB/AAR-88/09), Washington, DC: NTSB.

National Transportation Safety Board (1993a) *GP Express Airlines Flight 861* (NTSB/AAR-93/03), Washington, DC: NTSB.

National Transportation Safety Board (1993b) *Scenic Air Tours Flight 22* (NTSB/AAR-93/01), Washington, DC: NTSB.

National Transportation Safety Board (1994) *GP Express Airlines N115GP* (NTSB/AAR-94/01), Washington, DC: NTSB.

National Transportation Safety Board (2004) *American Airlines Flight 587* (NTSB/AAR-04/04), Washington, DC: NTSB.

National Transportation Safety Board (2009a) *Colgan Air, Inc. Operating as Continental Connection Flight 3407* (NTSB/AAR-10/01), Washington, DC: NTSB.

National Transportation Safety Board (2009b) *US Airways Flight 1549: Group chairman's factual report of investigation cockpit voice recorder* (Docket no. SA-532; Exhibit no. 12), Washington, DC: NTSB.

New York Times (1987) 'F.A.A. begins review of standards for pilots', 22 November.

Sullenberger, C.B. III (2009) 'Statement before the Committee on Transportation and Infrastructure', US House of Representatives.

Tempest, S., Starkey, K. and Ennew, C. (2007) 'In the death zone: a study of limits in the 1996 Mount Everest disaster', *Human Relations*, 60(7): 1039–63.

Turner, V.W. (1969) *The Ritual Process*, Chicago: Aldine.

US Department of Transportation (1998) *Profile: Regional jets and their emerging roles in the U.S. aviation market.*

US Government Accountability Office (GAO) (2005a) *Commercial Aviation: Structural costs continue to challenge legacy airlines' financial performance* (GAO-05-834T).

US Government Accountability Office (2005b) *Commercial Aviation: Bankruptcy and pension problems are symptoms of underlying structural issue* (GAO-05-945).

Yu, R. (2008) 'United flight canceled when pilot says he's too upset to fly', *USA Today*, 23 June.

15 Social dreams of the financial crisis

W. Gordon Lawrence

The present financial conundrum

A Social Dreaming Matrix with two sessions (Matrix 1 and Matrix 2) was convened at the Working Men's College, Camden Town, London, in July 2009. The working hypothesis employed was that whatever the conscious, historical and rational reasons for financial institutions, the resulting contemporary financial crisis is occurring because banks and related institutions have been blinded to the demands of their original purpose because of their unconscious thinking and ideology, which borders on delusion.

In the 1970s and 1980s there was a change in the governance of British banks. Margaret Thatcher's Conservative government freed the banks from regulatory constraints. Later, Gordon Brown, as chancellor to the Labour prime minister Tony Blair and as subsequent prime minister himself, implemented Thatcherite financial market reforms and deregulation. The lobbying financial district of the City of London always had argued for deregulation. This was to put all faith in the market ideology, even though the notion of unregulated capitalism had been stringently questioned by George Soros (1998), and the global economy exposed as a myth by John Gray (1999).

Social Dreaming

Social Dreaming was discovered at the Tavistock Institute of Human Relations in 1982. It is a complementary method to traditional, psychoanalytic dream analysis, rather than being in opposition to it, for it takes a different vertex on dreaming by focusing exclusively on the conscious and unconscious thinking and knowledge embedded in the dream narrative and revealed in a Matrix. This is to use the idea of the 'sphinx', the mythical searcher for truth in solving the riddles of humanity, yet symbolising flawed humanity, by embracing an objective, sociocentric, scientific posture to reality (Bion 1961/1994: 8).

The classical oedipal vertex on dreaming examines the pair relationships that analysands experience in their autobiography and takes an egocentric mental posture by asking the question 'What does the dream mean for me?' The result is that the world of dreaming has become 'gagged and bound by the world of "I" and "me"' (personal communication, N. Symington, 1998).

Social Dreaming redresses this perspective by asking the question 'What does dreaming mean for humanity as evinced through the systems from which participants are drawn?' This entails a shift in the perception of dreaming from the autocentric subject of psychoanalytic dreaming to the allocentric, which is to see the dream as an object existing in its own right (Schachtel 1959: 98).

Further distinctions are that oedipal dreaming is conducted in a one-to-one situation, whereas Social Dreaming is carried out with many people present. Sessions last for an hour. A matrix rather than group is used for containing the dreaming because it mirrors in waking life 'the matrix of the undifferentiated unconscious' while asleep and dreaming (Ehrenzweig 1967).

To discover Social Dreaming, one had to be blind to what was previously known of dreaming and the dynamics of groups in order that one might see what only the Social Dreaming Matrix (SDM) can discover. The thrust of the SDM is towards the unknown, not towards the irrelevance of what is known. To discover the unknown and potential of Social Dreaming, it is necessary to replace the memories, certainties and understanding of historical methods of dream analysis with a 'not-knowing' mental posture that acknowledges the existence of relativity, complexity, synchronicity, uncertainty and mystery. Social Dreaming captures the internal, mental dream drama structured by the unconscious thinking that takes place because of the manifest, rational drama of life's actions – the unconscious and manifest mutually informing each other.

At the July meeting, thirty people participated, drawn from organisational consultancy, banking, the legal profession, psychoanalysis, business, writing and poetry. The *raison d'être* of the SDM was to explore dreaming that occurred during the financial crisis. It had a purpose: 'to transform the thinking, both conscious and unconscious, and the knowledge embedded in the dream narratives (dream thoughts) by means of free association and amplification to find links between the dreams, and in that process be available for new thoughts and thinking' (Lawrence 1998, 2003, 2005, 2007, 2010).

Selection of social dreams, and free associations/amplifications of Matrix 1

In the Matrix, members present dreams spontaneously and others make associations with and connections to these dreams. A Social Dreaming host introduces the task, monitors time and provides interventions in support of the task. Here, dreams and associations will be noted and connections developed in terms of the financial crisis.

For ease of reading, in the following

> *dreams* are in italics;
- indicates free associations by matrix members; and
notes the hosts' interventions.

The first Matrix opened with a dream about cheese:

There are some sheets, they are kinds of cheese, soft and hard; where is a third kind of cheese?

Am with my sister, brother-in-law and father; my father sticks a knife through his own head. We are in my father's house which is full of riches and jewellery. There are also clothes left in a heap. I think to steal some of it and think that there is so much here the theft may not be discovered.

I am in the city of Oxford and take a diversion through a street market. I am looking for an agate stone, but when I look closely I see it is made of plastic. I am late for the show and separated from my mother who is ill with cancer. The organisers of the show are running an audition for the show. I decide to audition and I sing 'You Are My Sunshine'. Mother is now dying and my desire to be part of the show creates a conflict with caring for mother.

•   Fakes in the antique market. Why do we value old things?

We are fleeing in the street. I am holding a wallet full of money, but the money looks different, it is printed in different colours and is of different sizes becoming dark brown. I cannot sort the money out. I am wondering whether money has been lost.

Anxiety about relying on things which cannot be relied on.

'Neverland' [Michael Jackson's ranch]: *there is a money machine that does not work. Gordon* [the host] *comes along and kicks the machine which starts working and produces money. I think a money dispenser is like a urinal.*

A man changes into a woman because of a genetic disease. A prize in the form of pink and blue beans, the pink beans are given to the boys and the blue ones to the girls, but all the beans are made of plastic. Is it a mess?

A memory of sitting in the 2nd row at the Wigmore Hall [a London concert venue] *and seeing a figure in the row in front dressed as a man. I realise it is dressed as a woman; feeling of revulsion.*

•   Zeus would appear in another form in order to seduce.
There is a link between change and the Credit Crunch where things appear to be the opposite of what they are.
•   All that is solid melts into thin air.

There is Gordon [the host] *with a large multi-ethnic crowd in a huge arena at first, but then the place appears very small and they are lost. They find their way out through a plastic sheet and they find a room. There is a museum down a stairway; the flaying of Marcia is taking place; he has no skin, but he carries it on his arm.* [The contemporary sculptor Damien Hirst has a skeleton of a man carrying his skin over his arm.]

There is a Madonna having light coming out of one of her breasts. Somehow she seemed oversexed. The question came to mind: what if women were geneti- cally modified to produce cheese? Not a comfortable idea.

- The *Metamorphoses* of Ovid is a work about change.
- \# These seem to be metaphors for the financial market. There is the idea of change and transformation, where basically nothing is quite what is expected to be.
- In the film *Il Gattopardo* (The Leopard) there is a scene in a cow shed where a young girl is made to touch a bull's genitals; it is very uncomfortable.
- A connection between the word 'chocolate' and 'currency' in the Argentin- ian culture. It also brings to mind the story of a couple, friends from Argen- tina, who decided to go into farming, got cows and land for pasture and went into cheese and milk production. However, after a while they got into finan- cial trouble and eventually they went bankrupt because they were not able to play with time and capital. [Domestic metaphor for the banking crisis.]

Each session of the Matrix was followed by a Dream Reflection Dialogue (DRD). In each DRD, participants took part in a dialogue about the dreams and associations. Here the results of the two DRDs are put together in the discussion of each Matrix session below.

Selection of social dreams and free associations/amplifications of Matrix 2

I am in a huge cave with my mother and sister. There is a lake with fish and I am taking a path while fish are playing and jumping. One fish jumps against the rock and dies, but it cannot be caught because the path collapses. I want to call the Fire Brigade, but I don't know the address. One sister stands there, but the second sister falls down a cavern.

I am parked near a hotel. A bison runs at full speed towards me. It misses me narrowly. I look for the car, but it has gone. The manager of the hotel reassures me and shows me a lake with boats moored in a line. I follow the manager in the boat and we take a round trip on the lake. When we stop there is a bicycle on the left-hand side, but as I try to get to the bicycle the boat takes off too soon before I can get to the bicycle.

I am coming out of a building; I find my car is gone and I feel a dispropor- tionate anxiety.

- The idea of control, the bicycle, horse, natural forces, loss of control.

A doctor, or a surgeon, extracts a white golf ball out of my throat. Some time later (in real life) I was diagnosed with hypothyroidism.

We are in a big room. I am disoriented while there is a social dreaming con- versation. An insect comes very close and it looks as if it is made with jumbled wire. I try to kill it but I cannot get it. I feel as if drunk; a woozy feeling.

- Plato wrote about the cave; all that could be seen were the shadow reflections, never the full picture. [Reality perceived by the unaided senses may be a shadow of reality.]
- There is a sense of something being taken away from us and of feeling very woozy.
- Dreams are like bundles of wires and of intestines.

I am sinking in the sea and I see an angel fish. I find I am in a cave under water and I see something coming through from the back of the cave. I move towards it for a closer look and I see it is like a black cat, or a jaguar with a bloody mouth.

\# Financial managers are all-powerful and discharge their anxiety into the customers, who keep on repaying the banks enormous amounts.
- The jaguar; the black panther. The political Black Panthers had no one fighting for them but themselves.
- I am reminded of the film *Ratatouille*. The cook is a mouse hiding under the hat of someone else.
- I am thinking of the work of Anish Kapoor [a famous contemporary Indian sculptor trained in London].
- The Holocaust.

I am on a boat, in an industrial landscape. On the shore there is a village, looking very much like an old Dutch village. I go into a room of a house full of beautiful, rich plates and many other rich things. A man tells me that there is gold somewhere else and I start to realise that the plates are not as valuable as I first thought.

I am walking on an old pavement made of old and new stones worked together with water jetting out of a pipe and I make attempts to stop it.

There are cars travelling on an old road. I realise I am actually driving an aeroplane and Charles Kennedy [a British politician who represents a Scottish constituency] *is sitting beside me. I ask him whether people in Scotland are angry. He says no, not as they could be.*

We overtake the cars at a very busy traffic junction. It's a six-lane flyover, a spaghetti junction and now we are on a motorcycle going fast. We crash into a road sign (road side?) and a bunch of kids start laughing at us. I get up and tell the kids, 'Why are you laughing? It's our job to crash into things. Is there any place you would like us to crash into?'

It's a party. Bill Clinton makes a beeline towards me. I think to myself if I am going to have sex with him I would want it to be vaginal, not otherwise. I succeed in avoiding him.

- Condoms are made of latex-plastic.
- Sex and power.
- Black panther.

I am in a car, a Jaguar, going the wrong way in a six-lane highway. I am very afraid, sitting in the back. The driver is a large, black civil rights activist. The man and other arrive at the house where there is a party full of Black Panthers. The idea at the party is that plates need to be kept spinning in the air.

- I am reminded of the TV series *The Wire*; it has a complicated plot about society about to fall apart.

I am walking in the desert, a question is asked: 'What is compassion?' I don't know and I look for an explanation for something that I do not fully grasp. [Reference to the Desert Fathers?]

A dream about not understanding. There is Doria, a friend whose English is translated by a computer. At some point the machine becomes confused. The husband says 'It'll do' and shakes the machine and sings 'dododododo'. Perhaps singing would be easier.

- Translation often misses emotions and meaning.
- The language of finance is a foreign language.
- I am reminded of the Byzantium exhibition [an exhibition at the Royal Academy of Arts in London, October 2008 – March 2009].

There is a labyrinth made of cabinets with lifts going up and down, not stopping at the right place and in between floors. I feel anxiety and the idea that things are changing to 'I know you don't know' from 'no one knows', or 'I do not know and you know'.

- The stock market.
- I am thinking of a scrambled translation, not fitting in quality or compassion.
- The language we use to describe dreams is an old language: the Minotaur, the Cyclops.
- I am thinking of a wave of feelings of fragmentation.

I am in the bushes by Finchley tube station [in north London] *with a knife. What I find is not the Minotaur, but a roast chicken.*

I am in a building, possibly a hotel. I know where to go, but all access places, corridors and lifts have been changed. The place has had a metamorphosis.

- Ovid's *Metamorphoses*.
- There are fears not of the unknown but of the consequences of what is known. Someone said, 'We buy rubbish, we sell antiques.'
- # Maybe no one in this room knows the fear of losing everything.
- Perhaps there is nothing to lose.

Discussion of the first session of the Social Dreaming Matrix

The first dream of the first SDM, which was about 'sheets' of cheese, and the wish that the SDM produce a third kind, demonstrates that hope is being invested in the Matrix. Cheese is made by coagulating the milk of cows, goats, buffalo or sheep by adding rennet. It is a natural product with a long history of producing hundreds of varieties. It is a metaphor for the natural change in the composition of milk, belonging to a time when products of many kinds could be recognised for their goodness. The dream evoked the association 'Are we who are assembled here about to make a new kind of cheese?'

The second dream is the one in which logic is subverted. With the shock of the father's suicide, the rules of inheritance are replaced by stealing. Similarly, agate is made of plastic. This conflict of meaning is repeated in the dream of singing in a theatre show and looking after a dying mother ['You are my sunshine', a song of 1940; one of the two state songs of Louisiana]. This affirms life in the face of death, and might be a message that people will survive the financial crisis.

Cheese symbolises the human ability to create new products organically and is a metaphor for other human transformations such as 'quants' which were invented. The unintended consequences of the financial instruments, the 'quants', devised by the banks, was that though intended to take the risk out of reorganising shaky mortgages by parcelling them up and selling to other institutions, they failed because house prices in America tumbled. The debts became toxic. In a sense, the financial crisis is 'synthetic' because it was human-made but took little heed of the reality of markets. In the DRD, one member asked, 'Is this recession just a big, fat, smelly lie?'

There is a *conflict of meaning* for taken-for-granted objects and events. The dreaming subverts the logic of everyday life, or rather gives messages from the unconscious that everyday reality is having its logic subverted. What is fake, or real? Why do we value antiques, but sell rubbish? Later, dreams are seen as jumbled wire which the dreamer wants to kill to keep the 'reality' of the dream at bay. Is it the dreaming that is making us 'woozy', disorientated, or is it contemporary living? *Transformation* appears to be linked to magical processes, or sleight of hand, leading to a suspicion of plastic: is it real or not in what it symbolises?

Whereas plastic is tangible, financial profit is seen as intangible; for example, in the dream, the holder of a wallet of money is confused as to the colour of the notes and their value. The notes turn into a faecal colour, expressing what people feel about their loss of money and investments as a result of the crisis? In 'Neverland' the money dispenser does not work and is associated with ridding the body of urine. In the same dream, the wish in the Matrix to make the machine work is projected into the Matrix through reference to the host (i.e. the Matrix host, Gordon). The ambivalence felt about him as the object of transference is expressed through kicking the money dispenser.

Much later, there is the dream of a host (Gordon) being surrounded by a crowd (presumably the Matrix), emerging into a plastic tent which transforms into a room, then a museum where a flayed man is carrying his skin. This seems to be a commentary on the process of dreaming itself leading to infinite possibilities of meaning. The idea of 'Museum' is of treasures and curiosities of the past, and yields a man with no skin. Does losing skin, or shirt, mean losing the fundamental boundary between people? Does it follow that no skin means no person, means no mind, leading to the inability to think? This room change may be an expression of how dreaming can excavate reality through dream thinking.

The theme of human-made plastic runs through the Matrix in the dreams and associations, reappearing in different forms. The genetic disease that changes men into women is linked to a change in the colour codes for boys and girls, but again, the beads are made of plastic. The dream about sex changes is also disturbing in that the changes are felt to be not quite 'correct', causing discomfort in the viewer in the concert hall. Zeus, someone associates, would appear in another form to seduce. Are banking institutions being equated with Zeus? The dreamers are accessing a mythology of previous ages through their dreams and associations of gods. Dreams can be realised, as for example in *Billy Elliot*, which is a film about a working-class boy who becomes a star ballet dancer. The 'dream' is reality based, whereas the bankers' dreams of riches did not come true because they were out of touch with reality.

The mood of the Matrix changes with the reference to Lampedusa's *The Leopard*. This is about nineteenth-century Sicily and recounts the effects of Garibaldi's revolution on the aristocracy when money and people with new riches emerged. Tancredi, the Prince's nephew in *The Leopard*, says, 'If we want things to stay as they are, things will have to change.' The novel becomes a metaphor for the present crisis and how to survive it – for, in the same way, the current financial crisis is upsetting the distribution of money in contemporary societies and causing anxiety. The theme of the manipulation of money is ever-present in the Matrix, as is the useful and destructive consequences of plastic, i.e. 'plastic surgery'.

The uncomfortable image of the Madonna producing cheese from her breasts is linked by association to Ovid's *Metamorphoses*, which is about transformation and linked to an artist who works with the 'potential of materials'.

There is an association to 'Treblinka', symbol of the total annihilation of European Jewry, whose members were murdered not just because of their race but for their valuables. The idea of unconscious, 'animal spirits' comes through having to touch a bull's testicles. There is an association to friends who could not establish an economic farm. The implication is that ordinary people have the potential for managing their economic affairs but bankers are just as flawed as the farmer friends. Will bankers be able to change, or are they like the leopard's inability to change their spots? Hope is expressed in the last association given to the Matrix of the Buddhist who is attempting to attain balance in her self-sustaining farm – a perfect economic model.

The sense of annihilation in the Matrix was strong and the participants couldn't believe what had happened to them in the crisis. To be sure, they were all professionals and their income was barely affected. But pension schemes were shaky and credit difficult to obtain. The credit crunch was seen as being part of something larger. 'We live in a time which is a liquid phase for humanity where stem cell research, petrol crisis, global warming, bio-fuels, genetic engineering and financial resources are emerging to destabilise the world we have known'. Someone said, 'We are in a chaotic in-between moment.' There is *anxiety* in the Matrix expressed in the DRD in the following: 'Anxiety in defeat of money and men'. 'Poverty is more than the loss of money', 'Anxiety of buying antiques, or rubbish'.

There was a reference to alchemy (gold from dross), which is linked to 'the horrendous fears about what can happen in situations such as the one we are in', and expressed the panic of the dream Matrix.

The idea of unconscious 'animal spirits' (Akerlof and Schiller 2009) comes in having 'to touch the bull's testicles'. Whether the crisis is the result of animal spirits or the 'unseen hand' is questionable, for it seems to have been caused by bad financial management. This idea compares with farming friends who couldn't follow a sound economic model and failed. In contradistinction, there is a Buddhist woman who follows natural methods of farming and succeeds. The simple economic rules have not been followed by banks, unlike the eco-friendly farmers.

Interestingly, the link in Brazil between currency and chocolate brings the Matrix back to the beginning, when cheese is seen as a natural product and of quite different constituency to plastic.

Discussion of the second session of the Social Dreaming

The first dream of the second session of the Matrix is about danger in a cave with shadows and paths that collapse, resulting in a sister falling down; also, the idea of never leaving the cave, never growing out of being young and primitive. It also expresses being 'lost' by the participants, who cannot capture the fish (dreams) because the moment they start to associate, the path of thought that they are following crumbles and disappears. The wish to call the fire brigade is to invoke authority to resolve the issue through some appropriate body.

The dream about the bison could symbolise the United States and might be a reference to where the financial crisis began. There is a reference to means of locomotion as natural forces and losing control of them. The dream insect made of jumbled wire makes the dreamer feel drunk, out of control, expressing the participants' wish to engage with the unconscious of the dreaming.

The dream about a golf ball and subsequent operation is an example of dreaming being 'shadows of the future cast before' (Bion 1961/1994: 309), as is the dreaming predicting a collapsing world, chaotic roads and the loss of logic.

In the past, life was regarded as predictable and easy – with sea and angel fish. Now the fish (dreams) die in the pool of the cave. The wish to call the fire brigade is to invoke some external authority (transference) to save the situation. Then the dreaming becomes menacing, where a black jaguar with a bloody mouth expresses the idea that banking has become predatory, causing anxiety in its customers. What happened to the bank failures? Although the Black Panthers was a political movement, it does not mitigate the menace of the panther in people's minds; 'black panther' could represent shades of the sabre-toothed tiger that terrified primitive humans.

The dream about being on the lake and not reaching the bicycle has the connotation of escaping the financial crisis, but the boat continues around the lake; the crisis continues. The feeling of perturbation and panic felt about the crisis appears in the dreams about traffic. This is evident in the dreams about traffic on motorways with their accidents. Were the banks meant to crash?

The experience becomes mixed: Mickey Mouse and the painting of a suicide man; mouse-cooks and sculptors; the Holocaust and Berlin. Kapoor makes an interesting observation: 'the power of a work comes from its ability to accrue layers of meaning – whether, poetic, political, or historical' (Kent 2009). Can the same be said of dreams?

The Holocaust is an indication that the dreamers feel that they are facing annihilation by the financial crisis. The reference to the film *Ratatouille* expresses the idea that it is all a stew; one is not sure what it contains.

The dream of going into a house, in an industrial landscape, full of beautiful, rich plates, leaves the dreamer doubtful as to their actual value, expressing the growing doubt of the Matrix as to what *is* valuable and what is not. The dream of asking Charles Kennedy (the politician) whether Scots are angry has the reply, 'No, not as they should be!' This indicates that we ought to be angry about the financial crisis, but we are keeping quiet, denying our feelings. The participants feel subdued; feel that they can do nothing except accept.

The reference to Bill Clinton and sex is about whether it is a real experience, or just a form of mental masturbation. The reference to the Black Panthers and civil rights, and the idea of keeping plates in the air, may be about the wish to take action while financial services have been 'juggling with plates' which have now collapsed. Similarly, the reference to the TV series *The Wire* carries the belief of society falling apart. Perhaps the financial crisis has ushered in a period of dystopia, because everything is out of place and fragmenting after the utopia of spending on credit which fuelled the crisis. Again, this augurs shadows of the future.

What is 'reality during change'? was asked by a number of participants. 'Search for the real.' 'Testing what is real, what was real, what is next possible'? 'What is real in change?'

We've moved from a false sense of security, during the pre-crisis spending spree, to the experience of not *knowing what is real or false, truth or lie*, like the dream of valueless plates and the promise of gold. At the same time, someone had the insight, 'We know more about what is going on than we want to admit.' 'The horrendous fear about what can happen in situations such as we are in now.' 'Intimidation means search for some vehicle – animal, spirit, cave – in order to be proud in our system.' The tragedy is in knowing that our grounds for being proud are few.

There was a feeling of being 'inadequate' for the study of the subject of financial crisis, as shown in the following quotations: 'Confusion leading to powerlessness. Questioning everything.' 'Everybody is in a fog' and 'We're still in a fog.' Someone said, 'We're in an "in between" moment.' This was restated by someone as 'fear of the hidden monster' and by another as 'There's no longer a shape for money. No boundaries (skin) to form its future.' At the same time, another participant asked, 'Is it true? *Pecunia non olet*, money does not smell. Endless opportunities versus human limits.' 'We are silenced if we are not part of the club.'

Solutions to the financial crisis were not the task for the SDM. Its task was only to express the dreams and what had been learned from them, evidenced in statements such as 'Economics rampant, morality dormant.' 'The irrational fiancé' [love affair?]. 'Ambivalence about nourishment and physicality.' 'There is also ambivalence about plasticity and shape shifting.' 'We are in a liquid phase for humanity where stem cell research, petrol crises, global warming, bio-genetic fuels, genetic engineering and financial resources have become unstable and are in emergence.' Someone suggests, 'Daring to be visibly not-knowing'.

Lack of a moral and ethical framework in financial markets is evidenced. There is depression about this realisation. Now, in the twenty-first century, the world we previously experienced, which relied on rising values of property and easy credit, is under siege because of the financial crisis. The social upheaval of the loss of employment is facing more people: the hopeful young graduate finds it difficult to find a job, just as school leavers are facing unemployment.

The language of finance is a foreign language. In the labyrinth, lifts never stop on the correct floor. Anxiety is felt at the mismatch between expectations and results. Someone makes an association to the mismatch between dreams and reality. Dreams are an old language stretching back to the beginnings of human time. There is a dream of stabbing a roast chicken. If the present crisis is the roast chicken, we have difficulty in stabbing a live chicken because we cannot distinguish between the two, and therefore the financial crisis becomes unsolvable.

The dream of the translating machine indicates that machines cannot express emotions, and the hotel where all the access points are jumbled up is about the inability to understand the language of finance. The reference to Ovid's *Meta-morphoses* is to everything changing, with the result that we fear the unknown less than we fear the consequences of what we do know of the crisis which bought rubbish (sub-prime mortgages) and traded them as valuable antiques.

The Matrix was commented on. The transference issues appear in dreams, but not addressed face to face, which is appropriate to working with dreams in a Matrix. The felt corruption leading to the crisis was hinted at through the bad smells of cheeses.

A host says, 'No one knows the fear of having lost everything?' prompting the reply from the Matrix, 'Perhaps there is nothing to lose', which was the final observation of the second Matrix.

Reflections on the day

The process of Social Dreaming reveals the layers of meaning in a dream through the free associations and amplifications of Matrix members. The SDM uncovered the unconscious meanings being given to the current financial crisis, which has disturbed logic, as exemplified in the following analysis.

The causes of the world economic meltdown, the worst since the 1930s, have been well documented in a *Daily Telegraph* leader of 17 July 2009:

> Sir David Walker, appointed by the British Government, identified four.
>
> 1   Bank boards failed to identify the risks they were incurring.
> 2   Non-executive directors could not curb the powerful management of banks.
> 3   Short-term performance of bank employees was encouraged, fuelling their willingness to take risks.
> 4   Bank investors became caught in their greed, and failed to exercise stewardship.

The immediate result has been that governments have rescued banks by lending billions to them.

Whatever the conscious, rational reasons of financial institutions, the working hypothesis here is that, in the past decade or so, people with roles in banks and related entities have been increasingly motivated by unconscious thinking which has blinded them to risk, and purpose. Starting in the 1970s, there was a change in the authority of corporations and, therefore, most businesses in Britain. At this time, 'bosses' began to think that the business belonged to them, irrespective of shareholders, and the assets of the business were owned by the senior managers. The idea of stewardship began to decline as more and more business leaders became guilty of hubris, indeed arrogance, in their denial of reality.

The perceived greedy recklessness of bankers is felt to be irrational (animal spirits). While the press labels such behaviours as 'reckless', they may be due to being out of touch with reality through denial. The significance and con- sequences of irrational behaviour in financial institutions were the subject of the Social Dreaming Matrix described here. The dream thoughts – the furniture of the dreams – are embedded in the dream narrative. They show that people are profoundly disturbed about the consequences of this 'greedy recklessness'.

As was said in the DRD, everybody is still in a fog, with resultant confusion leading to powerlessness on the part of the citizen, who now has to question everything. Someone notes that poverty is more than the lack of money and another concludes that much change is sterile; endless possibilities are curtailed by human limits, but what is *real* in change becomes reality. We search for the *real*. We continually test what *is* real, what *was* real, and what is next possible. We are in a chaotic in-between moment in history but, at the same time, we may know more of what is going than we want to admit. Change is valid, necessary, possible. But is it achievable?

The reference to *The Leopard* illustrates the monumental changes to societies that have occurred before in history. In the novel, the protagonist Prince is witnessing the breakdown of Sicily with the arrival of Garibaldi. The status quo there is changing: the local mayor, originally a peasant, has more money than the Prince and has become a landowner. Members of the Prince's family are marrying out of their social class, but in the midst of this the Prince holds to his now outdated values with dignity.

The Leopard is a metaphor for the condition of nations experiencing the financial crisis, although the causal factor is ostensibly economic, not political. The result is the beginnings of a change in the life of citizens. In the United Kingdom, for example, because of the government bailouts for banks, each citizen has a tax burden of £3,000 that will take years to repay, even though as yet the enormous size of the crisis has still to hit Britain. By November 2009, 12,000 independent stores had closed since 2008; these stores had contributed £30 billion to the economy. A reduction in spending needs to occur but, as the Matrices demonstrate, there is as yet no recognition of the fiscal reality of the British economy. It has not registered in people's minds. Different groups are proposing to go on strike for more pay, including university professors and postal workers. It seems that the survival of the individual is more important than the country. Only 20 per cent of the population see the need for retrenchment. The remainder assume that the 'fantastic growth in public spending' of the previous decade is an entitlement. Sir Howard Davies, director of the London School of Economics, predicts that by 2014 Britain will be one of the major global profligates (*Daily Telegraph*, 16 October 2009).

Now, a year or more after the Matrix, a Conservative–Liberal coalition government in Britain has told the electorate the extent of public debt, arguing now for enormous cuts in government spending. Predictably, this government is blaming the former Labour administration for the national debt. For the government, the real culprits, the bankers, are not to be held fully accountable. The idea is that banks are too big and important for the national economy to fail. But this may be a myth yet to be tested in reality.

The SDM offered an opportunity to dream what *reality is experienced to be* as a commentary on life as it is. Rational thinking is disoriented by the financial crisis. Now is the time to think rationally, being cognisant of our unconscious perceptions, fantasies and wishes evoked in the SDM and the DRD – not self-indulgently hating bankers but, rather, trying to empathise with them to understand their unconscious motivation because of their ideology inspired by illusion. They have a critical role to play in the maintenance of economically sound societies.

References

Akerlof, G.A. and Schiller, R.S. (2009) *Animal Spirits: How human psychology drives the economy*, Princeton, NJ: Princeton University Press.
Bion, W.R. (1961/1994) 'On a quotation from Freud', in *Clinical Seminars and Four Papers*, London: Karnac Books.

Ehrenzweig, A. (1967) *The Hidden Order of Art: A study in the psychology of artistic imagination*, London: Weidenfeld & Nicolson.

Gray, J. (1998) *False Dawn*, London: Granta Books.

Kent, S. (2009) 'Anish Kapoor: Material world', *Royal Academy Magazine*, no. 104, Autumn.

Lawrence, W.G. (1998) *Social Dreaming @ Work*, London: Karnac Books.

Lawrence, W.G. (2003) *Experiences in Social Dreaming*, London: Karnac Books.

Lawrence, W.G. (2005) *Introduction to Social Dreaming*, London: Karnac Books.

Lawrence, W.G. (2007) *The Infinite Possibilities of Social Dreaming*, London: Karnac Books.

Lawrence, W.G. (2010) *The Creativity of Social Dreaming*, London: Karnac Books.

Schachtel, E. (1959) *Metamorphosis*, New York: Basic Books.

Soros, G. (1998) *The Crisis of Global Capitalism*, London: Little, Brown.

16 The consumer credit boom and its aftermath in Hungary

On the changing role of commercial banks

Sándor Takács

Introduction

In this chapter I explore how psychoanalytically informed research in organizations contributes to our understanding of financial institutions. In the history of the Hungarian financial sector there was a period of four years between 2004 and 2008 when mortgage-based consumer credit given to average-size households exceeded, as a sum total, the total of the previous fifteen years. Concomitantly, the role of 'customer care' employees in branch offices during the 'credit boom' changed from that of 'administrator' to that of 'sales representative', despite the official name remaining 'consultant'. Truly acting as a 'consultant' would reflect the primary task of banks more adequately, but to achieve this a manager's role would also have to change to include more listening and coaching.

In the first decade of the twenty-first century, the retail banking sector in Hungary has shown some of the hallmarks of a command-and-control, centrally planned economy, mixed with the negative consequences of extreme market competition, while using the phraseology of a socially sensitive, customer-driven Western service industry. I focus here on the theme of the changing role of commercial banks in a transitional, market-based capitalist system and its consequences for the way customers are managed, through the in-depth analysis of a major private retail bank in Hungary.

The current crisis is about change. Those organizations able to understand how their own practices contributed to the financial crisis and who find appropriate answers to its challenges may well become stronger and come out as winners. Banks have to learn to deal with primary-task-related anxiety in a mature way (avoiding the traps of denial, splitting, projection and other primitive social defenses). The first step towards this goal is for decision makers in banks to recognize their own role and the changes needed in it, in order to better contain the anxiety present in the system.

Commercial banks have increasingly taken over the function previously accomplished by other institutions (e.g. investment banks, financial consultants, insurance companies, even tax advisors). Events having no direct impact on everyday life some years ago might now have a crucial effect on financial portfolios, currency rates and/or debt levels on a daily basis, influencing our decisions, opportunities and threats.

Here, after defining my understanding of the systems-psychodynamic approach to organizations, I will offer the case of Retail Bank Hungary (a pseudonym) as an illustration of dilemmas also present in many other countries on the peripheries of global capitalism.

Theoretical background

Systems-psychodynamic analysis (or socioanalysis) of organizations is the activity of exploration, consultancy and action research which combines and synthesizes methodologies and theories derived from psychoanalysis, group relations, social systems thinking, organizational behavior and Social Dreaming (Bain 1999). Authors writing in this tradition frequently refer to social defense theory (Menzies 1960/1984), which explains, using psychological concepts, how overt structures governing individual behavior in organizations are developed. Menzies (ibid.) describes how the nurses' 'struggle against anxiety' related to the 'primary task' of their health organization led to the development of socially structured defense mechanisms. The research illustrates the ways various features of the organization, such as human resource management policies, operational procedures, and behavioral patterns, reinforce the individual psychological defensive needs of members as well as help in task accomplishment.

The concept of social defense links the individual (with his or her psychological defenses) to the collective. Disturbing intra-psychic conflicts and anxieties, often elicited in the course of taking up a role or joining an enterprise, are defended against as members collectively engage in psychological defenses such as splitting, denial, projection, rationalization and sublimation. Thus, many 'objective' features of organizational life symbolize the psychological needs of members. Over time, an entire social defense system builds up as organizational members enter into unconscious agreements in order to diminish the anxiety related to their primary task.

One of the most influential organizational development consultants, Edgar Schein, in his concept of organizational culture (Schein 1985), also talks about two modes of learning: problem solving and pain and anxiety reduction. The latter, he argues, accounts for the emergence of various features of an organization's culture, like rituals and patterns of thinking or feeling, based on beliefs and tacit assumptions 'that were learned originally as ways of avoiding painful situations.... We can think of parts of a group's culture as being social defense mechanisms' (ibid.: 178). According to his theory, the problem-solving and anxiety-reducing elements together – and, I would add, each in the other's context – are able to offer a more comprehensive understanding of organizations.

The unconscious and collusive nature of social defense mechanisms explains why certain of its elements are so dysfunctional for organizations. It is also important to differentiate between primary-task-related anxiety and anxiety created by the social defense system itself. Menzies (1960/1984), in her seminal article, notes that particular modes of defenses institutionalized in culture lead to less effective task performance and as a result serve as a secondary source of doubt and anxiety.

In this chapter I will define social defenses as implicit or 'taken-for-granted' patterns occurring at different systemic levels (individual, group, organization, society), frequently present in the form of social norms, roles or practices, etc. These defenses are formed unconsciously in order to regulate human behavior, usually as amendments for more explicit mechanisms, such as rules, policies, procedural regulations, and artifacts, serving the unconscious needs of different members by reducing the anxieties created for their particular roles at a particular time by the primary task of their organizational units.

These mechanisms are created by unconscious processes in which stakeholders of the system mutually reinforce certain patterns of meanings, beliefs, assumptions and values (possibly via an unspoken 'gentleman's agreement') which are used as the context for the explicit rules, for example the practice of performance evaluation (the central tendency in ratings) or the 'praxis' of professional communities (e.g. lawyers or academics). Such rules and their subsequent influence on the behaviors expected of employees, usually including ethical issues, have a strongly compelling character, including emotional labor (Hochschild 1983), which can be seen as the human cost of the social defense system.

Primary-task-related anxieties are usually first confronted at the boundaries of organizations. Stein (2008) offers a powerful metaphor for examining customer–employee relations in a post-industrial society, namely that of toxicity. Front-line service workers share a space with customers called the *boundary region*, which refers to the experiential or phenomenological dimension (Hirschhorn and Gilmore 1992: 105): 'boundaries aren't drawn on a company's organizational chart, but in members' minds'.

Crucial to the healthy functioning of the organization is the degree of permeability of its boundary regions: inadequately permeable boundaries may thwart effective work by restricting contact, and the resulting rigidity may preclude learning and adaptation. Too much permeability, on the other hand, may risk effectiveness by allowing over-intensive contact or invasion (Schneider 1991). Employees at the receiving end of toxicity frequently find themselves influencing others in a negative way, leading to a toxic work environment and resulting in further damage in the provision of service.

Organizational splitting

One particular defense mechanism in organizations is splitting, usually in combination with denial and projection. The psychoanalyst Melanie Klein (1946/1986) states that children are born with the two primary drives of love and hate. Splitting refers to the separation of the things the child loves (good, gratifying objects) and the things the child hates (bad, frustrating objects). Klein describes these as the 'good breast' and the 'bad breast'. The child experiences these abstract internalized 'breasts' as distinct, separate and opposite, although both belong to the one mother. The worldview associated with such splitting of good and bad is called the paranoid-schizoid position. All humans struggle throughout their lives to integrate the two drives into constructive social interaction, and one important step in childhood development is their gradual depolarization. Splitting as a defense mechanism is used to cope with doubts, conflicting feelings and anxiety, even in adulthood. It enables the individual to separate negative and positive feelings, thereby reducing the complex and contradictory feelings associated with them, and results in seeing things in 'black and white'.

Splitting in organizations is also described when different organizational functions are separated 'in the mind'. Krantz and Gilmore (1990) discuss the splitting of leadership and management into different ideologies, calling one extreme 'Heroism' and the other 'Managerialism'. In both ideologies the essential link between new or visionary ideas and the organizational apparatus required to realize them is broken. 'Our premise is that the driving motivation for unconscious adoption of these neutralizing social defenses is to avoid the doubts, uncertainties, and disturbing anxieties which are stimulated in the course of confronting the adaptive requirements of the emergent organizational environments' (ibid.: 7).

Scapegoating is a splitting mechanism used by groups (Stapley 2006). Tensions and anxieties faced by the group are located in a single person who is blamed. Problems, failures or mistakes are symbolically discarded by declaring the scapegoat 'all bad' and getting rid of him or her. No understanding of how and where the problems or mistakes were created or developed, no corrective mechanisms and learning are produced by this mechanism; only a quick and easy solution to decrease the immediate frustrations and tensions in the group.

Financial institutions and organizations in system-psychodynamic theory

Financial institutions have recently become the center of attention for researchers interested in the unconscious dynamics of organizations. Stein (2003), for example, focuses on the function of envy and organizational narcissism; Sievers (2003) elucidates some of the psychotic dynamics inherent in pension fund systems. According to Sievers (ibid.: 200), 'the world is reduced to an abstract world of money ... and the commoditized immortality to be gained by affluence is limited to a narcissistic love of self'. The related feelings, greed and envy (Stein 2000), do appear on the boundaries of financial organizations as toxic material (Stein 2008).

Wachtel (2003: 108) also discusses the contemporary culture of greed and envy: 'success is defined materialistically and possessions are sought largely as an end in themselves and serve for validating their worth and definer of their needs and desires'. He traces this phenomenon to the broken selfhood of the members of mass-consumer societies as a result of their lack of genuine human connection: 'money or material possession, or the status of one's job in our society comes to serve as substitute self-objects'. Seeking to sustain selfhood in this way is an esca-lating process: 'we need to get even more alienated from human sources of psychic nourishment as we need more money to buttress our self-esteem' (ibid.: 118).

Besides greed and envy, I would add (in the Hungarian context) the paranoid feelings of losing money (through secularization, or hyperinflation,[1] or other compulsory ways of financing the crashing state) as a potential source of anxiety. In the country's twentieth-century history we can find examples of all of these phenomena. As a result, the ratio of cash held by Hungarian households as com-pared to the total amount of cash in the country's economy is estimated to be triple of that in other Central Eastern European countries (HVG 2010).

The process of privatization (especially in its early-years' 'spontaneous', i.e. unregulated, form) has also led to properties that were in state hands being passed on to private hands without societal discourse or control. Being rich and having money has made people objects of suspicion. The resulting feelings of guilt are also largely repressed by those who are on the payroll of privatized companies. Guilt might be the repressed feeling of those who have work, when they compare themselves to those members of society who have become the vic-tims of systemic changes. These potentially ambivalent, anxiety-provoking, often unconscious feelings, combined with more rational aspects of dealing with money, are subject to being introjected as toxic material by employees at the boundary region.

My hypothesis is that the traditional social defense mechanism in banks (especially in Hungary) is splitting. Structures, meaning patterns and procedures are so directed that the rational and irrational (emotional) aspects of handling money are separated. Banks try to deal only with the rational elements and split off the bad, irrational part. All irrational elements are translated into, and assessed as, risk – rendering them one-dimensional, just like money – and are on the activity list of 'back office' functions (such as risk management, treasury, regulation and credit control). It is the 'front office' (sales and customer service) that has to deal with people.

The traditional physical layout of branch office spaces also reflects this split: even within the boundary region there is a clear separation of client area and banking staff. There are no gates or points of entry between the two. Physical contact is restricted, with high walls and glass in which there are only small holes for specific transactions: the passing of money, documents and written instructions, and the signing of contracts.

Larger banks tend to have a symbiotic relationship with governmental eco-nomic regulations and policies. Because of their economic weight, they have a strong influence on the stability of the national economic systems. Yet their operation is very much dependent on government policies, on the central bank and other central regulatory institutions. Changes in the regulatory framework have direct consequences for the terms and conditions of their services. Banks try to handle these 'irrational' elements with another kind of splitting, which finally appears in the banks' right to enact unilateral modification clauses of ser-vice contracts offered to their consumers and clients.

Research questions and methodology

In this chapter I will describe some of the social defense mechanisms of the sales organization of a major retail bank in Hungary. Although it enacts the main characteristics of splitting, since the previous period of credit boom subtler forms of splitting have been developed as a result of the changes in the bank's primary task. I would like to demonstrate how these social defenses contributed to the generation of new anxieties (leading to further emotional costs) and, finally, how existing patterns are inhibiting adaptation to the challenges the bank is facing, emanating from the recent financial crisis.

The material described here was collected during a developmental process at Retail Bank Hungary (RBH). It involved collecting and analyzing data at conscious and unconscious levels, placing emphasis on feelings, anxieties and unconscious processes, together with members of the organization in a process of defining action plans and evaluating their results ('action research' as defined by Long, 2004). Between 2008 and 2010 I worked at RBH as a member of a consulting team that designed and delivered a management development program for different levels of the management of the retail organization of RBH. The process consisted of defining developmental needs, carrying out developmental actions and evaluating results in several rounds. Here I will use as data my observations, interview transcripts, drawings by training participants (from sessions of role analysis) and projective identifications in my role as consultant – that is, how I thought and felt in the experience as a result of projections from the organization.

One particular method used as part of the developmental process was role analysis (Newton *et al.* 2006) or, more precisely, role consultation, which examines the complex interactive processes between the person and the organization in the context of the professional role. 'The organization is understood as an inner object, awareness of which can help the client to understand his or her professional role and to differentiate between fantasy, reality and illusion' (Sievers and Beumer 2006: 65).

Another possible method to uncover the unconscious feelings in organizations is to look at the organization/consultant interface, where these potentially threatening contents are usually projected through projective identification (Krantz and Gilmore 1985) or parallel processes (Smith 1984). Bain (1976) also suggests that the denied aspect of the *presenting problem* – that is, the 'personal link that connects presenter and problem' – is at first projected into the role that is desired for the consultant. The consultant might also enact these projections and 'fall from grace' (Redding Mersky 2001), hence giving information about the hidden forces present in the organization.

The developmental process

RBH is one of the big private commercial banks, with a substantial retail network across the country. The network consists of branch offices working under sub-area managers. These offices come under a few area managers who are responsible for the sales performance of their respective areas. The retail organization also has some central functions (product development, risk management, regulation, human relations, IT, etc.). The developmental program consisted of role analysis workshops and participants' own case analyses in group coaching. The commissioner of the project was the relatively recently (six months earlier) appointed head of the Retail Division. The program was launched at almost the same time as the problems in the financial sector came to the surface.

At the time that the new leader was appointed, employees characterized the network as a 'fear- and anxiety-based' culture. The antecedent for this was that in the previous period the former division head's main challenge was to change the service staff's role from that of 'administrator' to that of 'sales representative', with an increasing emphasis on branch office- and individual-level performance, compared to the previous, collectivistic reward system.

In the new system each branch office manager was measured on a percentage scale of a composite index of different sales targets (a quota combining investment stocks, credits, number of credit cards sold, new clients attained, etc.). There were also individual sales targets and commission schemes introduced for branch office staff. Based on a ranking on this composite index, there were incentive travel trips organized in every quarter of the year for the top 20 percent of performers, and there was a major trip to an exclusive location based on the year-end results.

Branch office staff played one of three different roles depending on their place in the status hierarchy: 'creditors', 'front-liners' and 'cashiers'. Creditors usually dealt with mortgage-based consumer credits; front-liners handled accounts and credit cards. Managers at all levels in the network (mainly former creditors) were nominated to their positions on the basis of their sales performance.

The planning and performance measurement system was unified and there were similar expectations set for each branch office, depending on the number of employees (which ranged from three to fifteen). The leadership style of the previous division head was quite authoritarian, based on goal setting, regular measurement of performance, but also on strong personal relations with branch office managers. As the organization grew very quickly, the personal impact of the leader slowly disappeared and area managers (and informally sub-area managers, responsible for the sales performance of a number of smaller branch offices, ranging in number from one to seven, depending on seniority and geographic conditions) took over the managerial aspects of running the retail network, without the charismatic leadership characteristics.

When the new head of the division was appointed, his first action was to replace those area managers who were perceived to have an autocratic management style. His vision was to introduce a 'coaching style of management' in the retail network. Our developmental program's aim was to support this vision. In the first round, it was offered to relatively fresh managers of small branch offices, because staff turnover in these offices had become measurably higher in recent years.

Results and analysis

The first part of the program was directed at the development of the management skills for relatively inexperienced branch office managers. Training groups consisted of eleven or twelve people meeting for four two-day sessions over a period of six months. The atmosphere in the training groups was at first defensive and not supportive (there were harsh jokes, a lack of clarity in describing their own cases, a lack of consideration for each other, etc.). There was no cohesion; several subgroups were formed according to gender, or top performers versus average performers versus beginners, for example. It was only after the third session, when we had the role analysis, that participants started to offer cases for analysis, discussed within a group coaching process. In the following, I will elaborate on some of the drawings where typical patterns of organizational splitting could be identified. A typical case will also be presented, supporting my hypothesis about the mechanisms of splitting.

Results of role analysis

One drawing depicted the bank as a gigantic system of cogwheels working against each other (the 'catapult' in Figure 16.1). The branch office manager ('Me' in the middle) had as his main task to mediate between two opposing forces, which seemed to be a mission impossible. The person who did the drawing explained:

> [C]entral departments have their 'ambitious' ideas and visions, pushing their new products and IT systems, while my colleagues see opportunities which could be used on the market, but these frequently move in the opposite direction. All the tension is on my shoulders.

The problem seemed to be that both parties see their own ideas as 'perfect' and the others' as 'completely bad', and there is no communication between the two. Splitting leads to a waste of time and energy: 'It is a time bomb and it will explode before we shoot!'

Many similar drawings represented the relation between branch offices and central functions as weak branch offices versus strong HQ; lack of communication; and HQ not taking into account branch offices' feedback. Central functions were seen as controlling, pushing, not listening, not interested and not reacting to the expressed needs of branch offices. In another drawing (Figure 16.2) the organization was an octopus, the branch office manager being one of its suction cups. As its creator explained, '[I]t has a big head, which does not see anything, just goes after its own ideas.... The arms have the information about the environment, but it is not conveyed to the head.' As one interpretation put it, 'the

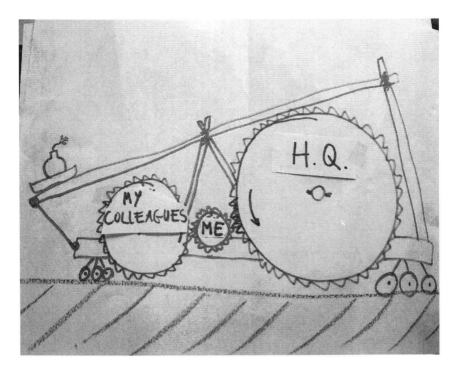

Figure 16.1 Picture 1: the organization as a counterproductive catapult.

narcissistic head is split from the rest of the body'. The result is that there are many lost opportunities; for example, the hidden treasures below the rock in the lower right corner of Figure 16.2 will not be reached.

Another type of drawing was about the lack of coaching or mentoring. Management was seen as exercising only administrative control (e.g. 'thunderstorms' or 'men with their lashes around us'). A newly appointed branch office manager drew a burning forest with all the trees in red and a strong green curved line separating it from the safe blue ship, referring to the breaking news about the financial crisis (Figure 16.3): 'I am thrown into a situation and I have to find the solution without any help. There is no coaching, no containment; as a little squirrel with lots of question marks, you have to find your way to the ship.' The theme of a highly idealized situation of being on the safe side, compared to the uncertainties of the present, also appears here as splitting.

The previously unexpressed feelings in the group, resulting in a collective denial frequently named in another context as complaining or 'social crying' (Takács 2009), could be resolved by surfacing the patterns of splitting. After recognizing the similarities at a deeper level, training group members found constructive ways of coping with tensions and started to value their differences, listening to and supporting each other. We also felt that group members began to

Figure 16.2 Picture 2: the octopus with hundred legs.

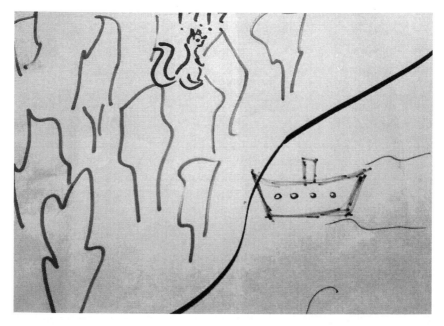

Figure 16.3 Picture 3: the burning forest.

relate to each other (and to us, as consultants) more positively and personally. The main lesson of our projective identifications also reinforced the message of the last drawing: that, with more containment, branch office managers would be able to handle their challenges much more easily.

A participant's case: the software testing exercise

Another expression of organizational splitting mechanisms can be found in the following case study put forward by a branch office manager during a group coaching session about 'how to motivate subordinates'. His office had been participating in testing a new software, the aim of which was to produce a shortlist of clients from an existing database. The final goal was to invite them to a personal meeting in the branch offices to 'activate dormant accounts'. Through the testing, the bank wanted to check whether data generated by the software were really worth using or if some improvements were required. The task was assigned to a few experienced front-liners in diverse locations.

The manager presenting the case intended this assignment to be for one of his best sales staff as a token of personal recognition and motivation. As the experience rolled out, the manager did not get any further information from central departments, though his employee was invited to several meetings. He felt a little bit 'left out' without being given any further details about the project. After a while, he heard from his area manager that it would be important to 'produce positive results' for organizational/political reasons, so it was a priority to follow up the project more closely. After discussing the matter with his colleague, it turned out that the data generated by the software did not produce the expected hit rate. So, the next motivational issue was whether he should attempt to influence his front-liner participant's written report.

Another dilemma was whether he should press for the test to be finished, which could frustrate his staff and would not be productive for his own office's actual performance, and write in the report the predictable negative results; or whether, alternatively, he should follow the informal suggestions of his area manager that 'the software was perfect, so it would be a mistake to disappoint higher-level decision makers'. Finally, he decided to follow his 'survival instincts', call an end to the testing and order a positive feedback report. This solution was also a consequence of the fact that during the test period the branch office's sales performance deteriorated (partly because of the testing, especially the 'bad data' that had taken too much time away from 'good, useful work'), so his area manager was increasingly pressing for better sales results.

As the primary task of the project was to give feedback to central functions, the manager – in order to calm his conscience – informally contacted the responsible departments in HQ, which reacted with the usual response: 'It is not a data problem, but a lack of sales skills and will. Why are you so negative again; why don't you just finish the test?' So finally he felt that he had to defend himself again from HQ. He wondered how the testing project turned from recognition into a defense of his best salesperson against attacks and how the primary task of 'improving the quality of the software' changed into scapegoating ('who is to blame for the bad results?').

Splitting mechanisms and their consequences

The observed patterns of splitting in role analysis drawings as well as in participants' cases are probably the results of deeper defense mechanisms operating in the organizational culture of the bank. Changing the culture and also the physical layout of the sales organization – that is, removing the impersonal, bureaucratic defenses – has led to increasing toxicity from the boundary regions. The system has preserved its splitting mechanisms through the division of work between the front office, whose role it is to manage relations with and consult clients (the emotional task) and the back office, whose role it is to manage risks, to carry out calculative and evaluative tasks (e.g. develop new products and services, prepare business plans based on market research) and manage resources (information technology, human resources). These tasks also have a strong influence on the quality of the direct contact with clients in the network, whose major task is to sell products and services and build relationships. The back office's major task is to detect and uncover 'adverse selection' of clients, and covertly, of front office staff.

This kind of division of work and decision making often leads to communication problems and conflicts, which, lacking proper handling, usually lead to mutual distrust and contempt. Information on new products and services (exact conditions, the details of their administration, etc.) does not filter down easily; there are frequent problems and inconsistencies within the information system.

Part of the communication problem is that there are completely different skills and competencies needed for back office and front office roles. For front-line staff it is less critical to have a finance background.[2] It is important to observe that the selection and training systems also reinforced splitting: by putting less emphasis on financial knowledge, the branch office staff are predestined to play a 'less qualified and manipulative role' compared with the back office perspective, with a lower status compared to central functions.

This division of work naturally leads to a psychological split. As the result of the communication problems and frequent changes in conditions, products and services, the emergent flaws and mistakes confronted by clients in the branch office are attributed to central departments. It is easier to blame the central departments for the decision that 'the credit application could not be accepted' or 'too high a price was charged', 'terms and conditions have changed', etc.

The more permeable the boundary is at the client/front office interface, the less permeable it becomes between the back office and the front office. In the 'sales' role, customer service staff members have to be empathetic and patient with clients. Customers are always 'right'. Staff have to accept it if the client 'knows things differently', be understanding if the client is frustrated because of mistakes, etc. By hiding their true feelings, consciously or unconsciously, they have to perform emotional work. These are the emotional costs of operating with outdated social defenses.

The main cultural patterns in the case presented were lack of communication from HQ about the process; lack of trust of branch offices towards initiatives coming from central departments; political considerations about giving feedback; constant performance pressures; changing priorities; envious attacks; and defensive reactions. The major frustration for the manager came from the fact that the very aim of the project was to give feedback in order to improve the software, which was to be introduced soon to 'help' the sales network.

Organizational splitting mechanisms finally result in distorted feedback. This mechanism at the organizational level led to a management that does not encourage constructive criticism (which is frequently labeled 'bad news'). Such feedback is usually heard as 'complaining' or 'finding excuses'. The role of branch office managers is to balance contradictory expectations and try to preserve the motivation of subordinates. This is another form of emotional labor, also as an additional cost of social defenses.

The envious characteristics of the organizational culture of RBH

Splitting as a social defense was also present in the planning processes of the sales network performance and the connected performance management system. The sales targets specific to products and services were based on central calculations, changing with external conditions and regulations. As a consequence, the sales network did not have a clear understanding of the business goals and strategy. Planning and goal setting followed a top-down breakdown of figures, based on a few principles that were defined centrally. The lack of transparency and involvement in the performance measurement system had led to a lack of trust in the measurement system.

The sales management system was built upon detailed measures of results and activity control, combined with regular feedback. Sales staff were confronted on a weekly basis with their performance, and there were quarterly campaigns as sales competitions. The most important indicator was the composite index, upon which the best performers were rewarded with incentives. This way, the reward system operated another splitting mechanism: the incentive trips gave a chance for top performers to build informal relations with each other, with central functions and with top management. These strong competitive forces divided designated 'good' branch offices from 'bad' ones, creating the conditions for envious feelings.

According to Stein (2000), and based on Klein's concept, envy involves the often unconscious feeling of ill will towards another whom one perceives to be more fortunate than oneself. Stein also postulates that 'envy is experienced most powerfully in relation to those on whom one is dependent' and that it involves a violent attack which is not concerned with self-preservation. 'Ironically, therefore, the envious attack invariably results in damage to both the attacked other and to the self' (ibid.: 199), or attacker. Social systems – not only individuals – may be characterized by envious attacks on perceived good and desirable qualities, leading to a chaotic and malfunctioning system in a way that goes beyond the role of any particular individual. 'Indeed, there is an ongoing process of recruitment of new members ... [who] are consciously or unconsciously tasked with the role of engaging in new envious attacks on others' (ibid.:. 203). These envious attacks may be targeted at positive and healthy links with others, at learning and at leadership.

The above tendencies of the envious organizational culture were tangible in the training groups and within the branch offices between front-liners and creditors (displayed by their not referring their clients to each other); branch offices envied each other's locations, results and clients. It was a practice (contrary to written policies) that whenever an existing client entered another branch office, his or her account was taken over in the computer system. Area managers were constantly attacked by their subordinates at the division headquarters. As consultants, we were frequently 'attacked' and our efforts undermined (for example, our training methods were criticized and questioned by some participants). The head of Human Resources, the person responsible for the program, was also frequently attacked (finally, she was even forced to leave the organization). These attacks became more frequent as we came to understand the deeper levels of the system.

The performance rating was a critical part of the self-esteem of branch office managers, so their self-evaluation depended on their standing in the composite index. As a consequence of the crisis, branch offices and certain sub-areas faced serious difficulties in meeting their business targets, so many of their managers suffered psychological problems (depression, nervous breakdown, psychosomatic illnesses and drinking problems), especially in areas where branch offices were too densely populated. Envious fights between big branch offices were well known, as their managers (playing also a sub-area manager's role) had to actually fight with each other for local resources.

Conclusions

The anxieties related to handling money are exacerbated in the context of an economy and society in systemic transition. Within a relatively short period (during the 1990s), Hungary moved from egalitarian values to extreme individualism; from low income and material differences to the emergence of formerly unthinkable fortunes and poverty; from guaranteed employment to double-figure unemployment rates. After twenty years, a dualistic society has developed, with strong separation of winners and losers in the political and economic changes. Relation to money under these circumstances has become even more ambiguous than in traditional capitalist systems with a history of gradual development of their institutions.

The analysis here has provided some evidence for the assumption that the division of work between the retail network and central departments, as well as planning and performance management systems of the bank in the context of social defense mechanisms that are based on splitting, reflect outdated assumptions about the primary task. Increasing emotional costs led to decreasing levels of trust and commitment, and a lack of knowledge and information sharing. The resulting problems are aggravated by defense mechanisms that turn differences within the retail network into rivalry and a projective interface for unconscious envious feelings. Frustrations result in an above-industry-average fluctuation rate, or as a consequence of the crisis (lacking alternative job opportunities) complaining and attacks.

This is a sign that the primary task of retail banks is changing: banks are increasingly striving to help people handle their money better. The physical part is that of handling money without substantial transaction costs, but it also means making wise decisions. As one bank advertisement put it, the bank was 'for those for whom the only interesting part of the world of finance is money'. The current financial and economic crisis has produced immediate pressures on banks and financial organizations. The Retail Bank's sales strategy had to be reformulated (from credits to collecting reserves), and a new approach in handling customers was introduced. Currently existing social defenses might well be the result of the previous leadership style and the environmental conditions favoring the giving of credit. Organizational splitting may have worked well for handling anxieties then, but it has led to a division in hierarchical levels, functions and locations, and a general communication breakdown. In order to attract new clients and to activate existing accounts, the organization has to learn to listen better, and contain the anxiety of customers and support them – and, as a precondition, managers must act similarly towards their subordinates, as must central functions towards the retail network.

Notes

1 After World War II, the Hungarian currency, the pengő, completely lost its value within eight months in 1946. This was without precedent in European history in the absence of any political manipulation. The mass hysteria evoked was the cause of the subsequent state interventions (nationalization of large, medium-sized and than small enterprises), securing the introduction of the forint, the current Hungarian currency.
2 The bank's human resource manager's tricky question for selecting branch office managers used to be: 'Who is a better candidate for a front-line banking job, an accountant or a butcher?' One would usually choose the accountant, because of his or her educational background, but in the selection process social skills are far more important: 'to be able to talk all day long and smilingly sell tough meat'.

References

Bain, A. (1976) 'Presenting problems in social consultancy', *Human Relations*, 29(7): 643–57.
Bain, A. (1999) 'On socio-analysis', *Socio-Analysis*, 1(1): 1–17.
Hirschhorn, L. and Gilmore, T. (1992) 'The new boundaries of the boundaryless organization', *Harvard Business Review*, May–June: 104–15.
Hochschild, A.R. (1983) *The Managed Heart: Commercialization of human feeling*, Berkeley: University of California Press.

HVG (2010) 'A rejtett gazdaság miatt túl nagy a készpénzállomány' (High cash ratios due to the grey economy), 26 January. Online, available at: http://hvg.hu/gazdasag/20100126_rejtett_gazdasag_keszpenzallomany (retrieved 26 January 2010).

Klein, M. (1946) 'Notes on some schizoid mechanisms', in J. Mitchell (ed.) (1986) *Selected Writings of Melanie Klein*, New York: Free Press.

Krantz, J. and Gilmore, T.N. (1985) 'Projective identification in the consulting relationship: exploring the unconscious dimensions of a client system', *Human Relations*, 38(12): 1159–77.

Krantz, J. and Gilmore, T.N. (1990) 'The splitting of leadership and management as a social defense', *Human Relations*, 43(2): 183–204.

Long, S. (2004) 'Action research, participatory action research and action learning in organizations', in Y. Gabriel, *Organizations in Depth: The psychoanalysis of organizations*, London: Sage.

Menzies, I.E.P. (1960) 'The functioning of social systems as a defence against anxiety', *Human Relations*, 13: 95–121. Reprinted in M. Kets de Vries (ed.) (1984) *The Irrational Executive*, New York: International Universities Press.

Newton, J., Long, S. and Sievers, B. (2006) *Coaching in Depth: The organizational role analysis approach*, London: Karnac Books.

Redding Mersky, R. (2001) '"Falling from grace" – when consultants go out of role: enactment in the service of organizational consultancy', *Socio-Analysis*, 3(1): 37–53.

Schein, E. (1985) *Organizational Culture and Leadership*, San Francisco: Jossey-Bass.

Schneider, S. (1991) 'Managing boundaries in organizations', in M. Kets de Vries and associates (eds) *Organization on the Couch*, San Francisco: Jossey-Bass.

Sievers, B. (2003) '"Your money or your life?" Psychotic implications of the pension fund system: towards a socio-analysis of the financial services revolution', *Human Relations*, 56(2): 187–210.

Sievers, B. and Beumer, U. (2006) 'Organizational role analysis and consultation: the organization as inner object', in J. Newton, S. Long and B. Sievers (eds) *Coaching in Depth: The organizational role analysis approach*, London: Karnac Books.

Smith, K. (1984) 'Toward a conception of organizational currents', *Group and Organizational Studies*, 9(2), June: 285–312.

Stapley, L.F. (2006) *Individuals, Groups, and Organizations beneath the Surface: An introduction*, London: Karnac Books.

Stein, M. (2000) 'After Eden: envy and the defences against anxiety paradigm', *Human Relations*, 53: 193–204.

Stein, M. (2003) 'Unbounded irrationality: risk and organizational narcissism at Long Term Capital Management', *Human Relations*, 56(5): 523–40.

Stein, M. (2008) 'Toxicity and the unconscious experience of the body at the employee–customer interface', *Organization Studies*, 28: 1223–41.

Takács, S. (2009) 'Social crying: complaining as a uniting force (the case of a retail bank in Hungary)', paper presented at the 26th ISPSO Annual Meeting and Symposium 'Differences at Work: Towards Integration and Containment', Toledo, Spain, June.

Wachtel, P.L. (2003) 'Full pockets, empty lives: a psychoanalytic exploration of the contemporary culture of greed', *American Journal of Psychoanalysis*, 63(2): 103–22.

17 Falling bankers and falling banks

A psychoanalytical exploration of the Phaethon motif and the fall in financial careers

Hans van den Hooff

Introduction

The increasing level of responsibility that bankers and business people take on as their careers progress does not necessarily go hand in hand with their psychological maturity. It is not uncommon for such a mismatch to develop into a full disaster, bringing serious suffering such as burnout, anxiety, panic or depression to the individual and sometimes also serious damage, such as financial loss and even bankruptcy, to the organisation. As an organisational consultant and an executive coach working psychodynamically, I have for many years worked with people in financial institutions. Mostly these were individuals with significant responsibility. From my training in Jungian psychoanalysis, similarities between many different cases of corporate rising and falling struck me and made me wonder if perhaps archetypal psychological mechanisms could be at work.

The literature on archetypal constellations in organisations is limited, but interest in this work seems to be growing. The number of publications on archetypes and complexes operating in organisations – as opposed to individuals – is limited. Moxnes (1998) has proposed a number of organisational archetypes and elaborated for each archetype a correspondence with Bion's basic assumption groups: dependency, fight–flight and pairing (Bion 1961). However, Moxnes studied the archetype primarily in the individual and not so much as a collective unconscious pattern of a group. Outside complex theory, the area of a collectively distorted reality function in groups has of course been widely studied. Bion's basic assumption theory and the notion of groupthink (Janis 1972) are well established. Not many authors have elaborated further on the theory of complexes in groups. However, there has been a recent upsurge of interest in this area – witness the edited collection Singer and Kimbles (2004). These authors – also building on Jung's concept of the complex – introduced the concept of cultural complex to study conflicts between groups and cultures in society. In the last part of this chapter, I will elaborate on this.

In this chapter, I will explore in particular the psychological image of 'the fall' in the Greek myth of Phaethon, who crashes down in his father's sun chariot. I look at the phenomenon of steep career-making and sudden falls as the enactment of an archetypal complex related to the motif of Phaethon. This flying motif is particularly apt to describe the unconscious dynamics in the financial industry, which, compared with manufacturing industry, lacks factories and warehouses and is therefore in a way more airy and less grounded. I propose that the archetype, which potentially lies dormant in the psyche, is more likely to become active in individuals coming from families with hidden trauma or other secrets than in individuals without such a background.

The structure of the chapter is roughly as follows. To illustrate the phenomenon of career-making in the financial industry and the fall from a clinical angle, I will introduce two clients:[1] Philip and Jonathan. Both men are bankers who for many years had successful corporate careers which were interrupted in each case by a sudden fall. Philip's case was extreme; Jonathan's was milder and more typical.

After introducing the cases, I will sketch two versions of the myth of Phaethon, namely those by Ovid and Euripides. After sketching the Phaethon myths, I will elaborate on the vignettes further and explore parallels between the myths and the case material. This will include some client dreams of flying and falling down. This exploration centres round the following aspects. With Ovid, the psychological drama centres on the son–father axis, including Phaethon's attraction towards the light and the father. In the 440-year-older version of Euripides, however, Phaethon's motivating forces are not only an attraction towards the light but also a repulsion from a home with secrets and partly incestuous relations to the female. A tentative conclusion from this comparison between myth and praxis is that the psychodynamics of the relatively unknown Euripidal myth correspond more significantly to clinical reality than the drama of Ovid's canonised version. In other words, the father–son dynamics alone are not enough to constellate the Phaethon complex. What is also at play psychologically is a needed and necessary break from home and the incestuous relation to the female.

In the last part of this chapter, I will elaborate how the Phaethon complex of the individual may infect the wider organization. I will discuss some of the effects of executive coaching and I will say a word or two about how executives who have increased awareness of their inner life can have a beneficial effect on their organisations.

The case of Philip

Philip was referred to me by Nicola, who is a human resources (HR) manager at a very large international bank. This bank has been sending clients to me for executive coaching for more than five years. Mostly, these have been senior professionals at vice-president level. Over the phone, Nicola told me that recently several people had started to complain that Philip's behaviour was becoming 'problematic'. He was described as 'self-conscious', 'abrasive' and 'selling himself too much'. He was said to evoke a lot of aggression in others.

Philip entered my consulting room dressed in a typical banker's suit. He said that he wanted help to understand why he is very good at starting things, such as a work project, only at a later stage to start destroying what was built. During the first couple of sessions Philip told me about his life and his career. He had started at the age of 25 to work in a junior position in a country-site office of a bank. He soon learned how to gain the confidence of wealthy customers and became a successful investment relations manager. Within a couple of years he became the bank's 'head of investment relations' for the whole of the country. He married and had two children. His good performance in the bank was noted in the job market and he was offered a more responsible position with an even bigger bank. His next job was to reorganise ways of working in the area of investment management. After that job, he also became a project manager for the merging of two banks. These are very complex, multimillion-euro projects that involve 80 hours' work per week and hundreds of project team members. He was leading these projects, working all the time, literally without any time for himself, his family or any other non-work-related activity except for an MBA study on which he was concurrently enrolled. One of these projects was starting up a new subsidiary of that same European bank in another continent. In the meantime he had obtained his MBA from an 'ivy league' business school.

Somehow a conflict developed between him and the bank that he was working for, and he left to join yet another bank, in an even more responsible position. For this last-mentioned bank he also carried out large-scale, high-profile change projects until recently, when he felt that the board members who had hitherto 'fathered' him (these seniors would always receive his calls and have time for him) started to not return his calls and to 'fence him out'. Also, very recently his marriage had broken up and he had got divorced.

The case of Jonathan

In contrast to Philip, Jonathan came to me on his own initiative. He had recently become a member of the board of management of a bank. Jonathan was responsible for strategy development. He came to me because he felt out of control in his work. He told me that he could not think clearly any more and that he felt that others had too much influence on him. Preparing for work on Sunday evening, he was often anxious about how he would be able to perform and keep up concentration and appearances the next day.

Jonathan's career had been very successful until some six months previously. After obtaining an MBA degree from a prestigious university, he had worked for a number of world-class and very respectable banks. The résumé that he had brought to me showed that he had changed employer every three years or so and that he had worked in different countries in different continents. After working and living for more than ten years in different countries and continents, he and his family had recently returned home for the education of the children. On the basis of his successful career, he was offered his current position on the board of management.

My first impressions of Jonathan were that he paid great attention to how he dressed and behaved. I found that his behaviour was at times mannered, over-polite and over-friendly. It was important for him to please me. His troubles at work seemed to centre on suggestibility – that is, he had lost the ability to find his own standpoint. When colleagues on the board suggested an idea or an initiative, he rarely found himself capable of formulating his own opinion about that proposal or idea. He could not concentrate on the problem or idea and he could not formulate his own idea, and could certainly not formulate a convincing authentic response. I noticed that in interaction with me he similarly seemed to have difficulty in finding his own standpoint, and I think that he was too sensitive to what he believed to be my suggestions. The way in which he talked about his job gave me a clear idea that he was hardly in touch with the day-to-day reality of the business and rather obsessed by unrealistic future business opportunities.

The atmosphere in Jonathan's parental home was tense, strange and chilly. His father was very remote towards him and there was an issue with sexuality around the father. The father had said that all kind of persons, including an uncle of Jonathan, are homosexual (which according to Jonathan he was not) and that Jonathan should stay away from them. Jonathan's mother was described as very timid, and from Jonathan's perspective she seemed absent and living in the shadow of his father. When Jonathan left home and began his studies at university, he was glad to leave a home with a highly disturbing atmosphere. It seemed he had not found a real father yet.

Ovid's Phaethon

Different versions of the myth of Phaeton have survived. The central part of all versions is that one day the young Phaethon, son of Helios, drives the sun chariot of his father. Phaethon is not capable of handling the horses and keeping the chariot on track. The whole enterprise gets out of hand; the chariot sets the world on fire while crashing down.

The most canonised version of the Phaethon myth is the one told by Ovid in his *Metamorphoses* (4 CE). In Ovid's version, the mother of Phaethon is Clymene, daughter of Oceanus. His father was the sun-god Phoebus ('Phoebe' is the name that Romans gave to Helios, to the sun and to Apollo). Once, when Phaethon was boasting about his high birth, another boy taunted him and said that Phaethon was not the son of Phoebus and that he was a bastard. Phaethon demanded the truth from his mother, Clymene, who swore to him that he was a legitimate son of Phoebus and advised him to travel to his father's palace to hear the truth from his own lips. Arriving at his father's splendid palace in the East and climbing the steep stairs, he went straight in. Phaethon explains that he has come to confirm his parentage. Phoebus gives the desired confirmation at once. Then Phaethon asks for proof, upon which Phoebus promises to fulfil as proof any request that Phaethon may make. Immediately Phaethon asks to drive the chariot. Then Phoebus delivers a highly dramatic speech to dissuade Phaethon, explaining that he is still too inexperienced to do so. Phaethon insists that his father keeps his promise. Phoebus sees that it is impossible to change Phaethon's mind and delivers a second speech now with instructions and advice about which course to take and how to handle the horses. Immediately after the second speech, Phaethon mounts the chariot. From the first, the horses realise the inexperience of their driver and leave their accustomed path. Phaethon loses control and looks down at the earth in terror. Ovid describes in great detail the wild ride, how the sun gets too close to the earth and the world fire that follows. Then Phaethon is hurled from the chariot as Zeus sends a thunderbolt to prevent a complete catastrophe from happening to the whole earth. Clymene travels to her son's tomb. Phaethon's sisters, the Heliads, are transformed into poplars and weep amber.

Euripides' Phaethon

Euripides' version of the myth, simply called *Φαεθον*, is much less well known than the myth from Ovid. Euripides wrote his *Phaethon* around 440 BC. Perhaps it is important to remember that this is thought to be the time of the first cities, the end of matriarchy and the beginning of patriarchy (see, for example, Mendelsohn 2002: 21). The principal source for the play fragments of Euripides' *Phaethon* is the fifth-century BC palimpsest parchment, Paris Bibliothèque National manuscript Gr. 107B (see Collard and Cropp 2008: 329). This parchment is badly damaged in parts. Diggle (1970) has examined all the manuscript evidence and offered many decipherings and interpretations. Using both Diggle and Collard and Cropp as sources, it is possible to reconstruct the *Phaethon* of Euripides as follows.

In the opening scene, Clymene delivers a monologue in which she makes it clear that she is now married to King Merops and that Phaethon, who until that day had no reason to doubt that Merops was his father, was the fruit of her liaison with Helios. She also speaks about the marriage that Merops is planning that day for Phaethon. Merops is also unaware of who Phaethon's father is. Phaethon now appears and displays dislike for the marriage that is planned for him and disbelief about Helios being his father. Clymene urges Phaethon to learn the truth from Helios himself by holding him to a promise that he made to her during their union, which was that he would grant any future wish to the future child. Next, a *parodos* (entrance song of the choir) follows in which housemaids sing a song announcing their joyful anticipation of Phaethon's marriage later that day.

Merops then urges his case for the marriage. The bride is to be one of Phaethon's half-sisters, one of the Heliads. Merops talks about a dowry. Phaethon's answer indicates that he does not care for the dowry (lines 158–159): 'Though he is free, he is a slave of his marriage bed, when he has sold his body for the dowry.' Merops also talks about old and young, succession and the need for another 'anchor' to increase the stability of government. Phaethon's answer indicates that he does not care for the fatherland (line 163): 'for the nourishing earth is a fatherland everywhere'.

Phaethon leaves the scene for Helios's palace. Merops assumes that Phaethon is leaving in search of his bride. Phaethon, however, wants to find out for himself whether Helios is his real father. Merops's wrong assumption about Phaethon's motive for leaving the palace creates a dramatic tension that lasts until the final scenes of the play, when everybody but Merops knows about the accident. In the next scene, a messenger – Phaethon's *paidagogos* – who had accompanied Phaethon to Helios's palace describes Phaethon's departure in the sun-god's chariot and the disaster that followed it. Clymene and the chorus greet the news with appropriate outbursts of mourning and despair.

In the following scene the smouldering corpse of Phaethon is on the stage. Clymene orders the maids to remove all bloodstains and to hide the corpse in the treasure chamber. Merops is heard approaching at the head of a group of girls, probably his daughters, who are singing marriage hymns and honouring the household gods with song and dance. Suddenly a servant rushes from the palace with the news that smoke is seeping out of the treasure chamber. Merops hastens inside. His cries are heard within.

Merops learns the truth from the *paidagogos* and threatens Clymene with death. In the final scene, an unknown mediator (maybe Oceanos, maybe Zeus, maybe Aphrodite) appears, who probably reconciled Merops and his wife. Perhaps (as elsewhere, text is missing) the Heliads are transformed into poplars and weep their wonted tears near the tomb of their brother.

Searching for father, escaping incest

With Ovid, the dramatic emphasis is on the wildness of the ride and the crash. The main motivating factor for the irresponsible ride is the confirmation that Phaethon is the son of Phoebus. In Ovid's version there is no dramatic tension in the family; there is no incestuous marriage to a half-sister. There is no stepfather. There is no pressure to prepare for succession. There is no attempt to bind him to the house. There is no Clymene who has a need to hide the body of the smouldering Phaethon from her husband. There is no conflict between Clymene and her husband.

In Ovid, Clymene and Phoebus are depicted almost as mortals and not as gods. Phoebus begs his son to give up his wish to drive the chariot but is helpless when Phaethon persists. Clymene is like any ordinary mother telling her son the truth, giving him motherly advice. But in the end she is helpless too and can only mourn his death. What drove Phaethon to this very bold ride? The motivation that Ovid gives Phaethon for his ride is Epaphus's insult and Phaethon's need to know his real identity. These reasons are on their own somehow not convincing enough. Why did Phaethon press on after Phoebus had made quite clear to him that he was his real father? There seems to be another hidden motive in the background, but Ovid did not give it. Some time after I had read the 'Phaethon' of Ovid's *Metamorphoses*, I read the fragments of Euripides' *Phaethon*, written about 450 years before Ovid. Here I found hints of more convincing motives.

In a way, Ovid's version is like the initial presentation of my clients when they come to see me after some kind of fall in their careers and wider lives. They describe the fall and sometimes the terror but have no idea what was happening to them on a deeper level and why. Many sessions later, a picture generally starts to develop, which, bit by bit, uncovers the motive forces that underlay their climb and fall. Somehow, Ovid's version is to Euripides' version as the initial presentation is to a more advanced state of the analytic coaching. Exploring the unconscious is like digging 400 years in history. It is as if what was lost by the generations between Euripides and Ovid is the same material that got lost in the client's consciousness during and after the corporate fall. The fascination with the father and the ride with the sun-chariot are less prone to oblivion than the subtler motif of the need to get away from having to marry a half-sister and the need to make one's own living (denying the dowry). Similarly, the fascination of the corporate climb and fall that clients experience is on top of their consciousness whereas the deeper motifs for career-making are hidden, at least at the beginning of coaching.

What can we make of the fact that in Euripides' *Phaethon*, the fall takes place on the day that he is supposed to marry one of his half-sisters, a Heliad? Could it be that this points to some incestuous energy from which escape is necessary? Having to enter into a marriage with a half-sister is taboo for mortals. The need to run away from this threat of incest is a convincing factor in his pursuing the mad ride in the chariot. What might this incestuous threat correspond to psychologically? What psychological incest do we need to break away from when we embark on our career?

Philip's case, continued

The obvious parallels between the Phaethon myth and the case of Philip are the blind drive, the importance of rising and the catastrophic fall. Also, during the rising phase of his career Philip seemed to have been dissociated from his negative feelings and to have been ruled by fiery impulses. This psychological constellation corresponds well with Phaethon's drive.

Another parallel between Philip and Phaethon emerged a month into the work. In one session, he told me that, just before he had married, when collecting his birth certificate, which he needed for the formalities of his marriage, Philip had found out that his supposed parents were not his real parents. It turned out that his parents had adopted him when he was a few months old and had never told him. So, almost in exactly the same way as in Euripides' Phaethon, around the time of his marriage Philip discovered that the person whom he had assumed to be his father was not really his father. Philip's case was worse, however, as his mother was also not his mother. A wider family was also lacking, because the mother had no more family and the father had no more family ties. No siblings, no cousins, no nephews or nieces. Thus, Philip was essentially a psychological orphan with an identity vacuum, without a name; his ambition could in part have been fuelled by his need to make a name for himself.

On the day that Philip had learned this deeply disturbing news, he cancelled the marriage and broke almost completely with his parents. When he found out that he had been adopted, the ground disappeared from under his feet. One could perhaps say that this discovery caused his need to create an omnipotent fantasy of control as a surrogate for the lost basis and grounding. He could not mentally symbolise this need as it was far too painful and he had no psychological help in those days. Therefore, he enacted the drama by taking the support of the 'horse called career' into his own hands. As all the environmental factors fell in place, the archetypes at the core of the Phaethon myth gained increasing autonomy and constellated a complex that completely eclipsed his wider ego consciousness and that directed his life for many years. His rising career was not his own conscious choice. It was not a result of thoughtful individual reflection. His career ascent was the unconscious acting out of an age-old psychological form that gained control over him.

After Philip found out that his father was not his father, he tried to locate his natural father but did not succeed. Clearly, the father archetype had not installed properly for Philip. His adoptive father was not really a warm and good enough father. His real father was not only totally absent, but also a mystery. Throughout his career, Philip had a strong need for recognition of his achievements by male authority figures. He told me very proudly how he had won the respect of members of the board of management of several of the banks that he had worked for. As his career progressed, Philip needed paternal recognition and was therefore comfortable with 'knowing his place'. Shortly before the fall, however, Philip was bypassing his direct superiors, thereby violating the unwritten rule. Maybe, psychologically, his direct superiors stopped being carriers of the father imago, just as his adoptive father had stopped carrying the father imago, as had Merops, the stepfather of Phaethon. It was not difficult to see how Philip's fall had accelerated to a crash when the same male authority figures that seemed supportive of him before had started to turn their backs on him because he had no more energy to deliver all those difficult projects.

In all versions of the Phaethon myth, as well as in the case of Philip, the need of the son for the 'fatherly', whatever that may be exactly, emerges clearly as a motivational factor explaining to an extent the otherwise incomprehensible blind attraction towards career climbing and the neglect of family life. The neglect of Philip's family life, which involved being a father to his own children, corresponded to the absence of his own father. But what about the female, what about the mother?

Philip's relationship with his mother was impaired, to say the least. It was unusual to hear the degree of coldness and detachment with which he spoke about her in the early phase of the coaching. When he used the words 'ice-cold', it did indeed become ice-cold in the consulting room. He told me that his mother never showed any emotion. In the aetiology of my client's problems, the cold mother played a very important role. In fact, much of the coaching work was about the relationship with his (adoptive) mother. An important transformation took place when he began to consciously realise how he had missed maternal caring. He started to get in touch with his internal wounds, which increasingly brought him in contact with his feeling function. Eventually he began to see how in a way his mother had her own big wounds, her Jewish family having been hit strongly by World War II. A couple of months into the coaching, having not spoken to her for years, he started to call her more often. He told me that the coaching had helped him to realise that the coldness of his mother had maybe resulted from causes beyond her control. Some images of his mother's childhood suffering increasingly helped him to become conscious of how he himself had suffered from his mother's distorted affect regulation. Together with this increasing feeling of contact with his own wounds, something important in the relationship with his mother developed. She even started to phone him, something that she had never done before. Also, Philip had traced his biological mother and, parallel to our work, he had deepened his relationship with her. She was a much warmer woman than his adoptive mother and was eager to develop their relationship further. Of course, both the development of the relationship with his adoptive mother and the relationship with his real mother developed slowly and with much stumbling. A further elaboration of how the relationship with the mother developed is outside the scope of this chapter. An important reason for sketching the complications in the relationships between Philip and his adoptive mother as well as with his biological mother is to illustrate how complications in the relationship with the maternal may go hand in hand with a flight into career which is also a flight to the father.

Jonathan, continued

Jonathan, the previously mentioned client who was suffering from suggestibility and therefore had difficulty in determining his own standpoint, told me that he had to fly a lot for his work and that he loved flying and aircraft. He also frequently dreamed about flying. I want to explore some of this flying-dream material because of its correspondences to the myth of Phaethon. In some dreams, Jonathan had difficulty in taking off; in others he crashed and there was a risk of explosions.

In the first couple of weeks, Jonathan dreamed about crashing planes. In one dream the emphasis was on the post-crash situation. The dream atmosphere was similar to Euripides' version of the Phaethon myth where the smouldering corpse of Phaethon is on stage and there is a danger of Merops's explosion:

> *An airplane flies at low altitude and crashes. Passengers who are paralysed by fear appear on top of the wings. I help several of them to get out of the plane by the wings. We are very anxious because we expect an explosion of the plane any moment. I want to run away but I also need to stay to give help. How many more passengers should I help? When is it enough?*

If we assume that the crashed plane somehow symbolises a part of the unconscious, the people leaving the crashed plane one by one could be seen as parts of the unconscious that are one by one brought to consciousness during the analytical coaching work. In that case, helping the passengers to get out is what his inner helper does and what we do in the coaching. The threat of the explosion points to a fear of an intense, unbearable, perhaps traumatic wound that might erupt from the unconscious during the analytic work. Perhaps this indicates a part of Jonathan that wished to run away from analysis, although there was no evidence for this in reality.

After many anxious flying dreams, he reported a flying dream that ended very well:

> *An airplane flies slowly through a street. It is not crashing but rather put down in a controlled manner. It has been expected, it is a very special environment. There are all kinds of different buildings: there is an Indian teepee but also a Hilton Hotel. I may choose where I will stay. It is a bit like paradise. The pilot had known all the time about this. A friendly lady comes to ask me what my first impressions are. I answer: very positive. It becomes clear that this place has been designed to give people a special space to develop themselves.*

Here, the Phaethonic dynamics seem to have become transformed into something quite constructive: a special place for self-development. The tepee–Hilton pair points to a dipole, with the image of a teepee pointing to nature and humanity, and the image of a Hilton Hotel pointing to culture and technology. This dream took place about a year after we started the work. It indicated the finding of authenticity and the individual standpoint that was previously unreachable.

The effects on the organisation

The in-depth executive coaching processes of Philip and Jonathan were for each of them accompanied by their discovering new aspects of their inner lives of which they had not been conscious before. It goes without saying that such a transformation potentially has a significant impact on how the executive does his or her work. The whole organisation can be affected. For example, in the area of recruitment the executive may reconsider which headhunters the firm will use or which managers should be involved in the screening of candidates. The executive will start looking for qualities in others that, through the coaching, they have discovered in themselves. There will be fewer and less powerful projections during the interview process. A more balanced promotion process will improve the stability of the organisation. In board meetings and in interactions with other parts of the organisation, the executive will be more aware of what is going on in him- or herself and in colleagues. All of this may greatly improve the quality of decision making and reduce the risk that irrational factors such as grandiose fantasies will lead the firm to ruin. The increased self-awareness of the executive tends to trickle down and change the organisation.

Particularly in cases where the client is the chair of the board, one can see very significant effects of coaching on the culture and performance of the organisation as a whole. It is not unreasonable to assume that competent executive coaching is one of the most efficient and effective ways of transforming organisations. As a management consultant I have been responsible for dozens of organisational change projects for large firms in international settings. Together with my colleagues, I have helped to organise and run very many workshops to 're-engineer' this or that strategy or business process. It is the experience of many of my colleagues and myself that dominant executives have an enormous influence on organisational change projects. These workshops were in general prepared thoughtfully by collecting market data and mapping the competitive position of the firm and the business processes. Large teams of analysts had done high-quality interviewing and data analysis. However, surprisingly often the logic of the data analysis, brainstorming and workshops pointed to a strategic direction that an influential board member 'did not like'. In no uncertain ways this executive would influence the project team and steer the recommendations for change in his or her direction. Often, the organisation as a whole would follow the dominant executive surprisingly meekly. Any academic understanding of the dynamics of organisational change cannot be complete without an appreciation of the excessive influence of dominant executives.

The question of how complexes of an individual leader influence the wider organisation is a central question in systemic organisational analysis and has been researched in depth (see, for example, Singer and Kimbles 2004). Although a broad exploration of this dynamic is outside the scope of this chapter, which focuses on the individual, it is understood that the psychological mechanism involves inductive dynamics such as projective identification. Through these mechanisms a leader may infect the organisation. In cases where the leader is largely in the grip of a myth, such as the myth of Phaethon, the whole organisation may become infected. The myth of Phaethon, for example, is an unconscious dominant that lies dormant in the unconscious of all the employees, ready to be activated when a dominant boss is under its fascinating spell. This is not dissimilar to viral or bacterial infections which can spread in groups. Through these mechanisms, archetypes such as the hero, the helper, being old, being young, etc. can install themselves in organisations. The psyche of human beings is prone to archetypal infection.

However, the same dynamics that constellate archetypal complexes in organisations can also operate in reverse mode. When the dominant leaders are freed from the grip of the myth, the spell that was put on the organisation may be lifted in its entirety.

On a final note, it should be mentioned that, not infrequently, executives who have been through a psychodynamic coaching process decide to leave the organisation to start their own firm, or make some such other significant career shift. They have come to see that such a redirection in their career will help them to fulfil their potential far more readily than staying with their existing organisation. Often these career changes are very beneficial to the individual. Whether or not they leave, life often becomes much more interesting for these executives.

Note

1 I gratefully acknowledge the willingness of the clients who have given me kind permission to use their cases in this publication. I have changed the names and some of the details of the biography of the clients to ensure their anonymity. Nothing has been changed in the dream material.

References

Bion, W.R. (1961) *Experiences in Groups*, London: Tavistock.

Collard, C. and Cropp, M. (eds) (2008) *Euripides Fragments*, Cambridge, MA: Harvard University Press.

Diggle, J. (ed.) (1970) *Euripides: Phaeton*, Cambridge: Cambridge University Press.

Janis, I. (1972) *Victims of Groupthink: A psychological study of foreign-policy decisions and fiascos*, Boston: Houghton Mifflin.

Mendelsohn, D. (2002) *Gender and the City in Euripides' Political Plays*, Oxford: Oxford University Press.

Moxnes, P. (1998) 'Fantasies and fairy tales in groups and organizations: Bion's basic assumptions and the deep roles', *European Journal of Work and Organizational Psychology*, 7(3): 283–98.

Ovidius (2004) *Metamorphoses I 747–79*, Cambridge, MA: Harvard University Press.

Singer, T. and Kimbles, S.L. (eds) (2004) *The Cultural Complex: Contemporary Jungian perspectives on psyche and society*, Hove, UK: Brunner-Routledge.

18 Melting the iceberg

Unveiling financial frames

Marc Lenglet

Introduction

When it comes to the description of financial markets, numerous difficulties arise: recognizing their role in contemporary societies may indeed imply the revision of accepted discourses. Whatever the difficulty may be in describing financial practices, it remains a definitive task, however, especially in times of crisis. Tett (2009) recently noted that six years ago a 'mapping' of the financial system based on available discourse would have revealed that several parts of its landscape remained barely covered. In fact, 'the Western financial system looked rather like an "iceberg" in media terms: one relatively small part of the system was visible, since it was extensively written about; a large chunk of activity, though, was submerged from sight, widely ignored' (ibid.: 6). The iceberg metaphor prompts us to look under the surface of the financial landscape in order to describe what really lies within terms such as 'liquid' order books, 'transparent' price disclosures, and all the devices that constitute the financial sphere.

If the social studies of finance still remain under construction, despite recent efforts (Knorr Cetina and Preda 2005; MacKenzie 2006, 2009; Preda 2009), I suggest that the constitutive elements generally used to describe the financial arena now need to be 're-embedded' through the study of mediating elements acting within financial organizations and institutions. The position in this chapter is rooted in the conviction that speaking about finance requires the disembedding of categories and models through the study of their application in the field, taking practices of everyday finance as an entry point – whether we find those in retail banking agencies, brokerage trading rooms, merger and acquisition departments, or elsewhere. In so doing, we soon get access to the abounding discourses that frame financial practices, precisely in the places where they develop.[1] Financial markets are organized with different languages, mingled with technical devices: computers managing order books, screens displaying prices, cables transmitting the flow of information, files recording client portfolios, procedures meant to organize the interactions between people and systems, together all contributing to the enactment of an original market materiality. The purpose of this chapter, which draws on social studies of finance, is to study how actors and rules contribute to the enactment of this materiality.

The compliance function's specific lens will be used here to gain a 'view from below'. This function, though excessively working with texts (directives, procedures and rulebooks), also works on codes (mostly codes of conduct applicable to situated practices), that is to say on specific languages with their own grammar and their own vocabulary. These normative languages help compliance officers to make constant shifts between texts intended to frame practices, and contexts giving rise to the reality usually described as 'the market'. Understanding how rules are enacted in the daily practices of financial markets may therefore help us understand what lies beneath the surface displayed by markets on the internet (websites allowing clients to transact in markets), in the papers (adds explaining how liquid the market is in order to attract investors), or even – for those markets that still exist as a physical place where buyers and sellers literally meet – what lies in the gestures, conventions and codes that lead to the making of a financial transaction.

The chapter is divided in two parts. I first provide (1) a series of examples describing what compliance officers do in the course of their daily duties. Discourses framing practices are articulated within the space defined by market contexts, which prompt (2) the formulation of a few remarks regarding the description of financial markets, in order to understand how we can access the underlying rules framing these entities. I suggest that greater attention should be paid to defining what a 'market context' is, and illustrate this position in describing the role of compliance officers as interpretive agents contributing to the framing of financial practices.

What do compliance officers do?

Compliance officers work on the definition of practices. Three examples will help us to understand precisely what is at stake with this function. In the following, I draw on long-lasting participant observation within a pan-European Paris-based brokerage house (hereafter referred to as Global Brokerage Services, GBS) that allowed me to gather data for a three-year period from October 2006 to September 2009.[2] Acting as a full member of a compliance department located within the main trading room, I studied practices at a time when the industry was experiencing great changes with the implementation of a new regulatory framework (the Markets in Financial Instruments Directive, MiFID, in November 2007). This was a period when rules were discussed, modified and reenacted.

Defining compliance

While the definition of the compliance function is clearly stated in regulatory texts, such as the UK Financial Services Authority's *Handbook* or the French Autorité des Marchés Financiers' *General Regulation*, its observation in a dedicated market context gives rise to further developments. Although regulatory regimes propose different definitions, the main objectives assigned to compliance officers remain the same: to ensure that services offered by investment firms, their management and employees are deployed in accordance with accepted codes of conduct, rules and regulations. Five tasks can therefore be derived from this principle to build the compliance agenda: enacting internal rules, training employees, providing advice, performing controls, and lobbying.

Compliance officers enact rules within the specific space relating to the company they work for: not only do they put in place compliance handbooks or dedicated procedures, but also they are constantly updating internal regulatory texts, as these meet the flow of regulatory innovation produced by regulators. The recent implementation of MiFID all over Europe implied that compliance officers had to redraft their sets of procedures once they had managed to understand precisely what was at stake within the new texts, and what had really changed. Once formulated, those rules had to be explained to the employees, so that they could implement them rapidly. During this phase, issues were raised regarding the modifications required by the practices, resulting in questions, IT developments, and the reconfigurations of organizational routines, depending on the degree of modifications required by the new state of the world described by the changed regulations.

Compliance officers also spend a great deal of time providing advice to market operators, for rules formulated in a procedure cannot, on their own, fully organize, order or frame the complexity of market materiality. In fact, it is certainly because rules remain principles in essence, even in the most meticulous of descriptions, that they cannot grasp the ever-changing states of markets. Depending on the context, rules can serve as frames to the understanding of the market reality; but in many occurrences the market reality may well overflow the fragile structures proposed by market rules and regulations. In such situations it is the compliance officer's duty to create and propose solutions, even when these may look incomplete or partly detrimental to the activity, as shown in the following series of examples.

'What shall I do now?'

The plot takes place within GBS's trading room on a Friday afternoon; it is 4.28 p.m. and some markets are about to close. On the Irish Stock Exchange it is the auction phase in which closing prices are determined. Denis, the head of program trading at GBS, pops up in front of Adam, one of the compliance officers, and says, 'I have a program on Dublin which will yank the market ... [the] client has sent an order for 200 to 500 per cent of the volumes at best, on 45 stocks of the index.... What shall I do? You have two minutes.' Denis's customer has sent an instruction that at first sight seems possibly erroneous, asking for volumes that are apparently not available in the order book. As a result, the operator does not know what to do: should he accept the order and try to execute it, or should he refuse the instruction?

Such a situation, drawn among the everyday events taking place in a trading room, is both simple and complex. It is simple because it raises an issue about the relationship between clients and intermediaries, and the agency that takes place in the exchange initiated by the client. It is complex because the sole instruction, when referred to the specific market context, looks like nonsense: it is the closing auction and in a very short period of time markets will not allow any new orders to be processed, which technically means that the operator will no longer be able to 'work' the order. At this particular moment the sizes available in the order book are two to five times smaller than the volume requested; the main issue here is not that the client will not see his instruction completely fulfilled (which remains a strong probability), rather that this order will definitely move the market (Denis uses the expression 'yank off', which gives a good image of the order book's ecology once the order bolts down to the market). Furthermore, the client's instruction is 'at best', which means with no price limit. Technically speaking, prices can move a great deal of ticks (the unit used for each financial instrument) and really fast, as the market algorithm determining the closing price will face some kind of disequilibrium in his calculation, and make the final price appreciably different from the one that would have been calculated otherwise.

These are the most visible elements that would probably come into consideration when the order is sent for execution, but other dimensions come into play here: in fact, the client has a right to see his instructions executed. He would have signed a contract with his broker when their relationship effectively began – the broker being an intermediary on whom he would most likely rely for an important part of his business. If the operator does not accept the instruction, then the client may lose some money and make the broker liable for such a loss: not only could he prosecute his broker for not having abided by his order but also he could use this event to impair the broker's ability to fulfil other clients' needs. Potentially, the situation could be very damaging to the broker's reputation, a determining element for him to gain access to clients and, therefore, commissions. On the other hand, the broker has a duty to prevent market abuses: regulations are adamant that practices intended to artificially fix the price of an instrument must not only be transmitted to the market but, moreover, disclosed to the regulator so that it can eventually look deeper into the situation, and sanction the contravening market participant. Complying with the client's instruction could make the broker liable for any results that would come about as a consequence of the instruction being sent to the market. And in the end, other market participants (both brokers and fund managers, for example) may criticize the decision made within GBS, as all the prices would almost surely be impacted – which is a strong possibility here, because of the context, where the characteristics of the order (a basket trade on all the underlying shares constituting the index, 'at best') do not allow any margin of appreciation to the operator.

The market context, opening with the sending of an apparently bizarre instruction by the client, materializes in the form of the indirect interaction taking place between the client, the operator and his compliance officer. This interaction, located in a specific place and a defined time-span, involves different devices such as phones, computers and screens, rules and regulations, prices, market conventions and market participants. All those elements gather and rely upon each other, articulating around the practice that will or will not be activated, once a decision is made. While seeking advice, the operator needs to feel that he will be backed by the compliance officer should there be an investigation. At the same time, if the compliance forbids the trade, then it may be easier for him to explain to his client that 'compliance is not happy with it; I'm very sorry, lad, can't do'.

What we see here is that the compliance function, dedicated to the framing of practices within the space and time of the organization, has to make a quick decision, the issue of which will take place in a rather uncertain context. The compliance officer has to manage many aspects relating to the trade: not only its most visible parts, but also the mid- and long-term consequences that may be associated with this decision. These are of a regulatory nature (will the broker be sanctioned?) but also relate to the effects of the decision on the image of the institution (how will the market react?). Finally, the issue of the trade is not sure at all. What if, in the meantime, other orders are being sent to the market and displayed on Denis's screens? The compliance officer has less than two minutes to make his decision: he faces uncertainty, and is quite convinced – drawing on his past experience and understanding of the rules and regulations, both added to the other elements pertaining to the context – that the market will not be able to absorb the order, which will as a consequence have a huge impact, draining liquidity and moving prices almost instantaneously.

Although there is now a broad literature on financial markets, looking either at their institutional structures (Fligstein 2001) or at their constitutive parts (Callon *et al.* 2007), *market contexts* remain scarcely described. With this first example, we somehow see the development of a chemical precipitation, where associated entities pertaining to and participating in the market get articulated. These entities can be of many different kinds, and answer to different ontological regimes (whether human or non-human). Their common characteristic is that they hold together during a certain period of time, in a certain place. During this process of precipitation, entities are actualized, that is to say either attached, detached or stabilized in the given environment: the time-span during which the plot as a whole takes place can be described as the market context.

Performing control over error accounts

Another situation may help us understand the very specific nature of compliance and the way it inscribes its action beneath the surface of the market. In our first example the compliance officer is put in a situation where he acts as a resource for the market operator. But while providing advice, he may also act as a controller and sanction operators who misbehave. Defining misbehaviour may not, though, be simple as one might think: once again, it all is about the context and the apprehension of available elements of appreciation. The example we take hereafter is the control of 'error accounts' that are used in order to register gains and losses generated from mistakes that may happen as the result of misunderstandings or system defaults. The question is about the way the operator communicates (or not) to his client that the order he sent generated a loss or a gain resulting from the execution capacities of the market, in the specific case where the order was not executed as it should have been. Such situations can occur, for example, when there is a misunderstanding between the sales trader who spoke with the client and the trader who executes the order.

The scene takes place in October 2006; the customer, from First Finance Capital (FFC), makes a late call to Sarah, her account manager. The fund manager at FFC had earlier received the research published by GBS on the Japanese food industry, and wants to discuss some points with the sales trader. After the conversation, Sarah transfers her customer to John (a sales trader) so that he can instruct the purchase of 25,000 Asahi Breweries shares executable the following day with strict conditions ('You take at 1,750 close to the opening; it may rise quickly'). The next morning, though, John realizes that the order was not correctly recorded, owing to a system error; deciding to execute the order immediately, he notices that the market, already active for 45 minutes, is falling, owing to a set of bad economic circumstances that had not been foreseen. John manages to execute the order for an average price of ¥1,735 per share, which allows him to record on his error account a gain of ¥375,000 (approximately €2,300 at that time). The following week, and while he was looking into error accounts in the course of his routine controls, Adam, the compliance officer notices the anomaly and addresses a written reminder to John, who should have admitted to the client that the gain was due to the system error and the resulting late execution:

> After investigation, I remind you that you must be transparent with your client. If your execution price is better as a result of a mistake, you must inform your client and leave him with the choice to be answered: the asked price or the effective price. In such a situation, it is not your responsibility to determine which price should be applied. Thanks for complying with this position in the future.

The reminder sent by Adam, expresses the idea that the degree of knowledge between the broker and its client must at least be equal, and certainly not detrimental to the latter. Contrary to what operators tend to believe ('When you lose, you take the loss; when you win, you give it back'), the question asked is about the asymmetry of information at the precise time when the order is acknowledged by the broker, in the given market context. Here, the compliance reinstates the practice within its elementary context, referring to a principle of action (market operators shall not take advantage from an asymmetry of information). In this example, we see how compliance officers manage to 'refuel' practices with norms, through the performance of routinized controls. It is very important to note that the way practices are explained heavily draws on the ability of the compliance officer to understand the context in its different constituents: not only the act of receiving, transmitting and executing an order, but also the way the interaction is effected, the channels used by the operator, including the different devices (here the IT system) that in some way contribute to the enactment of the context.

These contexts, which can also be seen as events or situations, represent the market: they speak in the name of markets and account for them. It is their succession that gives the market its own reality, its flesh and its very specific embodiment (Cooren 2006). The chemistry metaphor makes perfect sense here: at a given moment, an event may 'precipitate' a series of agencies that were arranged in a specific setting, acceptable or not with regard to the normative framing. The precipitation will fix some elements of the agencies and make them crystallize, while letting others free in the surrounding liquid: the market context will be reconfigured in its own ecology and result in a different state, allowing for future market contexts.

Framing practices: the case for 'indications of interest' (IOIs)

If compliance is about putting norms into practice, making sure that the market frames hold together each time a disturbing event happens, crystallizing elements of the market context, then the persons in charge of the function also act as field legislators. The framing capacity of compliance officers does not come into effect only when an operator seeks advice, or during the performance of control procedures. Taking stock of past situations, or the development of practices, may show that wide areas of activities in markets are not covered by any specific rule; and it is not because texts do not exist that compliance officers are not entitled to make them exist within the defined space of their own institution. Practices may well be shared over European markets; however, the degree of precision of regulatory texts may still vary from one country to another. MiFID brought some homogenization over several topics, ranging from execution services to the management of conflicts of interests, but those remain principles governing areas of activities. Some practices may still be accepted in some countries, while not being imaginable in others;[3] sometimes, innovative practices are shared between market participants, while not being inscribed in a regulatory text. In fact, the link between practices and normative texts may well exist but in a rather marginal fashion: the precise nature of this link remains subject to discussions whenever situations materialize by way of precipitation.

Such is the case in France with 'indications of interest' (IOIs). The name refers to 'messages sent between investment firms to convey information about available trading interest' (CESR 2010: 6). Among the different issues raised by the use of such IOIs stands the question of the materiality of the underlying positions they are resting on: a broker may well advertise an interest in a position that does not exist, in order to generate a flow of orders for a dedicated stock. Until at least 2009, no specific text regulated such IOI practices in France: the point is important in an industry where the processing of information remains a high priority. Operators could therefore display buying or selling interests with no materiality at all, trying to attract customers through the display of overgrown liquidity. At GBS the management decided that, as a matter of practice, IOIs should be framed with a dedicated procedure. Charles, the CEO, explains:

> I'm trying to hire compliance who show a capacity to understand the business, I mean I'm waiting for him to take initiatives when there are true compliance issues. Not only as an employee hired in order to check and help as indicated by the texts, but rather a person who'll be in a position to suggest important evolutions as regards our practices.... Take the case for IOIs: well, there are no texts here; our compliance officer addressed the issue and we implemented our own procedure on these. I know it's not a popular procedure among sales traders, but I feel much more on the right track, even though I know some of my competitors will just take advantage of that, and continue to bullshit the market.

Financial markets offer spaces for the development of framed practices. Sometimes, as shown in this example, compliance officers are in a position to change the architecture of practices, inventing internal regulations that enact a different kind of market reality. The reason why actors may wish to act under further restraints is not always clear, but the view exposed by Charles, that he feels 'on the right track', reveals a very specific relationship to the idea of what markets should be with regard to the common good and the related representations. The very essence of compliance officers also appears here: siding with market operators, they provide the frames that may be missing in order to conduct the business in a respectful way. This raises issues linked with the specific morality infusing markets that, as a result, is at stake. Engaging compliance with employees in markets through the framing of their practices means that when the operator decides to transact, the decision is already framed with a whole set of norms, some of these being enacted in the gesture of practice, in the field.

In this respect, markets are collectives, as defined by Callon and Latour (1981): variable geometry entities leading to the attachment and detachment of devices, practices and texts activated either by people or by machines. In the confrontation of entities, one of the actants may take advantage and 'decide' to act or react, and thereby produce or improve a further stage in the situation. When this happens, the market context acquires a further thickness, requiring further layers of ethnographic description.

Describing financial markets: how can we melt 'cognitive icebergs' down?

Following the iceberg metaphor proposed by Tett (2009), and in an attempt to understand what lies beneath the surface of financial markets, we need to recognize that our descriptions are critical in allowing us to access places that are scarcely taken into account in mainstream finance. Several attempts have recently been formulated in order to renew our understanding of financial markets: among these, Smith (2007), Muniesa (2009) and Ortiz (2009) all provide useful insights that contribute to the study of financial markets within an anthropological paradigm.

Financial markets and the definition of practices

Taking options markets as an example, Smith (2007) underlines the importance of contextualized descriptions, because financial instruments traded in these markets seem heavily dependent on the structure of the market, the kind of exchange that thereby takes place, and the equipment (whether social or material) in which exchanges are grounded. Getting access to the complexities of finance with a view to providing a concise account of what really happens in market-places may indeed require some further engagement from researchers: '[I]f one is to understand how meanings and rules enable and constrain the market's practices and how these practices in turn fashion these meanings and rules, one needs to participate in these practices' (Smith 2007: 34). The constant surge of events constituting the flow of market materiality is too complex to be looked at from one or the other bank of the river. Swimming in market liquidity may well be necessary in order to find out what constitutes the stream of financial transactions.

The metaphor is fully significant: resituating a contextualized experience of markets depends on the volume of intuitions the observer effectively accesses, and these may best be felt when directly experienced by the person translating the intuition into a representation. It is exactly what Smith explains in his own account of markets as definitional practices:

> Second hand accounts while informative and useful are not sufficient in themselves. In order to recognize and follow the correct paths, one must often first experience what it means to be lost. Formal analytic market models may work for solving various economic problems, but they seldom, if ever, embody the behavioral complexities essential for a sound sociological account.
>
> (ibid.)

The view expressed here reinforces the idea that ethnography remains a powerful means of investigation, especially within fields that are ontologically thick, depending on several layers of agencies involving both humans and non-human entities.

Challenging representations and practices, revealing sub-conversations

The proposed framework, suggesting that markets should not be seen as plain entities but rather studied with a view to rediscovering their contextualized nature, has been illustrated with different examples. Those restitutions, showing how interactions between humans (clients, sales, traders) and non-human entities (devices, instructions, rules) crystallize on a continuous basis in the everyday life of markets, allowed us to outline some aspects of the work of compliance officers. In the last part of my contribution I would like to discuss the role played by this function within contemporary financial markets, and the conditions allowing them to perform the framing of financial practices effectively.

Looking at the financial industry from below reveals a wide network of agencies and interactions involving numerous participants that usually do not form part of the accounts and descriptions provided, either in the media or in academia. In this underworld economy, constituting the effective assemblage making finance happen as the reality it is, compliance officers play a role that has not yet been thoroughly underlined. Shaping practices through the performance of a dedicated language, rooted in norms, they indeed have the power to indicate, like a compass, where operators shall direct their own behaviours with reference to acceptable (if not accepted) rules. Working as interpretive agents performing the discourse of norms in situations where uncertainty rules, compliance officers offer a unique standpoint for the observation of how markets are constructed, and the specific type of performativity that may develop in such environments.

Performativity has been a widely debated subject in social studies of finance, from the foundational proposals made by Callon (1998) up to more recent accounts (MacKenzie *et al.* 2007). A relationship that has not really been looked into, however, is the agency between performativity and normativity. Both are concepts that have experienced parallel development, as shown by Sandra Laugier (2004). The qualification of speech-acts by Austin (1962) happened against a background of legal thinking, particularly in relation to the texts of Hart on the concept of law.[4] If we acknowledge with De Goede (2005: 7) that we should try to understand finance 'as a discursive domain made possible through performative practices, which have to be articulated and rearticulated on a daily basis', then there may be no need to look anywhere but in the discourse articulated by compliance officers. The very specific way in which they try to combine texts and contexts within financial organizations, making constant shifts between the two realms, certainly shows how financial activities get arranged, especially when rules seem to be partial, faulty or unfit with regard to the available context. If we agree that compliance officers enact some kind of speech-act meant to frame practices and enact a specific kind of market materiality, we need to make sure that the market operator will receive this speech effectively. After all, it is not because the compliance, acting as an authorized officer, says how the practice is to be oriented that the operator will follow this expression. Ensuring conditions of felicity for compliance speeches, so that these can be reflected in speech-acts, effectively active in the course of the interaction materialized in the given market context, indicates directions for future research.

Despite the importance of regulation as a field of inquiry for economic sociology, studies of regulating functions have been scarce. Among them, works on

auditors or risk officers can be found, but whenever it comes to permanent con-
trollers or compliance officers, it is very difficult to find detailed accounts of
what these functions do, how they organize, and the purposes with which they
act. Looking into these functions can, however, help our understanding of financial markets: they are definitive depositaries of generic normative texts (the laws
and regulations which most of the time account for principles of action), which
they help disseminate in specific practical contexts (the trading room or the retail
banking agency, places where practices take root and develop). This dissemination contributes to the institutionalization of legitimate practices aimed at reducing the risks to reputations supported by the activities. To do this, compliance
officers achieve the deployment of discursive and material devices (compliance
manuals, procedures, emails containing their advice, and training) helping
traders, salespersons or financial analysts to interpret rules; they also create
norms 'from scratch' when a market context is not clearly addressed in the available regulatory frame. Once produced, these devices need to be described, translated and interpreted so that market operators asking their compliance officer,
'And now, what shall I do?' can find an answer to issues and dead ends they face
in their day-to-day practices. Compliance therefore appears as a sub-textual
function organizing the discourse of finance.

The notion of *sub-conversation*, developed by Nathalie Sarraute in 1956, in a
manifesto entitled *The Age of Suspicion*, will serve as a comparison here. Trying
to redefine the art of writing in the twentieth century, Sarraute suggests that the
New Roman should draw on the ability of languages to carry intentions with
them, intentions that sometimes will access a further state of complexity when
becoming embodied in an action. Referring to those underlying intentions, Sarraute explains that

> speeches have the necessary qualities to capture, protect, and carry in the
> open those subterranean movements that are at once impatient and afraid.
> They have their own flexibility, their freedom, the rich shimmering of their
> nuances, their transparency or their opacity.
>
> (1956: 102, my translation)

If we agree that financial actors deploy a specific speech, we may then wish
to follow these speeches and try to see how they carry the underlying intentions
framing financial markets. In our studies we shall not limit ourselves to a single
kind of conversation, but rather try to take into account the diversity of codes
framing financial places, whether they are expressed in gestures, languages,
moral principles or legal rules of conduct, all providing their influx to the
deployment of practices. Doing so, we may recognize financial markets as entities giving rise to a whole original set of sub-conversations, meeting precisely
where exchanges take place, in renewed market contexts.

Conclusion

Since the mid-1980s, markets have been dematerialized, the result of which is a greater level of difficulty in representing exactly what they are. Accordingly, turning back to some kind of materiality, reinstating the interactions that invigorate their reality and the codes governing such agencies, may help us melt down the cognitive iceberg hiding the roots of contemporary finance. What is usually not seen, and therefore remains below the surface of financial activities, is the body of norms framing those activities, especially as they are embedding actions in a delineated stream that remains unnoticeable, while being paradoxically available there at any time. Studying those norms and the ways they are deployed, developed, added or integrated to the course of action may help our understanding of how finance is made. In such a task it may well be easier to begin with functions such as compliance, which carries sets of norms, texts and other elements intended to organize the financial world. Resituating the plenum of agencies available in given market contexts, which I have been describing as basic constituents of the market materiality (more or less developed, more or less ontologically thick), should definitely help us better apprehend the density of markets.

Notes

1 Providing new descriptions remains critical to really understanding the ecology of financial markets; they cannot be reduced to the mere expression of 'interests' themselves accounting for 'rational agents'. Even with the recognition of the limited character of such rationality, and its recent recalling as a way to better explain the sub-prime crisis (Akerlof and Shiller 2009), we still are not sufficiently equipped to unfold financial markets.
2 Company and personal names have been changed in this chapter for the sake of anonymity.
3 Such is the case with 'liquidity contracts', which are recognized as an accepted market practice in some countries but not necessarily legal elsewhere.
4 Hart is indeed mentioned by Austin in a note (1962: 7).

References

Akerlof, G. and Shiller, R. (2009) *Animal Spirits: How human psychology drives the economy, and why it matters for global capitalism*, Princeton, NJ: Princeton University Press.

Austin, J.L. (1962) *How to Do Things with Words*, Oxford: Oxford University Press.

Callon, M. (1998) *The Laws of the Markets*, Oxford: Blackwell.

Callon, M. and Latour, B. (1981) 'Unscrewing the Big Leviathan: how actors macro-structure reality and how sociologists help them to do so', in A. Cicourel and K. Knorr Cetina (eds) *Advances in Social Theory and Methodology: Towards an integration of micro- and macro-sociologies*, Boston: Routledge & Kegan Paul.

Callon, M., Millo, Y. and Muniesa, F. (2007) *Market Devices*, Oxford: Blackwell.

Committee of European Securities Regulators (CESR) (2010) *Micro-structural issues of the European equity markets*, Call for evidence/CESR 10-142, 1 April.

Cooren, F. (2006) 'The organizational world as a plenum of agencies', in F. Cooren, J.R. Taylor and E.J. Van Every (eds) *Communication as Organizing: Empirical and theoretical explorations in the dynamic of text and conversation*, Mahwah, NJ: Lawrence Erlbaum.

De Goede, M. (2005) *Virtue, Fortune, and Faith: A genealogy of finance*, Minneapolis: University of Minnesota Press.

Fligstein, N. (2001) *The Architecture of Markets: An economic sociology of twenty-first-century capitalist societies*, Princeton, NJ: Princeton University Press.

Knorr Cetina, K. and Preda, A. (2005) *The Sociology of Financial Markets*, Oxford: Oxford University Press.

Laugier, S. (2004) 'Performativité, normativité et droit', *Archives de Philosophie*, 67(4): 607–27.

MacKenzie, D. (2006) *An Engine, Not a Camera: How financial models shape markets*, Cambridge, MA: MIT Press.

MacKenzie, D. (2009) *Material Markets: How economic agents are constructed*, Oxford: Oxford University Press.

MacKenzie, D., Muniesa, F. and Siu, L. (2007) *Do Economists Make Markets? On the performativity of economics*, Princeton, NJ: Princeton University Press.

Muniesa, F. (2009) 'The description of financial objects', *Anthropology Today*, 25(2): 26–7.

Ortiz, H. (2009) 'Embarking on financial industry research: a response to anthropologists' common methodological concerns', *Anthropology News*, 50(7): 25.

Preda, A. (2009) *Framing Finance: The boundaries of markets and modern capitalism*, Chicago: University of Chicago Press.

Sarraute, N. (1956) 'Conversation et sous-conversation', in *L'ère du soupçon. Essais sur le roman*, Paris: Gallimard.

Smith, C.W. (2007) 'Markets as definitional practices', *Canadian Journal of Sociology*, 32(1): 1–39.

Tett, G. (2009) 'Iceberg and ideologies: how information flows fuelled the financial crisis', *Anthropology News*, 50(7): 6–7.

Part III
Capitalism

19 Pathology of the capitalist spirit

David P. Levine

Introduction

Speculative movements in asset prices have been a common occurrence in the history of modern, or capitalistic, economies. While the effects of such movements may be restricted to the markets in which they occur, it is also possible for them to affect other sectors of the economy, and to have adverse consequences for employment, income and welfare. This happens when speculation undermines the circulation of money and finance in a way that makes it difficult for producers and consumers to acquire the credit they need to support their activities. With the growing sophistication of financial markets, the tendency towards speculative movements is enhanced by the development of new and more complex financial instruments.[1] This process tends to further disconnect the creation of claims over wealth from the capacity of capital investment in real assets to produce wealth. The difficulty of sustaining this disconnect over time eventually leads to a downward adjustment in asset values, the magnitude of which is no more limited by their real potential to produce wealth than was the original upward adjustment we refer to as a speculative boom.

During a speculative boom the belief spreads that prices can only continue to rise and that the circumstances leading to the current inflation of asset prices differ in some fundamental way from those that fueled earlier bull markets. This latter belief makes it unnecessary to consider the historical record, which would show that all speculative processes must come to an end, that they are all based on faith rather than fact, and that once belief falters, prices will not return to their 'normal' levels but will fall until wealth has been destroyed more than in proportion to its fictional production by the bidding up of the prices of assets representing claims over it.

Thus, the recent financial dislocation begins with the belief that housing prices cannot fall and have no upper limit, and that therefore there need be no link between the debt incurred by the homeowner in purchasing a home and any ability to service that debt, given that the rapid increase in the house's value assures a growth in wealth unconnected to income from work. Here, as always, belief expresses an underlying hope, which is the hope to be freed from the limitations of reality so that life can be radically different from our experience of it, in this case so that we may have a life in which income from work will not limit gratification. The speculative boom occurs in a space where memory is dismissed and the past and present radically disconnected.

The problem is compounded because, given the possibility of reselling mortgage debt, the lender need not incur whatever risk is acknowledged to be embedded in questionable mortgage loans, but can instead pass that risk along to whoever purchases the mortgages, bundles of which are now recreated as marketable assets in their own right. In other words, the speculative movement is fueled not only by a denial of history but also by a shifting of responsibility onto others. This also shifts the entire process outside the realm of reality, which is a place where all assets must be owned by someone and actions have consequences. One consequence of this process of the creation of what have been termed 'toxic' assets is that the speculative process now takes on an added purpose, which is to transfer the toxic assets to others, something that, at least on a psychic level, can be thought of as an end in itself rather than simply an unfortunate byproduct of the effort to get rich quick.

For those interested in the psychodynamics of capitalism, the language that opposes real to financial assets will prove suggestive, hinting as it does at the division of the world of economic affairs into real and fantasy worlds, while emphasizing the complex relationship between the two. We will recognize the power of fantasy in the know-no-limits quality of speculative movements, which in this respect clearly indicate that the bonds of the real have been negated and that we have therefore moved into an alternative universe governed by hope and fear, and by the denial of the boundaries that establish the finiteness of the self in a world of others.

Speculative movements operate within a larger system of thought and experience, the system driven by what Max Weber refers to as the spirit of capitalism. Weber summarizes what he refers to by that term in the following way:[2] 'Man is dominated by the making of money, by acquisition as the ultimate purpose of life. Economic acquisition is no longer subordinated to man as the means for the satisfaction of his material need' (1904–5/1992: 53). Use of the term 'spirit' to refer to this domination by the end of moneymaking suggests that what we are concerned with is the factor within the organism (whether conceived as an individual unit or as a larger social system) that brings it to life. In other words, the idea that there is a capitalist spirit in Weber's sense of the term is the idea that the organism is animated by moneymaking and that without the prospect that it will see its accumulation of money increase, the organism lapses into a lifeless state. If we are to understand the psychic meaning of speculative movements, we must understand the part they play in a drama of the life and death of spirit.

Once we consider the speculative movement an expression of the forces shaping fantasy life, and therefore as an attack on reality, we can understand its destructive potential. At the same time, however, once we consider the link to fantasy, we cannot see in these movements simply a destructive process from which the real economy must be protected. This is because fantasy's attack on reality is an expression of the human creative potential – indeed, of that peculiarly human capacity to create reality as it might be by negating reality as it is. If we have the power to negate, the relevance of history does indeed fade. And this power applies above all to the self. Indeed, it is the power of self-creation that denies history and drives the speculative boom.

In the fantasy embedded in the speculative process, self-creation takes on a specific purpose, which is to dismiss the unacceptable and painful reality of the impoverished self in favor of a fabricated reality in which the self is rich beyond measure. What distinguishes the operation of this fantasy in the speculative movement from the way it might function elsewhere, and assures that its attack on reality does not express the creative impulse, is the idea that we can enter into a new reality without the characteristic human creative activity: work. Those caught up in speculative processes are essentially engaged in watching their wealth magically increase. The dominance of magical thinking tells us that the creative force is not to be exercised by the individual through work, but rather is to be invoked by an act more akin to prayer.

While capitalism represents the release of man's creative potential, it needs to be understood as the source not only of the destruction that creates a new world, but also of the destruction that does not.[3] It is the latter that I will refer to here as the pathology of the capitalist spirit, a pathology that is not, however, produced by the introduction of an alien organism into the body of a system otherwise a stranger to it, but by its own immanent development. More specifically, I will suggest that within the capitalist system, the specific mentality expressed in the speculative movement represents a kind of pathological trend that indicates a regression from more to less mature forms of thought, from reason linked to work in the direction of magical thinking linked to the attempt to invoke a higher power. In the following, I consider the underlying fantasy that shapes the capitalist spirit and some of the consequences of allowing the free and full expression of that fantasy in our social institutions. To do so, I begin with a brief account of the organizing ideals and institutions that constitute a capitalistic economy.

Capitalism

Capitalism is the economic system that emerges when the idea of private property is instantiated in institutions and ways of life, especially in the form of a legal system in which wealth and the means for producing it (land, labor and capital) are privately owned. The idea that animates the capitalist system is self-regulation. A capitalist economy is one in which what is produced, how it is produced and how output is distributed are all primarily determined by a system of private transactions governed by private ends rather than by external authority in the form of the state. This contrasts sharply with earlier systems of economic arrangements in which what can be produced, how it is to be produced and by whom, and the terms on which exchanges take place are all subject to strict regulation. The destruction of this older system constitutes land, labor and capital as commodities to be disposed of at the discretion of their owners.[4]

The older system was organized to assure that the economy would serve the ends of the community (Tawney 1962: 23). Regulation of economic life served both to protect the member by instituting a communal obligation to secure his or her welfare, and to subject the member to that strict control associated with the dictates of what Marx and Tawney refer to as a moral order. In particular, it assured adhesion of the member to an order of higher and lower, dominant and subordinate. The destruction of the older order transformed the member of the community into the independent property owner and citizen. The rise of a modern economy separated individuals one from another, eroded their sense of mutual commitment and turned them inward rather than demanding that they concern themselves with the group and the greater good it represents. This freed the individual to make living in the world express what Christopher Bollas (1989) refers to as his or her 'unique presence of being'.

We might follow Donald Winnicott in speaking of the two orientations towards others – one typical of the newer order, one of the older world – as creativity and compliance. Winnicott (1986) associates being alive with the first of these two orientations. When what we do represents only our adaptation to a reality predetermined for us, then we are not alive in his sense of the term. What Winnicott refers to as creativity in living 'indicates that he who is, is alive' (ibid.: 39). Being alive means leading a life shaped by an inner force, one usually referred to in the language of the self. When what we do is shaped by this inner force, then, in Winnicott's language, doing expresses being, and our lives are determined, at least in some significant part, by the presence of the self.

The connection of being alive to the self suggests a connection between the self and the idea of an animating spirit. Indeed, since its spirit is the factor within the organism that brings it to life, in a modern society this spirit is the self. The economic system we refer to as capitalism is the expression of the liberation of the self to pursue its interests however it chooses to define them. Private ownership is the institution that makes this possible, at least so far as economic affairs are concerned. Private ownership, especially of capital and labor, which defines capitalism, does not in itself, however, imply domination by the spirit of acquisition. What is also required is the attachment of self-interest to the goal of the endless accumulation of wealth, or that 'boundless greed for riches' to which Marx so vividly draws our attention.

Greed and self-interest

In attempting to understand the relationship between self-interest and greed, we might begin with the observation that to pursue self-interest means to establish a special relationship between the internal and external worlds, one in which the inner world shapes conduct and relating in an especially powerful way. More specifically, to pursue self-interest means to have interests that are not fully determined by external factors. This immediately suggests a connection to greed, which represents a refusal to accept the limits external reality places on the expectation that our desires will be satisfied. Understood in this way, greed is about the emergence of an inner world and a determination of conduct and relating originating in that inner world, and this implies a connection between greed and what Winnicott refers to as being alive and feeling real. This line of thought is consistent with Joan Riviere's description of greed as 'an aspect of the desire to live' (1964: 26–7; see also Hyatt-Williams 1998: 46).

What Riviere refers to here must, however, be a life of a special kind, since we can imagine creatures whose lives are not marked by greed, but rather proceed within well-defined limits. Evidently, what Riviere has in mind is a peculiarly human sort of life, one in which the organism has, in the words of Harvey Kaplan, 'broken loose from the original instinctual drive and lost [its] original instinctual motivations' (1991: 514). What has replaced the original instinctual motivation is a freedom from it and openness to forms of satisfaction not limited by it. This openness is sometimes confused with greed, and, especially in its most primitive forms, does constitute a relationship with the world that knows no limits and in that sense could reasonably be considered a form of greed. Yet it would be a mistake to confuse this primitive form with the acquisitive instinct Weber equates with the spirit of capitalism.

When we are driven by greed, our goal is to incorporate all the good things into the boundary of the self. This expresses the infant's original orientation towards the world, which is not one of self and other but of a more fluid interchange between internal and external, an interchange in which relating is organized around processes of internalization and externalization with the goal of taking in what is good and getting rid of what is not. The goal of our original greedy self is to consume the good as a way of demonstrating that no limits exist to the domain of the self, or, in other words, to establish the dominance of the self over its world (creativity) rather than the dominance of the world over the self (compliance). This urge becomes adult greed when the individual is unable to develop an alternative to incorporation as a way of establishing his or her existence in the world as a determining factor. For such an individual, the alternatives are limited to two: either I dominate all objects in the world or they dominate me. True adult creativity requires a middle ground where the individual's orientation towards external reality allows him or her to be and have a self in the world of others. The drive to overcome all limits the reality of other persons place on the connection of the self to the good object by merging the self with that object and excluding others from it marks the conflation of greed with self-interest.

It follows from these considerations that the attachment of greed to self-interest is a complex matter. The main issue that must be addressed if we are to understand it, however, should be clear enough. It is the matter of whether the organism's original urge to incorporate resolves itself into the development of a finite self with finite ends, or continues to dominate the organism throughout its life without any real modification to take into account the presence of others.

Otto Kernberg has argued that the primary factor standing in the way of this transition is the absence within the individual of a 'harmonious world of internalized object-representations' (1976: 74). We can briefly summarize this argument in the following way. The development process for which incorpora-tion is the first step seeks to create objects in the inner world in relation to which the individual can secure a sense of well-being. Failure to establish an internal object world adequate to this task leaves the individual with an excessive dependence on external objects for the needed emotional inputs (Kernberg 1986: 246). Failure to establish a harmonious inner world does not express only a deficit in the presence and power of good internal objects, however; it also indi-cates an excessive power of the destructive or bad objects, including those rapa-cious objects bent on depleting the good object of all the good it is capable of providing. This intensifies the dependence on others, who must also be available as containers for projection of the destructive impulses that dominate internally.

One expression of excessive dependence on external objects is what Kernberg refers to as 'relentless greed' (1980: 136). Psychologically, the premise of greed is that the worth of the self equals the worth of objects attached to it. This is a natural extension of the individual's inability to find in the inner world an ade-quate basis for creating a conviction that his or her self has value. The lack of intrinsic value demands that value be acquired from outside. Thus, any failure to form an attachment to the external good things would expose the true condition of the inner world, which is the absence of a valued self there.

This suggests how we might understand greed in relation to self-interest. Spe-cifically, it suggests that self-interest expresses greedy desire when the self is intrinsically of little interest, and the individual seeks to offset the pain induced by this situation by forming an attachment to things that are made valuable by an authority outside the self. In doing so, the self seeks to have its worth measured not by an intrinsic standard but by the accumulated value of the things attached to it. Thus, the pursuit of greedy self-interest indicates not that too high a value is placed on the self but that the value placed on the self is too low.

Through projection, the individual who is possessed of a devalued self experi-ences others as unworthy of respect and justifies their treatment as so many means to the end of his or her self-aggrandizement. Greedy desire means that the indi-vidual has little or no capacity to treat others with respect for their integrity as sep-arate and different selves existing in their own right. The result is the rapacious self-interest that marks the spirit of capitalism as Weber characterizes it. And, so far as we identify self-interest with greed, we must find in the self a dangerous force that must be subject to strict control (regulation), if not altogether repressed.

Greed means that neither desire nor self-interest is subject to any internal limits. By contrast, the mature individual defines for him- or herself what is and is not of interest; and this activity of self-definition is also the activity of limit setting. Where, instead, what is of interest is defined externally as all things others deem of value, such limits do not hold, and the process of limitless accu-mulation is the result. So far as the individual has developed a capacity for limit setting, he or she has also developed a tolerance for regulation, which is an expression of limit setting, but now at the level of institutions and policy. Sim-ilarly, the attack on regulation at the level of institutions is simply an attack on any expectation that the individual can and will set limits for him- or herself.

Money

While the process of limitless accumulation might target any and all things in the external world, it is really the value of those things that is coveted, and because of this, one thing stands out as greed's special object: money. Money is the ultimate measuring unit for the external, or we might say objective, value of things, and it is also a claim over things of value (what we use to pay for them). With money, it becomes possible to make acquiring value the end of economic activity rather than merely the means to acquiring things that we need. Thus, according to Christopher Columbus, 'Gold is a wonderful thing! Whoever possesses it is lord of all he wants. By means of gold one can even get souls into Paradise' (quoted in Marx 1867/1967: 131–2). What this says, in symbolic language, is that money can solve the problem of the loss of connection with a loving object, and thus act as the means for retrieving a lost state of grace. The pursuit of money is the pursuit of that lost state and therefore an expression of loss.

With this in mind, it should be clear why money is greed's special object. This can lead to insight into one of the most notable qualities of capitalist economy: its tendency to replace the accumulation of real assets by financial assets as its primary end, and especially the tendency to support the fantasy that no work is needed to acquire greed's object, but rather that possession of a measure of that object will magically result in the acquisition of more, that money has an intrinsic creative power.

The idea that money has an intrinsic creative power is nowhere better expressed than in Benjamin Franklin's *Necessary Hints to Those Who Would Be Rich* when he observes how 'money can beget money, and its offspring can beget more'.[5] This fantasy is true, of course, so far as the individual can expect his or her money to grow at the rate of interest. But what is true for the individual is not true for individuals taken collectively, since we cannot together become wealthy if we do no more than lend our money to each other. That we cannot do so expresses the dependence of the monetary on the real; and it is precisely this dependence that the constituting fantasy of capitalist economy denies by insisting that money is intrinsically productive. Failure to acknowledge this dependence leads to the destructive processes so common in the history of capitalist economies.

Attributing magical powers to money expresses the wish that, in acquiring money, we ourselves might come to possess such powers. Psychically, this fantasy contains the deeply rooted hope that desire will produce its object, which is a form of the wish that desire and its object can be merged into one. By contrast, work represents the renunciation of this hope and its replacement with the idea that through work we can create what through wishing we cannot. But for this to happen, gratification's object must undergo a transformation from the infinite to the finite; it must become something we can produce through work. We must give up our primitive greed and the form it takes in adult life.

Regulation

While we are in the habit of treating capitalism as a system organized around the celebration of self-interest, what we find on closer inspection is that the celebration of the self, and especially of its interest in the acquisition of wealth, does not raise interest in the self to the level of a social norm; rather, it assures that no interest must be taken in, or attention devoted to, the self. This is because any interest in or attention devoted to the self can only affirm its lack of worth. In other words, what passes for interest in the self is the massive societal effort to distract attention from it, specifically by focusing attention on the fabricated self made up of external things and the external connection to them we refer to in the language of ownership. In this world, the purpose is not to be a valued self, but to own one. It is this pathology of the capitalist spirit that poses such a powerful barrier to government regulation.

It can, with reason, be argued that the wealthy oppose government regulation because they see in it an attack on their wealth and the fabricated self it is acquired to support. Yet given the intensity of the attack on regulation, we need also to consider the possibility that it may represent a defense against a powerful unconscious need to be regulated. If this is the case, then the intensity of our hatred for government may be a measure of the intensity of our desire to be governed, which is in turn an expression of the dominance internally of a dependent and needy self. When this needy self is projected onto others, the attack on government understood as a potential source of welfare for them simply expresses the externalization of the internal attack on the internal needy self. Those who attack government, then, do so in part because they imagine it will provide others with what they themselves cannot have: care for their needy and dependent selves. The powerful aggression involved in the attack on the self is also projected onto government, which is experienced as a dangerous and destructive force that makes people needy and dependent so they will become vulnerable to its harmful intent.

So far as the attack on regulation expresses an unconscious need to be regulated, and therefore to control and repress a needy self, the factors driving the attack on regulation may also foster an unconscious desire to destroy the economic system, which is the system of the production and circulation of goods required to satisfy need. Here, it is important to consider the possibility that the movement against regulation may be intended, however unconsciously, to achieve what is usually thought of as an unintended consequence: placing the economic system at risk.

That an attack on the economic system is implicit in the financial disorganization fostered by deregulation is clearly expressed in the connection of financial disorganization to the tendency to replace real with financial assets and the associated fantasy that what represents and measures wealth, money, is wealth. We will find, implicit in this substitution, a significant measure of contempt for the real, which suggests the presence of a powerful impulse to attack and destroy it. So far as the acquisitive instinct represents a retreat into fantasy, it can be thought to be driven by the conviction that reality (true gratification) is unobtainable, a conviction that can easily develop into an attack on reality, especially so far as it is imagined to be a source of gratification for others, a possibility that can be reduced or eliminated by shifting the toxic assets onto them and, ultimately, by destabilizing the financial circulation on which the reality of the system of economic satisfactions depends.

The speculative movements that lead to economic dislocation represent the results of a system in which internal regulation is not effective and external regulation is not allowed. As was suggested above, the speculative movement can be understood as a flight from the inner world fueled by the fantasy that we might merge the self with the good object by possessing all of the good things. But it is also fueled by an unconscious desire to destroy the system that creates the good things. It follows that to regulate speculative movements is both to destroy the hope that the wish embedded in them can be fulfilled and to block the destructive impulse they represent.

While it could be argued that institutions organized to assure self-regulation require the absence of government intervention, this is not in fact the case. Rather, those institutions cannot survive unless conduct is regulated in a way that protects their integrity. The need for regulation to protect the integrity of institutions is more marked the more self-interest is attached to, or confused with, greed. This is because its attachment to greed makes self-interest a drive to violate all limits, especially those that protect the integrity of others. External regulation, then, is needed because self-regulation is not possible.

Love, admiration and envy

Must the destructive effects of greed be accepted as an inevitable part of our collective experience? In part, I think, the answer to this question must be yes. Greed is not the invention of capitalist institutions; rather, those institutions are simply one way in which society channels greed so that its destructive potential is limited (see Levine 2008). This does not mean, however, that we must accept the hypothesis that destructive forms of greed must dominate social institutions and the interactions taking place within them. As I have tried to suggest, the destructive forms of this impulse only dominate where the intrinsic value of the self cannot be reliably established. If this is correct, then, in attempting to address the problem of the destructive consequences of greed, we should turn not only to law and institutions, but also to those factors that shape the inner world and determine whether it is or is not that harmonious world of object representations the absence of which turns the original impulse to negate into destructive forms of greed.

Destructive forms of greed express the inability on the part of the individual to make a positive emotional investment in the self. The inability to do so in turn expresses the conviction that having and being a self is a threat to relatedness and therefore to being loved. This conviction is not, however, intrinsic to having a self, but originates in object relations in which the loss of love is experienced as a consequence of self-expression. It follows that where this interpretation of object relations dominates, it is likely the conclusion will be drawn that, by removing the real self and replacing it with a surrogate, there is at least the hope that the loving object that has been lost will return. If the presence of the self makes us unworthy of love, then getting rid of the (true) self creates the possibility we might become worthy of love.

For some, the possibility exists that the lost object can be found and love retrieved. But for others this is not the case. Where the return of the loving object is not considered a possibility, there develops a need to find substitutes for it. Among substitutes, two are of special importance in understanding the pathology of the capitalist spirit: admiration and envy. Indeed, it can be argued that the confusion of love, admiration and envy marks the presence of the pathology of spirit that leads to destructive consequences of the kind associated with financial disorganization.

Alice Miller draws our attention to the 'tragic link between admiration and love' that plays such a large role in the pathology with which we are concerned here. She suggests that where this link dominates, the individual 'seeks insatiably for admiration, of which he never gets enough because admiration is not the same thing as love', but only a 'substitute gratification' (1979/1986: 330). Seeking admiration as a substitute for love expresses the need to direct attention away from the self that is judged unworthy of love, and towards the fabricated self, which, while equally unworthy of love, is well suited to gain the admiration it is hoped will dispel the feelings associated with the loss of love. Indeed, it is in being admired by others that this fabricated self takes on a semblance of reality. The semblance of reality born of admiration secures the individual's attachment to a self that is fundamentally alien in that it is owned by others. Attachment to an alienated self expresses and intensifies the loss of the self, and in this sense reenacts the object loss that creates the problem in the first place. This self-sustaining process is the psychic core of the speculative process operating at the level of economic systems.

The connection between seeking admiration as a substitute for love and object loss suggests how admiration may also be linked to the power of envy, which, as Miller suggests, begins as envy of the object relations of others, or more specifically with the perception that others are loved and understood while we are not. Seeking admiration expresses envy when its primary purpose is not to secure the reality of the fabricated self but to destroy the self in others. The pain of envy can be moderated if envy can be shifted onto others, which it can so long as we are admired by them rather than forced to admire them. And this is possible so long as they are made to bear the onus of the loss of love and love's object, and we are not. This transfer of loss is enacted in the financial system as the production and sale of toxic assets, which represent the badness originating internally. The overpowering impulse to be admired and envied by others expresses the profound absence of objects capable of love and understanding and therefore the impossibility of internalizing a loving and empathic object relation.

Conclusion

To ameliorate the problems associated with this pathology, we must limit the incidence of object loss or, if that is not possible, counter the interpretation of object loss as the result of the presence of the self. While object loss can result from many factors, including the contingencies of illness and death, culturally systemic forms of object loss have systemic sources and express constituting ideas about self and other embedded in institutions. In particular, they express the idea that the self is inherently a locus of greedy desire and therefore a threat. Forms of self-repression aimed at coping with this threat only exacerbate the problem it represents.

This has an especially debilitating expression in the way children are perceived as the locus of greed, especially the projected greed of their parents. This perception places children in a double bind. Their perception by others as the locus of greed invites an attack on their neediness and thus fosters both explicit and implicit forms of abuse and neglect. At the same time, this attack on the child's neediness becomes a way the parent can use the child to serve the parent's narcissistic ends, including those driven by greed. Thus, once the use of the child as container for parental greed is set in place, the path has been cleared for a full and unrestricted expression of the parent's greed, at least within the context of the family, all in the name of the repression of the child's destructive impulses.

On an institutional level, this use of the child as container for adult greed is well expressed in the movement in schools towards an ethic of service, which imposes on the child the self that must negate itself if it is to become worthy of love. The ethic of service has this meaning so far as it targets the child's greed and treats it as a destructive force that must be repressed. But this meaning is even more powerfully embedded in the urge to make the child a container for the adult's greed, which justifies the attack on self-expression sometimes associated with the idea of service. To be sure, the eagerness that many students have to participate in various forms of service, in part at least to offset their experience of an internal greedy self and to participate in a drama of displaced responsibility for destructive impulse, expresses how well adapted they are to the tendencies dominating in the larger society. And because of this, we can say that the problem begins neither in the family nor outside, but in both locations, and therefore in a larger spirit of the time, expressed for example by the idea that the family must come first, which simply means the subordination of the child to it and the necessity that the child experience its own narcissistic needs as a danger to its objects and therefore to itself.

With this in mind, we might consider the following conclusion regarding social policy aimed at limiting the power of destructive greed. The purpose of such policy should not be to suppress greed through moral education but to assure that neither family nor civil society becomes a setting for the exercise of narcissistic domination. The purpose of social policy would be, then, not to assure that the family must come first, but rather that priority must be given to the welfare of its members, without which the family cannot accomplish the work designated for it, which is to be a setting in which (1) the child can develop unencumbered by the repressive impulses associated with his or her use as a container for adult greed, and (2) the adults can also live together without sacrificing their connection to the reality of self and other but, on the contrary, in a way that secures that connection.

Notes

1 It is also possible to bundle claims over financial assets representing direct claims to real assets so that the new assets claim to the productivity of real assets becomes indirect.
2 A vital element in the capitalist spirit as Weber defines it has more and more faded from the scene, and that is the element of worldly asceticism, or the 'strict avoidance of all spontaneous enjoyment of life' (1904–5/1992: 53). For a further discussion of this aspect of the spirit of early capitalism, see Levine (2008).
3 The former is the unity of creativity and destruction, or 'creative destruction' that Joseph Schumpeter (1934) sees as the central feature of capitalist development. On the link between creativity, change and destruction, see Winnicott (1971), Benjamin (1988) and Levine (1999).
4 Karl Polanyi (1957) refers to these as 'fictitious commodities', a term that captures some of the fantasy element so prominent in the shaping of capitalistic economy.
5 Quoted in Weber (1904–5/1992: 49).

References

Benjamin, J. (1988) *The Bonds of Love: Psychoanalysis, feminism, and the problem of domination*, New York: Pantheon Books.
Bollas, C. (1989) *Forces of Destiny: Psychoanalysis and the human idiom*, London: Free Association Books.
Hyatt-Williams, A. (1998) *Cruelty, Violence, and Murder*, Northvale, NJ: Jason Aronson.
Kaplan, H. (1991) 'Greed: a psychoanalytic perspective', *Psychoanalytic Review*, 78(4): 505–23.
Kernberg, O. (1976) *Object Relations Theory and Clinical Psychoanalysis*, New York: Jason Aronson.
Kernberg, O. (1980) *Internal World and External Reality: Object relations theory applied*, Northvale, NJ: Jason Aronson.
Kernberg, O. (1986) 'Factors in the treatment of narcissistic personalities', in A. Morrison (ed.) *Essential Papers on Narcissism*, New York: New York University Press.
Levine, D. (1999) 'Creativity and change', *American Behavioral Scientist*, 43(2): 225–44.
Levine, D. (2008) *Politics without Reason: The perfect world and the liberal ideal*, New York: Palgrave Macmillan.
Marx, K. (1867/1967) *Capital*, vol. 1, New York: International Publishers.
Miller, A. (1979/1986) 'Depression and grandiosity as related forms of narcissistic disturbances', in A. Morrison (ed.) *Essential Papers on Narcissism*, New York: New York University Press.
Polanyi, K. (1957) *The Great Transformation: The political and economic origins of our time*, Boston: Beacon Press.
Riviere, J. (1964) 'Hate, greed, and aggression', in M. Klein and J. Riviere, *Love, Hate and Reparation*, New York: W.W. Norton.

Schumpeter, J.A. (1934) *The Theory of Economic Development*, Cambridge, MA: Harvard University Press.

Tawney, R.H. (1962) *Religion and the Rise of Capitalism*, Gloucester, MA: Peter Smith.

Weber, M. (1904–5/1992) *The Protestant Ethic and the Spirit of Capitalism*, trans. T. Parsons, London: Routledge.

Winnicott, D. (1971) *Playing and Reality*, London: Tavistock Publications.

Winnicott, D. (1986) *Home Is Where We Start From*, New York: W.W. Norton.

20 Trust and the global financial crisis

Douglas Kirsner

Trust is crucial for the economic system. However, trust in the financial system to be efficient, self-regulating and ultimately beneficial for all has been massively undermined by the global financial crisis. As Nobel Prize laureate in Economics Joseph Stiglitz underlined,

> Even in a market economy, trust is the grease that makes society function.... In the current crisis, bankers lost our trust, and lost trust in each other. Economic historians have emphasized the role that trust played in the development of trade and banking.... The big lesson of this crisis is that despite all the changes in the last few centuries, our complex financial sector was still dependent on trust. When trust broke down, our financial system froze.

> (2010: 289)

It is no exaggeration to say that human societies rest upon mutual trust to keep them together. People need to trust others not to deliberately harm them and to behave reliably. In the absence of a breach, we mostly do not think about this. We continue to pursue our goals, assuming all will go well provided we put in the effort, intelligence and resources. But we depend upon the underlying system to be sound. Normally, we proceed on the assumptions of confidence that the earth will not give way or that we will not be hit by a large wave from out of the blue. We make similar assumptions about the economic system not collapsing. Generally, we need to trust our systems, which is another way of saying that we have confidence in them not to betray us.

Although a significant part of the recent global financial crisis (GFC) is a crisis of loss of confidence and trust, there are also some further characteristics. The current crisis is unprecedented in size, depth and scope, extending to institutional defaults and sovereign debt. It has impacted at lightning speed in far-flung countries around the world. For many, following the boom of 2002–7 the GFC came unexpectedly as if a visitation from out of the blue – from outer space. Actually, it was correctly predicted, but not by the right kind of people: those mainstream economists central to the running the US economy. Stiglitz recalled his experience at an economics conference after the bubble had burst in 2008 when a chorus of central bankers told him that nobody had predicted the collapse. Despite the fact that Stiglitz and others at the conference were on record as predicting it, Stiglitz realized that what the central bankers meant was that 'nobody with credibility' had predicted it. So, this should be seen in terms of the roles of the central institutions of economic power and theory on which they are based.

For mainstream economic leaders, it was as though there were no real immanent root causes that produced what they thought of as a 'once-in-a-career event' at most. There seemed no systemic causes. Yet many others panicked, sensing that the system was not sufficiently stable to guarantee their investments. The mathematical, scientific economic modelling of efficiency theory that excluded human motivations and responses failed to support the centre of the system or forestall the collapse of pivotal icons of economic faith and stability. As Stiglitz discovered in the research for which he was awarded his Nobel Prize, although the neoclassical models assume the efficiency of markets except in particular instances of market failure, the opposite is the case. Models may assume perfect information and rationality from which to generalize but in reality the information is imperfect because workers, products, resources and situations differ in qualitative as well as quantitative ways. Because a world with perfect information differs markedly from a world with imperfect information, the former was not a viable model for the latter (Stiglitz 2010: 239–42).

Invariably, model makers miss critical conditions that occur only rarely but do in fact occur. Rarely are the users of the model aware of all the conditions tested or of the rare conditions under which the model creates disasters, as in the case of the BP Deep Horizon well of 20 April 2010. Although economic models give a seemingly positive answer, such as a calculation, in reality they provide only hypotheses created by earlier observations of specific conditions, actions, reactions, tested in a variety of environments to determine conditions under which the hypothesis may or may not be true. Today, many answers are model driven. However, a model should not be confused with an answer. Such confusion lies at the heart of the kind of thinking that has got us to where we are today! It seems that mainstream economists have assigned robotic characteristics to those who are the 'market'. They have pigeon-holed human characteristics based on false or incomplete information about populations of flesh-and-blood humans. Many other aspects of humanness operating in social systems have not been included in these models.

One such operating component of humans is the human capability for problem solving and creating entirely new future conditions at rapid rates (Jaques and Cason 1994). Today those creations move through the global network in nanoseconds – no wires attached! By missing key assumptions, such as the importance of non-economic factors, or by making erroneous assumptions, such as perfect information or rationality, they bring about wrong and harmful results. The internet allows such rapid communication and dissemination of information that the psychological factors of euphoria, mania, fear and panic are not contained and spread swiftly, 'calming' or 'exciting' the market.

Because the market is not simply a mathematical entity, both economic and non-economic factors make an impact. An important non-economic component is what John Maynard Keynes labelled 'animal spirits'. In its original Medieval Latin sense it meant 'of the mind' but has become transformed to mean what Akerlof and Shiller in their recent book, titled *Animal Spirits*, call 'a restless and inconsistent element in the economy. It refers to our peculiar relationship with ambiguity or uncertainty. Sometimes we are paralyzed by it. Yet at other times it refreshes and energizes us, overcoming our fears and indecisions' (2009: 3–4). As Shiller (2009) commented elsewhere, 'it refers also to the sense of trust we have in each other, our sense of fairness in economic dealings, and our sense of the extent of corruption and bad faith'. Trust, which dismissed doubts about others, was crucial to animal spirits.

> Keynes sought to convey the message that swings in confidence are not always logical. The business cycle is in good part driven by animal spirits. There are good times when people have substantial trust and associated feelings that contribute to an environment of confidence. They make decisions spontaneously. They believe instinctively that they will be successful, and they suspend their suspicions. As long as large groups of people remain trusting, people's somewhat rash, impulsive decision-making is not discovered.
>
> Unfortunately, we have just passed through a period in which confidence was blind. It was not based on rational evidence. The trust in our mortgage and housing markets that drove real-estate prices to unsustainable heights is one of the most dramatic examples of unbridled animal spirits we have ever seen.
>
> (Shiller 2009)

Shiller adds another important factor related to trust. The new, far more complex system of granting credit meant more intermediation in the markets, more complex arrangements with innovations in housing mortgages, securitization and derivatives, including the shadow banking sector.

> The more complex the transaction the more trust is needed to sustain the transaction....
>
> The trust in the innovative lending practices was excessive; now that trust is replaced by deep mistrust. The wreckage of formerly towering financial institutions is all around us.
>
> (ibid.)

Trust is dependent on psychological factors. Indeed, psychology plays a key role in the work and direction of economies. Psychological confidence is essential to the functioning of the market. Consumers and investors behave differently depending on their confidence or concern.

In the GFC, as Stiglitz stated, 'the trust and confidence that underlie the banking sector evaporated' (2010: 3). Confidence, trust and faith in the system are crucial to understanding waves of euphoria and mania, which push the markets upwards, and the panic and fear that bring them down. The past few years of easy credit have allowed Ponzi schemes to rise to immense proportions and then collapse like houses of cards around the world. Faith in the financial institutions has been too great to the point of illusion or delusion, while scepticism and panic can cause collapse. The central importance of psychology is underlined by the way self-fulfilling prophecies can pull the market down through initial panic, leading to increasing panic. In boom times, when the economic system seems to produce ongoing growth and development, the psychology is hidden or muted; the market then seems to have an inevitable upward dynamic all of its own. It is then that many people simply assume that things will continuously improve and pay little attention to the market except to reap their profits. It is seen simply as a taken-for-granted fact of life that needs little explanation, certainly not a psychological one. The bubble may not look like a bubble in an economy on the rise when economic rational-ism and economic greed seem sufficient to explain increasing euphoria. Yet this assumption requires explanation, if only because there are busts as well as booms.

When things go well, the system seems to be producing results on its own, akin to what Adam Smith called the 'invisible hand' of the market in his classic work of 1776, *The Wealth of Nations*. All that was required was a free market in which each would pursue his or her own ends, which ipso facto would also produce the best for the whole community. This concept of the coincidence of individual and social aims formed the basis for the value of self-regulation of the market under laissez-faire capitalism. However, people lose faith in this invisible hand when there are busts, or after bubbles such as the recent credit bubble. Belief in the stability of the system that has been taken for granted is vital when the system seems under threat. Our psychological attitude, best defined by whether or not consumers and investors basically trust the system to be safe and secure, has consequences. Crises are not mainly the result of purely economic factors. As Akerlof and Shiller assert,

> The idea that economic crises, like the current financial and housing crisis, are mainly caused by changing thought patterns goes against standard eco-nomic thinking. But the current crisis bears witness to the role of such changes in thinking. It was caused precisely by our changing confidence, temptations, envy, resentment, and illusions – and especially by changing stories about the nature of the economy.
>
> (2009: 4)

Banks were regarded as the most robust part of the system before they went beyond their traditional roles and became clearly involved in easy credit schemes. The necessity for trust was such that governments needed to intervene to guarantee banks. If there is not some fundamental guarantee that banks can be trusted in difficult times, then consumers will shift their money away.

Our attitude or approach towards the economy is fundamental to its functioning. As Bob Roach, chief investigator for the US Senate Committee investigating the collapse of Goldman Sachs, put it, we need a system that will operate far differently, 'because in the end people have to have faith that the system will work for everybody, not just for a group of insiders. And if that faith and confidence isn't resorted, we're going to have a lot of problems' (Australian Broadcasting Corporation 2010).

Taxpayers and consumers need to feel assured that guarantees of bailouts do not gravely impact on the real wider economic system in which they have a major stake. This means that if governments, and therefore taxpayers, need to guarantee the banking system with possible bailouts, then governments have an appropriate major role in regulating that system. Stiglitz notes the irony that 'the way the model of American individualism worked was that people took responsibility for successes but showed little sense of accountability, or responsibility for the failures or the costs imposed on others' (2010: 282). This is far from a trust-inducing situation, which requires taking responsibility for all outcomes. Moreover, there is a fiduciary relationship between investment banks and their investors that requires oversight through laws and regulations. As Akerlof and Shiller conclude about the role of regulation in capitalism,

> We had forgotten the hard-earned lesson of the 1930s: that capitalism can give us the best of all possible worlds, but it does so only on a playing field where the government sets the rules and acts as a referee. Yet we are currently not really in a crisis for capitalism. We must merely recognize that capitalism must live within certain rules. Indeed our whole view of the economy, with all of those animal spirits, indicates why the government must set those rules.
>
> (2009: 173)

The behaviour of the financial industry and institutions itself affects the financial and economic system and demonstrates the need for external regulation. Group or collective culture has significant characteristics. Herd mentality, identification with leaders, regression, splitting, projection and like behaviours are par for the course in groups and organizations. The implementation of policies or aims is often at considerable odds with the laudable aims of many institutions, such as the Church, the United Nations or corporations (Long 2008). Self-evidently, trustworthy institutions cannot allow systematic fraud and corruption to rule, and therefore need transparent structures, regulations and oversight to prevent this.

The financial system has shown that it cannot be relied upon to regulate and prevent fraud and that the required faith and confidence of investors to keep that system going means government involvement to assure trustworthy institutions. The financial system, including banks, can no longer be detached from the economic system (if they ever should have been), especially given the limited data upon which the models that have propped up the financial system have been based. As Akerlof and Shiller observe, in their attempts to clean up macroeconomics and make it more scientific, the standard macroeconomists have imposed research structure and discipline by focusing on how the economy would behave if people had only economic motives and if they were also fully rational.

(2009: 168)

These economic models assume that people always act rationally and from only economic motives, and that therefore the financial system should be self-regulating. However, if the models took psychological factors into account, there would need to be government involvement and regulation (ibid.: 173). As Gillian Tett observes, the financial system itself has many silos within it. Different departments of banks vie with each other with little oversight, and regulators themselves have many silos within their organizations. The connection with reality was both tenuous and tendentious: 'The chain that linked a synthetic CDO [collateralized debt obligation] of ABS [asset-backed security], say, with a "real" person was so convoluted, it was almost impossible to fit that into a single cognitive map – be they anthropologist, economist or credit whizz.' This disconnect was not noticed because credit was considered to be so technical that only experts could deal with it, and it was 'a classic area of social silence' (Tett 2009: 299).

This area of social silence illustrates how far illusion replaced reality in the financial system. Many bought the illusion that it was axiomatic that the new financial instruments would of themselves contribute to stability and growth. But far from adding to the stability of the system, the new financial instruments contributed to the illusion of the financial alchemy that the compound of infinite market liquidity and continuous market innovation would keep wealth increasing (Nesvetailova 2010: 143). Stiglitz also uses the alchemical metaphor: 'Modern alchemy entailed the transformation of risky sub-prime mortgages into AAA-rated products safe enough to be held by pension funds. And the rating agencies blessed what the banks had done.' The banks then became gamblers. Thinking they had passed on the risky assets they held, they were 'caught off guard' when the market collapsed (Stiglitz 2010: 6).

One major form of illusion in the financial system has been that peculiar combination of knowing and not knowing: 'turning a blind eye' to what was going on. Many, both within and outside the financial system, had turned a blind eye to what was going on. It is a dim awareness that is diminished by an awareness of the displeasure involved in facing it, and an attitude that can only engender mistrust. British psychoanalyst John Steiner focused on the idea of having insight but at the same time turning away from it and misrepresenting it. Steiner discussed the mechanism of turning a blind eye, which occurs when 'we seem to have access to reality but choose to ignore it because it proves convenient to do so' (1985: 161). According to Steiner, this conveys the right kind of ambiguity about how conscious and unconscious the knowledge is:

At one extreme we are dealing with simple fraud where all the facts are not only accessible but have led to a conclusion which is then knowingly evaded. More often, however, we are vaguely aware that we choose not to look at the facts without being conscious of what it is we are evading. These evasions may lead to a sense of dishonesty and to various manoeuvres which deny or conceal what has happened by creating a cover-up.

(ibid.)

But what are the characteristics of mutual trust and trustworthy systems? The financial system needs to be robust in structure, believable, and to merit confidence, i.e. be trustworthy. Humans need to be able to trust in the system for society to function. Trust is far more than a feeling. It is a state that engenders bringing people together to work, bond and create futures. To function effectively, institutions and organizations need to induce trust and not suspicion and mistrust. That trust needs to be based on values, which it cannot be assumed the market will automatically enact.

Our fundamental dependence upon trustworthy systems and mutual trust is most evident in the breach. Wars can bring at least broad sections of nations together in fighting a common enemy. But the common enemies in economic crises such as the Great Depression and the global financial crisis can be less clear, and with immediate consequences for us in terms of employment, even financial survival. The GFC brought the advanced capitalist world dangerously close to collapse. The US economy was in 'freefall' in October 2008 (Stiglitz, 2010: 27), with attendant consequences. With the collapse, rescues and bailouts of key icons, confidence in the financial system itself to ensure safety and the certainties of basic necessities of life have been under serious challenge. Banks have played an ambiguous role: as both providers and repositories of value at the same time as those that have undermined this value. Banks have been blamed, and governments have intervened to save the banks and the system, at least for a time. As Stiglitz concluded, 'today only the deluded ... would argue that markets are self-correcting and that society can rely on the self-interested behavior of market participants to ensure that everything works honestly and properly – let alone works in a way that benefits all' (2010: 219).

Individuals and societies act on the basis of crucial taken-for-granted assumptions. The biggest one is that we live in a trustworthy social system, that we trust the underlying system to endure. We assume regularity in the natural or physical world and assume that it is sufficiently benign as to not threaten us so that we can get on with our lives normally. As Sigmund Freud maintained, human unhappiness emanates from three sources: from the external world, the ravages of the body and, most painfully, from other people (1930/1961b: 76–7). Earthquakes and tsunamis remind us of our intense vulnerability to nature. Death and illness in ourselves or those close to us tell us again how fragile individual lives can be. Our fear of each other has meant that we establish societies, social contracts, laws and regulations so as to set up systems we can trust that help to guard against deliberate harm to each other. The handshake induces trust by showing the other that there is no weapon. In order to protect ourselves from each other and from nature, we need to be mindful of their dangers and not deny them. This means that we need to be realistic about what is normal; succumbing neither to panic nor to euphoria, either in life or in the market. This is what Freud termed the 'reality principle', which served the pleasure principle but often not in the short term. In *Beyond the Pleasure Principle* (1920/1955b), Freud suggested that the pleasure principle, which holds that we seek the immediate gratification of our drives, must be modified with the advent of civilization by the reality principle, which involves the subservience of the pleasure principle to the demands of reality. This is demonstrated in the development from the immediate satisfaction of childhood immaturity to the delayed satisfaction or resignation of adult maturity.

Freud is often regarded as being solely focused on the mental life of the individual, but this is mistaken. Freud saw an inseparable link between individual and the collective: individual psychology was at the same time 'social psychology as well' (Freud 1921/1955c: 69). Reality contrasts with illusion and fantasy, and involves social bonding. For Freud, turning away from reality defines neurosis, which has collective as well as individual significance. Freud notes that neurosis involves not just withdrawal from reality but withdrawal from society. Reality involves being social, living together with others in the human community; and neurosis involves cutting the bond with society:

> The asocial nature of neuroses has its genetic origin in their most fundamental purpose, which is to take flight from an unsatisfying reality into a more pleasurable world of phantasy. The real world, which is avoided in this way by neurotics, is under the sway of human society and of the institutions collectively created by it. To turn away from reality is at the same time to withdraw from the community of man.
>
> (1913/1955a: 74)

The neurotic person utilizes illusion or fantasy with its hallucinatory pleasure, and numbing of the pain involved in confronting what is really going on. According to Freud, this is not a simple misperception to be corrected by pointing to the facts. There is a pay-off in keeping away from reality; the fulfilment of a wish in fantasy, an investment in this pleasure. Freud's work *The Future of an Illusion* (1927/1961a) was a trenchant critique of religion as a major form of wish fulfilment that kept us from confronting and dealing with reality. For Freud, the religious worldview, built on wish and illusion, had its basis in the mainsprings of childhood emotion, which he contrasted with a scientific approach built upon real issues and how best to deal with them.

Past decades have seen a denial of reality in the financial system which has significantly undermined trust. After the 1987 stock market crash, I wrote an article on the role of illusion and other psychoanalytic aspects, including splitting, projection and manic denial (Kirsner 1990). Recently, Morante summarized his argument that

> an important psychological factor underpinning the crisis was the collective need to escape the reality of an increasingly complex and vulnerable global

world and find an illusory refuge in the ownership of money and property. On the trail of a favorable economic cycle, financial operators, regulatory authorities and the public colluded in the illusion, which eventually developed into something akin to a psychic retreat, that financial markets would provide effortless and everlasting wealth and home ownership to an increasing number of people. The paper considers how omnipotence, illusion and the absence of the father/authority figure as the psychic representative of reality fostered a manic wave of rampant optimism, greed and overconfident investors.

(2010: 4)

The recent denial of reality that undermined trust included the self-serving fraud of using easy credit and new financial instruments as a means of, for example, bundling junk assets with real assets; unquestioned faith in economic efficiency models of the market which proclaimed that it would sort itself out through self-regulation; and faith in the world of derivatives in failed attempts to postpone any rendezvous with reality into the indefinite future.

The scope of these recent temptations to deny reality is enhanced and magnified by the socio-economic context of the contemporary post-industrial world. Accelerated technological and social change has led to vast and fast interconnections, with decreasing time for reflection and thought about such immense changes and their consequences. This involves reconfiguring how the economic system operates, with the largest, very diverse world economies coming together as G2, G8 and G20 in attempts to deal with common global financial issues. There have been immense shifts in production from the West to developing countries such as China and India, making the world 'flat', as Thomas Friedman (2007) argues. The system became global, with a number of centres such as China and the European Union, instead of being unipolar with the United States as central. A significant factor that has promoted illusion is the emergence of a major driver of the world economy: a new chimeric entity designated by economic historian Niall Ferguson and economist Moritz Schularick (2007) as 'Chimerica'. Ferguson explains: the most important thing to understand about the world economy over the past decade has been the relationship between China and America. If you think of it as one economy called Chimerica, that relationship accounts for around 13 per cent of the world's land surface, a quarter of its population, about a third of its gross domestic product, and somewhere over half of the global economic growth of the past six years (Ferguson 2009). Although this 'symbiotic relationship' appeared as a 'marriage made in heaven', since one half saved while the other half spent, it was based on shaky assumptions that should lead to impending divorce.

China promoted its competitiveness by artificially keeping its currency from appreciating by acquiring a large dollar reserve, and has successfully encouraged saving. Conversely, US consumers massively overspent with easy credit, including new financial instruments that bundled together junk and real assets and passed the debt down the line until it could be postponed no more, leading to defaults

(Ferguson and Schularick 2009). But the landscape has changed: whatever happens, there is now a pronounced tilt to the east, since major shifts have occurred in the structures of the economies of what is produced where. The United States consumes and spends far more than it produces, and seemingly risk-free easy credit and high leverages made it seem that tomorrow would never come.

In terms of the organizational conditions within institutions, trust between people in working towards common goals is as important as the damaging effect of mistrust between people working together in any role (colleagues, parents, spouses, managers, politicians, etc.). For Elliott Jaques, trust involves 'the ability to rely upon others to be truthful and to behave in a helpful and understanding way' (2002b: 177). As he shows, if the organizational conditions are dysfunctional and obscure, then there is great potential for destructive conflict. Jaques suggests, 'Good managerial systems bring out mutual trust and commitment in people. Bad systems breed extreme self-interest' (ibid.). Bad organization is 'paranoiagenic' – that is, it gives rise to persecutory anxiety, stirring suspicion and mistrust. Our substantial stores of paranoid anxiety are ready and waiting to be aroused and spread into working relationships, and thereby destroy trust. Trust concerns confidence between people: the ability not only to have faith in each other, but, as suggested by the etymological root, to suffer for each other. (Faith's etymological root 'to abide' has the earlier meaning of 'suffering for' (Jaques 2002a: 252).) Jaques defines mutual trust as

> relationships in which individuals can rely on each other not to engage in doing damaging, harmful, or injurious things to each other. Injurious shares the same etymological root as justice, namely the Latin *ius*, to join or link. To do harm to another person is to injure that person, and doing injury inevitably breaks the link. It is fundamentally unjust. Thus it is that to be true, trust must be mutual: it is concerned with relationships, with justice as mutual linkage and joining together.
>
> (2002b: 251)

Etymologically, the concepts of 'trust', 'confidence', 'credit', 'faith', 'fidelity' are all related to each other in meaning and involve the psychology of working and bonding together in terms of truth or reality. 'Trust' has the same derivation as 'true', from the Old English *triewe*. Fidelity is derived from the Latin *fidelitatem*, which relates to 'faith', which in turn is derived from 'trust'. 'Confidence' derives from *confidenzia*, 'firmly trusting'. Credit comes from the Latin *credere*, 'I believe'. Belief involves commitment. This obviously relates to how credit is a transaction with another person, where the person giving credit believes in the process. Perhaps they have faith in it. Credit and confidence are foundations for holding the global financial system together. We need to trust others not to harm us in order for social institutions to function. As Akerlof and Shiller state,

> Economists have only partly captured what is meant by *trust* or *belief*. Their view suggests that confidence is rational: people use the information at hand

to make rational predictions; they then make a rational decision based on those rational predictions. Certainly people often do make decisions, confidently, in this way. But there is more to the notion of *confidence*. The very meaning of trust is that we go beyond the rational. Indeed the truly trusting person often discards or discounts certain information. She may not even process the information that is available to her rationally; even if she has *processed* it rationally, she still may not *act* on it rationally. She acts according to what she *trusts* to be true.

(2009: 12)

The GFC has been traumatic for a large range of people on whom it has impacted in terms of loss of property, jobs, income and security. The effect is not just physical but psychological. A sense of some control over the main direction of one's life is important to a sense of identity and optimism about the future. But the failure of trust has been especially dramatic in the GFC. As Burkard Sievers argues, trust involves vulnerability: 'The greater the risk trust has to "absorb" the greater the capacity required to cope with the loss when one's trust is violated' (2003: 31).

The dissociation of the broader economic system from the financial system is, especially in boom times, an illusion that feeds an inevitable fall at the end of the bubble. Galbraith (1987a) explains that in a stock market, real estate or art boom,

[t]here is increasing participation by institutions and people who are attracted by the thought that they can take an upward ride with the prices and get out before the eventual fall. This participation, needless to say, drives up prices. And the prices so achieved no longer have any relation to underlying circumstance. Justifying causes for the increases will, also needless to say, be cited by the sadly vulnerable financial analysts and commentators and, alas, the often vulnerable business press. This will persuade yet other innocents to come in for the loss that awaits all so persuaded. For the loss will come. The market at this stage is inherently unstable. At some point something – no one can ever know when or quite what – will trigger a decision by some to get out. The initial fall will persuade others that the time has come, and then yet others, and then the greater fall will come. Once the purely speculative component has been built into the structure, the eventual result is, to repeat, inevitable.

Apart from its socio-economic structure, the market is, importantly, a repository of our wishes. Nine months before the 1987 stock market crash, John Kenneth Galbraith observed, in an article published in January 1987 about parallel circumstances with the 1929 crash, 'There is a compelling vested interest in euphoria, even, or perhaps especially, when it verges, as in 1929, on insanity. Anyone who speaks or writes on current tendencies in financial markets should feel duly warned' (1987a: 62). Galbraith also notes that, throughout history,

[n]othing so gives the illusion of intelligence as personal association with large sums of money. It is, alas, an illusion. The mergers, acquisitions, take-overs, leveraged buy-outs, their presumed contribution to economic success and market values, and the burden of debt that they incur are the current form of that illusion.

(ibid.: 65)

According to Galbraith, nothing is really new in the world of finance, and the controlling fact is 'the shortness of the public memory, especially when it con-tends with a euphoric desire to forget' (ibid.: 66). If he were with us today, I imagine he would be signally unimpressed by the financial instruments of the New Economy which have helped to delude investors about the galloping dis-tance from 'underlying circumstance'. Trust in any truth in the system would be absent.

Just after the 1987 stock market crash, Galbraith suggested that recent years had seen an outbreak of 'financial dementia' in Wall Street, with the lessons of the past going unheeded.

People and institutions were in the stock market in these last five years, some in the belief that it would go up for ever, some in the equally innocent conviction that their own peculiar financial genius would allow them to get out before the fall. This is the pure speculative situation.... Anything, or even nothing, can trigger the eventual, inevitable and very rude rush to get out.

(1987b)

Galbraith would have agreed with George W. Bush's assertion in July 2008, 'Wall Street got drunk' (Doyle 2008).

The close connection between society and the financial system needs to be acknowledged so that the self-validating economic models are based on realities rather than carefully restricted theories based upon limited criteria. A widespread sense of basic trust goes beyond the necessary recognition of flawed assumptions involving the autonomy and self-correcting nature of the free market into trust-ing the wide range of factors involving trust between Wall Street and society.

This chapter has focused on the centrality of trust and trust-inducing institu-tions in the foundations of the economic and financial systems in societies. The situation facing the world at the GFC raises some fundamental issues about how to erect and maintain a secure foundation of trustworthy institutions. Many of the old divisions of left and right have disappeared, as it is now indisputable that the state needs to be involved with regulating the economic system. What is the relation between economy and the state and what are the future optimal roles of the national state and combinations of states? The answer is not so much in the proportion of state versus market but the foundation of what will promote mutual trust, human bonding and progress. What kinds of codes are optimal to be trust-inducing across societies? The recipe involves a spectrum where creativity is encouraged together with respect and a sense of fairness. A multidisciplinary approach to understanding the future economic system needs to go beyond economic models and other silos. At the very least, trustworthy institutions prevent deliberate harm – they would target fraud and manifest unfairness. These past years have seen not only gigantic fraud on the part of companies such as Enron and pyramid sellers such as Madoff, but also immense compensation for executives involved with corporate failure in the first place. People are prepared to accept genuine mistakes and accidental harm but their sense of fairness is offended when leaders profit from their own bad actions. It also requires greater complexity in going beyond the national level to trustworthy agreements between nations that are sustainable. As Stiglitz recently concluded,

> An environment of bitterness and anger, of fear and mistrust, is hardly the best one in which to begin the long and hard task of reconstruction. But we have no choice: if we are to restore sustained prosperity, we need a new set of social contracts based on trust between all the elements of our society, between citizens and government, between this generation and the future.
>
> (2010: 208–9)

References

Akerlof, G. and Shiller, R. (2009) *Animal Spirits: How human psychology drives the economy, and why it matters for global capitalism*, Princeton, NJ: Princeton University Press.

Australian Broadcasting Corporation (2010) 'One shitty deal', *Four Corners*, 14 June. Online, available at: www.abc.net.au/4corners/content/2010/s2926600.htm (retrieved 18 October 2010).

Doyle, L. (2008) 'Bush: "Wall Street got drunk and now it's got a hangover"', *Independent* (London), 24 July. Online, available at: www.independent.co.uk/news/world/americas/bush-wall-street-got-drunk-and-now-its-got-a-hangover-875780.html (retrieved 1 November 2010).

Ferguson, N. (2009) 'What "Chimerica" hath wrought', *The American Interest Online*, January–February. Online, available at: www.the-american-interest.com/article.cfm?piece=533 (retrieved 18 October 2010).

Ferguson, N. and Schularick, M. (2007) '"Chimerica" and the global asset market boom', *International Finance*, 10(3): 215–39. Online, available at: www.jfki.fu-berlin.de/faculty/economics/team/persons/schularick/Chimerica_and_the_Global_Asset_Market_Boom.pdf (retrieved 1 November 2010).

Ferguson, N. and Schularick, M. (2009) 'The great wallop'. Online, available at: www.niallferguson.com/site/FERG/Templates/ArticleItem.aspx?pageid=221 (retrieved 18 October 2010).

Freud, S. (1913/1955a) *Totem and Taboo*, in J. Strachey (ed. and trans.), *The Standard Edition of the Complete Psychological Works of Sigmund Freud*, vol. 13, London: Hogarth Press.

Freud, S. (1920/1955b) *Beyond the Pleasure Principle*, in J. Strachey (ed. and trans.), *The Standard Edition of the Complete Psychological Works of Sigmund Freud*, vol. 18, London: Hogarth Press.

Freud, S. (1921/1955c) *Group Psychology and the Analysis of the Ego*, in J. Strachey (ed. and trans.), *The Standard Edition of the Complete Psychological Works of Sigmund Freud*, vol. 18, London: Hogarth Press.

Freud, S. (1927/1961a) *The Future of an Illusion*, in J. Strachey (ed. and trans.), *The Standard Edition of the Complete Psychological Works of Sigmund Freud*, vol. 21, London: Hogarth Press.

Freud, S. (1930/1961b) *Civilization and Its Discontents*, in J. Strachey (ed. and trans.), *The Standard Edition of the Complete Psychological Works of Sigmund Freud*, vol. 21, London: Hogarth Press.

Friedman, T.L. (2007) *The World Is Flat: A brief history of the twenty-first century*, New York: Farrar, Straus & Giroux.

Galbraith, J.K. (1987a) 'The 1929 parallel', *Atlantic Monthly*, January: 62–6.

Galbraith, J.K. (1987b) 'What tact the press showed!', *New York Times*, 22 December.

Jaques, E. (2002a) *The Life and Behavior of Living Organisms: A general theory*, Westport, CT: Praeger.

Jaques, E. (2002b) *Social Power and the CEO: Leadership and trust in a sustainable free enterprise system*, Westport, CT: Quorum.

Jaques, E. and Cason, K. (1994) *Human Capability: A study of individual potential and its application*, Falls Church, VA: Cason Hall.

Kirsner, D. (1990) 'Illusion and the stock market crash: some psychoanalytic reflections'. *Free Associations*, 19: 31–59.

Long, S. (2008) *The Perverse Organisation and Its Deadly Sins*, London: Karnac.

Morante, F. (2010) 'Omnipotence, retreat from reality and finance: psychoanalytic reflections on the 2008 financial crisis', *International Journal of Applied Psychoanalytic Studies*, 7: 4–21.

Nesvetailova, A. (2010) *Financial Alchemy in Crisis: The great liquidity illusion*, London: Pluto.

Shiller, R. (2009) 'Animal spirits depend on trust', *Wall Street Journal*, 27 January. Online, available at: http://online.wsj.com/article/SB123302080925418107.html (retrieved 18 October 2010).

Sievers, B. (2003) 'Against all reason: trusting in trust', *Organisational and Social Dynamics*, 3(1): 19–39.

Steiner, J. (1985) 'Turning a blind eye: the cover up for Oedipus', *International Review of Psycho-Analysis*, 12: 161–72.

Stiglitz, J. (2010) *Freefall: America, free markets, and the sinking of the world economy*, New York: W.W. Norton.

Tett, G. (2009) *Fool's gold: How unrestrained greed corrupted a dream, shattered global markets and unleashed a catastrophe*, London: Little, Brown.

21 The financial crisis

Exploring the dynamics of imagination and authority in a post-industrial world

Larry Hirschhorn

Introduction

This chapter explores the psychodynamics of the recent financial crisis. I argue that we have reached a state of economic development where creativity is a productive force, and imagination is the human activity that propels creativity. The market, I suggest, has become the projective screen for our imaginative capacities. But at the same time, the market itself creates systemic risks that require the exercise of authority and the subordination of imagination to rules and regulations. The result is a tension between imagination and authority. When poorly managed, this tension leads to crises.

The chapter is divided into eight sections. In the first, I argue that the 2007–8 financial crisis was less the result of imprudent decisions and more the result of what are called 'systemic risks'. In the second, I link the idea of systemic risk to what we call within the system psychodynamics tradition, 'the group as a whole' and the problem of authority. In the third, I suggest that markets are attractive to the mind not because they are rational but because we project onto them our capacity to imagine. I suggest this is so because increasingly imagination has become a 'productive force' in the economy.

In the fourth section, I suggest that imagination as a psychic function integrates what Freud (1911) called the pleasure and reality principles, and that this integration takes psychological work to sustain. It is therefore prone to break down into one or the other of its constituent parts. When the pleasure principle wins out, the culture takes on a narcissistic color, and the sense of entitlement replaces the respect for authority. I suggest that the behavior of some bank and financial-firm executives and their employees reflected this sense of entitlement.

In the fifth section, I argue that in our valuing of imagination, we therefore risk succumbing to the pleasure principle, which brings us into conflict with the authority system we need to manage systemic risks. But the authority system's legitimacy is based on the useful work accomplished by the reality principle. Authority expresses the important idea that we must keep our narcissism and impulses in check in order to participate productively in the social world. *We experience a conflict between the reality and the pleasure principles instead of their integration in imagination.* In the sixth section, I explore the learning from two innovations that William Halton introduced to the Group Relations conference: the resource planning and marketplace events. I show how members' experience in these events suggests that as imagination is broken up into its constituent parts, the reality principle and the pleasure principle each become social defenses for the other. In the seventh section, I suggest that we replace the idea of social psychology with the idea of psychosociology, a term our French colleagues use, because, increasingly, social and political conflicts are the result of the projections of our mind onto society. The meaning of the classic tension between markets and central planning has been transformed. In the final section, I summarize my argument.

The roots of the financial crisis

I think there are two competing explanations for the financial crisis. The first is that investors were imprudent and took unnecessary risks; the second is that investors were prudent but fell prey to what are called *systemic risks*, risks that arise from the interactions of all marketplace participants. I propose rejecting the first explanation and accepting the second. Of course, in using the term 'investors', I do not mean all investors. Some financial institutions were neither prudent nor imprudent. They were predatory, creating financial instruments they knew were destructive. I want to focus on the larger class of naive investors – individuals, institutions and fund managers – who did not understand the destructive nature of these instruments.

The prudent investor

Consider the following six pieces of evidence that such investors were acting prudently. First, many of the institutions that bought mortgage-backed securities presumed that their ratings by the rating agencies were realistic and meaningful. Second, the quantitative models that Wall Street firms and the ratings agencies used to estimate risk did not predict massive defaults on mortgages. Third, many people believed that housing prices in different parts of the United States were only weakly correlated. This meant that you could hedge your investments by buying mortgage-backed securities on mortgages that had originated in different regions. This belief turned out to be unfounded, but surely it reduced the risk investors felt in holding any pool of securities. Fourth, a pool of securities was divided into three tranches, each less risky than the one below it. Investors presumed that the markets were pricing risk appropriately so that an institution could limit its risk and its return by buying the first tranche. If it wanted a higher rate of return, it could buy the second or third tranches.

Fifth, institutions could buy insurance policies in the form of credit default swaps to protect themselves against declines in the value of their investments. It was certainly not evident before the crisis that their counterparties, like the insurance company AIG, would not be able to make good on these policies when the housing market collapsed. That is why only a limited number of people 'shorted' the housing market. Sixth, interest rates were very low. That meant that pension fund managers who were under pressure to insure that pension liabilities could be funded in the future had to seek out securities that paid a higher interest rate and were therefore riskier. It was paradoxically prudent for them to do so.

Systemic risk

So let's consider the second explanation. Investors were prudent, but the financial system as a whole created risks that individuals did not anticipate, precisely because these risks arose from the interactions of all buyers and sellers. Consider the follow analogy. A crowd is standing on an outdoor balcony one story up from the street. If one person in the crowd leans on the railing of the balcony, he is taking no risk, but if everyone in the crowd leans on the railing at the same time – say, they are all looking for the source of smoke they see in the distance – there is a great risk that the railing will break and that people will fall off the balcony onto the street below. The risk of leaning against the rail is prudent from the individual's point of view, but imprudent from a systemic point of view. Any one person creates only the smallest additional risk when he or she joins the group leaning against the railing, but when they all do so, the risk spikes.

Indeed, there is good reason to believe that the system for *regulating* the financial markets itself increased systemic risk. It is not only that the markets failed, but, equally important, market regulations amplified market failure (Friedman 2010). Consider the following two examples. First, the Basel II regulations allowed banks to hold less capital against outstanding debt if the capital was in the form of instruments backed by the government. Since Fannie Mae, though a private corporation, was believed to have the backing of the federal government (and this turned out to be true), banks could originate mortgages, sell them to Fannie Mae, which in turn could sell them back to the banks as mortgage-backed securities. These securities supported more loans, more leverage than the original mortgages themselves. This is one reason financial institutions were operating with what in retrospect appears to have been too much leverage.

Second, the Department of Housing and Urban Development, beginning in 1994, directed Fannie Mae and Freddie Mac to buy back sub-prime mortgages from mortgage originators. This was a social policy designed to increase home ownership among poor people and minorities. It reflected both the Democratic and the Republican Parties' belief that extending home ownership was a way to spread the 'American dream' as well as win votes for the party in power. Fourth, the Federal Reserve Bank, partly in response to the dotcom bust in 2000, kept interest rates very low. This led investors to seek out securities with higher returns than were afforded by Treasury Bonds. Such securities by definition were at greater risk of defaulting.

I bring up these examples not to attack regulation per se, but to highlight that no one was considering the regulatory environment as a system in its own terms that set the boundary conditions for market behavior and channeled it along certain lines of activity. The regulatory system, rather than reducing systemic risk, increased it.

The group as a whole

Let's look at the financial regulatory system from a group dynamics point of view. I think we can say that to create a good regulatory system we must take as our starting point the 'group-as-a-whole' viewpoint. To protect the people standing on the balcony there must be some way of reducing the risks that everyone will be leaning on the rail at the same time. Someone, for example, should be monitoring the rail and the number of people leaning against it. In psychodynamic systems terms, this viewpoint means that we are looking at the *boundary* conditions that shape what goes on within any system.

Now we also know that from a group dynamics perspective, when you take up a group-as-a-whole perspective you must immediately ask who is authorized to establish these boundary conditions. Who is the traffic cop that tells a person not to lean on the rail? This is why in our group dynamics work we are always attuned to the constituents of authority. We want to know how the ground rules were established and by whom, and whether they are experienced as legitimate and psychologically containing. This suggests that the failure to recognize the regulatory system as a system was a failure to consider issues of authority. As an investor described in the book *The Big Short* by Michael Lewis (2010) suggests, many perspicacious investors assumed that there was a 'grown-up' in charge of running the financial system who assured that risk was not grossly mispriced. This was an assumption that they learned – to their chagrin, but also to their profit – was wrong.

Now, it is common to argue that one reason the grown-up was absent was that Alan Greenspan, the former head of the Federal Reserve Bank in the United States, believed, along with many other influential academics, business people and journalists, that markets are self-regulating. Markets will 'automatically' price risk correctly. Following our argument, this means that a believer in the self-regulatory power of markets agrees to dispose with or avoid issues of authority. This is why Karl Polanyi, the great critic of the concept of the self-regulating market, labeled this concept and belief as 'utopian' (1957: 3). In any concept of utopia, it is presumed that issues of power and authority never emerge. This is what makes the setting a utopia.

Why markets are attractive to the mind

One conventional conception is that this belief in markets as self-regulating is based on the idea that markets are rational, that the appeal of markets is linked to their ability to calculate, through the aggregation of millions of decisions, prices that reflect real costs and actual demand.

I want to make the strong hypothesis that this view is mistaken. Markets appeal to the human psyche for much more fundamental reasons. *Most importantly, the market is the psychological repository for the experience of our capacity to imagine.* We project into the market our imaginative capacity. Consider, for example, the ways in which in discussing strategy we use the word 'vision' to signify how the markets are apprehended. The idea is that the market is not simply what is front of us; it is not the count of houses and cars for sale, but is instead a potential of what might be ahead of us. Indeed, this is how financial analysts understand the stock market. A share price is the value of dividends and capital gains discounted from the future to the present. In this sense the stock market is experienced as a soothsayer or prophet, and of course prophets communicate through their visions.

The reality and pleasure principles

A good vision for a business has three distinct features. First, by definition it is not yet present in our experience. Second, apprehending it gives us pleasure; it expresses how our desires might be fulfilled. Third, if it is to be meaningful as the instigator for a strategy, it must bear some logical relationship to reality as we currently experience it. It cannot simply be fanciful.

Perhaps you will recognize in these features of a vision, what Freud called 'the two principles of mental functioning', which he labeled the 'pleasure principle' and the 'reality principle'. The former shapes our thinking along the lines of a dream. It takes place in the register of what he called the 'primary process', where feelings, wishes and our associations to them link our ideas together. The latter takes place in the register of the 'secondary process', where logic and cause–effect reasoning shape our thinking.

Following Charles Rycroft, the psychoanalyst, we can define imagining as that process which integrates these two ways of thinking (Rycroft 1968, chapter 8). To envision in a way that is fruitful, we have to come into touch both with what we desire and with the practical challenges of achieving it. Artists in many fields face just this challenge. To do inspiring work, they have to come into touch with their desires – what gives them pleasure. But to do good work, they have to subordinate their impulses to the principles of craftsmanship – the rules that define what is quality.

The imagination in economics

Richard Bronk, author of *The Romantic Economist: Imagination in Economics* (2009), makes the case that there is an underlying but repressed vein of romantic thought in economics. For example, Alfred Marshall, the great economist who established the theory of the firm and the role of markets in allocating resources, argued that '[e]conomic problems are imperfectly presented when they are treated as problems of static equilibrium and not of organic growth' (ibid.: 122). He used the metaphor of the 'forest' to describe an economy: young trees struggle for light, with some surpassing their neighbors to transform the forest cover as a whole. Nature as a metaphor is of course a classic romantic conceit. Other economists used metaphors that echo romantic conceptions of human nature. Schumpeter's entrepreneur unleashed the forces of 'creative destruction', while Keynes's investors were motivated by what he called 'the animal spirits'.

The beauty of markets

Let me also draw attention to a book, *Escape to the Futures*, by Leo Melamed (1996), who helped build the MERC futures exchange in Chicago into one of the most powerful exchanges in the world. The book is a story of his career at the MERC, first as a floor runner, then as a broker and trader, and finally as its CEO.

He titles the second part of the book 'The beauty of markets'. Beauty is, of course, one outcome of a fertile imagination. When we describe a work of art or a Bach fugue as beautiful, we are announcing that these artistic products represent works of great imagination. The question for my purposes is what constitutes the market's beauty.

To understand this better, consider Melamed's paean to markets at the very end of his book:

> But the important effect of trading is that it keeps me linked to reality and truth. The beauty of markets, and for me their quintessential characteristic, is that they are the final determinant of veracity. Washington policy makers, Tokyo or Berlin ministers, officials of governments the world over can try to tell the world whatever they want, but the markets tell the world the truth ... their opinion doesn't count a tinker's damn unless or until it is endorsed by the market.
>
> (1996: 436)

One might see this as a paean to the rationality of markets, and partly it is. But the use of the term 'beauty' suggests that something else is also at play. What is beautiful about truth (two qualities that Keats' 'Ode to a Grecian urn', no less, equates) is its integrity: the degree to which, in the welter of apparent complexity, is revealed an ordering that is at once surprising and satisfying. It is not unlike the way in which mathematicians refer to certain proofs as 'elegant', because through a limited number of theorems, surprising truths connect what were once experienced as vastly different domains of mathematics. Similarly, the beauty of the market resides in the production of order out of what looks hopelessly complicated, if not random. It is not a simple ordering like dominoes lined up a row, but rather a rich ordering, like the woven pattern of a Persian rug. In this sense, Melamed sees the market as a work of art, and therefore the product of human imagination.

You might say that this proposition relies too much on the observation of a single, though very creative, entrepreneur. But in response to this objection I can make the following argument. This appreciation of order out of chaos has come to characterize a vast network of writing and scholarship on 'complexity', 'emergence' and 'self-organization'. Listen to two coauthors reflect on the idea of 'emergence' in complex systems:

> Part of the innate appeal of emergence is the surprise it engenders on the part of the observer. Many of our most profound experiences of emergence comes from those systems in which the local behavior seems so entirely

disconnected from the resulting aggregates as to have arisen by magic.... Examples of such dramatic disconnects, include photo-mosaic pictures, the order and persistence of beehives and foraging ant colonies through simple sets of localized signals, and the stability of a market price generated by the often chaotic and heterogeneous efforts of traders.

(Miller and Page 2007: 45)

Indeed, those in the group relations field often marvel at the unconscious 'music of groups', the way in which a work leader spontaneously emerges out of a chaotic group and its members then freely organize themselves around this leader to do good reality-oriented work.

Projecting our imagination

One question is why the fascination with complexity, with order of out of chaos. Partly this represents the advance of science. But I think the resonance these ideas have had suggests that we are at a stage of cultural development where we feel impelled to project out our imagination into the material world. *We see it in markets, groups and nature.*

Let me say this in another way. Marshall McLuhan (1967) had a novel conception of technology. Technological devices were, he thought, extensions of the human body (he called them 'outerings') through which we greatly amplify what our puny body can do alone. So, for example, the wheel is an 'outering' of the foot; the lever, the outering of the hand; the telescope, the outering of the eye. Freud, in *Civilization and Its Discontents* (1929), similarly notes, 'With every tool man is perfecting his own organs, whether motor or sensory, or is removing the limits to their functioning.... Man has, as it were, become a kind of prosthetic God.' In this sense, we can say that the market as a technology is becoming the outering of our imaginations. We see in the market both the expression and the extension of our creativity.

Richard Bronk (2009: 10) references the following verse from a poem by the romantic poet William Wordsworth, a poem that uses the idea of 'nature' as a metaphor for the imagination:

...a blue chasm; a fracture in the vapour,
A deep and gloomy breathing-place through which
Mounted the roar of waters, torrents, streams
Innumerable, roaring with one voice.
...but in that breach
Through which the homeless voice of waters rose,
That dark deep thoroughfare, had Nature lodg'd
The Soul, the Imagination of the whole.

This points to the following hypothesis. In the industrial revolution, nature, still undomesticated, was the enemy of the machine and thus the repository for what was both mysterious and creative. Economics in the industrial age, however, took up the machine metaphor, so that what we think of as *desire* became *utility*. Pleasure-seeking was like engineering: one looked to 'optimize' utility in the face of limited resources But as we enter the post-industrial revolution, with nature fully domesticated, the market now becomes the repository for what is mysterious and creative, and economists are turning to 'behavioral economics' to overcome their engineering conception of human desire.

Imagination as a productive force

Why have we projected the imagination in this way? One hypothesis is that this reflects a change in the economic underpinnings of society. It is common to note that we live in a knowledge economy, but of course there is much knowledge work that can be commoditized and automated. What counts today is creativity, not simply knowledge, and indeed economists speak increasingly about the 'creative economy'. To use Karl Marx's phrase, imagination itself has become a 'productive force' (Marx and Engels 1938), and in this sense it has been intensified.

If this is true, it would shed some new light on the emergence of the market orientation over the past thirty years. The impetus to deregulate markets, particularly in the Anglo-Saxon world, did not simply represent a simple seesawing between markets and planning akin, for example, to the way in which the Gilded Age in the United States gave way to Progressive Period, or the 'Roaring Twenties' to the New Deal. Instead, it reflected a deeper social and economic trend that we need to understand if we are to avoid the kind of economic crisis we currently face.

The vicissitudes of the imagination

The breakdown of imagination

I have argued, along with Charles Rycroft, that imagining synthesizes the pleasure and reality principles. But as every person learns, whether he or she is a poet, musician or painter, it takes great discipline and work to sustain this synthesis. Imagining readily breaks down under the press of this difficult work. We are vulnerable to either overvaluing our impulses and wishes, or overvaluing the techniques that constrain us. In the first instance the resulting work is self-centered; it cannot communicate meaning to others. In the second, it is dull and uninspiring.

If imagination has been intensified, if we demand more of our imagination, the resulting stress can separate out the two principles of mental functioning. The synthesis breaks down. Like the walker on a tightrope, imagination is held in the tension between two sides. Any slackening leads to a fall. This suggests that in the breakdown we are at risk of elevating either the reality principle, hence emphasizing our conformity, or the pleasure principle, hence overvaluing our impulses and desires. Scholars and writers have paid a great deal of attention to the latter. Both Christopher Lasch in his work on the culture of narcissism (1991) and Howard Schwartz in his work on political correctness (2001) have explored this terrain.

Political correctness

Howard Schwartz's work is instructive here. His critique of political correctness derives from his assumption that political correctness is an assault upon the father. Political correctness, rooted in an attack on white male privilege, renders institutional authority and its associated standards suspect. These standards are seen not as objective, as rooted in some activity, function or craft, but as vehicles for protecting the unearned privileges of white male elites. Programs for increasing diversity, for example, which at one point were grounded in sensible ideas of fairness and equal opportunity, instead became instruments for attacking all performance standards.

Schwartz describes the psychoanalytic background for this development by characterizing it as anti-oedipal. The attack on institutional authority is nourished by a fantasy, socially constructed but unconsciously held, that mother will love us no matter what we do, that father's claim to authority is therefore illegitimate and that all we need is mother. Rather than providing us with a route to love through accomplishment in the world, we see father as usurper of what mother could give us if only he allowed her to. He calls this anti-oedipal because instead of winning mother by identifying with father, we presume that our impulses are worthy in their own right because we are worthy in our own right. We are entitled to love without working for it. This is the sense in which his conception of political correctness joins the earlier critique of the 'culture of narcissism'.

Entitlement versus greed

This same psychodynamic can provide some insights into aspects of the financial crisis. There has been a presumption that the crisis was stimulated by greed, but I want to draw attention instead to feelings of entitlement. Consider the following. Goldman Sachs set aside $7 billion in salaries and end-of-year bonuses in 2008 after the government gave it $6.1 billion in bailout money. About $1 billion went to its 343 partners. Surprised and taken aback by the public's angry response, the firm required that its executives give some fraction of the bonuses to charity.

Similarly, when, in early 2010, the federal government sought to impose a large fee on banks, Goldman Sachs hired a lawyer to challenge the ruling 'all the way to the Supreme Court'. As a *New York Times* editorial of 23 January 2010 said,

> The push-back against the fee underscores bankers' peculiar sense of entitlement. They feel entitled to the public support dished out by the Treasury,

the F.D.I.C. and the Federal Reserve. Yet they do not believe they should be made to contribute toward the effort to save the economy from their reckless behavior.

The *Times* editorial reflected wide puzzlement. Why did these institutions and their leaders have no sense of proportion? I don't think that the answer is greed. It is not that these banks and their employees felt they could never have enough or get enough. Instead, they felt disrespected. This feeling arises when people believe that authority is illegitimate. It is as if the banks' leaders and the financial firms' partners are saying, 'Who do you think you are to tell me what to do?' In this sense, these responses meant that the banks simply did not accept the institutional and legal framework within which they were operating. They were free agents and creatures of their own making. They were not connected through a network of obligations to other institutions; hence, they experienced neither guilt nor shame over the damage they helped create.

Psychoanalytically, greed is linked to hunger and feelings of dependency. By contrast, entitlement is linked to indignation and feelings of self-sufficiency and is a protest against the demand for a relationship. The entitled person has a right to satisfy an impulse or wish not because of the impulse's urgency but simply because it is *the person's own* impulse. Like the practitioners of political correctness, the banks and the financial institutions were acting as if they should be honored for who they were, titans of finance, not for what they had either created or, in this case, destroyed.

The breakdown of imagination

Let us return to the concept of systemic risk. As our interdependence grows, we are increasingly vulnerable to one another's decisions. We need mechanisms of coordination and planning to help manage these risks. But these mechanisms mean that individual impulses and wishes must, in the service of a stable world, be repressed. In other words, we need to rely more heavily on the reality principle.

But there is a danger here. Under the press of authority, the imaginative function can break down. In response to the suppression of pleasure, people may respond to the imposition of authority with dependence or counterdependence. If the former, people subordinate to authority and conform; if the latter, people overvalue their impulses and attack authority. Each response inhibits creativity.

We can interpret the post-World War II critiques of capitalism as reflecting each of these possibilities. Consider the argument that Abraham Zaleznik, the psychoanalyst and management thinker, lays out in his classic book *The Managerial Mystique* (1989). He argues that management as an art has been devitalized. The good manager no longer feels 'the fire in the belly', but is concerned above all with process, with the orchestration of meetings and deliberations without regard to their outcome. What counts is how matters appear, not what they mean. In the terms we are using here, the reality principle supervenes, and the manager is focused, obsessively, on adaptation and conformity. In this case, the reality principle dominates the pleasure principle and the art of management is mystified. It is voided of meaning, and reduced to a technique.

You will undoubtedly recognize in this argument the critique of the technocrat and the admonishment that corporations are without souls. This point of view dominated criticism of advanced capitalism in its early post-World War II phase. The 1960s counterculture was partly a counterargument to this trend, represented most forcefully in such books as Theodore Roszak's *The Making of a Counterculture* (1963), Charles Reich's *The Greening of America* (1970) and Betty Friedan's *The Feminine Mystique* (1963). This development in turn gave rise to a third phase of critique, expressed in such concepts as 'the culture of narcissism' and the theory of political correctness, both of which we have already referenced. In this last way of thinking, the organization, far from being soulless, became a playground for the projection of impulses. If we take this literature as representing aspects of real experience, it suggests how difficult it has been to sustain the integration of the reality and pleasure principles in advanced capitalism.

Learnings from group relations conferences

Let me also turn your attention to the creative work done by William Halton (2004, 2005) in extending the groups relations conference model. He has introduced two new types of events: 'resource planning' and 'marketplace' events. In the former, the conference staff authorize a small group of members, the management group, to work with the membership in planning a series of learning sessions based on the members' learning needs. (I am simplifying the description here.) The managers ask resource groups, each composed of some subset of the members, to plan and deliver these learning sessions. The presenting challenge is for the management group to win the cooperation of the resource groups and for the resource groups to accept the authority of the management group. There is the risk that the resource groups will spin off as independent entities 'doing their own thing'. Describing one conference, Halton writes:

> Resource group A members were upset that some of their needs had been left off the list by the assessors. At first they were frightened of management and requested consultancy about whether it was safe to ask the management group to remedy this omission. Later, they came up with a plan that would solve the various dilemmas facing management, but management rejected the plan on the grounds that the group was too aggressive in the way they presented it. The group were then unwilling to allow management into their room.
>
> Resource group B completed the inventory of their resources quite quickly and handed the list to management. They then withdrew into an isolated self-idealization in which they explored their own group process. They failed to cooperate in creating the plan or in contributing to the resolution of the system's problems.

Resource group C also contributed a list of their resources, but because a member of management was rude to one of them, they went on strike and refused further cooperation.

The system fell apart. Crowds of observers gathered in the management room. Arguments proliferated; the time available for running the events diminished; ambitious schemes were progressively cut back; learning needs had to be curtailed amid further arguments.

(2004: 12)

By contrast, in the marketplace event, subgroups form spontaneously and are given the opportunity to plan a presentation for the other members on any topic of their choosing and to be customers for the other groups' presentations. One rule is that all members of a group must be present when their group gives its presentation. The initial feeling in response to the task is a manic one. There is excitement that can stimulate thoughts about sexuality. For example, Halton describes one group that decided to offer an eau de Cologne scent that would improve a person's sex life.

But more importantly, what can happen is that the unpredictability of the marketplace itself – who will come to whose presentation and what they will think of it – leads the different groups to merge, so that now only one group, the membership as whole, is called upon to plan and deliver a series of scheduled events.

Describing one marketplace event, Halton (2004) writes:

The separate groups collapsed quickly into one organization with a leader, who set up a corporate project of making a promotional film to attract tourists to their town; one group was to make the video, another the brochures, a third to plan distribution and so on.

These two outcomes lead Halton to a provocative formulation. In response to the resource planning event, people enact a marketplace (each group is independent and can its own thing), and in response to the marketplace event the groups respond by creating a resource planning event. They decide to allocate time and effort through a collective process.

Thus, each event becomes a social defense against the other. In the marketplace event, the excitement gives ways to anxiety about its unpredictable nature. This leads members to combine forces and centrally plan their activities. This is not unlike companies forming surreptitious oligopolies, or traders trying to corner a market. In the resource planning event, authority's impingement on the freedom and potential creativity of resource group leads them to undermine the management group and to strike out on their own as entrepreneurs.

The new politics and the concept of psychosociology

The tension between the reality and pleasure principles inherits and transforms the historic political tension between markets and central planning. This tension grew out of, and was expressed by, the 'class struggle'. Workers and their allies attacked markets because they resulted in low wages, adulterated food and old people living in poverty. Their unions, and in Europe their political parties, aimed for a 'social' democracy in which a citizen's political rights were matched by everyone's right to a fair share of economic resources. At the same time, capitalists resisted government intrusions and defended their right to dispose of their property according to their own interests and objectives.

Today, this tension takes place first and foremost on the psychological plane. Under the press of authority and the burdens of living with systemic risk, we project onto the state the reality principle and onto the market the pleasure principle. We split off the two. This tension first lays a claim on our minds, before it results in an expression of some material or political interest.

This has two implications. First, we can use neither the market nor the state imaginatively. We deprive each side of the compensating principle it needs. Second, social conflicts today result from the *projections outward* of this inwardly experienced tension. This is why political conflicts in the United States, for example, have an increasingly cultural cast. Political wars and culture wars converge. I want to suggest that we need a new term for thinking about this terrain. The term 'social psychology' points to the way psychological processes are socialized. Let me propose instead the term 'psychosociology', a term our French colleagues use, to express the idea that social conflicts are psychologized. They are the projections outward of psychic forces. In this environment, it becomes increasingly difficult to link the historical concepts of 'interests' and 'interest groups' to political conflicts.

In *The Future of an Illusion*, Freud suggests that the intellect would not necessarily succumb to the instincts. 'The voice of the intellect is a soft one, but it does not rest until it has gained a hearing. Finally, after a countless succession of rebuffs it succeeds' (1928: 53). Perhaps we could amend this proposition by offering up the hope that imagination, fully realized, in which the reality and the pleasure principles are integrated, might provide the soil in which instinct and the intellect converge. This might feel utopian, as if civilization itself could become a work of art, but it may provide a hopeful direction.

In sum

The financial crisis has exposed a serious tension between the pleasure and reality principles. We need the former for creativity, the latter to manage systemic risks. Each entails, but is in tension with, the other. The cultural task is to integrate the two so that creativity takes place in a context in which legitimate authority can be exercised. But regression takes place readily, taking the form of the culture of narcissism and political correctness on the one side, or conformity and a devitalized organizational life on the other. We need to develop a new psychosociology to fully understand the implications of these developments and to create organizational and social systems that allow the imagination to flourish.

References

Bronk, R. (2009) *The Romantic Economist: Imagination in economics*, Cambridge: Cambridge University Press.

Freud, S. (1911) *Formulations on the Two Principles of Mental Functioning*, in *The Standard Edition of the Complete Psychological Works of Sigmund Freud*, vol. 21, London: Hogarth Press.

Freud, S. (1928) *The Future of an Illusion*, in *The Standard Edition of the Complete Psychological Works of Sigmund Freud*, vol. 21, London: Hogarth Press.

Freud, S. (1929) *Civilization and Its Discontents*, in *The Standard Edition of the Complete Psychological Works of Sigmund Freud*, vol. 21, London: Hogarth Press.

Friedan, B. (1963) *The Feminine Mystique*, New York: W.W. Norton.

Friedman, J. (2010) 'A crisis of politics, not economics: complexity, ignorance, and policy failure', *Critical Review*, 21: 127–83.

Halton, W. (2004) 'Developments in group relations: exploring the managed and unmanaged environment', unpublished paper, 30 November.

Halton, W. (2005) 'Consulting to institutions', unpublished note, April.

Lasch, C. (1991) *The Culture of Narcissism: American life in an age of diminishing expectations*, New York: W.W. Norton.

Lewis, M. (2010) *The Big Short: Inside the doomsday machine*, New York: W.W. Norton.

McLuhan, M. (1967) *Understanding Media: The extensions of man*, London: Sphere Books.

Marx, K. and Engels, F. (1938) *The German Ideology*, London: Lawrence & Wishart.

Melamed, L. (1996) *Escape to the Futures*, New York: John Wiley.

Miller, J.H. and Page, S.E. (2007) *Complex Adaptive Systems: An introduction to computational models of social life*, Princeton, NJ: Princeton University Press.

Polayni, K. (1957) *The Great Transformation*, Boston: Beacon Press.

Reich, C.A. (1970) *The Greening of America: How the youth revolution is trying to make America livable*, New York: Random House.

Roszak, T. (1969) *The Making of a Counterculture: Reflections on the technocratic society and its youthful opposition*, Garden City: Doubleday.

Rycroft, C. (1968) *Imagination and Reality*, New York: International Universities Press.

Schwartz, H. (2001) *The Revolt of the Primitive: An inquiry into the roots of political correctness*, Westport, CT: Praeger.

Zaleznik, A. (1989) *The Managerial Mystique: Restoring leadership in business*, New York: Harper & Row.

22 Profit as organizing meaning

The financial industry and the dynamic theory of multiple function

Ian S. Miller

Observing the financial industry and its component firms introduces psychodynamic consultants to a difficulty in spanning two unique experiential worlds of training and practice. On one side are the dangers of our own observational transference distortions from within psychoanalytic conventions of certainty and ambivalence. On the other side are the dangers of overvaluing the rationality of profit making from within the systemically bounded and self-assured contexts of firm, business socialization and training. Conceptually, the relation between psychoanalysis and business appears as a contrast of opposites. Psychoanalysis is anchored in the study of irrational conflict and anxiety. It is identified with the value of reflection upon the fluidity and ambivalence that characterize individuals and organizations in the passionate clash of experience, motivations and values. Finance, however, is identified with the value of decisive action under the appearance of certainty and rationality in the drive for specifiable deliverables profitable to the firm and its agents. The values of each discipline may be understood by considering the contexts and roles of the other (Mead 1972).

This chapter draws on my experiences both as a psychoanalytically trained business consultant and through participant observation in MBA training. Informed by the MBA experience, I examine the boundaries of finance industry rationality and irrationality through a psychodynamic lens focused upon the centrality to firms of profit making as a meaningful and rational enterprise.

Within business, profit making is a purposive and lived reality. Close to the dictionary definition of 'the real', reality in this sense is what actually exists or occurs. The rational interpretation of what exists based on individual and group reasoning is what makes sense in a given firm's situation, contextualized by conditions both internal and external. The fundamental management tool of SWOT analysis (strengths, weaknesses, opportunities and threats) acknowledges this reality as it focuses upon a business's internal strength and weakness together with external opportunity and threat.

However, this conventional business understanding of reality is at variance with the broader construction of multiple intra-psychic realities as viewed through a psychodynamic lens. Business reality dovetails with the 'reality principle' of psychoanalysis only to the extent that 'the search for satisfaction does not take the most direct routes but instead makes detours and postpones the attainment of its goal in attunement with the constraints of the external world' (Laplanche and Pontalis 1973: 379). The reality of business is always limited – constrained by the business context.

Nobel Prize laureate Herbert Simon observed that within business organizations, rational, sense-making behavior is continually defined and contextualized by the boundaries and limits imposed upon individuals and work units by the task constraints of business. In the service of productivity both within and across an industry's firms, the 'real' is limited to a construction shaped by organizational authority, and the immediacy and utility of action (Simon 1977).

Here, I seek to clarify both the scope of reality from within the organizational context of the profit motive and the limits of rational behavior within that context. Exploring decisions under the profit motive from the perspective of this limiting and bounded rationality, I conclude by suggesting a systemic, psychodynamic framework drawing on Robert Waelder's classic psychoanalytic paper 'The principle of multiple function' (1976), useful in business consultation for interpreting the activities of financial firms and markets.

Contextualizing inquiry

In the beginning, for the psychodynamic consultant, is the clarification of what James (1981) termed 'the psychologist's fallacy' – that is, the mistaking of the consultant's viewpoint for the perspective of the client. Within the psychoanalytic context this points to the recognition of the consultant's own transference distortions. Not only do such distortions predestine the consultant's arrival at questionable conclusions, but they also heighten the resistance of the client, closing down his or her openness to the business value of psychodynamic understanding.

Within the financial world, receptivity to psychodynamic understanding already begins as a 'hard sell', owing to the interaction of two very different cultures. In its interpretive understanding of the larger world beyond the consulting room, psychodynamic interpretation has often construed the profit motive and its aggressive drives in line with their genetic origins, i.e. as oral, anal and phallic. Traditionally, money and profit have been linked to the aggressive, tragic and pointless emptiness of greedy pursuits (Fenichel 1938; Fromm 1941; Wachtel 2003).

Psychoanalytic reflections focused upon profit with its attendant and unattainable narcissistic fantasies of happiness and fullness have therefore agreed with contemporary critiques of consumerist society rather than either with neutral observation or with furthering the purposes of business (Jackson 2005; Lasch 1979; Kasser *et al.* 2004). Yet the pragmatic question for the psychodynamic consultant – trained interpretively and furnished with biological, developmentally accented metaphors for human behaviour – is whether this singular perspective achieves value for the client in furthering understanding.

The psychodynamic observation of business must begin by clarifying its audience. Its intention as cultural critique describes both a different trajectory and a different receptivity than its intention as a potentially useful bridge between psychodynamic thought and business. To achieve this latter goal, psychodynamic interpretation must inquire into its desired effect.

Interpretive conviction within the client's experience is at the core of psychoanalytic interpretive efficacy (Ferenczi and Rank 1986). Otherwise, interpretation diminishes the value of psychodynamic formulation and provokes resistance. The bottom line is whether psychodynamic consultants wish to observe critically from outside the business world or wish to contribute to organizational understanding from within the boundaries of business organizations.

The limitation of psychodynamic reflection to the examination of the unsustainable gratifications of profit making forecloses psychodynamic contribution within the executive suite. It closes off the openness of business managers to psychodynamic contributions related to the psychodynamics of organizational systems while confirming psychoanalysis as a closed system; limited to its own scope of knowledge. In this sense, the limitation of psychodynamic interpretation to value-based condemnation of profit making in this way may serve a professional transference while heightening potential clients' resistance.

In so doing, such limitation enacts a social defense that confirms part of our own conceptual system while rejecting another – that is, a psychodynamic interest in organizations and groups dating back to Freud's 'Group psychology and the analysis of the ego' (1921). Functionally, this social defense serves both to judge a different identity system (namely, that of business) and to make certain that our own identity is repugnant to those we reject. In so doing, we protect ourselves from recognizing limitations in our own scope of knowledge as we split off our own ambivalence about profit in celebration of our interpretive capability.

This may well be because in practice we are ambivalent. I am reminded of a supervisory discussion early in my career by a respected senior analyst on the recognition of his own deep transferential interests in the elegant restaurant experiences described by his wealthy patients. He addressed his envy as well as the irrationality of his professionally driven valuation of knowledge acquisition over wealth acquisition. Ultimately, our supervision group recognized that both knowledge and wealth might each be the vehicles both of greed and of envy, but anxiously joked that the restaurant experiences sounded good. Money indeed may facilitate pleasant experience – though we may be ambivalent, professionally, in admitting it.

Instead, defensively, psychoanalysts may hold moneymaking in faint contempt, taking satisfying intellectual refuge in knowledge of money's developmental ordure. As psychoanalytically inclined consultants, we may cringe enviously at others' undiminished drive towards profit in our own unacknowledged shame within a profit-obsessed society of avoiding more profitable labor, as we judge business to be insufficiently intellectual to measure up to our own truly meaningful values and standards.

The consultant, like his or her clients, is 'more human than otherwise' (Sullivan 1953). Yet as we negotiate a turbulent global reorientation of finance and wealth, and as economic concerns permeate even casual discussion, it is understandable that the uncertainties beyond the boundaries of our own discipline cause us to fall back defensively upon habits of interpretive judgment and a worldview that distort rather than clarify new and anxiety-provoking experience. Alternatively, it might be said that the psychodynamic valuation of knowledge is an economic choice based from within the activities defining our professional identity. This is a choice radically different than the performance-based identity model common in finance (Akerlof and Kranton 2010).

In the end, as psychodynamic consultants to business, we make a focal choice. The present chapter explores the business firm as a meaningful social system rooted in the profit motive. It continues, linking potential turbulence within the larger business and financial communities as the unknown effects of multiple subsystems' interactions, beyond the limits of discretely bounded rationalities.

The profit-making firm as a meaning-making social system

The starting point of this broader psychodynamic inquiry is the firm. The firm, as abstraction, is more specific than its synonyms 'organization', 'dynamic system' or 'institution'. The firm is motored by profit. Profit is the firm's purpose and motivation. The prime movers of the firm's input, throughput and output processes are its profit margin, cash flow and bottom line.

For the psychoanalyst and systems-oriented consultant, this compression of knowledge to a single, concrete motivation feels incongruous – like a hard stop to inquiry. Yet it came to me as a freeing epiphany sometime in the middle of my first semester in business school.

I had elected to study for an executive MBA to expand my understanding of the business world to which I consulted. Attempting to keep my head above water in accounting, finance, marketing and entrepreneurship courses, the profundity of profit as a starting point in my new, yet circumscribed world of study suddenly made sense. It meaningfully organized experience. It provided grounding for that ubiquitous and never-defined business term, 'value'; it organized, for most of my colleagues, why we were studying: to profit or gain. Profit was the universal motivation. Obviously, its unit of measurement was money.

With this recognition, which emerged from innumerable equations, spreadsheets, research reports, rejections of correct answers written in pencil rather than ink (to teach us that the basic standard of competency is what the manager insists upon, affirming his or her authority), evaluations based on the performance of dysfunctional teams rather than individual merit, and the pain of what seemed never-ending and pointless work, I had begun to learn through experience.

Adrift in my initial business school socialization, I had felt rudderless. Doctoral and professional studies, professional practice, were worlds away from this experience. As an MBA student, I was instructed that I was an ignorant new recruit. I felt deskilled and experienced grief at my loss of identity.

'What will you be after two years?' we were asked in business school orientation. The obvious answer: 'an MBA'. It would be several years until I understood the underlying gravity of this self-evident pep talk. It extended beyond the simple 'Master's degree' as proof of study and anchor of personal identity. If we succeeded, our magical wish for mastery of the unknown would be the yield of a two-year ordeal.

Profit was the key. It securely integrated the unknowns of markets, employment, government intervention, globalization, GDP, and our futures as Masters of Business. Profit appeared in the finance class as an assumption anchoring the 'terminal values' of a depreciated asset long after its productive use. Profit appeared in my team's decision to recycle an earlier paper written on Chinese wind farming to another assignment. The risk of receiving a lower grade was leveraged against our team's calculation of profit – our calculation that a merely passing grade would not materially affect our cumulative average. Why produce newer work when it would not profit us? We were pleased with ourselves. We were thinking like MBAs. Through similar experiences I learned that while profit was nominally extrinsic as reward, the joys of profitable action were also intrinsic.

Profit was a flexible and utilitarian tool. It securely provided the bottom line as our shield in defending against too much confusing information. In this sense, through doing, we were learning 'bounded rationality' – a manager's limitation of informational inputs in the service of making a decision good enough for a particular strategic purpose (Simon 1977). As students, we often studied the constraints of the educational process in which we had enlisted – our own approximation to the firm; and using the compass point of systemic profit, were able to navigate it more safely and efficiently.

Of course, profit is a limiting value. In the cold light of economic recession and a questionably sustainable future, business professionals and educators have begun to address MBAs' lack of preparation in negotiating complexity in ignoring 'life-affirming values, collective welfare and ecological limits' (Gladwin and Berdish 2010); and here, business's internal critique begins to approximate broader social critique. Yet, in practice, 'cash is king' and opportunities are continual.

It was only through participant observation as a psychoanalyst in the business school that I learned the powerful demand of competing systemic realities upon the mind, behavior and spirit. My experience within the business school corresponded with descriptions of individuals' behaviors within firms as highly constrained and conditioned by the firm's controlling task. Reflecting on his experience as CEO of AT&T, Chester Barnard writes, '[T]he individual loses his preeminence in the situation and something else, non-personal in character, is treated as dominant' (1968: 9).

Business school taught me that the consultant's initial focus on central organizational dimensions of mission and goal may be misplaced idealizations. These are higher-level concepts, derivative of the firm's basic, if implicit, purpose: profitability. Profit is the firm's implicit constant, linked to competitive advantage and customer desire.

The centrality of profit is the psychodynamic consultant's unthinkable known. Though the purposive and conscious focus of our clients, our own professional orientations may subordinate profit to one of many possible business outputs. Instead, psychoanalytic consultants may begin, in consideration of business's wider and more abstract systemic goals – the firm's value and mission – as we move to considerations of structure, strategy, skills, staffing, systems and style (Waterman *et al.* 1980).

While we are conscious of profit as important, its simplified perception as an outcome variable presents us with a distorted orientation to the breadth of the firm's psychological situation. Unmindful of material profit's centrality, perhaps because of our own dedication to a different form of profit in knowledge, we again risk the psychologist's fallacy in substituting our own viewpoints for those of our client business people and their organizations (James 1981).

Recent negative sentiment about outsized remuneration in the finance industry bears little correspondence either to financial firms' purposes or to the profit-driven purposes of a firm's employees. The experiential centrality of profit is what business school teaches in its preparation of managers for the firm. Indeed, the certainty of profit making may be the deciding factor whether to follow a firm's original business model or to 'loot' the firm by making large payments to stakeholders in the certainty that debt repayment will fall to others (Aklerof and Romer 1993).

Profit is the Occam's razor of business organization – its most parsimonious bottom line. How organizations profit through risk is a dominant theme in human history (Bernstein 1998). Contemporary complaint that Goldman Sachs's professionals operate sometimes within the organization and sometimes within the government that regulates the firm is hardly scandalous. Indeed, the business model and success of Price Waterhouse (now part of PricewaterhouseCoopers, PwC), both in the United Kingdom and in the United States, is based on a similar interchangeable model of regulated and regulator spanning more than a century (Allen and McDermott 1993).

Seizing the opportunity, maximizing the firm's utility to the customer, is how profit is made. Sometimes, as in Goldman's complex business alliance with AIG and the US government, profitability and competitive advantage trump all else (Morgenson and Story 2010). Experientially, this is what business school teaches.

While intrinsic motivation may be a subsidiary benefit of employment, an incoming student's choice of investment banking derives from its material benefits, beginning with the recruitment process on elite university campuses. Forty percent of Princeton's 2005 and 2006 undergraduate classes entered financial services. Fifty percent of Harvard's 2005 class competed for investment banking and management consulting jobs. Not only do top-seeded banking firms offer monetary inducements but their reputations for seeking 'the best and the brightest' burnish the externally derived self-perceptions of students from elite universities. Election to a specific, highly valued firm confirms social status; and separates, as much as front office from back office, the best from the 'also-rans' (Ho 2009).

The evolution of finance from an industry among many to the predominant industry shaping twenty-first-century America reflects the enormous social cachet attached to employment by a finance firm (Davis 2009). It suggests that the entrant, once successful in competing both with other members of his or her graduating class and with competitive colleagues within the firm itself, is among the conventionally validated 'smartest guys in the room'. Such arrival often begins with preparation at preschool and continues through adolescence. Socially, it means that one is at the top of one's game, at the pinnacle of what matters, even if this is a product of social attribution and practiced attitude rather than personal competency (Stern 2010).

Once on board, as Herbert Simon (1977) observes, each subsequent decision becomes conditioned by the demands and purposes of the firm. The employee's election to enter the system is his or her last freely chosen decision, within the scope of activities he or she presents for use to the firm for its purposes. Individuals subordinate their energies to the directions and orientations of the firm. Within finance, that's about making money. And making money is a 'blood sport': the rules of the game, including the innovative and publicly misleading, leverage-reducing reporting of finances by Lehman, are known both within and between firms (Hughes 2010).

The profit motive in organizational context

During the growing collateralized debt obligation crisis in the years before Lehman's collapse, I had become intrigued by the uniform prediction, individually disclosed by each of several clients working in various sectors of the financial industry, that a collapse was coming, and with dangerous worldwide ramifications. As a psychoanalyst, I asked, 'Why didn't persons "in the know" say or do something?'

The clients uniformly chided me for my naiveté and explained that everyone was participating, but that if one firm withdrew from the activity, another would capture its market share. They explained that the system was about competitive profitability across firms. Were an individual, even at managing director level, to question the wisdom of continued trading, even as a precipice approached, it was likely that he or she would be seen as a weak link and treated accordingly. Therefore, it was full speed ahead for everyone.

Consensual reality from within the organization is always a subset of a larger reality. In my experience, several versions of reality may operate consciously to organizational actors. Within the specific role context and definition of organizational position and authority, a seemingly irrational action in relation to the broader world might make perfect sense as rational behavior within the organization. This seeming split is carried in the mind of the actor and may be knowable to the outside observer from the context of multiple interviews within organizational consultation or psychotherapy, but, when surfaced consciously, continues to make rational sense if it accords with organizational goals and constraints. When one is operating within organizational role, behavior that might seem irrational to the individual as a 'civilian' makes perfect sense in the role of organization member (Newton *et al.* 2006).

A few years later, economist Paul Wilmott (2009) illustrated this dynamic within investment banking. While retail brokers preached the conventional wisdom of 'asset diversification' to their clients, encouraging clients to build a portfolio on a balanced market basket of assets, the analysts who recommended these assets to these same brokers made their claims in virtual uniformity across individual businesses and industry. Market investment decisions made by financial analysts were herdlike and the result was that retail customers' choices followed suit.

Wilmott observed that acting in uniformity with the organizational group, while in role, made better economic sense for stock analysts than acting independently on the diversity of their possible judgments. The rationality of this behavior is based in the profit motive. Quite simply, because bonus payments are based on group rather than individual performance, there is safety in numbers when bonuses relate to group productivity.

Basing his argument in probability, Wilmott demonstrated how a freely thinking individual with a better winning streak than his colleagues must add his wins to his colleagues' losses. His own win joins his colleagues' losses and he suffers both their diminished bonus and their social stigmatization for thinking differently than they. On the other hand, if he loses when the group wins, he is faced with termination. It is more prudent for brokers and traders to fail as a group than to succeed individually – even if individual success helps the bank to increase return and to decrease risk.

The sensible response within this system, with behavioral parameters set by the firm's profit-making incentive structure, is not to deviate from the behavior of others but to follow the herd. The result is that the interests of financial analysts may vary greatly from the wisdom of diversification, as taught in finance class. The same philosophy is shared both by 'Main Street' shareholders and their consultant stockbrokers.

That the very brokers in the same organization as their analysts are guided by essentially uniform rather than diversified information describes the systemic limit of irrationality: what makes sense within one systemic subunit does not make sense within another. However, such systemic irrationality may make little difference to the organizational goal of profit making if it does not ultimately affect the conduct of buying and selling stock, which generates both broker and analyst salaries! In this manner, organizational irrationality may make no appreciable difference until a tipping point is reached between interactive social systems, with shareholder and retail client realization that their investment selections may be determined by subgroup interests other than their own.

What appears irrational at the retail level is anything but irrational at the level of analysts, where the behavior makes sense within the bounded context of profit making by the industry's internal standards. Learning such bounded rationality is implicit in learning the job: what seems irrational in the larger system is rational within the smaller group – just as I learned in business school.

My clients' experiences, like Wilmott's observations, reflect the internal life of a financial firm mirrored in the behavior of employees. Consistent with the profit motive of the firm, both examples remain remarkably attuned to the profit and incentive structure of the organization. No matter that they are vilified as greedy. From within the internal perspective of their world, bankers actually do act like 'the smartest guys in the room'. Within the bounded rationality of the firm and industry, the limited universe of considerations that condition behavior, what appears from the outside to make little sense is really crystal clear. The breakdowns begin when the givens of one system are unknown to another system that is reliant upon it.

Uncertainty and the smartest guys in the room

The collateralized debt obligation (CDO) is a brilliant financial solution to a difficult problem – and as metaphor for our financial system's destabilization, approaches classical psychoanalytic description in its florid dynamics. It removes liability from the balance sheet and jettisons it into the cosmos. Firms' painful internal balance sheet pressures are externalized; and through this action the individual organization again feels relief and the freedom of movement. The problem, as described by my consulting clients, would be the coming 'shit-storm'. And so it was.

The CDO, like many new financial instruments, was mathematically modeled. It was developed as a financial algorithm tested and burnished by the best and brightest, but it foundered as its assumptions proved incorrect (Jones 2009). The industry-wide financial belief that 'nearly any asset could be priced and traded' in a globalized world's increasingly free markets worked as computer models but it broke down disastrously in operation (Sender *et al.* 2010).

The Bank of England got it right when it observed in 2009 that effective, rational practices within firms interacted with dangerous consequences for the economic system in which the firms operated (Haldane 2009). The world shook, anticipating a new Great Depression. Economic assumptions, from those taught to MBAs in finance classes to those occupying the smartest guys on Wall Street, had become questionable: markets were inefficient and extremely volatile (Mandelbrot and Hudson 2004). The bounded rationality of the firm had reached its limit.

And within the financial world a remarkable shift occurred, hidden in plain view within the new, politicized popular split of Wall Street and Main Street. Bounded rationality as one of the firm's characteristic executive functions, channeling the indomitable drive of profit seeking, turned to a new opportunity in the relations between firm and government. Firms across the globe sought and found refuge in governmental regulation and bailout. Some, like Lehman, failed; but others, infused with new government funding, soared. Governments themselves, like that of Greece, sought creative securitization of assets as an off-balance-sheet method of stabilizing their economy.

Bounded rationality appeared to have reached the limits of its power at the level of financial firms' systemic participation in relation to creative financial instruments. Yet despite the systemic collapse and rescue of markets by governments, the smartest guys, as guardians of firms' decision making, turned their bounded rationality to the traditional relation between financial firm and governmental regulator, just as they had historically, in the consulting business model of Price Waterhouse. Some, as in the case of Goldman, pushed hard on weaker organizations like AIG (Morgenson and Story 2010) or marketed their securitization services to governments, like that of Greece, desirous of their creative services. Others developed financial instruments allowing investors to bet against the survival of these same companies and governments (Schwartz and Dash 2010). All of this makes sense within each organization, as long as the organization operates within national and international regulatory legality.

Multiple function within profit-seeking organizations

The 'Great Recession' of 2007–9 provides psychodynamic organizational consultants with a dramatic industry- and firm-based parallel to the model of systemic equilibrium suggested by Robert Waelder in his paper on the 'multiple function' of the ego's executive function (1976). While Waelder's original conceptual model relates specifically to individual human functioning, its utility to the functioning of firms and industries is readily apparent. In fact, Waelder's model of ego executive functioning is an elegant bridge that spans managerial concepts of SWOT analysis with deeper psychodynamic levels of organizational decision making. Waelder describes individual executive function as the continuous permutation of multiple subsystem actions, with the maximization of all subsystem demands as the systemic ideal only momentarily, if ever, realized.

Executive decision making extends over two discrete spheres of action that Waelder construes as 'passive' and 'active'. The passive sphere is the ego's management of all effects from prior action permutations. For Waelder, passivity is analogous to receptivity in that the ego receives and accommodates the inputs from four discrete dimensions. The first of these dimensions is internal, emanating from the drives and actions of the organizational infrastructure. These correspond, within the language of management, to the structure, staff, systems and skill described by Waterman *et al.* (1980), and act as constraints upon present decision making and action. The second dimension corresponds to the past decisions enacted by the organization's executivem and corresponds to the style and strategy categories described by Waterman *et al* (ibid.). The third dimension received by the organization hails from the external world, with the resonant effect of its earlier strategic decisions. Finally, the fourth dimension corresponds to patterns of organizational behavior unique to the organization, repetitive at different moments in organizational history. Minimally, this correspondence mirrors the continuing presence of an organization's superordinate vision – a continuing ideal, inspirationally repetitive and never fully realized, in organizational life (ibid.).

Waelder's 'passive' function corresponds directly to Keynes's insight in *The General Theory of Employment, Interest, and Money* that both disappointed and successful past expectations continuously constrain the firm in its determination of present expectations (Keynes 2008: 35). Waelder's 'active' functions correspond to decision making in the Keynesian present and are the scenes of bounded rational action.

As within Waelder's passive functions, the active sphere covers four dimensions: the 'internal' drive and infrastructure of the firm; its management of external stimuli – similar to those seen as opportunity and threat within SWOT analysis; its own active balancing of current decision-making considerations; and the effect of historical repetition upon decision making.

All told, Waelder's description adds value to SWOT both by doubling its considerations and by making the continuous rebalancing of internal and external operational forces determining a firm's context of bounded rationality, the focus of ongoing organizational reflection.

Waelder's contribution to executive reflection – psychodynamic consultation's cardinal value to business firms – provides a tool, understandable within the language of management, to troubleshoot both the residual effects of a profit-making firm's past internal and external acts, and the effect upon present decision making from within the firm's (1) capabilities and capacities, (2) the firm's self-representation, (3) the operative forces of the world external to the firm, and (4) the firm's ability to learn from the past in avoiding future mistakes.

Conceptually, from a broader systemic perspective Waelder's model extends to the interaction of multiple firms. While the full range of systemic actions and consequences remain unknowable, what can become known, through Waelder's model, are: (1) the functional efficacy of new, higher-level organizing entities such as regulatory bodies within the finance industry; and (2) how systemic interactions of industry players will become incorporated into firms' ongoing activities. These too will be subject to firms' own histories, capabilities both past and present, and constraints of bounded rationality.

Conclusion: the increased value of a systems psychodynamic SWOT

SWOT analysis, separating strategic business choices into both the strengths and the weaknesses of factors internal and external to the business, is a ubiquitous component of introductory business school education. While its developmental origins are obscure, it is generally credited to A. Humphrey of the Stanford Research Institute (Morrison 2009).

SWOT is flexible in that it is easily grasped. It divides the internal capabilities of an organization into strengths and weaknesses. It divides the external business environment into opportunity and threat. SWOT therefore provides a snapshot in time within a business organization's strategic planning.

However, as the current financial crisis reflects, today's business challenges extend beyond the clarity of SWOT's initial inquiry, to consideration of internal and external contexts that determine the continuing life or demise of businesses and industries. Necessarily, deeper inquiry requires consideration of organizational phenomenology, in the freedoms and limitations of firms' bounded rationalities, linked to the incentivizing motivation of profit.

Walder's dynamic concept of the ego both parallels and extends SWOT in addressing the organization as a system in continuous balance both internally and in relation to the external environment. Extending beyond the individual firm, a larger systemic ego may also describe the industry within which the firm is located, as it interacts dynamically both with its component subsystem firms and with systemic egos external to the industry, such as nation-states and global regulators.

Two significant examples illustrate, capturing the attention of the investment world in the first months of 2010. The first example reflects the indebtedness of countries, counties and municipalities as a result of the financial crisis. Greece, for example, struggled with the effects of the finance industry's derivative products upon its outsized level of debt as global attention turned to Germany in the role of the eurozone's potential white knight. Yet Germany's range of economic action relative to Greece was constrained by the desires both of its electorate and of its legal system (Peel 2010). From the perspective of interactional, systemic 'Egos', three agents engaged: 'Banking', 'Greece' and 'Germany'. Additional complexity might also be included, with agents such as the eurozone and the International Monetary Fund. Dynamically, the 'Ego' Banking engages with the 'Ego' Greece, which engages with the 'Ego' Germany, each at a particular time and under particular conditions of action.

For the dynamically informed management consultant or strategist, the momentary, individual frames of a fast-moving dynamic process become discernible through the lens of a SWOT aligned with the principle of multiple function as managerial data for decision making and action.

Too often, decision makers' frames of reference become too tightly constrained by the bounded specificities of the work task. A second example illustrates. My own attention, in the writing of this chapter, centered on expanding psychodynamic consultants' thinking about the financial industry. This required a certain limitation of focus, the equivalent of imposing boundaries on the scope of inquiry. However, in the spring of 2010, as the chapter was being edited, the US government's Security and Exchange Commission brought a suit against Goldman Sachs in relation to the marketing of the 'Abacus' derivative product (Story and Morgenson 2010). While the essential facts of this matter had been published months before (Morgenson and Story 2009), what was new and emergent was the systemic action of the United States as regulator toward Goldman, as the institution under regulation.

The event underscored the high significance of the enduring engagement of systemic interactions between finance industry and governmental regulators. This, after all, is at the heart of the financial business model. Indeed, much of the rational behavior within discrete financial firms is in direct relation to external regulation (Akerlof and Romer 1993; McDonald 2009).

While my focus on the finance industry had recognized the larger systemic interaction between finance and regulators, I located this relationship at the periphery rather than at the center of financial industry considerations. In my own process of writing, paralleling the strategic considerations of managerial planners, the significance of regulators as external agents critical to financial decision making was limited in my analysis. However, for the consultant, as for the manager, emphases are often a function of emergent conditions when what is known, but preconscious, becomes significant.

With the government's legal initiative related to Goldman, an always operative but momentarily quiescent systemic relationship achieved momentary significance. Beyond the bounded rationality of profit making, beyond the utility to governments, firms and individuals of CDO investment, the media brought into sharp focus the ongoing systemic conflicts and compromises between financial firms and government regulators. Where the Ego 'Banking' had engaged the Ego 'Greece' in the first example, the second example contrasted the Ego 'Banking' with a different systemic Ego, 'Government Regulator', always known as an actor but momentarily waiting its turn onstage.

The systemic expansion of the dynamic Ego provides the value of great elasticity to the conventions of SWOT. This expanded SWOT extends the psychodynamic functioning of individuals to the organizations within which individuals function, which are conditioned by similar passive and active conditions reflective of individual/group/organizational infrastructure, decision making, ideals and the external world.

Waelder's multiple function provides a key to understanding the discontinuities between organizational subsystems, allowing for both rational and irrational behaviors, ultimately determined as useful or harmful, by their cumulative effects. Such analysis provides a sophisticated, continuous extension of SWOT, attuned to the systemic dynamics of firm, industry and economic system.

Recognizing the utility to business organizations of psychodynamic constructs requires that the psychodynamic consultant enter into the phenomenology of business and workplace as a meaning-making social system. Like all applications of psychoanalysis beyond the consulting room, this may engender both personal and systemic anxieties, but reflects in practice the systemic utility of psychoanalysis in the world of organizations and social systems.

References

Akerlof, G. and Kranton, R. (2010) 'It is time to treat Wall Street like Main Street', *Financial Times*, 25 February: 9.

Akerlof, G.A. and Romer, P.M. (1993) 'Looting: the economic underworld of bankruptcy for profit', *Brookings Papers on Economic Activity*, Microeconomics no. 2: 1–72.

Allen, D.G. and McDermott, K. (1993) *Accounting for Success: A history of Price Waterhouse in America 1890–1990*, Boston: Harvard Business School Press.

Barnard, C.I. (1968) *The Functions of the Executive*, Cambridge, MA: Harvard University Press.

Bernstein, P.L. (1998) *Against the Gods: The remarkable story of risk*, New York: John Wiley.

Davis, G.F. (2009) 'The rise and fall of finance and the end of the society of organizations', *Academy of Management Perspectives*, August: 27–44.

Fenichel, O. (1938) 'The drive to amass wealth', *Psychoanalytic Quarterly*, 7: 69–95.

Ferenczi, S. and Rank, O. (1986) *The Development of Psychoanalysis*, Madison, CT: International Universities Press.

Freud, S. (1921) 'Group psychology and the analysis of the ego', in *The Standard Edition of the Complete Psychological Works of Sigmund Freud*, vol. 18, London: Hogarth Press.

Fromm, E. (1941) *Escape from Freedom*, New York: Rinehart.

Gladwin, T.N. and Berdish, D. (2010) 'MBAs unprepared for a morally complex future', *Financial Times*, 8 February. Online, available at: www.ft.com/cms/s/df5c80e2-1452-11df-8847-00144feab49a,dwp_uuid=ebe33f66-57aa-11dc-8c65-0000779fd2ac,print=yes.html (retrieved 27 October 2010).

Haldane, A. (2009) 'Rethinking the financial network', Bank of England Address to the Financial Student Association, Amsterdam, April.

Ho, K. (2009) *Liquidated: An ethnography of Wall Street*, Durham, NC: Duke University Press.

Hughes, J. (2010) 'Fooled again', *Financial Times*, 19 March: 7.

Jackson, T. (2005) 'Live better by consuming less: is there a "double dividend" in sustainable consumption?', *Journal of Industrial Ecology*, 9: 19–36.

James, W. (1981) *The Principles of Psychology*, Cambridge, MA: Harvard University Press.

Jones, S. (2009) 'Of couples and copulas', *Financial Times*, 24 April. Available at: http://xinkaishi.typepad.com/a_new_start/2009/04/ft-of-couples-and-copulas.html (retrieved 27 October 2010).

Kasser, T., Ryan, R.M., Couchman, C.E. and Sheldon, K.M. (2004) 'Materialistic values: their causes and consequences', in T. Kasser and A.D. Kanner (eds) *Psychology and Consumer Culture*, Washington, DC: American Psychological Association.

Keynes, J.M. (2008) *The General Theory of Employment, Interest, and Money*, BN Publishing: www.bnpublishing.net.

Laplanche, J. and Pontalis, J.B. (1973) *The Language of Psychoanalysis*, New York: W.W. Norton.

Lasch, C. (1979) *The Culture of Narcissism*, New York: W.W. Norton.

McDonald, L. (2009) *A Colossal Failure of Common Sense*, Reading, UK: Ebury Press.

Mandelbrot, B. and Hudson, R. (2004) *The (Mis)Behavior of Markets*, New York: Basic Books.

Mead, G.H. (1972) *Mind, Self, and Society: From the standpoint of a social behaviorist*, Chicago: University of Chicago Press.

Morgenson, G. and Story, L. (2009) 'Banks bundled bad debt, bet against it and won', *New York Times*, 24 December.

Morgenson, G. and Story, L. (2010) 'Testy conflict with Goldman helped push A.I.G. to precipice', *New York Times*, 76 February: 1. Online, available at: www.nytimes.com/2010/02/07/business/07goldman.html?pagewanted=print (retrieved 27 October 2010).

Morrison, M. (2009) 'History of the SWOT analysis'. RapidBI's Weblog – OD, L&D. Online, available at: http://rapidbi.wordpress.com/2008/12/29/history-of-the-swot-analysis/ (retrieved 27 October 2010).

Newton, J., Long, S. and Sievers, B. (eds) (2006) *Coaching in Depth: The organizational role analysis method*, London: Karnac.

Peel, Q. (2010) 'Stability not solidarity at root of response to debt crisis', *Financial Times*, 19 March.

Schwartz, N.D. and Dash, E. (2010) 'Banks bet Greece defaults on debt they helped hide', *New York Times*, 25 February. Online, available at: www.nytimes.com/2010/02/25/business/global/25swaps.html?_r=1&dbk (retrieved 28 October 2010).

Sender, H., Guerrera, F. and Tett, G. (2010) 'The hindered haircut', *Financial Times*, 27 January. Online, available at: www.ft.com/cms/s/0/3e18cd5c-0ab2-11df-b35f-00144feabdc0. html (retrieved 27 October 2010).

Simon, H. (1977) *Administrative Behavior*, 4th edn, New York: Free Press.

Stern, S. (2010) 'Danger, men at work', *Financial Times*, 6 February.

Story, L. and Morgenson, G. (2010) 'For Goldman, a bet's stakes keep growing', *New York Times*, 17 April.

Sullivan, H.S. (1953) *The Interpersonal Theory of Psychiatry*, New York: W.W. Norton.

Wachtel, P. (2003) 'Full pockets, empty lives: a psychoanalytic exploration of the contemporary culture of greed', *American Journal of Psychoanalysis*, 63: 102–21.

Waelder, R. (1976) 'The principle of multiple function: observations on overdetermination', in *Psychoanalysis: observation, theory, application. Selected papers of Robert Waelder*, ed. S. Guttman, New York: International Universities Press.

Waterman, R. Jr, Peters, T.J. and Phillips, J.R. (1980) 'Structure is not organization', *Business Horizons*, 23(3): 14–26.

Wilmott, P. (2009) 'Bonus Babies', *New York Times*, 11 February. Online, available at: www.nytimes.com/2009/02/11/opinion/11wilmott.html?_r=1&em=&pagewanted=print (retrieved 27 October 2010).

23 Anti-oedipal dynamics in the sub-prime loan debacle

The case of a study by the Boston Federal Reserve Bank

Howard S. Schwartz

Like most major disasters, the American sub-prime crisis of 2008 had multiple causes. I will look at only one element of this causal matrix, consisting in some psychological dynamics that led to loans being made to people who, it should have been known, would not be able to pay them back. I make no claim that this was the dominant cause of the financial disaster; the question that interests me is not financial but psychological.

I want to explore why what should have been known was not known. My point will be that the psychological configuration within which the loans were made did not recognize, or at least did not take seriously, the kind of information that goes into the calculation of financial risk. Such assessment must be based on an objective analysis of cause and effect, within the context of an agreed framework of rationality. But the psychology within which the loans were made understood their meaning as moral imperatives, and as ends in their own right; the objective analysis of the consequences that would be likely to follow from the granting of the loans was not part of the picture. Moreover, the moralistic analysis gained power because it placed the objective assessment of risk under a moral cloud and made it psychologically insupportable. The irony, of course, is that the moralistic way of seeing things helped to create a situation that, even regarding those who were supposed to be the beneficiaries, was catastrophic, economically and morally, as well.

My main focus will be on an influential study in the period leading up to the financial crisis. This was a study by the Boston branch of the Federal Reserve Bank that was first reported in 1992 (Munnell *et al.* 1996). Perhaps more than any other, it was taken as proof that there was racial discrimination in mortgage lending, and it led to a loosening of the criteria used to assess creditworthiness among black mortgage applicants.

The Boston Fed study

Unlike many previous studies that had reported different rates of loan acceptance by race, this study corrected for standard credit criteria. Using a sample of Boston-area mortgage applications, it found that the standard criteria explained about two-thirds of the difference between white and black, or Hispanic, rejection rates. Even after this correction, however, minorities seemed to be rejected at a rate of 17 percent, as opposed to only 11 percent for whites. This difference, they claimed, must be caused by racism. That conclusion was taken by many as a definitive answer to the question.

For instance, an article in the *Wall Street Journal* ran under the headline 'Boston Fed Finds Racial Discrimination in Mortgage Lending Is Still Widespread' (Thomas 1992). Similarly, the Office of the Comptroller of the Currency is quoted as asserting, 'Definitive – changes the landscape', and Richard F. Syron, president of the Federal Reserve Bank, of Boston said that it '[c]omports with common sense, no more studies needed' (Brimelow and Spencer 1993: 4).

But as more skeptical analysts quickly found out, the study was seriously and egregiously flawed. For example, Day and Liebowitz (1998) reported that the data were replete with glaring errors. In some cases these were errors that should have been noticed by anyone checking over the data, such as negative interest rates. In some cases the data would have been seen to be erroneous by any economist who was paying attention. For example, a mortgage application that indicated in one variable that the mortgage had been rejected, while another variable indicated that it had been sold on the secondary market, would have to be an error. When Day and Liebowitz ran the analyses with the obvious errors removed, the hypotheses of discrimination were not supported.

Another study found that the results were due to outliers. Forty-nine of the seventy banks under study had rejected no minority applicants at all. Two banks were responsible for over half of the rejections. One of these was a minority-owned bank and the other had an extensive minority outreach program (Schweitzer 2009: 56).

The point to be made here is that the discovery of these errors, which any graduate student would have been trained to spot, and which were rapidly found by outside observers, had no impact on the course of the governmental movement that the study was used to support. It was as if the propelling forces were independent of their presumptive analytic base.

A particularly striking example of this disconnect, at the individual level, was offered in *Forbes* magazine by Peter Brimelow and Leslie Spencer (1993). In order to refute the charge that blacks defaulted more, the study intended to take account of comparative default rates. What they found was that there was no relationship between the racial composition of census tracts and the default rates, which indicated to them that black and whites were equally likely to default.

But Brimelow and Spencer, interviewing Alicia H. Munnell, Boston Fed senior vice president and the chief researcher, pointed out that there was a serious flaw in this interpretation of their data. If there had been discrimination resulting in blacks getting loans even though they met the criteria, that would have meant they had been subjected to stricter criteria and therefore that their default rates on approved loans should have been lower. The fact that their default rates were the same meant that the ordinary criteria used for mortgages worked just fine, and the study therefore provided no evidence of discrimination. But consider the following remarkable exchange:

'[That] is a sophisticated point', says Munnell, questioned by Forbes. She agrees that discrimination against blacks should show up in lower, not equal, default rates – discrimination would mean that good black applicants are being unfairly rejected. 'You need that as a confirming piece of evidence. And we don't have it.'

FORBES: 'Did you ever ask the question that if defaults appear to be more or less the same among blacks and whites, that points to mortgage lenders making rational decisions?'

MUNNELL: 'No.'

Munnell does not want to repudiate her study. She tells Forbes, on reflection, that the census data are not good enough and could be 'massaged' further: 'I do believe that discrimination occurs.'

FORBES: 'You have no evidence?'

MUNNELL: 'I do not have evidence.... No one has evidence.'

(Brimelow and Spencer 1993: 4)

But Brimelow and Spencer's point was not sophisticated at all. On the contrary, there could have been nothing more basic. That it had not been anticipated in the study reveals something about the loss of critical functioning in the study's design and analysis.

What is more important is Munnell's statement 'I do believe that discrimination occurs.' For what could that belief have been based on? The study, corrected for the impact of default rates, did not support the conclusion. She admits this, but believes it anyway. This belief, like the 'common sense' that Syron believed was supported, was independent of the study, as we can see from the fact that the undermining of the empirical conclusion was not taken to bear upon it.

This was no small matter. Subsequent to the publication of the study, moves were taken to transform the credit approval criteria to increase the number of minority loans that would be approved. This was most notably accomplished through a mandated relaxation of standards imposed by the Department of Housing and Urban Development on Fannie Mae and Freddie Mac, the 'government-sponsored entities' that bought mortgages from the original lenders (Schweitzer 2009), thereby absolving them of the risk.

The point to be made here is that the proponents and the critics of the view that discrimination was at work were living in two separate, incommensurable worlds. Between these worlds, some facts could be agreed, but the interpretations of these facts were entirely different. I would like to suggest that they were apprehended through different frameworks of meaning. In the absence of an agreed framework of meaning, it was inevitable that one worldview, in this case the view that discrimination was at work, would dominate the other by the mobilization of political power.

The argument I want to put forward is that the outcome of the political clash between these two frameworks was determined by a great deal of psychological weight. The view that the cause of inequality was discrimination was a moralistic view, which brought the other view under moral attack. The alternative view, based on a rational calculation of consequences, could not overcome such an attack because its own premise was undermined. It could not offer defense, but only reason, yet reason itself had come under attack and was not able to defend itself. This points to a difficulty in our society far deeper and more threatening than the financial crisis itself.

In what follows, I will lay out the differences between these two frameworks of meaning. I will try to explain how reason itself comes under attack, and why it cannot defend itself against its moralistic opponent.

I have discussed the dynamics of these two frameworks elsewhere (Schwartz 2003, 2010; Schwartz and Hirschhorn 2009), and will reprise here the rudiments of the perspective, adding elements necessary for this particular purpose. I refer to these dynamics as oedipal and anti-oedipal psychologies.

The oedipal worldview

For psychoanalytic theory, the process of socialization, of how an individual becomes a member of society, is rooted in the Oedipus complex. In the classic formulation, the child begins life in tight connection, boundaryless fusion, with a loving and apparently omnipotent mother. This creates a condition in which the child experiences itself as being the center of a loving world. Freud calls this 'primary narcissism'. But the child experiences this as being disrupted by the father, who has a relationship with the mother that does not revolve around the child.

Here, the father represents external reality, which of course does not revolve around the child. This is known to the father, who builds his role out of his association with external reality, endeavoring to keep it at a distance from the family, maintaining its boundary, so that within the family the intimate manifestations of maternal love can safely operate, and within which he will have earned himself a secure place.

But, according to the classical psychoanalytic account, the child hates him for his intrusion and wants to kill him. Doing so will enable the child to get father out of the picture and resume his fusion with mother. Yet killing father is not in the cards; he is big and powerful and the child is small and weak. What is the child to do? In the paradigmatic case, the alternative chosen is idealization and then introjection. Instead of demonizing the father for his relationship with the mother, the child idealizes him, as someone who has won mother's love, and who can serve as a model for the child's own pursuit of someone like mother. He brings the father into himself, which means developing the capacity to see the world as the father sees it. This gives the terms with which the father justifies his position with mother and rules the child's claim, in this specific incestuous case, invalid. Thus begins the process of internalizing the impersonal rules of society and the associated understandings of reality, codified in the common meanings embedded in language. Lacan refers to this as the symbolic order.

The core to this commonality of meaning is the 'paternal function', which is the capacity to see oneself from a standpoint that does not give us any special place, that does not belong specifically to any of us, and that therefore is available to all of us. I call this 'objective self-consciousness'. I use the word 'objectively', not in the sense of seeing oneself as one actually is, but as an object – that is to say, from the perspective of someone who does not have a special emotional connection with us. It is developed through history, and is constantly under revision.

The objective framework may be said to exist at a number of levels of abstraction. At the highest level we have reason, logic and mathematics, which we may think of as the structure of objectivity. These make possible the development of lower levels of abstraction, including the various laws and norms of society, that can be collectively comprehended, learned, negotiated, applied and revised.

The objective framework is what makes it possible to codify and comprehend the network of exchange relationships that form the structure of society. These are a set of widely accepted interlinked hypothetical propositions, most basically what Gouldner (1960) called the *norm of reciprocity*, of the form 'If A does X, B will do Y.' In such propositions we can place ourselves in either the A position or the B position. This has made it possible for people to be mutually predictable and comprehensible to one another, and to coordinate with each other.

Members of the society understand that other members will use this framework in the design of their own behavior, and hence they are dependent on this regularity. This understanding creates a generalized responsibility to act in accordance with these expectations, whether as norms that hold true for all members of the society, or as roles, which hold true for persons having specific functions. In this way, objectively established regularities are reinforced by moral and ethical motivations, but they are not any less objective for that.

The objective framework is not developed for its own sake. It serves subjective purposes. In the Freudian presentation there is an implicit promise that if one becomes like father, one can have someone like mother. In other words, if you do what you're supposed to do in the objective world, you can attain your own desideratum, in the form of the world revolving around you as it did when you were an infant. Freud refers to this condition as the ego ideal. Hence, the objective framework gives us what we need to accomplish things collectively and cooperatively, while at the same time we each pursue the ego ideal, as we define it.

Now, the ego ideal is never fully realized; the world is not our mother, but objective self-consciousness make it possible to reconsider our behavior and the structure of exchange within which it occurs, and to reconfigure these to better attain the object of our desire. This leads to progress in the way we live our lives. It also makes it possible for us to account for, and to take responsibility for, the fact that we have not attained the ego ideal. It makes it possible for us to accept limitation and imperfection and to cope with frustration, to understand why we cannot have what we want just because we want it. These are perhaps no less important in determining the way we experience life, as we shall see.

All this comes together to form a certain form of meaning that we can call oedipal.

But notice that while something is surely gained in this resolution of the Oedipus complex, something is also lost. What is lost to objectivity is primary narcissism – the sense of one's cosmic importance, of being the center and the meaning of the world that fusion with mother originally meant.

Yet primary narcissism remains within every one of us, and from that perspective the rage against the father, and hence against the social rules and common understandings that he represents, remains as well. This makes possible another form of meaning, which is in a sense the opposite of oedipal meaning, and consists in the rejection of the father and his intrusion into our fusion with mother.

Within this form, the power of father is illegitimate. He has taken mother by force and the rules and understandings through which he justifies his place are only a subterfuge to conceal and further his domination. There is no objectivity, but only the imposition of his subjective will and desire.

It is a lie, in other words, that we are not unique unto ourselves, occupying a special and central place in the universe. Reason, operating as it does through shared understanding that gives no special place to anyone's particular experience, cannot serve to limit our sense of importance, since it is itself based upon that very premise. We do not need to subordinate ourselves to this lie of our insignificance; all we need to do is get rid of the liar. Expel him and his works, and the connection with mother can be restored. Then the infinite power of her love and goodness will make life perfect for us.

Here again a world is structured, but the structure is the mirror image of oedipal meaning. Expel the father, rather than identify with him; undermine his claims to legitimacy, rather than make sense of them. Do this and the perfect world of mother's love will be restored.

This is the basis of 'political correctness'.

Political correctness (PC) operates on the premise that there is no objective reality and hence that the achievements of the father in making reality amenable have been merely the means through which he has stolen mother's love. The ethics of PC are based on identification with those from whom her love has been stolen. The father should be hated for his theft, and the oppressed, which is to say those from whom he has stolen love, should be loved in compensation.

We are talking here about a permanent state of protest against the imposition of the father's order, which is to say order based on common understandings and objective rules (Schwartz 2010). This protest can be the leitmotif of a person's being, and a very different basis of meaning. I will call it anti-oedipal meaning.

What we can see here is a difference of ontology. The structure of the world is fundamentally different in the anti-oedipal worldview than in the oedipal. The oedipal world is indifferent to us as individuals, and structured by objective social rules that apply to all of us. These rules are impersonal and we can hold them provisionally, but we rely on them and we know others will do so as well. This enables us to predict each other's behavior and creates our idea of rationality, based on this shared view of the world. Moreover, we depend on their doing so. A person's goodness or badness is determined by their behavior; it is a function of how they measure up to these rules and accept their responsibility to do so.

In the anti-oedipal world, the basic structural element is the conflict between the *I* (Mead 1934) and the *not-I*. For the individual, the I is not only good, but the basis of all determinations of goodness. Therefore, the not-I is bad. Hence, the basic structural elements are not objective, impersonal rules, but moral conflicts in which good forces contend with bad forces.

These designations of badness and goodness are absolute and cannot be changed by behavior. Good persons can do bad things, but this is because they have been forced to do so by bad forces, and they are therefore exculpated; their goodness has not been called into question.

And these bad forces include those objective, impersonal rules. As we have seen, their premise is that we see ourselves in a way that would apply to anyone. But the premise of the I is that it is unique, and *sui generis*. Nothing else is like it. Thus, what are called objective rules are experienced as not-I, and indeed as an affront to the I. They imply its limitation and subjugation; they represent a kind of death. In the name of life, and righteousness, they are to be destroyed.

It is very obvious that all of this will result in a very different interpretation of the meaning of creditworthiness.

The meaning of creditworthiness in the oedipal and anti-oedipal worldviews

In the oedipal worldview, creditworthiness is not a moral designation but an economic calculation that represents the risk undertaken by someone making a loan. To be sure, whether someone fulfills their obligations may be used to evaluate them morally, but in this case it does not enter into the equation in a moral way. If there were a moral determination at issue, other morally relevant facts would be brought into consideration, such as what the person spent his or her money on. But no such facts are included. Instead, what is included is that, given certain empirically determinable circumstances, a certain percentage of people will not repay their loans. And this is entered into the equation, without moral commentary, as another objective fact.

By contrast, in the anti-oedipal worldview, creditworthiness is an entirely moral concept. If someone is a member of a group that is understood as having been victimized by the father, that person is morally entitled to restitution. This often goes by the name of 'social justice'. As we saw, in the oedipal worldview, moral considerations enter in a non-moral way. By contrast, within the anti-oedipal worldview, economic factors enter in, but in a non-objective way. When data can be used to support the moral case, they are mobilized and employed; when they cannot, they are ignored or distorted until they do. That is the reason the economic calculations brought forward in the Boston Fed study could be so easily corrupted and abused, and why there was so little critical scrutiny applied to them.

Closing the gap

The claim that the anti-oedipal worldview was responsible for the abuse of the research process in the Boston Fed study calls for further demonstration. For that purpose, I will turn to a guidebook called *Closing the Gap: A guide to equal opportunity lending*, produced by the Federal Reserve Bank of Boston (1993) in the aftermath of the 1992 study, and intended to enunciate the conclusions to be drawn from it. According to Liebowitz (2008), it was clearly intended to be taken as speaking for the Federal Reserve System.

Closing the Gap manifests the tension between the oedipal and anti-oedipal views, but ultimately the former is subordinate to the latter. A look at the way their position was structured in this publication reveals much about the way this view of the world played out in the bank's program recommendations. Two considerations are particularly significant.

In the first place, in accordance with the morality play ontology that structures the anti-oedipal worldview, it denies the independent validity of objective economic considerations, and indeed redefines them as oppressive elements, essentially as racist. Second, it idealizes the minority groups in whose interest, supposedly, the loosening of credit standards is going to be accomplished. What it is essentially doing, therefore, is redefining the concept of creditworthiness in moral terms: taking the previous refusal of credit as a moral assault, which the loan is intended to rectify.

The undermining of objectivity

The subordination is actually rather explicit, and is evoked in a number of ways. For one thing, *Closing the Gap* provides sidebars that lay out the thrust of the bank's position by citing authorities. For example, it quotes Lawrence B. Lindsey, identified as 'Member, Board of Governors of the Federal Reserve System', as saying, 'The regulatory issues in the 1990s will not be limited to safety and soundness, but will increasingly emphasize fairness: whether or not banks are fulfilling the needs of their communities.' Notice that the universality of application is not seen here as 'fulfilling the needs of their communities', which the oedipal framework would expect. Rather, this is set in opposition to something called 'fairness', which must mean that those 'communities' represent specific groups whose interests have been subordinated in the past and which now, in the interest of goodness, should be furthered. Who these specific communities are is defined in another sidebar:

> Editors' Note: A 1992 study of mortgage lending by the Federal Reserve Bank of Boston analyzed the effects of race on denial rates for blacks and Hispanics in the Boston metropolitan area. However, around the country, members of other racial and ethnic groups may also experience credit discrimination. For editorial purposes, it was necessary to select a single term to refer to underserved borrowers. In this publication, the terms 'minority'

or 'minority group' are used to refer to borrowers, including blacks and Hispanics, who are not members of the dominant culture in a particular lending area.

And it is clear that there is muscle behind this program. Here is another sidebar:

> **Did You Know?** Failure to comply with the Equal Credit Opportunity Act or Regulation B can subject a financial institution to civil liability for actual and punitive damages in individual or class actions. Liability for punitive damages can be as much as $10,000 in individual actions and the lesser of $500,000 or 1 percent of the creditor's net worth in class actions.

The seriousness of these penalties must be taken into consideration in order to understand the subordination of objectivity to this moral program, which is accomplished in other, more indirect ways. Most importantly, the meaning of the term 'discrimination' becomes indeterminate and impossible to pin down, but loses none of the opprobrium or the threat attached to it.

Thus, the authors acknowledge that 'discrimination' may be of three types:

> For the purposes of this publication, we distinguish among three types of discrimination: overt, intentional discrimination; subtle, deliberate discrimination; and unintentional discrimination.

They acknowledge that 'Overt discrimination in mortgage lending is rarely seen today.'

> Discrimination is more likely to be subtle, reflected in the failure to market loan products to potential minority customers and the failure of lenders to hire and promote staff from racial and ethnic minority groups.

Students of organizations will understand that, the penalties for 'discrimination' being as serious as they are, a bit of preemptive selective hiring and promotion will be useful as a defense, and will therefore be prudent, whether or not it serves a rational business purpose. Notice, however, that this has not been said. A policy has been moved along here by innuendo, not through conscious reason, and in this regard may again be said to be an undermining of the objective.

But for present purposes, what is most interesting is the third form of 'discrimination':

> Unintentional discrimination may be observed when a lender's underwriting policies contain arbitrary or outdated criteria that effectively disqualify many urban or lower-income minority applicants.

What can 'arbitrary' and 'outdated' mean here? The term 'arbitrary' could mean simply that there is no reason for the criteria, but any bank would not need to be told this. In the oedipal view, rules are supposed to be specifically crafted to accomplish a purpose, and in that sense are not arbitrary at all.

It is the sense of the instrumental character of the rules – their purpose in enabling people to gain their objectives through behavior that makes sense for that purpose – that is missing here.

The point is that within the anti-oedipal framework, the gap between the person and the ego ideal has been rendered anomalous. There is and can be no good reason why one simply cannot do as one wants and be loved for it. The idea that one must become like father has revealed itself as paternal propaganda. Instead of being the route to the ego ideal, the paternal legacy of rules is seen as what is blocking the enjoyment of maternal embrace.

The idea that these rules are the product of objective observation and rational utilitarian calculation is no longer present. Within the anti-oedipal worldview those considerations are not recognized. But deprived of that rationale, such rules are simply expressions of the dominant culture – one way of doing things, of no distinctive merit, rather than another. That is the sense in which they are seen as arbitrary here.

In the absence of any more substantive critique, the other term of opprobrium, 'outdated criteria', can only mean those criteria that the times, moved by whatever political and moralizing currents prevail, now call for abandoning. Here again, what is missing is the idea that the rules have a purpose that is better furthered by one set of rules than another, and that changes in rules are the result of rational consideration of which rules are more likely to attain that purpose.

What it is critical to see here is that reason counts for nothing in these matters, and standing on the ground of reason can only lead to trouble. And this is in a matter where getting a judgment wrong can mean heavy fines and opprobrium. The next paragraph spells out what must follow from this:

> While the banking industry is not expected to cure the nation's social and racial ills, lenders do have a specific legal responsibility to ensure that negative perceptions, attitudes, and prejudices do not systematically affect the fair and even-handed distribution of credit in our society. Fair lending must be an integral part of a financial institution's business plan.

Thus, insofar as lending is based on rational criteria, those criteria are redefined, when they stand in the way of political and moral currents, as 'negative perceptions, attitudes, and prejudices'. Indeed, it is not going too far to say that skepticism about the unlikelihood of a person with a poor history of loan repayment paying their loan would be classified as prejudice under these designations.

This has much to do with the way political correctness was able to carry the day in the issue of relaxing lending criteria. It set rational justification of the rules, based on objective considerations, as deeply immoral and, potentially, dangerously illegal. Discrimination could have been anything. It had nothing to do with intent, and could have represented criteria that had, for reasons that could not have been foreseen or predicted, come to be seen as 'outdated' or 'arbitrary'. But it was no less punishable for that. Few could have been expected to stand in the face of such potential criticism, and these low expectations were not, in the event, exceeded.

Idealization of the oppressed

The anti-oedipal worldview is structured by the tension between the forces of badness, represented by the father, whose rules are arbitrary and self-serving, and the oppressed, who represent the forces of goodness. The maternal forces operate here as love for the oppressed. In the oedipal worldview the father was conceived to have the mother's love, and that is the sense in which he was idealized. In the anti-oedipal view it is the oppressed who have the mother's love, and hence it is they who are idealized.

The anti-oedipal worldview preserves and defends the individual's uniqueness and spontaneity. Idealization takes the form of the belief that whatever the idealized one naturally and spontaneously does is lovable. Mother's love attaches to him because he is who he is. The proper response to him, therefore, is to see him in the best possible light. Negative behavior can be acknowledged here, but it must be attributed to forces outside of his control: his environment, discrimination, and so on. Anything but unconditional love, including judgments made on the basis of universalistic criteria, is seen as bad: bigotry, prejudice and the like.

Idealization of the oppressed implies demonization of anything that would deny their absolute uniqueness and impinge on their spontaneity. All rules do that; they are therefore anathema and should be undermined. That can be seen in the form of the treatment of exceptions to the rules of creditworthiness.

These are of critical importance because of the fact that the crisis was caused by people being unable to pay the mortgages they were awarded under the loosened criteria, which took the form of authorizing and mandating exceptions to the rules that would otherwise have been applied. The exceptions, that is to say, were a cause of the crisis.

In evaluating their use, we have the benefit of hindsight. We are not looking at them to ascertain their validity; they were not valid. Rather, what is important is to understand how that invalidity entered into the system.

The main point is that these exceptions were not treated as exceptions, but as the bases of policy in their own right. For example:

> Even the most determined lending institution will have difficulty cultivating business from minority customers if its underwriting standards contain arbitrary or unreasonable measures of creditworthiness.
>
> Consistency in evaluating loan applications is also critical to ensuring fair treatment. Since many mortgage applicants who are approved do not meet every underwriting guideline, lending policies should have mechanisms that define and monitor the use of compensating factors to ensure that they are applied consistently, without regard to race or ethnicity.

But the matter of consistency must be seen as a term of art, since the exceptions became a major factor in evaluating loan applications only when the move was made to maximize lending to minorities. Consistency can only mean that if an exception has been made for anybody, on a certain basis, that basis should be available to everybody. In this way, the exception becomes the rule.

Again, they say:

> Special care should be taken to ensure that standards are appropriate to the economic culture of urban, lower-income, and nontraditional consumers.

This refers back to the idea that the choice of cultures, and hence of the rules they follow, is arbitrary. This again says something about exceptions, in the form of difference from instrumental norms, determining the thrust of policy.

Moreover, such policies should be made known to minority mortgage applicants:

> To ensure fair treatment, it is important that the lending institution document its policies and practices regarding acceptable compensating factors. If an institution permits flexibility in applying underwriting standards, it must do so consistently. Management should consider developing a checklist for loan production staff to ensure that all allowable compensating factors are requested of the borrower (such as explanations of late debt payments or a demonstrated ability to carry high housing costs). The checklist will also make loan production staff aware of the institution's commitment to serving borrowers who may not meet traditional underwriting standards.
>
> Informed borrowers are more likely to ask loan production staff about ways to enhance their applications. Thus, another way to encourage consistent treatment is by clearly communicating the institution's lending policies and underwriting standards to the public.

If we look at the substance of these exceptions, the idea that they have been transformed into policy is again manifest:

> In reviewing past credit problems, lenders should be willing to consider extenuating circumstances. For lower-income applicants in particular, unforeseen expenses can have a disproportionate effect on an otherwise positive credit record. In these instances, paying off past bad debts or establishing a regular repayment schedule with creditors may demonstrate a willingness and ability to resolve debts.

Part of the application of the program has become a mandated optimism about the willingness and ability of the applicant to repay the loan. Thus, simply establishing a payment schedule is supposed, by itself, to demonstrate such willingness and ability. Similarly:

Successful participation in credit counseling or buyer education programs is another way that applicants can demonstrate an ability to manage their debts responsibly.

Summary and conclusion

In the oedipal view, the function of the lending institution is to connect lender and borrower in a way that benefits both of them. The rules of creditworthiness function to ensure that mutuality of benefit, based on the premise that borrower and lender will operate within an objective framework of shared normative and legal understanding.

Thus, in the oedipal worldview, based on objective rules of exchange, the idea that a loan is to be repaid is part of the definition of a loan; in the anti-oedipal worldview, it is not.

In the anti-oedipal worldview a loan is an expression of love, existing by itself and without regard to consequences. In the final analysis, the function of the lending institution is to express love of the oppressed by giving them money, calling these gifts loans, and to look for ways in which this can be accomplished. The rules of mutual understanding are not seen as a framework that ensures mutual benefit and minimizes risk, but as obstacles, and every care is undertaken to find ways around them. Characteristics of the lender that have been established to minimize risk are seen as violations of culture and the imposition of alien understandings. They are replaced by an idealization, which effectively assumes that borrowers should be seen in the most favorable light. The loan is to be made not if certain qualifications are passed, but if circumstances can be imagined in which the application of the qualifications may be considered not fair. Indeed, skepticism about this reversal may be seen as representing a bigoted attitude that itself constitutes discrimination.

But the result we have seen follows from the premise. The anti-oedipal worldview is based on the assumption that objective reality does not exist and that the rules developed to take it into account are impositions and agencies of aggression. Yet there is an external world, and violation of the prudential rules that keep us safe cannot be without consequences, for the borrower as much as for the lender.

The anti-oedipal framework does not recognize rules, but only exceptions to rules. In accordance with the premise that identifies the individual with his uniqueness, exceptions are supposed to replace rules as the organizing principle of society. But this would be an impossibility. Exceptions are exceptions to rules; there cannot be exceptions unless there are rules.

The anti-oedipal framework offers itself as an alternative form of social organization, but it undermines itself. What it presses towards is not an alternative form of social organization, but chaos. This is a fact that, in our anti-oedipal times, needs to be taken seriously.

References

Brimelow, P. and Spencer, L. (1993) 'The hidden clue', *Forbes*, 4 January.

Day, T.E. and Liebowitz, S.J. (1998) 'Mortgage lending to minorities: where's the bias?' *Economic Inquiry*, January: 1–27.

Gouldner, A.W. (1960) 'The norm of reciprocity: a preliminary statement', *American Sociological Review*, 25: 161–78.

Liebowitz, S. (2008) 'Statement of Stan Liebowitz before the House Subcommittee on the Constitution, Civil Rights, and Civil Liberties Hearing on Enforcement of the Fair Housing Act of 1968', 12 June.

Mead, G.H. (1934) *Mind, Self, and Society* Chicago: University of Chicago Press

Munnell, A.H., Browne, L.E., McEneaney, J. and Tootell, G.M.B. (1996) 'Mortgage lending in Boston: interpreting HMDA data', *American Economic Review*, 86(1): 25–53.

Schwartz, H.S. (2003) *The Revolt of the Primitive: An inquiry into the roots of political correctness and primitive feminism*, Piscataway, NJ: Transaction.

Schwartz, H.S. (2010) *Society against Itself: Political correctness and organizational self-destruction*, London: Karnac.

Schwartz, H.S. and Hirschhorn, L. (2009) 'Organization and meaning: a multilevel psychoanalytic treatment of the Jayson Blair scandal at *The New York Times*', *International Journal of Organization Theory and Behavior*, 12(3): 441–74

Schweitzer, P. (2009) *Architects of Ruin*, New York: HarperCollins.

Thomas, P. (1992) 'Boston Fed finds racial discrimination in mortgage lending is still widespread', *Wall Street Journal*, 9 October: A3.

24 Capitalist imperatives and the democratic capacities' constraint

An examination of the interface of modern capitalist markets with the world's largest worker-owned corporation, the Mondragon Corporation of Spain

Laura Yu

Introduction

This chapter contributes to a socioanalytic understanding of capitalist imperatives by exploring the interface of market pressures and the democratic participatory environment of the world's largest worker cooperative: the Mondragon Corporation of Spain. In recent decades, Mondragon's expanding growth and market interactions have challenged its important organizational balance between achieving competitiveness in the global market and maintaining the centrality of workplace democracy. The dynamics of this contentious balance are explored through application of a framework called the 'democratic capacities' constraint' to several examples of how formal policies developed to support the democratic environment have shifted to allow the organization to become increasingly supportive of market competitiveness. As a means to look deeper into how and why market imperatives propel these shifts at Mondragon, a socioanalytic perspective is utilized to shed a new light on the effects of market pressures on the organization. In particular, a focus on how the anxiety caused by this organizational tension may be a force at play in perpetuating these shifts highlights both the difficulty of, and potential strategies for, maintaining the integrity of the democratic workplace at Mondragon and beyond.

Balancing market competitiveness and a democratic participatory environment at Mondragon

Founded in 1956 in the Basque region of Spain, the Mondragon Corporation is a for-profit, business-based socioeconomic initiative that was developed with a focus on workplace democracy and maintaining a healthy democratic participatory environment (Mondragon Corporation n.d.). Mondragon was founded by a Catholic priest named José María Arizmendiarrieta, known as Arizmendi, whose experiences living through the Spanish Civil War and later witnessing the destruction brought by World War II inspired him to found the cooperatives as means to 'create a better society, at least in part, through the way we do work together' (Cheney 2002: 38). Arizmendi's beliefs in what a successful, sustainable cooperative needed were shaped through his study of the history and experiences of different cooperatives around the world. One key belief was that the cooperative would need to engage with the market while protecting organizational values and integrity – in other words, to 'participate in, yet be somewhat buffered from market forces' (ibid.: 40). This desired balance was also described as creating a 'third way' between 'individualistic capitalism and soulless collectivism' (as quoted in Whyte and Whyte 1988: 237). While some of Arizmendi's writings demonstrate an obvious distaste for the capitalist system, referring to it as a 'social monstrosity' and as 'fueled only by egotistical and material desires' (as quoted by Whyte and Whyte 1988: 238), Mondragon's founder also acknowledged that 'co-operativism is not to do the opposite of capitalism' and it cannot afford to turn a blind eye to the useful features of capitalism – especially its efficiency (ibid.: 238).

Mondragon has been upheld both as a triumph that represents a future for society (e.g. MacLeod 1997; Morrison 1991; Herrera 2002) and as a 'myth' that does not represent significant differences from a capitalist firm (e.g. Kasmir 1996; GEO 1996), and many shades in between. The following brief overview illustrates that Mondragon represents neither a perfect model for the future nor a failure in its commitment to workplace democracy, but is truly an organization struggling with its mission to maintain a 'third way'. Mondragon's success has been widely applauded with regard to both its commitment to workplace democracy and its financial success. Over its more than fifty-year history, Mondragon has grown from a small manufacturing cooperative to a group of 256 subcompanies and bodies that produce a wide variety of goods; from machine tools to elevators to household appliances. With over 90,000 employees and annual revenues of over €16.7 billion, this growth has been stunning (Mondragon Annual Report 2008). In addition to its financial success, Mondragon has also been praised for its high productivity levels, which have been related to its commitment to workplace democracy (e.g. Mondragon Corporation n.d.; Jackall and Levin 1984). At Mondragon, democratic participation 'has been, is, and will continue to be the determining factor in the establishment of all institutionalized policies and practices' (Herrera 2004: 59). Mondragon's worker-owners hold substantial decision-making power in relation to important changes or additions to Mondragon's institutionalized procedures. Central to this is the structure of the supreme decision-making body of Mondragon, the General Assembly, which requires participation in decision making based on 'one person, one vote'.

While the elective process is a key factor in maintaining workplace democracy, Mondragon's founder recognized that democracy could not be limited to the 'formalities and administrative expedients of the elective process' and that strong support of the democratic organization requires many institutionalized financial, educational and social procedures and substructures (Arizmendi 1984 as quoted in Whyte and Whyte 1988: 239). The health of the democratic participatory environment at Mondragon has been further supported through the development and maintenance of its Basic Cooperative Principles, which are central both to its organizational model and to its identity (Mondragon Corporation n.d.). These ten Principles (in bold) and their relational structure are described on the Mondragon Corporation's website as follows:

> The core is occupied by **Education** as the basic mainstream principle that feeds and feeds off all the others, and the **Sovereignty of Labor**, which is shielded by the other five principles of an internal nature in each individual cooperative: **Instrumental and Subordinated Nature of Capital, Democratic Organization, Open Admission, Participation in Management** and wage **Solidarity**. The outer ring features the three principles that are related to the cooperatives external projection: **Inter-Cooperation, Social Transformation** and **Universal Nature**.
>
> (ibid.)

Several of these Basic Cooperative Principles and examples of the structures that have been developed to support them will be examined in this chapter. However, as will also be shown, these essential support structures have been eroded in recent decades through an increasing shift of focus towards market competitiveness. This shift has been called a 'profound organizational transformation' at Mondragon, where the very meaning of participation has changed (Cheney 2002: 154).

In the key text examining the impact of capitalist market forces on Mondragon, *Values at Work*, author George Cheney finds that Mondragon has experienced overall declines in participatory decision making (2002: 148). More specifically, Cheney describes a fundamental shift away from a worker-owner form of participation to an external, customer-centric form of participation which he refers to as the 'marketization' of employee participation (ibid.: 34). This shift is correlated to Mondragon's increasing competitive expansion over the decades: growing from a local market, to a Spanish market to a European and global market (Cheney 1997: 73). Market pressures especially increased since the 1986 admission of Spain to the European Union and the 1992 reduction of trade barriers in the Union (Cheney 2002: 41). This increasing expansion and competition in the global market has increasingly challenged Mondragon in its ability to maintain its democratic environment (Cheney 2002; Gunn 2000; Errasti *et al.* 2003). Certainly, there are pressures on all organizations to maintain certain key values in relation to market pressures, yet for Mondragon 'the challenge of maintaining cooperative values in a corporate context is one of its greatest preoccupations' (Cheney 2002: 11).

Capitalist imperatives and the democratic capacities' constraint

In order to further lay the foundation of this chapter and to build understanding of what the capitalist imperatives are and why they exist, a break away from common conceptions of capitalism is necessary. While common definitions of capitalist markets connote opportunity and choice, others have defined capitalism's unique imperatives of accumulation and profit maximization as detrimental to a healthy functioning democracy (for example, see Bowles and Gintis 1987; Bowles *et al.* 1993; Wood 2005).

Ellen Meiksins Woods' *The Origin of Capitalism* (2002) explores how the emergence of capitalism brought forth a unique combination of imperatives, including competition, accumulation, profit maximization and increasing labor productivity. She characterizes these as requirements to interact with the market for the basic means of social and material life. This tendency under capitalism to privilege the profit motive over a social motive is explained by Karl Polanyi in *The Great Transformation* as 'mean[ing] no less than the running of society as an adjunct to the market. Instead of economy being embedded in social relations, social relations are embedded in the economic system' (1944: 57).

From this perspective a particular concern for organizations committed to workplace democracy like Mondragon is how the characteristics of the capitalist division of labor tend to promote the opposite traits required of a democratic culture by the way they 'concentrate information, information processing and decision-making skills' for an elite group and promote a sense of political ineffectiveness as well as discrimination for a majority of people (Bowles and Gintis 1987: 133; also see Solomon and McChesney 1993). Further argued is that while democracy requires insuring maximum participation by a majority of persons, capitalism requires minimal participation by the majority of persons because of the profit-maximizing drive (Bowles and Gintis 1976: 54, 68–103). These imperative pressures of capitalist markets have been held in check by government and non-governmental laws and regulations that protect our rights (e.g. Michelman 1994). However, even when regulations are present and enforced, to protect social, political and environmental rights, history has shown that the capitalist imperatives of ever-increasing profits can be difficult to constrict. In this relationship, Polanyi illuminates an interesting flaw in the capitalist logic: the very regulations that must be put in place to harness the more detrimental compulsions of capitalism are 'incompatible with the self-regulation of the market, and thus with the [capitalist] market system itself' (1944: 130).

While the preceding discussion provides a very simplified overview of some of the unique challenges of capitalist imperatives in relation to democratic processes, it provides a helpful framework for understanding the tension between market forces and Mondragon's democratic environment. This framework is further developed in applying and expanding the concept of the *democratic capacities' constraint*, as first conceived by Bowles *et al.* in *Markets and Democracy* (1993: 31). In the authors' conception the requirements of the democratic process – specifically, training members in the functions of participatory governance – can constrain the competitiveness of the democratic firm in relation to its capitalist firm counterparts (ibid.). While the authors limit their definition of the *democratic capacities' constraint* to the aspects of reduced competitive advantage due to the requirements of developing and training members in the functions of participatory governance (ibid.), in the following exploration of some of the changes at Mondragon in recent decades, the concept is extended.

Mondragon's shift toward greater market competitiveness has been marked by a wide variety of changes in policy and practice. Some examples include increasing numbers of temporary (non-member, non-voting) workers (Kasmir 1996: 158); the growing size of the cooperatives, adding to the real and perceived distance between worker-owners and management; and the increasing numbers of joint ventures between the individual cooperatives and non-cooperative firms (Cheney 2002: 71–5). In 1991, Mondragon even saw a name change: from the 'Mondragon Cooperative Group' to the 'Mondragon Cooperative Corporation' (ibid.: 49). Returning to the point emphasized by Mondragon's founder that democracy must be supported beyond the elective process and equally support institutionalized financial, educational and social substructures to be effective; the next section looks more in depth at examples of institutionalized processes and policies from each of these three areas. These are: changes in the role of education, the expansion of the wage ratio (a set ratio of pay between lowest- and highest-paid workers) and the diminishing role of the Social Councils (advisory bodies representing the worker-owners).

Role of education

The importance attached to education and training has been a key foundational value at Mondragon, rooted in the founders' belief in education as key to human development, progress and maintaining the democratization of power (Mondragon Corporation n.d.; Whyte and Whyte 1988: 240). Education's role as a key value is visible through its central position within the Basic Cooperative Value structure at Mondragon (Mondragon Corporation n.d.). The role of education has extended beyond formal education, such as that provided by the university faculties and professional schools, to lifelong training initiatives that are specifically designed to build the skills needed for democratic participation. Emphasis has also been placed on assuring that quality education and information is provided in order to continually improve the worker-owners' ability to participate effectively in decision making (Herrera 2004; Toth 1995). Mondragon has also supported education through extensive investment in formal education and its structuring of the worker councils, which actively involve, train and engage worker-owners in the range of managerial procedures from strategic planning to development activities, and in decision making (Toth 1995).

Shifts in the role of education

The past decade has seen many changes at Mondragon in regard to the way it dedicates time and resources toward education. In particular, Cheney observed that while the philosophical social and practical aspects of training are still present, they are taking a back seat to financial, technical and job-specific training (2002: 134–5). Here the democratic capacities' constraint can be applied in its original conception. The time and resources required to develop a workforce that is educated in democratic decision-making process as well as the critical thinking skills needed to review and debate policy changes can be considerable, and therefore prohibitive of the democratic organization's ability to compete with a capitalist firm (Bowles *et al.* 1993). As the success of the cooperative model requires a central commitment both to human development and to the development of effective communication skills to support the democratic process (e.g. MacLeod 1997: 82), significant departure from the support of this emphasis on the role of education threatens to erode the quality of the democratic environment.

Role of capital

The role of capital as subordinate to the social well-being of the worker-owners of Mondragon is also a key Basic Cooperative Principle. This principle translates into practice at Mondragon via democratic, direct participation by worker-owners in both organizational and financial management. This 'people over profit' principle has been a driving value in the development of some of Mondragon's most distinguishing policies. Perhaps the most notable example of this policy in action is that the primary objective of the cooperatives is to create jobs (Schweickart 2002: 68; Whyte and Whyte 1988: 70). Another striking example of this principle is in the policy that half of all surplus profits are allocated to a 'social fund' in the central bank for retirement, medical, social security and unemployment benefits while the remaining half is allocated for investments such as new start-ups, research and development, and community infrastructure (Mondragon Corporation n.d.; Carrier n.d.). Yet another of Mondragon's unique financial policies and an important support of the democratic environment is that of Wage Solidarity. Wage Solidarity is upheld through a structure of democratically agreed-upon wage ratios between the worker-owners at the top of the pay scale (such as executives) and those who make the minimum wage on the pay scale (such as factory workers). Wage Solidarity for many years meant that the top management of the cooperatives could only make a wage three times as much as the least qualified of the worker-owners. While today this ratio ranges from 3:1 to 9:1 in some cooperatives, with an average of 5:1, these ratios are still far below the ratios represented by some capitalist firms, which can get as high as 400:1 (Herrera 2004). The relationship between equitable pay policies such as Wage Solidarity and democratic participation appears to be symbiotic. While employee-owned and -managed organizations have been shown to more equally distribute income, wealth, power, prestige and privilege as compared with capitalist counterparts (Onaran 1992: 45), Wage Solidarity is also viewed as a critical component in maintaining the cohesiveness of the worker-owners. A positive relationship between greater perceptions of pay equity and participation in decision making in the cooperatives has been linked (Rhodes and Steers 1981).

Shifts in the wage solidarity policy

A 1991 change to the Wage Solidarity policy at Mondragon, which linked some top managers' salaries to 70 percent of the global market value, was met with criticism by some worker-owners concerned about the impact on organizational trust and internal solidarity (Cheney 2002: 134). While management sees more competitive wages as essential to remaining competitive in the market, the allocation of material benefits is also core to worker-owner perceptions of fairness in the organization (ibid.: 134). Here, an application of the democratic capacities' constraint can be broadened to include the issue of competitiveness in retaining top talent in non-capitalist firms. While Mondragon's Wage Solidarity structure remains largely intact, concerns expressed by worker-owners over these changes have highlighted the question as to how far policies essential to the quality of democratic participation can be compromised in the name of increased competition in the market.

Role of social structures and policies

While there are many examples in the broad category of social substructures that support the democratic environment at Mondragon, one that stands out in the literature is a unique social innovation of the cooperatives called the Social Council. According to the Mondragon Corporation website, the Social Council acts as an advisory and consultative body in representing the worker-owners as a whole before the authorities of the cooperative. Social Council members are elected based on areas of activity and how many members a cooperative has. Official functions include providing advice, information, negotiation and social monitoring. A worker-owner summed it up as follows:

> Essentially, while the central Social Council does not make decisions, it can have considerable influence. When it cannot find agreement to resolve concerns with the organs of government, it can bring the issue to the General Assembly where sometimes it has won, other times it has lost.
>
> (Whyte and Whyte 1988: 134)

In their book *Making Mondragon*, authors Whyte and Whyte put forward a broader interpretation of the Social Council's role as complementary to the role of the Governing Council: The Governing Council is designed to represent the members as co-owners, and the Social Councils are designed to represent the interests of members in the role of worker (1988: 213–14). Cheney brings an understanding of the role of the Social Council similar to that of Whyte and Whyte, though he specifies the Social Council's explicit 'concern for safety, hygiene, remuneration, and personnel issues' (Cheney 2002: 60). An example of the Social Council in action helps to further illustrate how its role can be used to represent the interests of worker-owners. When worker-owners at the Ulgor Cooperative were presented with plans to update a refrigerator assembly line, some worker-owners objected that the engineers had drafted the plan without considering or changing the dehumanizing characteristics of the conveyor-belt assembly line. The feedback from the Social Council resulted in the design team redrawing the plans to make them more acceptable (Whyte and Whyte 1988: 211).

Shifts and struggles in the role of the Social Council

Again, as with the examples of financial and education policies and practices at Mondragon, the unique and critical role of the Social Council has shifted over the years. In fact, the role of the Social Council at Mondragon seems to have a long history of tension and flux. While it started out with a purpose similar to that of a union in regard to the issues it addressed at the cooperatives, during a difficult period of economic adjustment for the cooperatives in 1979 and 1980, some said that the Social Councils went beyond their legitimate function as an advisory body by acting more like a union (Whyte and Whyte 1988: 38–41). However, in Cheney's analysis of Mondragon's commitment to democratic participation, he finds that many of the cooperatives have increasingly neglected the Social Councils' role altogether (2002: 133). As a result, many worker-owners have developed a negative view of the Social Councils' role and effectiveness. One worker-owner explained it as 'like a trap from which we cannot escape: no one takes the social council seriously, so it never has the chance to get better' (ibid.: 60). Some members also shared the view that the Social Council has no power and simply 'rubber-stamps' the decisions of management, or that members feel uncomfortable challenging management through the Council (Whyte and Whyte 1988: 213). Again, the democratic capacities' constraint can be applied and expanded. Here, a technical explanation for the diminishing role of the Social Council may be related to the notion that the quickening pace of work constrains the time available for deliberations important to the democratic environment (Cheney 2002: 74–5). In other words, because time and resources are finite, Mondragon's dual commitment to democratic participation and competitiveness in the open market may at times condense down into balancing sacrifices: either some competitive advantage can be gained or some of the time and resources to support its participatory environment, such as meaningful time in the Social Council, must be sacrificed.

The framework of the democratic capacities' constraint has been broadened to lend insight behind the shifts in Mondragon's institutionalized policies and procedures that enable its increased market competitiveness while also providing some insight into how capitalist imperatives may be at play in propelling these shifts. The specific issues identified of (1) limited time and resources to dedicate to the education of worker-owners in democratic participatory processes, (2) the competitiveness of wages to attract top talent to the organization, and (3) time and role conflicts associated with fully engaging in important democratic deliberations and decision-making in the Social Council, have provided greater technical understanding of how the 'the trend toward greater reliance on markets of the past two decades has made it more difficult for initiatives in workplace democracy to survive' (Gunn 2000: 448; see also Cheney 2002). The technical reasoning for these shifts is often attributed to issues of financial integrity and even survival of the organization. Some managers have expressed concern that the competitiveness of the organization is a direct matter of organizational survival (Cheney 1997: 77–8); while some worker-owners have described the rising market pressures over recent decades as presenting the need to 'grow or die' (Cheney 2002: 69). While it is true that increasing global competitive pressures have resulted in a quickening pace of work and a decrease in the time available for democratic deliberations for some cooperatives (Cheney 2002: 74–5), beyond these technical reasons for the 'profound organizational transformation' there seems to be more going on below the surface.

The effects of tension and stress at Mondragon and recommendations for moving forward

As the tension between social and economic values has intensified over recent decades, along with the conscious or unconscious levels of anxiety and stress; another requirement for maintaining a democratic participatory environment has gained importance: a certain level of emotional development of the organization members. As described by Donald W. Winnicott, a 'true democracy' requires 'sufficient maturity in the emotional development of a sufficient proportion of the individuals that comprise it for there to exist an innate tendency toward the creation and re-creation and maintenance of the democratic machinery' (1965/1990: 157). Over the years, Mondragon has been often recognized for such 'emotionally mature' traits as its ability to critique and modify its own experience (Cheney 2002: 62), its flexibility and 'willingness to abandon fixed ways for dealing with particular situations' (Whyte and Whyte 1988: 234), even to 'advance towards the edge of Chaos [to] a greater creativity – and in consequence a greater adaptability' (Lizarralde 2009: 36). Despite these examples of 'emotionally mature' traits on the part of the worker-owners of Mondragon, there is also an interesting gap in the literature in this area. There seems to be a disconnection in relating the 'ground-level' pressures and shifts experienced in the organization to the overarching conflict inherent in the organizational structure to 'participate in, yet be somewhat buffered from market forces' or to maintain a 'third way' (as quoted in Whyte and Whyte 1988: 237). Perhaps the silence around the connection between the shift within the organization and the broader task of balancing market pressures and social interests reflects an unconscious anxiety towards facing this connection. As the examples in the preceding section demonstrated, there is often no easy way to 'remedy' these conflicts without sacrificing either Mondragon's competitiveness in the global market or its organizational values as embodied in the Basic Cooperative Principles – both of which are critical to the organization's goals. In order to facilitate a deeper exploration into this absence, an application of a socioanalytic lens may provide a new way to understand and manage these tensions and dynamics.

On a very basic level, socioanalytic theory tells us that when a group's stress level rises, there is an associated increase toward the tendency to dispel this stress and anxiety (Bion 1961). As described in Wilfred R. Bion's *Experiences in Groups* (ibid.), a productive *Work Group* (W) becomes a *Basic Assumption* (Ba) group as a means of avoiding stress and anxiety (momentarily or indefinitely) that is associated with difficult key tasks. A W group is in action when a group is able to face, manage and learn from the anxiety that inevitably rises out of working together on the work task at hand (ibid.). Groups can have aspects of both modes operating at the same time, or swing rapidly from one mode to another. For example, when a W group feels that anxiety and stress have risen too much, the group can either 'hold' and manage the stress in order to stay with its work task or may defer into a Work Avoidance or Ba group mode (ibid.).

In applying these concepts to the example of Mondragon, an interesting hypothesis is illuminated. As the 'Work' of collaboratively participating in the management of the organization becomes increasingly stressful, Mondragon's worker-owners may be unconsciously employing a 'Basic Assumption' work avoidance tactic to relieve this stress. As noted above, there seems to be a missing dialogue regarding the conflicting pressures and resulting shifts experienced in the organization to the broader conflict inherent in the organizational structure to maintain (or find) a 'third way'. As these conflicts related to policy and the allocation of time and resources can often represent a choice between sacrificing either competitiveness in the global market or organizational values, it is understandable that there may be hesitation in bringing up or making these difficult, high-stakes decisions more consciously and collaboratively. However, avoiding facing these issues has 'allowed' the organizational policies and priorities to shift in support of greater market competitiveness. In allowing this shift to occur, Mondragon worker-owners may avoid taking responsibility for the shift occurring and can 'blame' management or the market. Further, in allowing this shift to 'just happen', they do not need to make the difficult decision to consciously sacrifice organizational values or, alternatively, income for the cooperatives.

In reflecting on both the capitalist imperatives and group tendencies towards the release and/or avoidance of stress and anxiety discussed in this chapter, it follows that the development of tools to distinguish W groups and Ba groups in action is important so that Mondragon might consciously weigh and make decisions regarding its social and market requirements. This recommendation to develop tools to manage stress and anxiety through the deeper understanding of Ba and W group behavior follows Susan Long's recommendation in *The Perverse Organisation and Its Deadly Sins*. Since healthy organizations depend on good communication, positive authority and role relations, and ethical processes, the use of socioanalytic concepts to explore the social 'underworld' can also provide critical tools in maintaining organizational health (Long 2008: 153). Beyond distinguishing between and better managing W and Ba groups, an understanding of these group tendencies can also result in the increased ability of the group to tolerate anxiety and stress as necessary. As Kenneth Rice states in *Learning for Leadership*, 'The major constraints on task performance ... apart from qualifications, time and cost, are the limited extent to which leadership can be taught and the willingness of members to tolerate the pain of learning' (1965: 178). The 'pain of learning', in other words, is the working through of the anxiety and stress of organizational tasks that are critical to the organization. Leadership must manage this anxiety and stress of the group in order to 'protect the internal subsystems from the disruption of the fluctuating demands from the outside; but it also has to promote those internal changes that will enable the enterprise to be adaptive and indeed proactive in relation to the environment' (Miller 1985: 248). Perhaps the reinvigoration of the Social Council is an appropriate forum for this learning and deliberation. In the absence of the tools to distinguish whether decisions are being made in order to dispel anxiety or made consciously and collectively for the long-term health of the organization, the current shift is likely to continue.

Wider application and concluding remarks

Understanding the impact of capitalist market imperatives in relation to organizations focused on maintaining workplace democracy is a discussion that expands far beyond the reach of Mondragon and of worker cooperatives in general. Mondragon is not unique in its use of work-avoidance or Basic Assumption Group behavior as a way to dispel anxiety in facing difficult decisions. Neither is Mondragon unique in its specific struggle to avoid decisions that may compromise either competitive advantage or policies and procedures that support the democratic participatory environment. Facing these issues, as with facing the most important issues in any organization, is always the most difficult work that a group does. The recommendation for Mondargon to train worker-owners in the difference between a W group in action and a Ba group as well as in how to manage these modes is proposed as an essential tool in working through these growing pressures and stresses. With external market pressures on Mondragon likely to increase, the tendency will be for a concomitant increase in the employment of work-avoidance tactics relating to these issues. Facing such increasingly stressful decisions is no small task for Mondragon or any organization.

In closing, I will describe an interesting juxtaposition of the challenge faced at Mondragon and the trend towards increasing market competitiveness as result of an effort to reduce anxiety. In the years following the economic depression of 2008, there has been growing interest in the United States in cooperatives as viable and more stable alternatives to recent economic uncertainty and stress. An article in *The Nation* touted cooperatives as a response to the economic crisis (Hill 2010). Another article notes that an increasing number of people are 'looking beyond the immediate response to the [financial] crisis and are trying to explore the possibilities for more radical changes that might help bring about a more just and sustainable economic system', and specifically the 'potential of co-operative effort to contribute to a renewal of our economic and social life' (McKenna 2010). Also noteworthy was the late-2009 announcement that the United Steelworkers Union (USW) and Mondragon would be jointly establishing manufacturing cooperatives that adapt to the worker-ownership model of 'one worker, one vote' (Witherell 2009). As USW international president Leo W. Gerard stated, 'Too often we have seen Wall Street hollow out companies by draining their cash and assets and hollowing out communities by shedding jobs and shuttering plants. We need a new business model that invests in workers and invests in communities' (ibid.).

As anxiety related to this environment of economic uncertainty increases, alternatives by which to reduce and relieve this anxiety are being sought. However, in this search it is critical that the motivations for change are clear. While cooperative structures can provide a real alternative to many of the effects of capitalism's more detrimental imperatives, they are hard work to maintain. Beyond the basic requirements of workplace participation, this chapter has shown how the additional work of maintaining a democratic environment amid constant market pressures can add additional and often difficult work for members. In other words, if the motivation to seek economic alternatives is driven by the reduction of anxiety, an endless 'grass is greener' cycle may ensue. However, when prepared with an understanding of group tendencies and a willingness of groups to work through the stress of the most important issues facing the organization, the elusive balance may be maintained.

References

Bion, W. (1961) *Experiences in Groups*, London: Routledge.

Bowles, S. and Gintis, H. (1976) *Schooling in Capitalist America: Educational reform and the contradictions of economic life*, London: Routledge.

Bowles, S. and Gintis, H. (1987) *Democracy and Capitalism: Property, community, and the contradictions of modern social thought*, London: Routledge.

Bowles, S., Gintis, H. and Gustafsson, B. (1993) *Markets and Democracy: Participation, accountability, and efficiency*, Cambridge: Cambridge University Press.

Carrier, D. (n.d.) 'The macroeconomic benefits of cooperative vs. capitalist ownership', Online, available at: http://davidcarrier.org/blog/wp-content/uploads/2009/06/mondragon-macroeconomics.doc (retrieved 27 October 2010).

Cheney, G. (1997) 'The many meanings of solidarity', in B.D. Sypher (ed.) *Case Studies in Organizational Communication 2: Perspectives on contemporary work life*, New York: Guilford Press.

Cheney, G. (2002) *Values at Work: Employee participation meets market pressure at Mondragon*, New York: Cornell University Press.

Errasti, A.M., Heras, I., Bakaikoa, B. and Elgoibar, P. (2003) 'The internationalization of cooperatives: the case of the Mondragon Corporation', *Annals of Public and Cooperative Economics*, 74(2): 553–84.

GEO (1996) 'Mondragon: model or myth?', *Grassroots Economic Organizing Newsletter*, issue 20, January–February.

Gunn, C. (2000) 'Markets against economic democracy', *Review of Radical Political Economy*, 32(3): 448–60.

Herrera, D. (2002) 'Laborem exercens, "traditional organizations" and the democratic Mondragón model', in *Work as Key to the Social Question: The great social and economic transformations and the subjective dimension of work*, Vatican City: Libreria Editrice Vaticana.

Herrera, D. (2004). 'Mondragón: a for-profit organization that embodies Catholic social thought', *Review of Business*, 25(1): 56–68.

Hill, S. (2010) 'Europe's answer to Wall Street', *The Nation*. Online, available at: www. thenation.com/doc/20100510/hill (retrieved 22 April 2010).

Jackall, R. and Levin, H.M. (1984) *Worker Cooperatives in America*, Berkeley: University of California Press.

Kasmir, S. (1996) *The Myth of Mondragón: Cooperatives, politics, and working-class life in a Basque town*, Albany: State University of New York.

Lizarralde, I. (2009) 'Cooperatism, social capital and regional development: the Mondragon experience', *International Journal of Technology Management and Sustainable Development*, 8(1): 27–38.

Long, S. (2008) *The Perverse Organisation and Its Deadly Sins*, London: Karnac.

McKenna, D. (2010) 'Co-operatives and the economic and environmental crisis', Jesuit Centre for Faith and Justice. Online, available at: www.jcfj.ie/analysis/analysismain/17/464-wniss63-co-operative.html (retrieved 25 March 2010).

MacLeod, G. (1997) *From Mondragon to America: Experiments in community economic development*, Sydney, Canada: University College of Cape Breton Press.

Michelman, I.S. (1994) *The Moral Limitations of Capitalism*, Aldershot, UK: Avebury.

Miller, E. (1985) 'Organizational development and industrial democracy: a current case-study', in A. Coleman and M.E. Geller (eds) *Group Relations Reader 2*, Washington, DC: A.K. Rice Institute.

Mondragon Annual Report (2008) Online, available at: www.mondragon-corporation. com/LinkClick.aspx?fileticket=d7ULZaqxbMI%3d&tabid=331 (retrieved 22 February 2010).

Mondragon Corporation (n.d.) Mondragon Corporation website. Online, available at: www.mondragon-corporation.com (retrieved 8 March 2010).

Morrison, R. (1991) *We Build the Road as We Travel*, Philadelphia: New Society Publishers.

Onaran, Y. (1992) 'Workers as owners: an empirical comparison of intra-firm inequalities at employee-owned and conventional companies', *Human Relations*, 45(11): 1213–35.

Polanyi, K. (1944) *The Great Transformation: The political and economic origins of our time*, New York: Farrar & Rinehart.

Rice, A.K. (1965) *Learning for Leadership*, London: Tavistock.

Rhodes, S.R. and Steers, R.M. (1981) 'Conventional vs. worker-owned organizations', *Human Relations*, 34(12): 1013–35.

Solomon, W.S. and McChesney, R.W. (1993) *Ruthless Criticism: New perspectives in U.S. communication history*, Minneapolis: University of Minnesota Press.

Schweickart, D. (2002) *After Capitalism*, Lanham, MD: Rowman & Littlefield.

Toth, W. (1995) 'The educative dimensions of workplace democracy', in S.M. Natale and B.M. Rothschild (eds) *Work Values: Education, organization, and religious concerns*, Amsterdam: Rodopi.

Whyte, W.F. and Whyte, K.K. (1988) *Making Mondragon: The growth and dynamics of the worker cooperative complex*, Ithaca, NY: ILR Press (Cornell University).

Winnicott, D.W. (1965/1990) *The Family and Individual Development*, London: Routledge.

Witherell, R. (2009) 'Steelworkers form collaboration with MONDRAGON, the world's largest worker-owned cooperative', United Steelworkers Union. Online, available at: www.usw.org/media_center/releases_advisories?id=0234 (retrieved 18 March 2010).

Wood, E.M. (2002) *The Origin of Capitalism*, London: Verso.

Wood, E.M. (2005) *Democracy against Capitalism: Renewing historical materialism*, Cambridge: Cambridge University Press.

25 Market masculinities and electronic trading

Matthias Klaes, Geoff Lightfoot and Simon Lilley

Introduction

On 7 April 2005 the London-based International Petroleum Exchange (IPE), a leading energy derivatives marketplace, closed its Brent and gas oil futures and options pits in order to force the move to electronically mediated trading. With this, open outcry trading disappeared from the City of London, with the exception of the London Metal Exchange. There had been considerable resistance to the introduction of electronic trading at the IPE. This found expression not only in the dismal take-up rate of electronic trading during the run-up to the closure of the pits, when a dual system was in operation, but also in more overt displays, such as walkouts by some traders.

The accounts of traders themselves unsurprisingly placed this reluctance to change in terms of their particular skills and the sympathies of such with the specific demands of trading in oil futures. Yet traders also agreed that moving towards screen-based technologies meant that people who could not survive in the raucous, physically demanding and masculine arena of the pits, such as 'gimps', 'dweebs' and women (Zaloom 2003), would be able to enter as full participants in the market, which was manifestly not the case within the pit environment. In the somewhat suspect discourse of electronic dominance upon which such a characterisation of events relies, technology would expunge the social restrictions on participation and on access to information that characterise pits. Technology's apparent enabling of equal access to market information would seemingly exceed constraints associated with those personal connections, gender patterns and physical prowess that mediated participation in the pits and its associated informational milieu.

In order not to fall prey to such easy simplifications, we argue in this chapter for increased attention to the ethnographic dimensions of market analysis, which allow for a fine-grained analysis of the gendered relationality of different trading technologies. We understand this gendered relationality in narrative terms, thereby seeking to move beyond the conventional accounts of market relationality in terms of transaction costs and social capital alone. Narrative analysis is starting to emerge as a mode of investigation with considerable potential in the field of feminist economics (see, for example, May 2006). Whereas May draws upon Joan Wallach Scott's (1996: 167) idea of 'culturally available symbols', and indeed the ways in which these are themselves drawn upon in particular settings, we go further and deeper in our mobilization of the notion of narrative to examine the ways in which such symbols of narrative are not only mobilized but also constructed in 'an icon of contemporary global high technology' (Knorr Cetina and Bruegger 2002: 906). In fact, we will argue that it is through the construction of narrative dimensions of market relationality that the gendered nature of both transaction costs and social capital become apparent.

At the heart of our account of financial markets as relational and gendered entities is the recognition that the seemingly neutral ground of the self-referential play of abstract signs of the market, which as such leave seemingly little room for a reality beyond themselves, opens up a gap that market players experience as a multidimensional lack. This concept of lack has recently emerged in the social studies of finance (Knorr Cetina and Bruegger 2000; Knorr Cetina and Preda 2004; see also MacKenzie 2006) and is central to our analysis. To elucidate market lack we revisit the psychoanalytic context of the concept to provide an essentially Lacanian but ethnographically inspired account of market relationalities. It is in response to this lack of the market that market masculinities find continued display across alternative trading technologies. Trading technologies, in short, cannot escape the gendered nature of social exchange, which is a point most relevant to the continued absence of women from those technologies.

Markets as relational and gendered entities

Financial markets drive home the point that the global marketplace is not premised on the exchange of tangible commodities and services. While elementary-level textbooks still frame market transactions in terms of apples and bananas, that which is being traded is in fact bundles of property rights in the underlying goods (cf. Coase 1960; Demsetz 1967). Financial markets are set apart from their commodity brethren mainly by the fact that the goods traded are assets, which are monetary in nature, and that innovation in these markets has brought forth trading of higher-level property right bundles in the form of derived property rights, better known as financial derivatives. While the underlying goods might remain traditional commodities or financial assets, derivatives are by their very nature intangible, and thereby their markets epitomise this Coasean conception in its purest form.

There is a further feature of financial markets that merits interest. They are arguably among the most heavily regulated spaces of economic activity one can find in developed societies. Given that financial markets are often portrayed as the closest real-world equivalent of the economic idealisation of a perfect market, the apparently central role of regulation in enabling their functioning reminds us of the activity required to engineer even an approach to perfection. A perfect market requires that atomistic competition obtains in the form of a large number of market participants, none of which is able to exert a significant influence on the market. It also requires that all relevant information is transparently shared among market participants, that these participants exert their buying and selling decisions in a rational manner, that there is a single market price that at any moment in time reflects the relative balance of supply and demand, and finally that there is a market for any relevant commodity. Commodities need to be understood here in their broadest sense, as being both timed and contingent – in other words, as including futures contracts, which entail an obligation to effect spot trading for the exchange of commodities at a later point in time (an obligation that can of course be traded out prior to this point in time, by any particular trader); and as including options, which allow for trades of discretionary exercisable rights, the exercising of which is likely to be contingent on the realisation of a particular state of the world.

While the existence of a requirement for contingent commodities has often been doubted and the possibility of persistently functioning markets thereof therefore derided as unrealistic (Kynaston 1997), there has, in recent years, been continuous innovation in financial markets, which has greatly expanded the range of tradable commodities available, such that an ever more arcane range of derived and contingent contracts have become possible.

Regulation of financial markets seeks to approximate the conditions of perfect markets beyond the mere acknowledgement and approval of the emergence of new derivatives. Implementation of trading technologies and algorithms seeks to ensure transparency of information, as do provisions against insider trading. Financial regulators closely scrutinise market data for 'irregular' trading patterns, and trading is suspended if price volatility exceeds certain margins.

It is not surprising therefore that a large proportion of financial trading takes place not in the anarchic-utopian realms of 'free' market exchange but in tightly controlled and tightly controlling companies which, being incorporated in various forms, run the various commodity, stock and derivatives exchanges. It is here thus that one comes to appreciate the scale of the 'visible hand' (Chandler 1977)[1] at play in the working of those markets and, given the central role of financial markets, in the working of market-based economies overall.

In fact, until their gradual demise in recent times, exchanges were characterised by the most visible hands of market makers and brokers operating on the trading floor under a regime known as 'open outcry'. Trading regimes in open outcry 'pits' epitomise the relational nature of markets as it is advocated by economic sociologists, who have long questioned whether and to what extent it is useful to abstract from the institutional nature of markets (White 1981, 2001; Baker 1984; Granovetter 1985; Fligstein 1996; Abolafia 1996).

Yet open outcry trading also stands for another feature of market exchange. While this trading regime is rapidly becoming extinct as a result of the diffusion of online marketplaces, it has provided stark examples of the gendered nature of trading. Feminist economists have long pointed to gender as a crucial dimension in our understanding of how markets operate (Ferber and Nelson 1993; Strassmann 1994). Few other economic institutions have as exclusively been the domain of men as trading floors, such as the recently closed International Petroleum Exchange (IPE), where, according to one of our informants, all of the close to 200 pit traders were men. He explains this extreme occupational segregation in the following terms: 'There are no women floor traders as the pits are powered by testosterone.'

Gender splits in trading are far from restricted to the IPE. 'In the time that I worked at the CBOT [the Chicago Board of Trade], the largest pit held 600 traders. Two were women. At LDF [a London dealing firm] ... there was one woman and 60 men' (Zaloom 2003: 270n5). Figures of this kind are perhaps surprising, but a little history makes them less so. The London Stock Exchange only began to consider applications for women members in 1973 (Kynaston 2001: 420). Such circumstances are precisely those in which the necessity of particular repertoires and displays of gender identity become seemingly essential to 'successful' job performance, with this 'success' obviously being largely defined by what social circumstance dictates as appropriate (McDowell 1996, 1997).[2] And the platform, the technology of exchange through which trade is enacted, is obviously a key part of this social circumstance.

Gendered repertoires of market exchange

Where a particular masculinity is operant as a 'compulsory' (McDowell 1996: 179), de facto mode of performance, repertoires open to those women who are allowed a place there are by implication also strictly delimited. The best of trading men are referred to by their peers as 'big swinging dicks' (McDowell 1996; Lewis 1989), while Kynaston (2001: 707) notes that nicknames applied to female traders include such niceties as 'Boiler' and 'Slapper'. Linguistic denominations of this kind exemplify Stoller's claim that the enactment of sexuality in 'discourse, symbolism and ... social practice' (McDowell and Court 1994: 235) turns around a fetishised image of the phallus as 'aggressive, unfettered, unsympathetic, humiliating' (Stoller 1979: 94). Scripts for performance available to women in such masculinised organisational settings fall into a limited number of categories.

McDowell (1996, 1997) describes a triptych of masculinities and a triptych of femininities seemingly available as City scripts. For men in high finance there seem to be two overarching scripts for the enactment of masculinity, with one of them further subdivided. Thus, in the world of corporate finance we witness the older *patriarchs* and the younger *princes* (McDowell 1996: esp. 1981–90), both bearing privileged educational and class backgrounds. In contrast, the third masculinity identified is primarily witnessed on the trading floor. It is a *macho masculinity*, inhabiting an environment that is 'noisy, aggressive and very pushy', as one of McDowell's (1996: 86) informants puts it (cf. McDowell 1997: 178–9).

In all three variants, though, despite a hint of the homoerotic surrounding the self-presentation of the princes, we glimpse a world organized around a compulsory heterosexuality. On the trading floor this takes the form of 'an idealised rampant heterosexuality that abhors both faithfulness and bi- or homosexuality' (McDowell 1997: 179). The three options available to women in these environments seem to be (1) to 'minimise their difference from the masculine norm through forms of disguise of their femininity and sexual attractiveness'; (2) to render 'status distinctions plain rather than gender differences indistinct' (ensuring that one is not confused 'with secretaries whose femininity, accentuated by dress is part of a gender performance in which "natural" attributes of a sexualized femininity are accentuated', often by always wearing a jacket); and, perhaps most interestingly, for a subset of the most successful women, particularly those in the vicinity of the trading floor, (3) to adopt a parodic, masquerading and potentially highly subversive performance of femininity which plays with rules and arguably challenges male dominance (McDowell 1996: 88–9; see also McDowell 1997: 181–203).

Masculinities and trading technologies

Faced with the heavily gendered world of open outcry trading regimes, what can we expect to happen to gendered patterns of exchange in a trading regime that tries to approximate the anonymous atomism postulated in the efficient market literature? Consider the screen-based trading regimes that have now largely replaced the trading floor. Would the switch to alternative trading regimes of this kind reshuffle the gendered performance repertoires available to those who engage in market exchange within such regimes?

On the face of it, replacing tightly knit social networks – access to which is subject to significant cultural and gendered barriers of entry and which rely on close bodily interaction and display – with electronic trading platforms appears to realise the perfect market ideal ever more closely. Co-present bodily interaction recedes behind the trading screen, screens themselves recede from the trading floor into a distributed network that may span the globe, and the public identity of the trader recedes into the anonymity of electronically realised public order books which, run in real time, realise the transparent immediacy of the law of one price. The advent of electronic trading platforms therefore appears to reassert markets as abstract entities that exhibit precisely those virtues ascribed to them by economists. The social network of interactions that sustains a dealership market becomes replaced by a web of trading screens linking up price and quantity signals of anonymous atomistic traders in a way sufficiently transparent to yield significant efficiency gains in comparison with floor trading.

A key organising concept to attend to these efficiency differentials has been the notion of transaction costs (Demsetz 1968; Stoll 2000). It has been argued, for example, that the replacement of a traditional dealership market by electronic trading reduces transaction costs as a result of the increased trading transparency thus achieved (Pagano and Roell 1996). Electronic trading systems are more transparent in that they make available more details of the order flow, such as the history of quotes and transactions, than was the case with floor trading. They thereby reduce informational asymmetries that may give rise to economic inefficiencies associated with adverse selection problems. Described in transaction cost terms, electronic trading should reduce the transaction costs associated with more traditional forms of trading, including open outcry.

The transaction cost narrative of increased transparency and reduced information asymmetries can be pursued into the realm of market genders via the notion of social capital, by addressing the particular relational structure of a trading technology in terms of the social capital that it embodies (cf. Bourdieu 1986; Coleman 1988).[3] If the ethnographic accounts from the trading floor are to be trusted, then the social capital sustaining open outcry trading is heavily gendered.[4] A move to electronic trading would allow for a more gender-balanced social capital structure associated with this new trading technology compared to pit trading, thereby allowing a more level playing field in terms of market participation. That, at least, is the promise implied by the suspect discourse of democratization attendant upon the virtual (see, for example, Hiltz and Turoff 1978). The concomitant move closer to the perfect market ideal may then be accounted for in transaction cost terms: the potential for shifting gender balance in the social capital underlying electronic trading would reduce transaction costs.

Overall, however, the notion of social capital prevalent in the economics literature is too blunt a tool for addressing the relationality of trading technologies since it does not extend to the narratives that facilitate and constrain this relationality. The gendered nature of trading technologies must be sought in the discursive horizon in which they are embedded. For although the shift from open outcry trading to that mediated more entirely by screen has been seen by those it affected most, the pit traders themselves, as redolent with potential for the acceptance of differing bodies and performances of a heavily gendered nature – a view utterly consistent with the simplification above – we should not be too optimistic about this potential being realised.

For while traders readily acknowledge that electronic trading could allow an increase in the diversity of market participants that would transcend the physical arena of open outcry pits of the heavily masculinised white male trader who defined himself in contrast to 'gimps', 'dweebs' and women (Zaloom 2002: 12), the 'could' is a big one. These are Zaloom's (2003: 266; see also Bailey 1996) impressions of walking into the electronically mediated, screen-based LDF dealing room:

> Walking down the left-hand corridor of the dealing room reveals soccer club posters, images of hot cars, baby photos and girly pix cut from magazines. Spare copies of Rupert Murdoch's tabloid, the *Sun*, are strewn about the room. The traders joked that the nipples of the topless page-three girl were sure indicators of daily market direction.

More fundamental factors seem to be at work in the gendering of trading regimes – factors that reach beyond the gendered nature of directly relational interactions among traders co-present in a pit. The traders in the LDF dealing room do not trade only with each other. Indeed, such trade, if it occurs at all, would generally constitute only a very small part of total activity. What they are dealing with is 'the market', and its universe of seemingly depersonalised signs. In other words, they appear to live the anonymity conditions sustaining those theories of the market that are abstract from its potential more direct, more traditionally 'social' relationality, by making prices and quantities the sole conduit for communication and interaction with other market participants. The gendered repertoires sustained in pit trading would naively seem to rely on personal contact and co-presence and the appearances and direct verbal and non-verbal communication that it enables. Would the bare semiotics of price and quantity provide sufficiently rich resources to maintain a symbolic system that sustains gendered interaction between traders and the anonymous market? Or are the scenes witnessed by Zaloom at LDF merely vestiges of conduct and moral codes that may not persist as the institutional set-up that seemingly enabled them recedes?

Lives of the market

Although trading partners are undoubtedly depersonalised by moves to more electronically mediated trading, in the vacuum of identities that appears to be left behind, the market seems to take on a life of its own. With the identity of market *participants* held at bay, the market itself becomes suitably and sufficiently animate and anthropomorphised to allow the trader to conduct his or her intimate relations directly with 'it', as a sentient entity in its own right. 'When I trade I try to find where the market hurts, what is hurting it' (trader's description included in Knorr Cetina and Bruegger 2000: 158).[5] But the anthropomorphised market is not a body so robust that it cannot be taken apart. Indeed, the nature of the market as signs, and seemingly signs alone, is both what enables its flow to take on the characteristics of an identity to which one can relate and the basis of its potential for disaggregation and disintegration (Lilley and Lightfoot 2006).

As Beunza and Stark illustrate in their discussion of a trading room post-9/11, traders in different fields (such as convertible bonds, equity arbitrage, customer sales) work at 'deconstructing the value of a stock or property into its constituent aspects, or properties' (2003: 140). Because the different desks use different means of determining these aspects, Beunza and Stark suggest that this leads to 'innovation' when they are reassembled. But this curious disassembly and bricolage, along with the dissembly often enacted through movement of that which is so taken apart and brought together, does not only occur at the level of the construction and deconstruction of products. It is also the essence of trading as ongoing practice. Or, as Zaloom (2002: 37) puts it, 'Traders act according to the narratives they build.'

To be clear here, these narratives are not only – indeed, not mainly – those of an outside world impinging on the market. Narrative is constructed from the market itself. Consider two moments captured in Zaloom's ethnography of a screen-based trading room. In the first, we witness the non-impact, indeed the eschewal, of the outside world within the trading place. During one of her visits, when a congressional speech by Alan Greenspan was screened on television, traders 'shrieked' for the trading room set to be switched off (Zaloom 2003: 267).

So much for external events. But what about the narratives within the signs, the signs within the signs, within the movements of the market itself? In our second example that we draw from Zaloom's work, we can begin to see why gendered repertoires of performance that take place within trading environments are not dependent upon merely the immediacy of a directly enacted machismo culture in circumstances of co-presence. Zaloom witnessed her screen-based traders imagining trading identities whose actions would render intelligible and personify the changing pattern of bids and offers; the 'Spoofer' being 'the most recurring' (2003: 267).

The Spoofer is a trader, or group of traders – real or imagined – trying to manipulate the direction the market is moving by creating spurious bids and offers. Once one is identified, traders can try exploiting the Spoofer's strategy for their own purposes by betting on the seeming predictability of the market's trajectory, predictability attendant upon the existence or imputation of the Spoofer. Alternatively, mimicking the machismo of the pit within the superficially less immediately gladiatorial environment of the screen, a trader could decide to confront the Spoofer by selling large quantities into his bids (or buying into his offers). The reputation of traders who manage to 'take out' the Spoofer rises as a result of success during what is regarded as 'one to one combat' (Zaloom 2003: 267).

Thus, in both Beunza and Stark's and Zaloom's accounts we see no essential, grounded attachment to any one set of signs, no matter how seemingly sophisticated; no privileging of an external, real reality. Instead, the ambiguities produced by the multiplication of ever more elaborate distillations of signs and the disjunctions and coincidences between them, the bluffs and invocations of bluff, merely produce additional opportunities for trade both in the products of the market and that 'symbolic capital' (Bourdieu 1984) in which traders seem equally interested: their reputation.

Market machismo: filling the gap

How, then, does the seemingly neutral ground of a market made up solely of disembeddable, disembodied signs enable perpetuation of gendered repertoires of performance that seemed easily explicable in terms of the actions of co-present others where the mere weight of masculine bodies and associated performances hold sway? Surprise at the perpetuation of the results of such circumstances turns in part upon misrecognition of the 'neutral' and in part upon misreading of the extent of that neutrality in even those circumstances which we have, up to now, described as intensely masculinised on the basis of what will turn out to be rather superficial grounds.

In any re-presentation of recalcitrant reality, selection is necessarily at work. And as feminism has long reminded us, the purported neutrality of rational accounts of the world, such as the self-immersed reflexivity of traders and the financial markets they inhabit, is predicated upon a particular version of the bloodless, calculative masculine as de facto norm (see, for example, Kerfoot and Knights 1993, 1994). This is the realm of the intellect, that cerebral place in which the seemingly (more) embodied and emotive feminine is strictly out of place. The very practice of this market *ratio*, in particular in the context of derivatives trading, seems on certain readings to require intensification of the break between the signs of the market and that which they would conventionally be seen to signify. For only then can one immerse oneself sufficiently *in signs themselves* to avoid entirely distractions from outside, distractions that serve to make those subject to them amenable to the sort of prediction associated with the deployment of strategy – deployment that itself provides potential for the deployment of (profitable) counter-strategy. The Spoofer, imagined or real, comes into being precisely upon such an understanding.

Eschewal of reality lurking beyond the signs of the market and its players is complete in accounts from the floor and, we would imagine, also from the screen. Traders, particularly the best traders with the most excessive resources at their disposal, seem at their happiest and 'most productive' when they adopt an ephemeral place, divorced from any 'outside', in which to carry out their business.

But signs qua signs constitute a world of *lack*, or rather a series of *lacks*. Nobody has explored this expression of signs as lack more assiduously than Jacques Lacan (1966, 1973; cf. Barzilai 1999) and, as Knorr Cetina and Bruegger (2000) have reminded us, recourse to his work allows a fresh perspective on the market as home for the 'Big Swinging Dick'. Close reading of the narrative repertoires of exchange reveals the phallus as an organising moment, which works both through its offensive presence in those accounts, and through its lurking absence. Finding himself on the wrong side of a lucrative trade, the trader who falls short of the standards set by the Big Swinging Dick thus ends up emasculated. Speaking with Lacan, the trader appears annihilated as the imaged embodiment of a lack first symbolically imprinted on the unconscious through the trauma of birth and the Freudian drive to be loved by the other that it gives rise to (Lacan 1966: 703–21; 1973/1998: 88–9; cf. Barzliai 1999: 196),

Where, then, do we encounter the lack(s) of the market in trading narratives? First, and most superficially, in the hypercompetitive settings in which trading occurs, traders are set targets, achievement of which determines a significant part of their remuneration and against which they are, for the majority of time, lacking, with this lack made immediately apparent upon the floor. Through accepting this lack as his[6] own, the trader is inserted into the market in a spiral of mimetic self-reflection, constantly valuing himself just as he constantly values potential and actual deals. But the trading self is not only valued in strictly financial terms. The star system of the trading floor (Knorr Cetina and Bruegger 2000: 154) insists that the trader evaluate himself against the model performance and behaviour of the Big Swinging Dicks, an evaluation through which a second dimension of lack is revealed, a lack of matching up to the model's performance and behaviour. From a Lacanian perspective, we can see the seeming madness of the trader's act, his disembedding of himself from a world of ordinary realities in which signs stand for things, as part and parcel of his self-lionisation and sacrifice as a hero or putative star:

The person who knows is indeed in such a perilous position, marked for failure and sacrifice, that he is led to feign madness, and even ... to be mad along with everyone else. Feigning madness is thus one of the dimensions of what we might call the strategy of the modern hero.

(Lacan 1959/1977: 20)

Trading, as traders themselves endlessly remind us in a rhetorical move that serves to aggrandise the quasi-magical, elusive nature of their thus obscured and sacramental practice, is not an activity that can be articulated through a series of expository rules and consequently learned from a book. It is rather, in every sense, a situated practice, and a practice in which competency can only be gained via immersion within the field of its play, which leads traders themselves to describe their practice as an art, not something that can be taught conceptually (cf. Abolafia 1996: 26).

In such accounts, this art of trading is not so much a description of activity as it is an epiphany to a whole way of being. This, then, is a third lack of the trading place, a lack of complete immersion in that place and its phenomenology, an inability to leave behind residual values that might lead to merely satisfactory performance and not winning, a lack of the character that trading requires. As Abolafia notes, 'the trading floor is not understood as a place to satisfice, foot drag, or merely survive as in other organizational settings. It is a place to win' (1996: 10); 'there is no career ladder for traders. There are only traders who make more and traders who make less in a continuous contest for wealth' (ibid.: 18). The visceral experience of living in the market is seen as essential, and an oft-cited rite of passage apparently occurs when one first feels the bodily pain of taking home a potentially loss-making position. This 'testing of character' (Knorr Cetina and Bruegger 2000: 154) that is constantly played out in the trading place permeates life around the floor as well. Indeed, the title of Lewis's book *Liar's Poker* derives from a bluffing game popular among traders and often played for exceedingly high stakes. Those unwilling to play at this level are seen to be lacking in the character also required for playing the trading game.

Thus, immersion in signs can be related to the particular machismo individuality that we witnessed above. To stay with the 'Human Piranha's' (Lewis 1989: 217)[7] ominous label, balls of steel seemingly enable the Big Swinging Dick to immerse himself in the spectacle of the market, in some senses *becoming* the movement of that market, both cause and consequence of market fluctuations (cf. Bay and Bäckius 1999) – to, albeit via congenital failure, fill the lack of the trading place with the individuality and certainty that seemingly attach to the organ of power: 'Nothing in the jungle got in the way of a Big Swinging Dick' (Lewis 1989: 52; cf. Stoller 1979). While an individual trader, perhaps emphasising the fragility of his masculine body and its exposure to the risks of violation in the jungle of trade, might talk about misfortunes suffered in deeply visceral, sexualised terms, redolent of the abhorrence of homosexuality we encountered earlier – 'I got shafted', 'I got bent over', 'I got blown up', 'I got raped', 'I got stuffed'/'The guy stuffed me', 'I got hammered', 'I got killed'

(Knorr Cetina and Bruegger 2002: 940) – the separateness that this masculinity offers, when it is not violated, when its fragility can be kept momentarily at bay, is just what is seemingly required to work with a depersonalised market of signs and signs alone – a place in which, ironically, real men seemingly rule. This is the metonymy of the trader as portrayed in populist accounts of this dynamic regime. and such accounts, with their lionisation of traders, are easily accepted by traders and enacted with force.

Speculative traders such as these Big Swinging Dicks, 'market makers' in the profound rather than the technical sense, do not necessarily enter the market to engage in a particular transaction. Rather, they seek to garner for themselves the position of central agency in the market by virtue of their superior detachment from the external, 'real-world' sources that supposedly drive the activities of 'investors'. They may or may not use this position to engage in particular transactions. That is something of a by-product, not definitional of the essence of the trading place.

Lewis (1989: 102–3) illustrates the masterly execution of such a strategy in his portrayal of a trader who finds that he is unable to take a significant position in the money market owing to his attempted action's impact upon the market rate. Whenever he raises his bid, the market rate moves beyond it. Exasperated, he turns to his line manager, who advises him to behave contrary to his intention by appearing in the market as a seller at the market rate, now apparently revealed as inflated and ripe for profit taking by his shifting tactic. As the rest of the market follows suit, demand collapses, price falls and the trader not only buys back his money at the lower rate, thereby making a profit, but is also finally able to trade his original position at the terms he originally desired – an exemplification of the whipping and driving (Lewis 1989) of the market enabled by its rendering as signs, and signs that can seemingly only be enacted by those who accept this semiotic reduction and both inhabit it and stand over it through the singularity of their phallic power.

Notes

1 Chandler is usually read as suggesting that the distinction between the visible and the invisible hand rests upon the coordination of the former by deliberative managerial action. Nevertheless, institutionalised settings such as exchanges that enable the seemingly invisible hand to hold sway are themselves extensively managed (see, for example, Kynaston 1997).

2 See also McDowell and Court (1994) and Kerfoot and Knights (1993, 1994).

3 See Fine (2001) and Sobel (2002) for critical assessments of the social capital concept, which we accept is a multifaceted notion that we employ here as a convenient shorthand for addressing the economically relevant gendering of trading technologies. Indeed, Bourdieu (1986) initially distinguished three forms of capital: economic, social and cultural (subsequently adding a fourth, 'symbolic capital', a term which we draw upon later in our account). The notion being mobilised here, and indeed in much of the economics literature that has drawn upon the notion, would seem to entail aspects of both social and cultural capital. We utilise the term 'social capital' in sympathy with its use in the economics literature.

4 Acknowledgement of the gendered nature of social capital is relatively recent (see van Staveren 2002; Norris and Inglehart 2003).
5 Such anthropomorphism is not of course solely to be witnessed in relation to electronically mediated screen-based markets. Its history is considerably longer. That said, there appears to be a discernible hyperbolisation of the anthropomorphism of the market as its constituent human parts are held further at bay and it, as an entity, becomes more proximal.
6 Following Zaloom (2003: 270n5), we adopt the masculine pronoun here for reasons of 'gender realism'.
7 The 'Human Piranha', who apparently coined the phrase 'Big Swinging Dick', was something of a hero to Lewis, despite his superficially unsavoury descriptions of the phenomenon: '*The Piranha didn't talk like a person.* He said things like "if you f***in" buy this bond in a "f***in" trade, you're "f***in" "f***ed"' (Lewis 1989: 83, original emphasis, our asterisks). His valorisation by Lewis, who expresses admiration for the, in his eyes, brutal yet fair honesty of the Piranha, is seemingly attendant here upon the consistent authenticity his ceaselessly expletive performance demonstrated (cf. Lewis 1989: 85).

References

Abolafia, M.Y. (1996) *Making Markets: Opportunism and restraint on Wall Street*, Cambridge, MA: Harvard University Press.

Bailey, C. (1996) 'Virtual skin: articulating race in cyberspace', in A. Moser and D. MacLead (eds) *Immersed in Technology: Art and visual environments*, Cambridge, MA: MIT Press.

Baker, W.E. (1984) 'The social structure of a national securities market', *American Journal of Sociology*, 89: 775–811.

Barzilai, S. (1999) *Lacan and the Matter of Origins*, Stanford, CA: Stanford University Press.

Bay, T. and Bäckius, P. (1999) 'Reiterating experimentation: inventing new possibilities of life', *Emergence*, 1(3): 71–83.

Beunza, D. and Stark, D. (2003) 'The organization of responsiveness: innovation and recovery in the trading rooms of lower Manhattan', *Socio-Economic Review*, 1: 135–64.

Bourdieu, P. (1984) *Distinction: A social critique of the judgement of taste*, London: Routledge.

Bourdieu, P. (1986) 'The forms of capital', in J.G. Richardson (ed.) *Handbook of Theory and Research for the Sociology of Education*, New York: Greenwood Press.

Chandler, A.D. (1977) *The Visible Hand: The managerial revolution in American business*, Cambridge, MA: The Belknap Press of Harvard University Press.

Coase, R.H. (1960) 'The problem of social cost', *Journal of Law and Economics*, 3: 1–44.

Coleman, J.S. (1988) 'Social capital in the creation of human capital', *American Journal of Sociology*, 94: S95–S121.

Demsetz, H. (1967) 'Toward a theory of property rights', *American Economic Review*, 57: 347–59.

Demsetz, H. (1968) 'The cost of transacting', *Quarterly Journal of Economics*, 82: 33–53.

Ferber, M. and Nelson, J. (1993) *Beyond Economic Man*, Chicago: University of Chicago Press.

Fine, B. (2001) *Social Capital versus Social Theory: Political economy and social science at the turn of the millennium*, London: Routledge.

Fischer, C.S. (1992): *America Calling*, Berkeley: University of California Press.

Fligstein, N. (1996) 'Markets as politics: a political-cultural approach to market institutions', *American Sociological Review*, 61: 656–73.

Granovetter, M. (1985) 'Economic action and social structure: the problem of embeddedness', *American Journal of Sociology*, 91: 481–510.

Hiltz, S.R. and Turoff, M. (1978) *The Network Nation: Human communication via computer*, Cambridge, MA: MIT Press.

Kerfoot, D. and Knights, D. (1993): 'Management, masculinity and manipulation: from paternalism to corporate strategy in financial services in Britain', *Journal of Management Studies*, 30(4): 659–77.

Kerfoot, D. and Knights, D. (1994) 'The gendered terrains of paternalism', in S. Wright (ed.) *Anthropology of Organizations*, London: Routledge.

Knorr Cetina, K.D. and Bruegger, U. (2000) 'The market as an object of attachment: exploring postsocial relations in financial markets', *Canadian Journal of Sociology*, 25(2): 141–68.

Knorr Cetina, K.D. and Bruegger, U. (2002) 'Global microstructures: the virtual societies of financial markets', *American Journal of Sociology*, 107(4): 905–50.

Knorr Cetina, K.D. and Preda, A. (2004) *The Sociology of Financial Markets*, Oxford: Oxford University Press.

Kynaston, D. (1997) *LIFFE: A market and its makers*, London: Granta.

Kynaston, D. (2001) *The City of London*, vol. 4: *A club no more, 1945–2000*, London: Chatto & Windus.

Lacan, J. (1959) 'Desire and the interpretation of desire in *Hamlet*', transl. J. Hulbert (1977), *Yale French Studies*, 55/56: 11–52.

Lacan, J. (1966) *Écrits*, transl. B. Fink, New York: W.W. Norton, 1999.

Lacan, J. (1973) *The Four Fundamental Concepts of Psychoanalysis*, trans. A. Sheridan, London: Vintage, 1998.

Lewis, M. (1989) *Liar's Poker: Rising through the wreckage of Wall Street*, New York: W.W. Norton.

Lilley, S. and Lightfoot, G. (2006) 'Trading narratives', *Organization*, 13(3): 369–91.

McDowell, L. (1996) 'Body work: heterosexual gender performances in city workplaces', in D. Bell and G. Valentine (eds) *Mapping Desire: Geographies of sexualities*, London: Routledge.

McDowell, L. (1997) *Capital Culture: Gender and work in the city*, Malden, MA: Blackwell.

McDowell, L. and Court, G. (1994) 'Missing subjects: gender, power, and sexuality in merchant banking', *Economic Geography*, 70: 229–51.

MacKenzie, D. (2006) *An Engine, not a Camera: How financial models shape markets*, Cambridge, MA: MIT Press.

May, A.M. (2006) ' "Sweeping the heavens for a comet": women, the language of political economy, and higher education in the U.S.', *Feminist Economics*, 12(4): 625–40.

May, A.M. (1997) *Capital Culture: Gender and work in the city*, Oxford: Blackwell.

Norris, P. and Inglehart, R. (2003) 'Gendering social capital: bowling in women's leagues?', paper presented at the conference 'Gender and Social Capital', University of Manitoba, 2–3 May.

Pagano, M. and Roell, A. (1996) 'Transparency and liquidity: a comparison of auction and dealer markets with informed trading', *Journal of Finance*, 51(2): 579–611.

Sobel, J. (2002) 'Can we trust social capital?' *Journal of Economic Literature*, 40: 139–54.

Stoll, H.R. (2000) 'Friction', *Journal of Finance*, 55: 1479–1514.

Stoller, R. (1979) *Sexual Excitement: The dynamics of erotic life*, New York: Pantheon.

Strassmann, D. (1994) 'Feminist thought and economics; or, what do the Visigoths know?', *American Economic Review*, 84: 153–8.

van Staveren, I. (2002) 'Social capital: what is in it for feminist economics?', Institute for Social Studies Working Paper 368, The Hague: Institute for Social Studies.

Wallach Scott, J. (1996) 'Gender: a useful category of analysis', in J. Wallach Scott (ed.) *Feminism and History*, Oxford: Oxford University Press.

White, H. (1981) 'Where do markets come from?', *American Journal of Sociology*, 87: 517–47.

White, H. (2001) *Markets from Networks*, Princeton, NJ: Princeton University Press.

Zaloom, C. (2002) 'Ambiguous numbers: technology and trading in global financial markets', paper presented at the Social Studies of Finance Conference, New York, 3–4 May. Online, available at: www.coi.columbia.edu/ssf/papers/zaloom.doc, (retrieved 12 March 2007); revised version published as Zaloom (2003).

Zaloom, C. (2003) 'Ambiguous numbers: trading technologies and interpretation in financial markets', *American Ethnologist*, 30(2): 258–72.

Conclusion

26 Money, finances and capitalism

Issues in organizational life for now and the future

Susan Long and Burkard Sievers

Introduction

This book is the first of its kind, being an attempt to look 'beneath the surface of money, finance and capitalism' from a socioanalytic and sociological stance. The authors have written from theoretical positions that regard the usual logic of the mathematical modelling of the finance industry as limited. It is limited because it takes little, if any, account of the human beings who develop and utilize these models. Through action research, case studies and evidence from consulting interventions in a variety of countries, the authors in this book have raised serious questions about the nature of thinking, planning and action in the financial industry. All these activities are strongly influenced by unconscious and 'unthought' group and organizational dynamics emergent from collective human motivations and emotions.

The stories told and arguments posed in this book mean that we should question any blind singular dependence on the assumption of rationality that lies behind much thinking in economics. What is required in addition is an understanding of organizational dynamics, the development of reflective thinking and the capacity to question and explore the 'groupthink' (Janis, 1972, 1982) or other social defences that so readily develop when anxieties or other intense human emotions are not contained. Only through a deeper understanding of collective behaviour, its meaning and expression, can the powerful resource that is human emotion be used in creative rather than destructive ways to support technological developments and economic thinking and theories.

The authors in this book have examined systemic problems within organizations primarily by examining their pathologies. Yet to understand societal dynamics as perverse (Long 2008) or psychotic (Sievers 2006), for example, is not to 'psychologize', or unthinkingly transfer terms from individual psychology to the social level. The perverse or psychotic states of mind are descriptive of systems dynamics that can be expressed through the behaviour of individuals or of the organization as a whole. Or they might even be expressed through the whole social fabric of a given culture at a given time.

The system dynamic of capitalism appears to be the current cultural container for the development, growth and continuation of money and global financial systems. In this final chapter we will look, from a socioanalytic perspective, at some of the implications of this changing politico-economic system, with its failings as well as its more constructive possibilities for the future of work organizations. In doing this, we will look at what we see as the basic dynamics of markets, money and the financial sector, building from our own work and the work in this book. We explore capitalism as a cultural container and add some implications for organizations towards the end of the chapter, considering how socioanalytic thinking should proceed in the future in relation to these issues.

Capitalism

Capitalism, with its economic stance based on competition within global financial markets and its political stance based on private ownership of capital, looks likely to continue to be the major global influence for the future despite its inherent failings, many of which have been broached in this book. Perhaps the question is not so much the failure of capitalism, but its reconstitution for a changing world where non-European or Western cultures will predominate and where the free market system may have to give way to a different kind of government intervention (Kaletsky 2010).

The nature of markets

One of the central pairings of our time is that between the institutions of consumer and producer of services and commodities (Long 2008). We use the term 'institution' in the sense of 'a custom that for a long time has been an important feature of some group or society' (*Webdictionary.co.uk*). Economic relations between people and groups are centred on and defined in terms of these institutions: around buying and selling; valuing, crediting and exchanging. They are the central institutions in the market. This pair – the consumer and producer – define each other. They are in many ways a mirror image of each other – a pair that is co-determined, co-existent and co-dependent. Psychologically and metaphorically, they are somewhat like mother and child, existing in cooperation, each defined in terms of the other, mutually dependent in existence. Just as a mother is a mother only in so far as she has a child, a producer is only that in relation to a consumer, and a consumer is co-dependent on a producer.

But there are other players in the market. For example, there are the market observers and reporters: those who study the markets and might advise members of the consumer and producer institutions and the groupings within. Particularly important are the regulators, those who develop and enforce laws with respect to market activities. The regulators play an important 'third' in the market. They intervene between the producers and consumers much as the father (psychologically) intervenes in the otherwise insular relation between a mother and infant (Winnicott 1971; Lacan 1970), introducing a world external to the pair. This 'third' position intervenes to bring a broader reality to the pair, who might otherwise remain removed from it because of their intense interdependence.

The market as an institution is age-old and basic to human society. Commerce between groups has been practised since tribal times and has been critical to the development of city-states and nations. But if we were to look at institutions across time, we could say that it has transformed and increased in importance over the past few hundred years since industrialization, and in the West with the decline of other institutions such as organized religion, an agrarian society and the feudal social system. These latter institutions are based on authority hierarchies with a basic assumption of dependency (Bion 1960). The market, however, especially as it has been instituted in capitalism, is based on the pair (of producer–consumer), where relations are forged according to supply, demand and finance. Authority or power is involved only tangentially according to the social and economic systems that govern the way capital is created and distributed. That the authority of the regulators, for example, has been minimized or even evaded through the ideologies surrounding free markets stems from the influence and ascendency of the producer–consumer pair as not simply central but narcissistically independent, as if they require no governance, only Adam Smith's 'invisible hand'.

Capitalism is an economic system based on the private ownership of capital – that is, money used to create more money. It differs from a system where commodities are simply sold by producers to consumers in so far as 'the capitalist system is one in which producers are employees, and do not themselves own, or have the means to buy, their own equipment and materials' (Kilcullen 1996). Employees thus sell their labour, and the owner of the means of production reaps the surplus value of commodities: the value beyond what is paid for raw materials, production costs and labour. At least, this was the analysis made by Marx. However, in our complex twenty-first-century economies those who eventually gain are not simply the owners of equipment and materials – for example, owners of small businesses with very small margins or none at all beyond providing the owner with a wage fall into this category – but that collection of capitalists who control large corporations and financial institutions (Bakan 2004) and to a much smaller extent, paradoxically since Marx, to the workers themselves through superannuation investments and government investments to fund health and social services (Sievers 2003). Through this process, capitalism has become a process that does not simply underpin an inequitable class system – although the vestiges of its history are there – but has inveigled itself so that even the formerly so-called repressed classes depend heavily upon it for their well-being and are consequently invested psychologically in its continuance. This is even when they are not gripped by 'false consciousness' and are aware of the hold the system has on their choices.

This complexity is increased by the presence and growth of financial markets. These markets deal in financial products based on estimates about the future prices of commodities, interest rates, international currencies and, indeed, other financial products.

Under capitalism, the market is a complex system of roles including:

1   producers (not in the sense of Marxist labour but in the sense of those cor-
     porations and investors that gain capital from commodities, services and
     virtual financial products) who also consume;
2   consumers, who may also be investors and producers;
3   regulators, such as governments;
4   observers and commentators who sway opinions and decision making;
5   lobbyists and other stakeholders.

In many senses, markets are virtual large groups or, more correctly, virtual collectives of roles (Dalgleish and Long 2005). They are not organized hierarchies
or bureaucracies. Their leadership is emergent and may change from instant to
instant. They tend not to obey the dynamics of work or even political organizations, but those of unstable complex systems such as weather or traffic systems
or populations in ecological systems (Ball 2004; Kaletsky 2010). Despite their
being made up of individuals who reflect, learn and make decisions based on
evidence or whim, their systemic nature is not managed. They are networks.
Their internal regulation, like that of a biological population, is directed (not
consciously, but through system dynamics) towards their survival and reproduc-
tion, not towards the interest of individuals or subgroups, which can be readily
sacrificed. Like biological populations, they may become destabilized and move
into self-destructive modes such as we have seen during several 'bubbles' such
as the IT bubble of the early 2000s and the 2008–9 international financial crisis.
In the latter case, strong government intervention was required to bring back
some stability.

Free markets are a key catch-cry for conservative governments and groupings
who laud individual choice. They are seen as part of social evolution towards
individualism and away from collectivism with its strong government presence.
The irony here is that capitalist market dynamics do not in fact protect most individuals, but eventually lead to inequalities. In fact, recent research implies that
both extremes, of capitalism and socialism, reduce wealth.

> Sorin Solomon and colleagues at the Hebrew University of Jerusalem in
> Israel have shown that attempts to enforce a worldwide equality of wealth
> are apt to make that wealth dwindle uniformly to zero ... and have shown
> that once markets become global, there is an increased risk of all the wealth
> getting concentrated in one place.
>
> (Ball 2004: 278)

But markets, especially financial markets, are important systems for work
organizations and there is a strong desire to predict and control them – certainly
to gain from them and protect against the risks they pose. Although organizations put a lot of effort into examining their investment risks, such endeavours
are somewhat akin to meteorology. Some predictions are increasingly sophisticated, but, as with weather and climate change, control of the system is near-
impossible and the human complicity in causality is intertwined with deeply

entrenched ways of doing things. Chapters 10–14 of this book all examine the idea of risk control, discovering the unconscious social dynamics that increase risks. These go unrecognized by purely economic models.

> One of the dreams of entrepreneur economists is to develop a theory that can predict the ups and downs of the market before they happen. This would allow traders to make profits indefinitely, buying and selling exactly when their calculations tell them the time is right. Real traders – at least, those with a serious understanding of market dynamics – have long since given up on this idea. They know that it cannot be achieved. Indeed, the impossibility of making completely accurate forecasts is enshrined in one of the central tenets of economics: the 'efficient market hypothesis'. One way of stating this hypothesis is that it is not possible to predict future stock prices from previous values.
>
> (Ball 2004: 247–8)

Recent years have shown that failure to note this hypothesis leads to dangerous assumptions entering the mathematical models underlying market predictions, leading traders to believe they can engage in risk-free trading. One such failure was made by Long Term Capital Management, a hedge fund in the United States in the 1990s (Dunbar 2001; Stein 2003). Pride and belief in their flawed investment strategies together with their ability to draw other financial institutions into their wake led to a near-global financial disaster (Long 2008). Malkiel (2003: 5) says, '[A] definition of efficient financial markets is that they do not allow investors to earn above-average returns without accepting above-average risks.'

Kaletsky (2010) provides an argument, however, that even such central tenets of economics as the efficient market hypothesis are based on ideology rather than fact. He argues that in the years leading up to the 2007–8 world financial crisis, the free-market ideologies dominating right-wing politics were based on fantasies that markets were inherently stable and self-rectifying, even if unpredictable in detail, and that financial busts and booms were due to interferences or problems in the markets that delivered random fluctuations around past prices. That is, markets were considered as basically self-correcting but sometimes contaminated:

> EMH [the efficient market hypothesis] asserted that financial markets could never cause or amplify economic instability. On the contrary, because financial markets were the most competitive of all markets and allowed investors to trade on future events with options and other derivatives, the prices set in these markets would, by definition, incorporate the best possible analysis of all available information. If financial markets failed to reflect efficiently the best possible analysis of both current and future conditions, this could only be because of excessive regulation, or insider trading, or lack of transparency of some other kind. EMH did not claim, of course, that financial markets would always be right about the future, because unpredictable

events would always occur, but it did assert that no investor could consistently outwit the market. Better still, from the ideological standpoint, EMH
proved that no government official or regulator could allocate resources
more efficiently, or make better guesses about the future, than the financial
markets themselves.

(Kaletsky 2010: 176)

Conversely, Kaletsky demonstrates how capitalism itself is unstable and, as a
complex system, requires the right mix of market dynamics and government
intervention in order for it to adapt to changing circumstances. Adam Smith's
'invisible hand', while allegedly expressive of self-correcting large system
dynamics, requires some guidance when unexpected systemic changes occur. In
this sense, the explanations of chaos theory become useful. Some changes swing
a system from long-term predictable outcomes – such as described in the random
walk idea of share price changes linked to the efficient market hypothesis, or the
long-term 50/50 outcome of coin tosses despite short-term irregular distributions
– into new, perhaps runaway, change.

The nature of group dynamics underlying human activity in markets

Part of the fantasy of prediction and control within complex systems lies in the
belief that human decision making can predictably and strategically be used to
modify parts of the system in a 'corralled' or limited way – that systemic 'on-
flow' can be predicted, with unintended consequences noted as risks and
avoided. The usual way of dealing with this is through the complex mathematical modelling of numerous relevant variables and their 'proven' levels of
influence. Socioanalysis takes the position that this is only partially possible.
First, there is always the issue of human motivation, attention and error – all of
which are fallible, as many chapters in this book demonstrate. Second, all new
ideas and combinations of ideas cannot be predicted because not only does the
whole system change quantitatively with new ideas and combinations, but the
whole system may change qualitatively at particular state-change boundaries.

Through the idea of an 'associative unconscious' or the 'unconscious infinite', we understand that all thoughts – and therefore the activities and construc-
tions that emanate from the thoughts that inform planning, implementation,
adaptation and evaluation – are connected to all other thoughts through networks
both of logic and of associations that are not traditionally logical. These networks occur at an unconscious level in cultures and operate as a basis for deep
linguistic structures (Chomsky 1968) or cultural assumptions (Bion 1960), for
instance, or proto-mental states (ibid.) and archetypes (Jung 1934–54/1981), as
well as all the implicate meanings held within these (Bohm 1980).

Linked to this is the idea of the 'containers' (Bion 1970) of ideas that provides finite semi-permeable boundaries within an infinite network where everything is linked to everything else with infinite combinations – semi-permeable
because ideas can move between different containers. They do this often in the

form of metaphors derived in one container (say the field of biology) and transferred to another container (say the field of psychology or organizational analysis), allowing new thoughts to emerge. The network of thoughts that we have described in its infinite form has within it several containers for limited groupings of thoughts. These may be broad fields of study, cultures or specific organizations, groups or even an individual mind. The container holds the thoughts in such a way that they can be thought about – so that thinking can occur.

This network or matrix should not be understood as a process of thought transfer or a para-normal phenomenon between individuals but as an instantiated symbolic system implicitly contained within collectives of human experience. It explains, for instance, the fact that the same new idea might arise in different places at more or less the same time even when there is no direct communication between the thinkers involved, only a shared general understanding of the field involved. What is common is the network of concepts and ideas present in a scientific or artistic field, for example, that is not only consciously available to the scientists and artists, but implicitly contains many other possible thoughts or ideas – that is, it demonstrates Bohm's (1980) idea of the 'implicate'. Chapter 15 in this book uses the process of a social dream matrix to bring to the surface ideas about the financial crisis that are part of the implicate thinking of citizens and Chapter 5 teases out the implicate ideas of financial leaders.

How does this relate to markets?

The rises and falls in share prices and the overall shape of the markets emerge from a multitude of influences. Socioanalytically, we can think of these as being in a pool of influences that are filtered through the system of symbols within the market discourse or language, including its mathematical models and ideological assumptions. These influences are crystallized into thoughts and impulses that lead to the buying and selling behaviours of traders. But to add to the complexity, players interact with the perceptions they have of other market players. A game of 'double guessing' ensues.

Many economists are aware that human irrationality and emotional impulses affect the way that markets operate. Most nonetheless believe that mathematical modelling provides the best way of understanding market dynamics. As socioanalysts, we are convinced that such 'systems analysis' needs also a deeper understanding of how unconscious social dynamics occur across a culture, and such dynamics are not readily symbolized in precise mathematical ways.

Actions within markets emerge from the unconscious thought matrixes of multiple market players, and subsequent actions of players emerge from this matrix. Individuals may use careful logical thinking and planning. They may also be influenced by illogical impulses or even calculating, corrupt and destructive impulses. However, overall market dynamics emerge from a matrix of influences, thoughts, impulses and behaviours. Such a broad matrix cannot be conscious to any one player or set of players. This is the understanding beneath Keynes's insights.

Keynes, in a sense, recognized the macroeconomy as what biologists, engineers, and mathematical physicists would today call a complex system. A complex structure, such as an ecological environment, the human body, or even a weather pattern, involves so many different components, all interacting in unpredictable ways, that its behavior cannot be analyzed by aggregating the individual movements of its atomistic parts.

(Kaletsky 2010: 162)

Institutions as complex living systems

How, then, can we understand the way that unconscious networks or matrixes operate in social systems? In this context, we can take an idea from the container 'biological sciences' and apply this to 'organizational studies'. An organization, then, might be regarded as analogous to a super-organism, or at least a super-system – the very hypothesis underlying earth systems sciences as explored in the Amsterdam Declaration (2001). This declaration states:

The scientific communities of four international global change research programmes – the International Geosphere-Biosphere Programme (IGBP), the International Human Dimensions Programme on Global Environmental Change (IHDP), the World Climate Research Programme (WCRP) and the international biodiversity programme DIVERSITAS – recognise that, in addition to the threat of significant climate change, there is growing concern over the ever-increasing human modification of other aspects of the global environment and the consequent implications for human well-being...

Research carried out over the past decade under the auspices of the four programmes to address these concerns has shown that:

The Earth System behaves as a single, self-regulating system comprised of physical, chemical, biological and human components. The interactions and feedbacks between the component parts are complex and exhibit multiscale temporal and spatial variability. The understanding of the natural dynamics of the Earth System has advanced greatly in recent years and provides a sound basis for evaluating the effects and consequences of human-driven change.

James Lovelock worked extensively for many years to establish the basic idea that the world was a single living system (Gribbin and Gribbin 2009). Although his 'Gaia hypothesis' has been challenged and modified, it is now well accepted in the earth systems sciences that exploration of the earth as a unitary system is required in order to understand the influence of humans on climate, biodiversity and population dynamics, among many other global systems.

We wish here to emphasize that organizations might also be regarded as self-regulating systems comprising physical, chemical, biological and human components, including human psychosocial structures and processes. This proposal is not new. Miller and Rice (1967) proposed such an idea many years ago when they described organizations as open systems transforming goods imported from the environment.

But building on and beyond the ideas of Miller and Rice, we can see that the fundamental nature of organizations lies not in the physical systems that include human manual labour, but in the knowledge systems that are part of human culture. The case studies examined in this book demonstrate and elaborate this (see Chapters 8, 10, 12, 16–18 and 23–25, for example). The fundamental nature of organization is based in thought, ideas, decision making, communication dynamics, trust, delegation, authority, power relations, and so on. Moreover, as Maturana and Varela (1972/1980) argue, the cognitive systems in organization are not so much open as closed self-regulating systems. New thoughts from the outside do not 'enter' the system so much as 'perturb' or 'disturb' it, causing the system to reorientate itself internally. Perturbing thoughts from outside make us rethink ideas we already have, make us re-evaluate our position and think the 'unthought known'.

Using the combined ideas of Kaletsky, Maturana and Varela, and Lovelock, we are presented with the possibility of an organization that is self-regulating in order to adapt and survive.

Capitalism as a self-regulating social system

Could the social-economic system known as 'capitalism' also be changing in an evolutionary way? Anatole Kaletsky's book *Capitalism 4.0* takes the perspective that capitalism is an adaptive system, 'an evolutionary system that reinvents and reinvigorates itself through crises' (2010: 3), rather than a static set of institutions or a system tied to one political ideology. His argument embraces the idea of basic human psychological characteristics that influence the economic and political institutions within capitalism.

> [T]wo basic human qualities are the competitive spirit (ambition) and the desire for sensual gratification and mastery of the material world (which can be described pejoratively as greed) ... there are two additional requirements: acceptance of profit and capital accumulation as motives with genuine moral legitimacy, as opposed to deplorable, although ineradicable, human vices; and the recognition of voluntary exchange and cooperation, rather than heredity and coercion, as the main organizing principles of economic life.
>
> (Kaletsky 2010: 41)

This is a sentiment echoed in Chapter 22 of this book. Kaletsky outlines four major phases in the growth of capitalism to date. The first period was crystallized in Smith's *The Wealth of Nations* and held the idea that if individuals pursued their own self-interest, within rules of trust and honesty, they could produce a system that gave mutual satisfaction to all. In the United States this was set within an ideology of laissez-faire where economics and government were seen as separate. Despite the presence of government intervention in the form of protectionism, the dominant ideology was of separation. Calling this era 'Capitalism 1', Kaletsky argues that it ended with World War I, followed by the Great Depression. Following these events, during 'Capitalism 2', the ideas of the economist Keynes gained ascendency. Governments were seen to be important as regulators of the economy and should be concerned with macroeconomic policies involving unemployment and interest rates. The main belief of Capitalism 2, he argues, was a belief that 'capitalism, if unguided by government, was ruinous and intrinsically unstable' (ibid.: 50).

All this changed again with the mass unemployment and economic crises of the 1970s. Stagflation – introduced as a new description – was a result. When the economy is working normally, stagnant economic growth reduces demand, which keeps prices low, preventing inflation. Stagflation can only occur when fiscal or monetary policy sustains high prices, and inflation, despite slow growth. Stagflation is normally blamed on the oil supply shocks of 1973, when OPEC cut its quota and prices quadrupled. However, several other shocks occurred:

- The United States went off the gold standard (Bretton Woods Agreement), which increased the money supply. This created inflation, as too many dollars chased too few goods.
- As prices rose, demand fell, and businesses cut back on production.
- However, the effect of the sudden surplus of dollars kept an upward pressure on prices even after the economy became sluggish. Ultimately, inflation rose to double digits.
- President Nixon instituted wage and price controls, throwing off the ability of the markets to self-correct.
- To fight inflation, the Fed kept raising the Fed Funds rate, reaching a peak of 20 per cent in 1979. However, it did so in a 'stop-go' fashion, confusing price-setters, many of whom kept prices high.

(Barsky and Kilian 2000)

Kaletsky calls the next period 'Capitalism 3'. As a result of the problems of the 1970s, the Reagan–Thatcher period began a period of ideology, following the work of Milton Friedman, around monetarism, free markets, individualism, small government and minimal government intervention. This led to massive corporatization and sometimes privatization of government services in the 1990s and the early twenty-first century. Capitalism 3, according to Kaletsky, is in its last throes, having been dealt a severe blow by the 2008–9 financial crisis. Heavy government intervention was required and many neo-Keynesian processes were employed. 'Capitalism 4', he claims, will see new private–public cooperation in thinking about macroeconomics.

The notion that all societal development should culminate in a modern market economy may be an ideological delusion (see, for example, the critique of 'American exceptionalism' explored by Hoggett 2009). However, whether or not one agrees with the specific analyses and predictions made by Kaletsky, his description of capitalism and its institutions as evolutionary accords with the notion of institutions as complex adaptive systems that evolve over time.

We began with the idea of markets as complex systems holding the central pair of producer and consumer with additional roles surrounding them, and introduced the analogy of the mother–infant pair. Regulators are analogous to the intervention of the father, understood in Lacanian psychoanalysis as bringing the law to the pair (Lacan 1970). Kaletsky's historical overview of capitalism resonates. He argues that in its different forms, via dominant ideologies of the times, capitalism has welcomed or rejected government intervention or cooperation. Without overburdening the analogy, it might be said that government and the law are in the place of the father, with the mother–child of the producer and consumer. Infants do begin their lives as consumers at the breast. But perhaps, even better, we might say that the family unit itself plays out the broader-level social symbolic dynamic between the collective found in government and the law and the private found in markets. Levy-Strauss did tell us that the incest taboo that created the possibility of family was as much about defining the power and inheritances of families as it was about sex and individual psychology.

It may be that no form of capitalism will eventually survive. New forms of collectivist ownership may emerge. However, we take the stance here that capitalism will most likely survive and evolve in the near future. Certainly the basic human emotions of competition and greed will continue to exist, and we had best discover ways to operate more ethically and humanistically within the capitalist system and with greater cognizance of unconscious social factors.

Implications for organizations

The socioanalysis of finance and capitalism is to a large extent a new but most important venture. Perhaps it is a sub-discipline in the making. There is ample evidence that during recent decades the realm of finance has not only dominated the global economy but has had a major impact on our daily lives, maybe creating the financialization of everyday life (Martin 2002; Langley 2009). We broadly seem to have made peace with capitalism in the West through ignoring its 'dysfunctions', many of which are enumerated in this book.

We are arguing here that organizations, institutions and capitalism itself are complex self-regulating systems. We add, from a socioanalytic perspective, that they are formed from unconscious human social dynamics. They change and evolve, but do so in line with inner historical and motivational forces.

So what might be some of the evolving aspects of organizational life that are illuminated by socioanalytic theories and methods?

1   First is the increased understanding of organizations as complex self-regulating systems. Although this understanding is realized in practices such as distributed leadership and collaborative process that allow for the influence of more organizational members from all levels of hierarchy in

decision making, this book also argues the need for clear authority and leadership. All this helps avoid the excesses of 'groupthink', perverse denial and the dominance of group psychotic mechanisms. Laura Yu's discussion of the Mondragon group's adaptation to the market economy (Chapter 24 of this book) looks at how some of these processes are challenged by the new climate.

2   Second is an increased understanding of unconscious dynamics in groups. Chapter 9 of this book, for example, looks at the irrational decision making behind deregulation, and Chapter 2 looks at the unconscious irrationality in the actions of bankers and other financial institution players. Reflective practice and the provision of reflective spaces for thinking about group process are necessary, along with management education in group and organizational dynamics.

3   As a third point, strengthened management-independent governance structures with responsible boards aid the performance of management through heightened accountability and the provision of an independent perspective to counter management 'blind spots'. These include the blind spots created by 'turning a blind eye' to issues that run counter to one's desires or expectations. Chapters 3 and 4 specifically deal with the perverse dynamics that emanate from organizational denial.

4   Fourth, clarity of task and role is critical to good organization (Newton *et al.* 2006; Van de Loo and Kemna, Chapter 13, this book). The exercise of good authority, immune to corruption and perverse dynamics, is enabled by continuous attempts to provide clear roles linked to clear tasks. The slide across the boundary to corrupted roles and tasks (Chapman 1999) begins with just one ambiguity. Although ambiguities are part and parcel of organizational life, what is important is the attempt to clarify and continually work with ambiguities in a constructive and collaborative way.

5   Fifth, an historical perspective is important, alongside a capacity to learn from experience. The balance between understanding long-term systemic dynamics and also taking account of changes as they occur is critical for organizational survival.

6   Greed and a connected sense of entitlement among those with money and power act as central motives in capitalism (see Chapters 2, 3 and 21 of this book and Sievers 2011) and might be said to be part and parcel of the capitalist state of mind. Although we do not suggest that such basic emotions as greed can or should be removed, we do believe that some social structures and dynamics can better contain, sublimate or use them constructively (see, for instance, Chapter 22).

7   The idea of risk has been largely left to the 'experts' (see Chapters 7 and 10–12). But risk in finance as well as in life is something that individual citizens need to judge.

8   Finally, organizations will have to enable new public–private cooperation. This will include new ways of developing multi-party collaborations across all sectors – a challenging prospect.

We hope that this book and its lessons will enable readers to question the meaning and dynamics of money, finance and capitalism and continue to explore the terrain 'beneath the surface'.

References

Amsterdam Declaration (2001) 'Challenges of a changing earth', Global Change Open Science Conference, Amsterdam, 13 July. Online, available at: www.grida.no/news/press/2187.aspx (retrieved 9 December 2010).

Bakan, J. (2004) *The Corporation: The pathological pursuit of profit and power*, London: Constable.

Ball, P. (2004) *Critical Mass: How one thing leads to another*, London: Arrow.

Barsky, R.B. and Kilian, L. (2000) 'A monetary explanation of the great stagflation of the 1970s', 27 January. Online, available at: www.fordschool.umich.edu/rsie/workingpapers/Papers451-475/r452.pdf (retrieved 9 December 2010).

Bion, W.R. (1960) *Experiences in Groups*, London: Tavistock Publications.

Bion, W.R. (1970) *Attention and Interpretation*, London: Tavistock Publications.

Bohm, D. (1980) *Wholeness and the Implicate Order*, London: Routledge & Kegan Paul.

Chapman, J. (1999) 'Hatred and corruption of task', *Socio-Analysis*, 1(2): 127–50.

Chomsky, N. (1968) *Language and Mind*, New York: Harcourt Brace Jovanovich.

Dalgleish, J. and Long, S.D. (2005) 'Management's fear of market responses', in E. Klein (ed.) *Relatedness in a Global Economy*, Madison, CT: Psychosocial Press.

Dunbar, N. (2001) *Inventing Money: The story of Long Term Capital Management and the legends behind it*, New York: John Wiley.

Gribbin, J. and Gribbin, M. (2009) *He Knew He Was Right: The irrepressible life of James Lovelock*, London: Penguin Books.

Hoggett, P. (2009) *Politics, Identity and Emotion*, London: Paradigm.

Janis, I.L. (1972) *Victims of Groupthink*, Boston: Houghton Mifflin.

Janis, I.L. (1982) *Groupthink: Psychological studies of policy decisions and fiascoes*, 2nd edn, Boston: Houghton Mifflin.

Jung, C.G. (1934–54/1981) *The Archetypes and the Collective Unconscious*, Collected Works, vol. 9, 2nd edn, Princeton, NJ: Bollingen.

Kaletsky, A. (2010) *Capitalism 4.0: The birth of a new economy in the aftermath of crisis*, London: Bloomsbury.

Kilcullen, J. (1996) 'Reading guide 6: Marx, *Capital*', *POL264 Modern Political Theory*, online, available at: www.humanities.mq.edu.au/Ockham/y6406.html (retrieved 9 December 2010).

Lacan, J. (1970) *Écrits*, London: Tavistock Publications.

Langley, P. (2009) *The Everyday Life of Global Finance: Saving and borrowing in Anglo-America*, Oxford: Oxford University Press.

Long, S. (2008) *The Perverse Organisation and Its Deadly Sins*, London: Karnac.

Malkiel, B.G. (2003) 'The efficient market hypothesis and its critics', Princeton University: CEPS Working Paper no. 91, April. Online, available at: www.princeton.edu/~ceps/workingpapers/91malkiel.pdf (retrieved 9 December 2010).

Martin, R. (2002) *Financialization of Daily Life*, Philadelphia: Temple University Press.

Maturana, H.R. and Varela, F.J. (1972) *Autopoesis and Cognition: The realization of the living*, Dordrecht, the Netherlands: D. Reidel, 1980.

Miller, E.J. and Rice, A.K. (1967) *Systems of Organization: The control of task and sentience boundaries*, London: Tavistock Publications.

Newton, J., Long, S. and Sievers, B. (eds) (2006) *Coaching in Depth: The organizational role analysis approach*, London: Karnac.

Sievers, B. (2003) ' "Your money or your life?" Psychotic implications of the pension fund system: towards a socio-analysis of the financial services revolution', *Human Relations*, 56(2): 187–210.

Sievers, B. (2006) 'The psychotic organization: a socio-analytic perspective', *ephemera*, 6(2): 104–20. Online, available at: www.ephemeraweb.org/journal/6-2/6-2sievers.pdf (retrieved 09 December 2010).

Sievers, B. (2011) 'Towards a socioanalysis of capitalist greed', paper presented at the ISPSO Annual Meeting 'Regeneration in Organizations – Psychoanalytic Perspectives', Melbourne, June.

Stein, M. (2003) 'Unbounded irrationality: risk and organizational narcissism at Long Term Capital Management', *Human Relations*, 56(5): 523–40.

Webdictionary.co.uk (n.d.) Meaning of 'institution'. Online, available at: http://webdictionary.co.uk/definition.php?query=institution&Submit=Find+Definition (retrieved 9 December 2010).

Winnicott, D.W. (1971) *Playing and Reality*, London: Penguin Books.

Index

Please note that page numbers relating to Notes will have the letter 'n' following the page number.